LATER STUART TRACTS

AN ENGLISH GARNER

LATER STUART TRACTS

WITH AN INTRODUCTION BY
GEORGE A. AITKEN

NEW YORK
COOPER SQUARE PUBLISHERS, INC.
1964

Published by
Cooper Square Publishers, Inc.
59 Fourth Avenue, New York, N. Y. 10003
Library of Congress Catalog Card No. 64-16741
Printed in the United States of America

NOTE

IT would be incompatible with the plan of this new edition of my friend Professor Arber's valuable *English Garner* to interfere in any way with his labours, beyond classifying the pieces contained in the collection in such a manner as to illustrate more fully the various topics on which they throw so much light. I have therefore contented myself with contributing to this volume an explanatory Introduction, leaving the text and the brief notes of the original edition as I found them. The only exception is the addition of the interesting Preface to the Eighth Volume of Defoe's 'Review,' which completes the series, and has never before been reprinted.

G. A. A.

CONTENTS

INTRODUCTION

UNDER the later Stuarts the newspaper press was in its infancy, and men who wished to influence public opinion on a question of the day usually published a pamphlet, which was read and discussed in coffee-houses, and was frequently answered by one or more pieces of the same nature. During the Civil War there were, indeed, various 'Mercuries,' which during their usually brief existence gave their readers items of news, together with animadversions upon the opposite party, but most of the controversy was carried on by means of isolated pamphlets.

After the Restoration the newspaper gradually grew in importance, but pamphlets remained the favourite medium for political controversy for more than half a century. Sir Roger L'Estrange, a prolific pamphleteer, started, in 1663, two weekly papers, the *News* and the *Intelligencer*, 'published for the satisfaction and information of the people.' These papers, written in defence of the Government, gave place in 1665 to the *Oxford Gazette*, which became the *London Gazette* in the following year, on the return of the Court to town after the plague. The *Gazette*, however, contained little but paragraphs of news, official notices, and the like, and when men's minds were agitated by the Popish Plot in 1679-80, a host of pamphlets appeared on either side. At the same time L'Estrange brought out controversial periodicals, *Heraclitus Ridens*, 'a discourse between jest and earnest, in opposition to all libellers against the Government,' and the *Observator*, which lasted for six years.

Party politics, questions of church government, economic problems, literary quarrels—everything in which men were interested, formed the subject of pamphlets. Many of these pieces were, of course, by forgotten scribblers, for the cost of production was slight; but they were also the means by which men like Marvell and Baxter made their views known to their contemporaries. In fact, the pamphlet fulfilled the purpose now served by a leading article in the *Spectator* or other influential paper, or by a letter from a public man in the *Times*. Sometimes the pamphlet was in verse, like Dryden's *Medal* or *The Hind and the Panther*, or (on the other side) Shadwell's *Medal of John Bayes*.

In 1695, the year after the final disappearance of the system of press licensing, rival newspapers, the *Flying Post* and the *Post Boy*, appearing on three days in the week, were started by George Ridpath, a Presbyterian Whig, and by Abel Roper, a Tory bookseller, who was sometimes assisted, in later years, by paragraphs from Swift. It was not until 1702, after Queen Anne's accession, that the first daily paper, the *Daily Courant*, appeared. The editor said he should relate only matters of fact, avoiding comment or conjecture, and the paper in no way took the place of the pamphlet. Daniel Defoe had already begun to produce that long series of tracts on questions of the day which was continued for thirty years; but he was essentially a journalist, and in 1704 he started the *Review*, of which some specimens are given in this volume. Defoe's paper is the forerunner of all the political reviews of to-day. Other papers, like Tutchin's *Observator* and Lesley's *Rehearsal*, which were constantly attacking each other, are now of interest only to the historian.

One of the attractions of the periodical essay, of which the fashion was set by Steele in the *Tatler*, was the avoidance of party controversy; but in later papers, such as the *Guardian*, Steele found, as he says, that 'parties were too violent to make it possible to pass them by without observation.' Even Addison was drawn into writing a *Whig Examiner*, besides one or two political pamphlets. Swift's work under Queen Anne illustrates very well the varied uses of the pamphlet. On behalf of the government he wrote the *Conduct of the Allies* and the *Remarks on the Barrier Treaty*, which were followed by many ephemeral pieces by himself or by 'understrappers' writing under his supervision. In the controversy with Steele he published *The Importance of the Guardian considered*, in reply to *The Importance of Dunkirk considered*, and *The Public Spirit of the Whigs*, in reply to *The Crisis*. To church controversies he contributed his *Project for the advancement of Religion*, and *Sentiments of a Church of England man*. A serious literary question was discussed in the *Proposal for converting, improving, and ascertaining the English Tongue*, while the *Predictions for the year* 1708 and other pieces formed part of a conspiracy of the wits against the astrologer Partridge. But convenient as was the pamphlet, Swift found it desirable to use also the more modern weapon, the periodical; and the *Examiner*, begun in 1710, contained a series of powerful political papers by him, and was continued by minor writers for four years.

This is not the place to discuss the pamphlets on literary subjects which appeared under the later Stuarts; but we may recall the fact that among them were Dryden's *Essay of Dramatic Poesy* (1668), Gildon's *Comparison between the Two Stages* (1704), several pieces by Dennis, Downes's *Roscius Anglicanus* (1708), Gay's *Present State of Wit* (1711), and Pope's *Essay on Criticism* (1711), all valuable to the literary student of to-day for the facts which they contain, and for the light which they throw on the way in which contemporaries viewed the writers or actors of that time.

The pieces contained in this volume illustrate fairly well the tracts of the later Stuart period. They were originally selected on account of their intrinsic merit rather than as illustrative of the literature of a particular time, and it would of course be easy to suggest many pamphlets which might have been included. But Petty as an economic writer, Defoe as a journalist, and Arbuthnot as a wit, writing on the side of the Government, are sufficiently representative. Swift is not directly included, but he was no doubt consulted in the writing of the *History of John Bull*, and his works are readily obtainable.

The first piece here given is one of a series of little books by Sir William Petty, whose publisher sometimes complained that the manuscript sent him 'made no sufficient bulk,' to which Petty replied, 'I could wish the bulk of all books were less.' Petty's own books certainly contain much matter in a little space. He was deeply interested in social problems, and his writings give the result of a wide experience of men and of affairs.

As a boy, Sir William Petty was interested in mechanics. He tried the sea, studied at a Jesuit college and at Dutch universities, and at Paris formed a friendship with Hobbes. For a time he followed his father's business as a clothier; then he wrote on education, invented a manifold letter-writer, and moved to Oxford, where he took the degree of doctor of physic, and lectured on anatomy. In 1652 he was appointed physician-general to the army in Ireland, and was found so useful in reorganising the service that he was asked to supervise the survey of the forfeited estates of Irish landowners, and ultimately to carry out the re-settlement in that country. After the Restoration Petty was in as much favour with Charles II. as he had been with Henry Cromwell; and he was knighted at the incorporation of the Royal Society (1662), of which he was one of the earliest members. Evelyn says of him: 'There is not a better Latin poet living, when he gives himself that diversion; nor is his excellence less in council and prudent matters of state. . . . There were not in the whole world his equal for a superintendent of manufacture and improvement of trade, or to govern a plantation. If I were a prince, I should make him my second counsellor at least.' And Pepys, after mentioning various distinguished men, says, 'But above all I do value Sir William Petty.'

The *Political Arithmetick* appeared in 1690, two years after Petty's death, but there had been a spurious edition in 1683. The book seems to have been begun about 1671 and finished about 1677. As early as 1662 Petty published a *Treatise of Taxes and Contributions*, and assisted Captain John Graunt in the preparation of *Natural and Political Observations upon the Bills of Mortality*. After various tracts on money, Petty published, in 1682, an *Essay in Political Arithmetick, concerning the people, housing, hospitals, etc., of London and Paris*, and *An Essay concerning the multiplication of Mankind, together with an Essay on the growth of London*. These were followed by *Another Essay in Political Arithmetick concerning the growth of the City of London*, and in 1687 by *Five Essays in Political Arithmetick*, and *Observations upon the Cities of London and Rome.*[1]

[1] A collected edition of Petty's *Economic Writings*, by Prof. Hull, was published in two volumes in 1899; several of the pieces mentioned above are

There was no census in this country before 1801, and Petty had to base his calculations on the Bills of Mortality, the statistics of the Chimney Tax, and the like. He was conscious of the imperfect nature of the data on which he worked, and he often resorted to guesses, but his guesses were wonderfully acute, and considering the difficulties in his way, his success was very marked. Frank and liberal-minded, Petty occupies a high rank as a writer on politics, and by virtue of his application of statistics to social questions, he was one of the founders of economic science in England. Evelyn seems to have done an injustice to Graunt when he said (*Diary*, March 22, 1675) that Petty was 'author of the ingenious deductions from the bills of mortality which go under the name of Mr. Graunt'; but Graunt, though entitled to most of the credit for that early work on vital statistics, was not an economist like Petty. There are many contradictions and reservations in Petty's writings, sometimes due to his not having shaken himself free from prevalent fallacies, and sometimes the result of prudential considerations as to what would be palatable; but in the main he was on the side of free-trade, and opposed to the prevalent belief that the wealth of a country is to be measured by the excess of its exports over the imports.

After Petty's death his widow was created Baroness Shelburne by James II. Their son, who was created Lord Shelburne, dedicated to William III. his father's posthumous work, *Political Arithmetick*, which had long remained unpublished because it ran counter to the French policy which had been in favour under Charles II. In the preface Petty

included in one of the volumes of Cassell's *National Library* (1888). A detailed Life, by Lord Edmond Fitzmaurice, appeared in 1895. An article by Mr. W. C. Bevan, in vol. ix. of the American Economic Association's *Proceedings*, should also be consulted.

says that the work was intended to show the baselessness of the prevalent fears respecting the welfare of England. The method adopted was 'not yet very usual.' 'Instead of using only comparative and superlative words and intellectual arguments,' Petty expressed himself 'in terms of number, weight, or measure,' using only 'arguments of sense,' and considering only such causes as have visible foundations in Nature. He began by showing that a small country, by its situation, trade, and policy, may be equivalent in wealth and strength to a far greater nation, and that conveniences for shipping eminently conduce to wealth and strength. An English husbandman earned but about four shillings a week, whereas a seaman's earnings (including food and lodging) were equal to twelve shillings, so 'a seaman is in effect three husbandmen.' Wise points in Dutch policy were Liberty of Conscience, the securing of titles to land and houses, and the institution of banks. Petty then proceeded to show that some taxes increase, rather than diminish, the wealth of a kingdom. If money is taken, by means of taxation, from one who spends it in superfluous eating and drinking, and delivered to another who employs it in improving land, or in manufactures, it is clear that the tax is an advantage to the state. The people and territories of the King of England are, naturally, nearly as considerable for wealth and strength as those of France. 'If a man would know what any land is worth, the true and natural question must be, How many men will it feed? How many men are there to be fed?' Petty came to the conclusion that the English people 'have, head for head, thrice as much foreign trade as the people of France, and about two parts out of nine of the trade of the whole commercial world, and above two parts in seven of all the shipping.'

The impediments to England's greatness were but contingent and removable. Many useful reforms could be effected. Might not the three kingdoms be united into one, and equally represented in Parliament? Might not parishes, etc., be equalised? Might not jurisdictions be determined? Might not taxes be equally levied, and directly applied to their ultimate use? Might not Dissenters be indulged? There were enough lands in the country to enable earnings to be increased by £2,000,000 a year, and there were employments available for the purpose. There was enough money to drive the trade of the nation, and capital enough in England to drive the trade of the whole commercial world.

Such are some of Petty's conclusions, worked out by the use of the figures which were to hand, or at which he guessed. The whole treatise is interesting because of the ingenuity of the arguments and the enlightened views of the writer. As he says, he showed (i) the use of knowing the true state of the people, trade, etc.; (ii) that the king's subjects were not in so bad a condition as discontented men would make them; and (iii) the great effect of unity, industry, and obedience on the common safety and on the happiness of the individual.

Petty's influence is very discernible in succeeding writers. Gregory King, Lancaster Herald, wrote his interesting *Natural and Political Observations and Conclusions upon the State and Condition of England* in 1696; extracts from it were published by Charles Davenant, but the work itself was not printed until 1801. Davenant wrote *Discourses on the Public Revenues and of the Trade in England* (1698); *An Essay upon the probable methods of making the people gainers in the Balance of Trade* (1699), and other treatises on finance and public affairs. But before these came Defoe's *Essay upon Projects* (1697), a work which is full of interesting information, and of enlightened suggestions on banking, bankruptcy, friendly societies, education, and numerous other questions of public import. This book, in which Petty would have delighted, is here represented by an eloquently worded extract on the advantages of the education of women.

For a right understanding of the pamphlets by Defoe given in this volume, some short account is necessary of the events which led to their production. The masterly *Appeal to Honour and Justice* should be studied by all who are interested in Defoe's course of action under Queen Anne.[1]

Defoe was about forty years of age in 1700, when Tutchin attacked William III. in a pamphlet called *The Foreigners*. As a boy, it was intended that Defoe should enter the Nonconformist ministry, and he was placed at the academy of the Rev. Charles Morton, at Stoke Newington, where he learnt several languages, and was well trained in English. But after a time the idea of the ministry was abandoned, and Defoe became a hose-factor in Cornhill. The accession of James II. brought fears of Popish aggression, and when the Duke of Monmouth landed at Lyme, Defoe, with some of his old schoolfellows, joined in the rising. He was fortunate enough to escape the fate which awaited many of his comrades at the hands of Judge Jeffreys after the Duke's defeat at Sedgemoor.

[1] There are lives of Defoe by William Lee, Wright, and others. Defoe's *Romances and Narratives*, with an introduction by the present writer, were published in 16 vols. in 1895. A large number of the pamphlets are included in Hazlitt's edition of Defoe's *Works* (1840-3) in 3 vols.

In the succeeding years Defoe followed his business, and made several tours through the country, studying the life and condition of the people. He was made a liveryman of the City, and established a dissenting congregation at Tooting, where he had a house.

Discontent at the acts of James II. grew in intensity, and when William of Orange landed in 1688 Defoe was among those who went to welcome him. At Henley he joined William's army, and in 1689 he rode as a trooper in a volunteer regiment which escorted William and Mary to the Guildhall. Subsequent years were less prosperous; speculations in foreign trade, which led to visits to Spain and France, involved Defoe in bankruptcy in 1692. A composition was agreed to, but his opponent Tutchin tells us that Defoe carried out his resolve that, though discharged, he would pay his creditors in full, 'as far as God should enable him.' He became owner of brick and pantile works at Tilbury; and as a reward for his services in joining 'with some eminent persons at home in proposing ways and means to the Government for raising money to supply the occasions of the war,' he was appointed Accountant to the Commissioners of the Glass Duty. The *Essay upon Projects* was followed by *A Poor Man's Plea* (1698), which dealt with the reformation of manners and the suppressing of immorality, questions which were just then engaging much public attention.

The publication by Tutchin, in August 1700, of *The Foreigners*, an attack on the King and the Dutch nation, led Defoe to write *The True-Born Englishman: A Satyr* (Jan. 1701), which was an immense success. In pointed doggrel verses he showed how the English were descended from many races:—

'From a mixture of all kinds began
That heterogeneous thing, an Englishman;
A *True-Born Englishman's* a contradiction!
In speech an irony! in fact, a fiction!'

The conclusion of the whole was that ''Tis personal virtue only makes us great.' 'I am one,' says Defoe in the Preface, 'that would be glad to see Englishmen behave themselves better to strangers, and to governors also: that one might not be reproached in foreign countries for belonging to a nation that wants manners.' The publication of the poem led to Defoe's introduction to William III., 'whose goodness to me,' he says, 'I never forgot, neither can forget; whose memory I never patiently heard abused, nor ever can do so.'

A new Parliament met in February 1701, with Robert Harley as Speaker. The majority was opposed to the King, and came into conflict with the House of Lords. Five Kentish gentlemen, who brought up a petition urging the House of Commons to give His Majesty such supplies as would enable him to provide for the interests of the country and assist his allies, were ordered to be taken into custody by the sergeant-at-arms, and were afterwards, on May the 13th, committed to the Gate-House prison, under the Speaker's warrant. Next day Defoe, accompanied by sixteen gentlemen, went to the House and delivered to the Speaker his *Legion's Memorial,* in which it was pointed out, in very plain language, that 'Englishmen are no more to be slaves to Parliament than to a king. Our name is Legion, and we are many.' The House seems to have been cowed; supplies were voted; Parliament rose, and the prisoners were released. Defoe's account of the whole matter will be found in his *History of the Kentish Petition.*

King William's death in March 1702 was a serious blow to Defoe. The friends of Queen Anne were among the Tories, and she was a strong churchwoman. War was declared against France and Spain in May, and in the new Parliament the Tories had a large majority. In November a Bill for the prevention of Occasional Conformity was brought in, but it was lost through the disagreement of the Lords. This bill disabled from holding their employments all office-holders who had conformed as required by the Act of 1673, but who afterwards went to any meeting for worship not conducted in accordance with the liturgy of the Church of England; it also made them liable to penalties, and debarred them from holding office until they had conformed for a year. Public feeling ran high; chapel windows were broken, and some of the more moderate bishops were accused of betraying their Church. Defoe followed up his *Enquiry into Occasional Conformity* by his famous pamphlet, *The Shortest Way with the Dissenters*, published on the 1st of December 1702. Writing ironically in the guise of an extreme churchman, he showed the absurdity of the prevalent intolerance by pushing the argument against Dissenters to extremes. The Church, he said, had been humiliated for fourteen years; she had too long harboured her enemies under her wing. 'The time of mercy is past! Your day of grace is over!' If James I. had rooted the Puritans from the face of the land they could not since have vexed the Church. The French king had effectually cleared France of Protestants: 'If ever you will leave your posterity free from friction and rebellion, this is the time!' Fines were useless; the proper remedy was a law that whoever was found at a conventicle should be banished, and the preacher be hanged. At first, such severity might seem hard, but the contagion would be rooted out.

It is not surprising that the pamphlet deceived many. Dissenters regarded it as an attack, and when it was found to be by a dissenter, they did not agree with the writer's views on Occasional Conformity. On the other hand, violent churchmen were furious when they found that the piece which they had greatly valued was a satire upon them. Defoe made an unavailing appeal to the Earl of Nottingham, the Secretary of State, in which he described himself as 'a zealous, faithful, and thankful servant of the Queen,' and offered to plead guilty if he might receive a sentence 'a little more tolerable to me as a gentleman than prisons, pillories, and such like.' A reward was offered for his apprehension, and the pamphlet was ordered to be burnt by the common hangman. Then Defoe surrendered, 'rather than others should be ruined by his mistake,' and in July 1703, after he had published *A Brief Explanation of the Shortest Way*, he was tried, fined, and ordered to stand thrice in the pillory, and to find sureties for good behaviour for seven years. Defoe again prayed to be excused from the pillory without result; but when the time came, it was found to be a triumph instead of a punishment, for the mob received him with enthusiasm. On the first day on which he stood in the pillory (July 19) he published *The Shortest Way to Peace and Union*, by which he meant common charity and tolerance, and *A Hymn to the Pillory*, where it is suggested that many of those opposed to him better deserved such punishment.

But Defoe had to go back to prison, and there he wrote various pamphlets, which need not be mentioned here. In September 1703 Harley wrote to Godolphin, the Lord

Treasurer, that Defoe was much oppressed with his usage at Newgate, and was willing to serve the Queen. If his fine were satisfied by the Queen's bounty, 'he may do service, and this may perhaps engage him better than any after rewards, and keep him more under the power of an obligation.' Some months later Harley, who had succeeded Defoe's enemy Nottingham, as Secretary of State, wrote to ask Defoe what he could do for him, and made arrangements for the relief of his family. In August 1704 Defoe was released from prison, when he published *A Hymn to Victory*. In his *Appeal to Honour and Justice* he describes his gratitude to Harley and to the Queen, by whose bounty his fine was paid, and he asks how he could ever act against those to whom he owed so much. The Queen, too, took Defoe into her service, and he was employed, at Harley's suggestion, 'in several honourable, though secret services.'

In the meantime Defoe had begun, on February 19, 1704, while in prison, the famous periodical known as the *Review*, a paper which lasted until 1713, and was the immediate forerunner of the *Tatler* and the *Spectator* and all subsequent periodical essays. The paper was at first called *A Review of the Affairs of France aud of all Europe, as influenced by that nation* ; it treated of politics, news, and trade, but there was also a lighter element, contrived to 'bring people to read with delight.' 'After our serious matters we shall, at the end of every paper, present you with a little diversion, as anything occurs to make the world merry ; and whether friend or foe, one party or another, if anything happens so scandalous as to require an open reproof, the world will meet with it there.' These essays on 'the immediate subject then on the tongues of the town' were called *Advice from the Scandalous Club*, or, later on,

Advice from the Scandal Club, and there were monthly *Supplementary Journals*. When the *Tatler* appeared Defoe welcomed Steele's lighter touch, and devoted himself more and more to politics.

The *Review* began as a weekly paper; after the eighth number it appeared twice a week, and after the eighth number of the second volume thrice weekly. The passing of the Stamp Act in 1712 brought the paper to an end in its original form; but it was soon revived, as a single leaf, and was published twice a week until June 11, 1713. Defoe wrote the whole himself, a truly marvellous feat when we remember that he was often travelling about the country, and that while the *Review* was appearing he wrote pamphlets and books containing, as he calculated, nearly five thousand pages.

The first volume dealt largely with the question of English Trade; and Defoe, answering criticisms on his carelessness respecting language and polite phraseology, said that while he was on the subject of Trade he felt free from the bonds of cadence and perfections of style; it was enough to be 'explicit, easy, free, and very plain.' In his second volume, struck by the growth of animosity and party fury, Defoe endeavoured to 'prevail on all people in general to study Peace,' and to beware of Tackers and Tories. In the third volume he dealt at length with the Union with Scotland. 'If I thought myself obliged, in duty to the public interest, to use my utmost endeavour to quiet the minds of enraged parties, I found myself under a stronger necessity to embark in the same design, between too much enraged nations.' Seeing that those carrying on the negotiations were at last approaching the subject in a spirit likely to lead to success, he felt he must do his part without doors, by attempting to remove national prejudices. With this object he wrote pamphlets, and went to Edinburgh, where he helped the Government by smoothing over difficulties for many months, both before and after the signing of the Treaty of Union.

The seventh volume of the *Review* was concerned with the controversy that arose out of the prosecution of Dr. Sacheverell in 1710. Defoe's writings against the 'exploded ridiculous doctrine of Non-Resistance' brought upon him many threats, but did not move him to change his attitude. 'You should first answer the argument,' he wrote; 'that is the best way of murdering the author! To kill him first is to own you could not answer him. If your doctrine of Non-Resistance will subsist, it will uphold itself; . . . for Truth will prevail.' But 'whether in this work I meet with punishment or praise, safety or hazard, life or death, *Te Deum Laudamus*.' He could not but feel it hard, however, that one who endeavoured to steer the middle course between all parties, and to press either side to pursue the public interest, should be maltreated by any, and still more by both sides. 'But so shall it fare with any man that will not run into the same excess of riot with any people.'

In the interesting preface to the eighth volume of the *Review*, Defoe again defended himself against attacks from those who might have been expected to be his friends. He consoled himself with the knowledge that he had always written his free and undirected opinions, and with the hope that the sincerity of his conduct would be yet cleared to the world. No ill-treatment could make him an enemy of the Dissenters, and he awaited a better understanding with patience and resignation. In the meantime he expressed his resentment at the Occasional Conformity Bill, which was a more barbarous measure than the Dissenters realised. 'The people I have served, and love to serve, cut my throat every day, because I will not cut the throat of those that have served and assisted me. . . . And now I live under universal contempt, which contempt I have learned to contemn.' He was called 'a fighting fellow'; but truth makes any man bold, and with a bad cause he felt he would have been a coward. 'In defence of truth, I think (pardon me that I dare go no further, for who knows himself?) I say, I think I could dare to die, but a child may beat me if I am in the wrong.' The hostility of the patriots of the cause he served did not move him, because he served 'the cause, and not the men.'

During the negotiations for a peace with France in 1712 Defoe wrote pamphlets in favour of 'a good peace,' with the result that he was charged with being a hireling. This, he said, 'was abominably false'; he had 'suffered deeply for cleaving to principles.' At the close of the year, and early in 1713, he wrote an opposition to the schemes of the friends of the Pretender, sometimes in very plain-spoken pieces, like *A Seasonable Warning and Caution*; sometimes ironically, as in *Reasons against the Succession of the House of Hanover*; *What if the Pretender should come?* and *What if the Queen should die?* As in the case of *The Shortest Way with the Dissenters*, the irony was misunderstood — really misunderstood by some stupid readers, and wilfully misunderstood by others who wanted an excuse for attacking the writer. It was held that the pamphlets were scandalous, wicked, and treasonable libels, and Defoe was committed for trial. Eventually, however, in December 1713, Harley—now Earl of Oxford—procured for him a pardon of 'all crimes and offences.'

Though Defoe did not approve of the terms of the Treaty of Utrecht, he thought it the duty of a loyal subject to make the best of it when it was signed; but when he wrote to that effect he was charged with being in the French interest, often, as he says, on the supposition that he was the author of pamphlets of which he knew nothing. His whole attitude is summed up towards the close of the *Appeal to Honour and Justice*: 'I was from my first entering into the knowledge of public matters, and have ever been to this day, a sincere lover of the constitution of my country, zealous for liberty and the Protestant interest, but a constant follower of moderate principles, a vigorous opposer of hot measures of *all* parties. I never once changed my opinion, my principles, or my party; and let what will be said of changing sides, this I maintain, that I never once deviated from the Revolution principles, nor from the doctrine of liberty and property on which they were founded.' And again: 'A constant, steady adhering to personal virtue and to public peace, which (I thank God! I can appeal to Him!) has always been my practice, will, at last, restore me to the opinion of sober and impartial men; and that is all I desire.'

The Earl of Oxford's fall in July 1714 was shortly followed by the death of the Queen and the accession of George I. Defoe's *Appeal to Honour and Justice* appeared early in 1715, and here we must leave him, merely noting that four years afterwards, when in his sixtieth year, he began, with *Robinson Crusoe*, the wonderful series of romances by which he is most widely known. For five years these books succeeded one another with astonishing rapidity; and besides the stories, he wrote books and pamphlets on historical and moral subjects, on commerce, on politics, on magic, and on literature. The busy life came to an end in 1731. He was too independent, and his views were too much in advance of his time, for him to be viewed with anything but doubt by mere party-men. One opponent, John Dunton, said: 'I cannot but own his thoughts are always surprising, new, and singular; and though he writes for bread, he could never be hired to wrong his conscience, or disgrace the quill, and, which crowns his panegyric, he is a person of true courage.'

Arbuthnot was a fellow-writer with Defoe in favour of a peace with France; but they had little in common. Defoe's position was naturally one of isolation; he was outside the literary circle of his day; and Swift and Pope, though he was writing on their side, mention him, on the rare occasions on which they refer to him, only in terms of opprobrium Apart from other reasons, he would be looked down upon as a Dissenter and as a man of the people, who was not a member of any university. In 1712, when the pamphlets given in this volume were published, Arbuthnot was a fashionable physician of forty-five, an intimate friend of Swift, Pope, and the wits in general, as well as of Oxford and Bolingbroke.[1]

Arbuthnot's father was one of the clergy who were expelled from their churches and manses at the Revolution in 1689, because he would not conform to the Presbyterian system. John, the eldest son, came to London, where he taught mathematics for a time, and then entered University College, Oxford. In 1696 he took the degree of M.D. at St. Andrews; in 1704 he was elected a Fellow of the Royal Society, and next year became Physician-Extraordinary to

[1] The fullest life of Arbuthnot is in *The Life and Works of John Arbuthnot*, Oxford, 1892, by the present writer.

the Queen. In 1706 he was a fellow-worker with Defoe in the endeavour to remove the prejudices against the Union entertained by the Scotch. In his *Sermon preached to the people at the Mercat-Cross at Edinburgh, on the subject of the Union*, he pointed out to his fellow-countrymen the intimate relations between Pride, Poverty, and Idleness, 'a worse Union a great deal than that which we are to discourse of at present'; the text was, 'Better is he that laboureth, and aboundeth in all things, than he that boasteth himself, and wanteth bread.' In due course Arbuthnot became Physician-in-Ordinary to the Queen, and enjoyed great influence at court; Swift more than once refers to him as 'the Queen's physician and favourite.'

Early in 1712 active negotiations were in progress with a view to the settlement of a peace with France, and Arbuthnot rendered material aid by a series of pamphlets which were afterwards collected under the title of *The History of John Bull*. They are often printed with Swift's works, but Pope said, 'Dr. Arbuthnot was the sole writer of *John Bull*.' On the 10th of March 1712 Swift wrote to Stella, 'You must buy a small twopenny pamphlet, called *Law is a Bottomless Pit*. It is very prettily written, and there will be a second part.' The piece was advertised in the *Examiner* for March 6, with the title *Law is a Bottomless Pit, exemplified in the case of the Lord Strutt, John Bull, Nicholas Frog, and Lewis Baboon, who spent all they had in a Law Suit*. Lord Strutt was the late King of Spain; John Bull, the English; Nicholas Frog, the Dutch; Lewis Baboon, the French King; Philip Baboon, the Duke of Anjou; Esquire South, the King of Spain; Humphrey Hocus, the Duke of Marlborough; and Sir Roger Bold, the Earl of Oxford. The lawsuit was, of course, the war;

John Bull's first wife stood for the late Ministry, and his second wife for the present Tory Ministry; his mother was the Church; his sister Peg, the Scottish nation. Arbuthnot tells very amusingly of the cause of the lawsuit; of its success, which made John Bull think of leaving off his trade to become lawyer; of his discovery that Hocus had an intrigue with his wife; of the annoying attorney's bill; and of the steps taken by the lawyers to persuade John Bull not to accept any composition, and so end the lawsuit. Arbuthnot first applied the name of John Bull to the English people. John was generally ruddy and plump; fond of his bottle, and generous with his money; an honest, plain-dealing man, but choleric and of inconstant temper. He was not afraid of the French, but often quarrelled with his best friends. In spite of good business capacity, he was careless about accounts, and was often cheated by partners and servants.

The second part of 'John Bull' was called *John Bull in his Senses.* On the 17th of March Swift wrote that it was 'just now printed, and better, I think, than the first.' It deals with the doctrine of non-resistance, the Barrier Treaty, Lord Nottingham's opposition to the Peace, and the arguments used by Marlborough, Godolphin, and Cowper, the guardians to John's three daughters by his first wife (War, Discord, and Usury), and by the King of Spain. *John Bull still in his Senses: Being the third part of Law is a Bottomless Pit,* was published in the middle of April. On the title-page was the misleading statement that this, as well as the two former parts, was by the author of the *New Atalantis*—Mrs. Manley, who was also a minor writer of Tory pamphlets. The chapters include an account of John Bull's mother (the Church of England), of his sister

Peg (the Scottish Church and nation), and her lover Jack (Presbyterianism); of the early quarrels of John and Peg; of their reconciliation (at the Union), and their subsequent disagreements. The remainder of the pamphlet relates to the Partition Treaty; to Oxford's services to his country; to Church troubles, and to the difficulties in bringing about a peace.

An Appendix to John Bull still in his Senses appeared in May. On the 10th Swift wrote to Stella, 'The appendix to the third part of "John Bull" was published yesterday; it is equal to the rest. I hope you read "John Bull." It was a Scotch gentleman, a friend of mine, that wrote it; but they put it upon me.' This pamphlet deals with the history of the differences between Church and Dissent, and with the Bill against Occasional Conformity. The last of the series was published at the end of July: *Lewis Baboon turned honest, and John Bull politician: Being the fourth part of Law is a Bottomless Pit.* Swift wrote on the 7th of August, 'Have you seen the fourth part of "John Bull"? It is equal to the rest, and extremely good.' The pamphlet treated of the discussions at the meeting at the Salutation Tavern (the Congress of Utrecht); of the settlement of accounts between John Bull and Nic. Frog; of the turmoil at home about the Succession; and of the private negotiations with France.

When Arbuthnot died in 1735, Swift said that the news struck him to the heart, and years afterwards Dr. Johnson wrote: 'I think Dr. Arbuthnot the first man among them. He was the most universal genius, being an excellent physician, a man of deep learning, and a man of much humour.' As Lord Chesterfield said, he placed his fund of wit at the disposal of his friends, without any thought of his own reputation, so that he was and is still generally undervalued. It is often difficult to separate his work from that of other members of the Scriblerus Club, to which he belonged. The historical student must needs study *The Conduct of the Allies*, *The Public Spirit of the Whigs*, and other pamphlets by Swift; but though these pieces are unrivalled for invective, the 'John Bull' series give an excellent idea of the more good-humoured side of the political controversy of the time.

G. A. AITKEN.

Political Arithmetic,

OR

A DISCOURSE

Concerning

The extent and value of Lands, People, Buildings; Husbandry, Manufacture[s], Commerce, Fishery, Artizans, Seamen, Soldiers; Public Revenues, Interest, Taxes, Superlucration, Registries, Banks; Valuation of Men, Increasing of Seamen; of Militias, harbours, Situation, Shipping, Power at sea, &c.: as the same relates to every country in general, but more particularly to the territories of His Majesty of Great Britain, and his neighbours of Holland, Zealand, and France.

By Sir WILLIAM PETTY,
late Fellow of the Royal Society.

London. Printed by ROBERT CLAVEL at the *Peacock*, and HENRY MORTLOCK at the *Phœnix* in St. Paul's Church-yard. 1690.

LET this book called *Political Arithmetic*, which was long since written [*about* 1677, *see p.* 29] by Sir WILLIAM PETTY deceased, be printed.

Given at the Court at Whitehall, the 7th day of November, 1690.

NOTTINGHAM.

To the King's most excellent Majesty.

SIRE,

WHILST every one meditates some fit offering for your Majesty, such as may best agree with your happy exaltation to this Throne; I presume to offer what my father, long since, wrote to shew the Weight and Importance of the English Crown.

It was by him styled Political Arithmetic, *inasmuch as things of Government, and of no less concern and extent than the glory of the Prince and the happiness and greatness of the People are, by the ordinary rules of Arithmetic, brought into a sort of Demonstration.*

He was allowed by all, to be the Inventor of this method of instruction, where the perplexed and intricate ways of the World are explained by a very mean piece of Science: and had not the Doctrines of this Essay offended France, they had, long since, seen the light [i.e., the *Essay* would have been printed in England, but for the French policy of CHARLES II.]; *and had sound followers, as well as improvements, before this time, to the advantage, perhaps, of mankind.*

But this has been reserved to the felicity of your Majesty's reign, and to the expectation which the Learned have therein; and if, while in this I do some honour to the memory of a good father, I can also pay service, and some testimony of my zeal and reverence to so great a King, it will be the utmost ambition of

SIRE,
Your Majesty's
Most dutiful and most obedient subject,
SHELBORNE.

The principal Conclusions of this Treatise are:

PREFACE.

FORASMUCH as men who are in a decaying condition or who have but an ill of their own concernments, instead of being, as some think, the more industrious to resist the evils they apprehend, do, contrariwise, become the more languid or ineffectual in all their endeavours; neither caring to attempt or prosecute even the *probable* means of their relief. Upon this consideration, as a member of the Common Wealth, next to knowing the precise truth, in what condition the common Interest stands, I would, in all doubtful cases, think the best! and consequently not despair without strong and manifest reasons, carefully examining whatever tends to lessen my hopes of the Public Welfare.

I have therefore thought fit to examine the following Persuasions; which I find too current in the world, and too much to have affected the minds of some, to the prejudice all, viz.:

The fears of many concerning the welfare of England.

That *the rents of lands are generally fallen*; that therefore, and for many other reasons, *the whole Kingdom grows every day poorer and poorer*. That formerly it abounded with gold; but now, *there is a great scarcity, both of gold and silver*. That *there is no trade, nor employment for the people*; and yet that *the Land is underpeopled*. That *taxes have been many and great*. That *Ireland*

and the Plantations in America, and other additions to the Crown, are a burden to England. That *Scotland is of no advantage.* That *Trade, in general, doth lamentably decay.* That *the Hollanders are at our heels, in the race for naval power: the French grow too fast upon both; and appear so rich and potent, that it is but their clemency that they do not devour their neighbours.* And, finally, that *the Church and State of England are in the same danger with the Trade of England.* With many other dismal suggestions, which I had rather stifle than repeat.

The real Prejudices of England.

It is true, the expense of foreign commodities hath, of late been too great. Much of our plate, had it remained money, would have better served trade. Too many matters have been regulated by Laws, which Nature, long custom, and general consent ought only to have governed. The slaughter and destruction of men by the late Civil Wars [1642–50], and Plague [1665], have been great. The Fire at London, and Disaster at Chatham have begotten opinions in the *vulgus* of the world, to our prejudice. The Nonconformists increase. The people of Ireland think long of their Settlement. The English there, apprehend themselves to be aliens, and are forced to seek a trade with foreigners, which they might as well maintain with their own relations in England.

The Improvements of England.

But notwithstanding all this, the like whereof was always in all places, the buildings of London grow great and glorious. The American Plantations employ 400 Sail of Ships. *Actions* [Shares] in the East India Company are nearly double the principal money [*the original nominal Stock*]. Those who can give good security, may have money under Statute interest. Materials for building, even oak timber, are [but] little the dearer (some cheaper) for [all] the rebuilding of London. The Exchange seems as full of merchants as formerly. No more beggars in the streets, nor executed for thieves, than heretofore. The number of coaches and splendour of equipage exceeds former Times. The public Theatres are very magnificent. The King has a greater Navy, and stronger Guards than before our calamities. The Clergy are rich, and the Cathedrals in repair. Much land has been improved, and the price of food is so reasonable as that men refuse to have it cheaper by admitting of Irish cattle.

And, in brief, no man needs to want, that will take moderate pains. That some are poorer than others, ever was and ever will be: and that many are naturally querulous and envious, is an evil as old as the world.

These general observations, and that men eat, and drink, and laugh, as they used to do, have encouraged me to try if I could also comfort others: being satisfied myself, that the Interest and Affairs of England are in no deplorable condition.

The method I take, to do this, is not yet very usual. For (instead of using only comparative and superlative words, and intellectual arguments) I have taken the course (as a specimen of the Political Arithmetic I have long aimed at) to express myself in Terms of Number, Weight, or Measure; to use only arguments of sense, and to consider only such causes as have visible foundations in Nature: leaving those that depend upon the mutable minds, opinions, appetites, and passions of particular men, to the consideration of others. Really professing myself as unable to speak satisfactorily upon those grounds (if they may be called grounds!) as to foretell the cast of a die [*dice*], to play well at tennis, billiards, or bowls (without long practice) by virtue of the most elaborate conceptions that ever have been written *de projectilibus et missilibus*, or of the angles of incidence and reflection.

The Author's Method and manner of arguing.

The nature of his Propositions and Suppositions.

Now the Observations or Positions expressed by Number, Weight, and Measure, upon which I bottom the ensuing Discourses, are either true, or not apparently false. And which if they are not already true, certain, and evident; yet may be made so by the Sovereign Power, *Nam id certum est quod certum reddi potest.* And if they are false, not so false as to destroy the argument they are brought for: but, at worst, are sufficient, as Suppositions, to shew the way to that Knowledge I aim at.

And I have, withal, for the present, confined myself to the Ten principal Conclusions hereafter particularly handled: which if they shall be judged material, and worthy of a better discussion; I hope all ingenious and candid persons will rectify the errors, defects, and imperfections, which probably may be found in any of the Propositions, upon which these ratiocinations were grounded. Nor would it misbecome Authority itself, to clear the truth of those matters which private endeavours cannot reach to.

CHAPTER I.

That a small country and few people, by its Situation, Trade, and Policy, may be equivalent in wealth and strength to a far greater people and territory. And, particularly, that conveniences for shipping and water carriage, do most eminently and fundamentally conduce thereunto.

THIS first principal Conclusion, by reason of its length, I consider in three parts: whereof the first is

That a small country and few people may be equivalent in wealth and strength to a far greater people and territory.

How one Man by Art, and one Acre of land by improvement, may be equivalent to many.

This part of the First principal Conclusion needs little proof: forasmuch as one acre of land may bear as much corn and feed, as many cattle, as twenty; by the difference of the soil. Some parcel of ground is, naturally, so defensible, as that an hundred men being possessed thereof, can resist the invasion of five hundred. And bad land may be improved and made good. Bog may, by draining, be made meadow. Heathland may, as in Flanders, be made to bear flax and clover grass; so as to advance in value from one to a hundred. The same land, being built upon, may centuple the rent which it yielded as pasture. One man is more nimble or strong, and more patient of labour than another. One man, by Art, may do as much work as many without it, viz.: one man with a mill can grind as much corn as twenty can pound in a mortar. One printer can make as many copies as a hundred men can write by hand. One horse can carry upon wheels as much as five upon their backs, and, in a boat or upon ice, as twenty. So that I say again, this First point of this general Position needs little or no proof.

But the Second and more material part of this Conclusion is that this difference in land and people, arises principally from their *situation*, *trade*, and *policy*.

A comparison of Holland and Zealand with France.

To clear this, I shall compare Holland and Zealand with the Kingdom of France; viz., Holland and Zealand do not contain above 1,000,000 of English acres. Whereas the Kingdom of France contains above 80,000,000.

Now the original and primitive Difference holds proportion as land to land: for it is hard to say that when these places were first planted, whether an acre in France was better than the like quantity in Holland and Zealand; nor is there any reason to suppose but that, therefore, upon the first plantation, the number of planters was in proportion to the quantity of land. Wherefore, if the people are not in the same proportion as the Land, the same must be attributed to the situation of the Land and to the trade and policy of the People superstructed thereupon.

The next thing to be shewn is that Holland and Zealand, at this day, is not only an eightieth part as rich and strong as France, but that it hath advanced to one-third or thereabouts; which, I think, will appear upon the balance of the following particulars, viz.:

As to the wealth of France, a certain *Map* of that Kingdom, set forth *anno* 1647, represents it to be £15,000,000, whereof £6,000,000 did belong to the Church: the Author thereof, as I suppose, meaning the rents of the Lands only.

That the Lands of France are to the Lands of Holland and Zealand as 8 to 1, in value.

And the Author of a most judicious *Discourse of Husbandry* (supposed to be Sir RICHARD WESTON) doth, from reason and experience, shew that lands in the Netherlands, by bearing flax, turnips, clover grass, madder, &c., will easily yield £10 per acre. So as the territories of Holland and Zealand should, by his account, yield at least £10,000,000 *per annum*: yet I do not believe the same to be so much, nor France so little as above said: but rather, that one bears to the other, as about 7 or 8 to 1.

The people of Amsterdam [*about* 160,000] are One-third of those in Paris or London [*about* 480,000]: which two cities differ not in people, a twentieth part from each other, as hath appeared by the Bills of burials and christenings for each. But the value of the Buildings in Amsterdam may well be half that of those of Paris, by reason of the foundations, grafts [? *piles*] and bridges; which in Amsterdam are more numerous and chargeable than at Paris.

The Buildings of Amsterdam are about Half the value to those at Paris.

Moreover, the habitations of the poorest people in Holland and Zealand are Twice or Thrice as good as those of France: but the people of the one, to the people of the other, being as 13 to 1; the value of the Housing must be as about 5 to 1.

The Housing in France above Five times in value of those in Holland and Zealand.

The value of the Shipping of Europe, being about 2,000,000 tons,

I suppose the English have	500,000
the Dutch	900,000
the French	100,000
the Hamburgers, and subjects of Denmark, Sweden, and the town of Dantzic	250,000
And Spain, Portugal, Italy, &c.... ...	250,000
	2,000,000

The Shipping of Holland Nine times that of France.

So as the Shipping, in our case of France to that of Holland and Zealand, is about 1 to 9; which, reckoned at great and small, new and old, one with another, at £8 per ton, makes the worth to be as £800,000 to £7,200,000.

The Hollanders' capital in the[ir] East Indian Company is worth above £3,000,000; where the French, as yet, have little or nothing.

The comparison of Holland and France in the Indias.

The value of goods exported out of France to all parts, is supposed to be quadruple to what is sent to England alone [£1,250,000]: and consequently in all about £5,000,000: but what is exported out of Holland into England is worth £3,000,000; and what is exported thence into all the world besides, is sextuple to the same [£3,000,000+£18,000,000=£21,000,000].

The Exportations of France and Holland is as 5 to 21.

The monies yearly raised by the King of France, as the same appears by the book entituled *The State of France*, dedicated to the King; printed *anno* 1669, and set forth several times by authority, is 82,000,000 of

The Revenues of France.

French Livers, which is about £6,500,000 sterling. Of which sum, the Author says that "one-fifth part was abated for non-valuers or insolvencies" so, as I suppose, not above £5,000,000 were effectually raised.

But whereas, some say that the King of France raised £11,000,000 as the One-fifth of the effects of France: I humbly affirm that all the land and sea forces, all the buildings and entertainments which we have heard by common fame, to have been set forth and in any of these seven last years [? 1671–77] needed not to have cost £6,000,000 sterling; wherefore I suppose he hath not raised more, especially since that were One-Fifth insolvencies, when the tax was at that pitch.

The taxes paid by Holland and Zealand.

But Holland and Zealand, paying 67 parts of the 100 paid by all the United Provinces; and the city of Amsterdam paying 27 of the said 67 parts: it follows that if Amsterdam hath paid 4,000 Flemish Pounds *per diem*, or about 1,400,000 Pounds *per annum* or £800,000 sterling; that Holland and Zealand have paid £2,100,000 *per annum*.

Now the reasons why I think they pay so much, are these, viz.:

1. The Author of the *State of the Netherlands* saith so.
2. The excise of victuals at Amsterdam seems to be above half the original value of the same, viz.: Ground corn pays 20 stivers the bushel, or 63 guilders the last. Beer 113 stivers, the barrel. Housing, one-sixth of the rent. Fruit, one-eighth of what it cost. Other commodities one-seventh, one-eighth, one-ninth, one-twelfth, &c. Salt, *ad libitum*. All weighed goods pay, besides the premises, a vast sum.

   Now if the expense of the people of Amsterdam, at a medium, and without excise, were £8 *per annum*; whereas in England, it is £7: then if all the several imposts above named raise it to £5 more; there being 160,000 souls in Amsterdam, the sum of £800,000 sterling *per annum* will thereby be raised.
3. Though the expense of each head should be £13 *per annum*: it is well known that there be few in Amsterdam, who do not earn much more than the said expense.

4. If Holland and Zealand pay *per annum* £2,100,000; then all the Provinces together must pay about £3,000,000. Less than which sum *per annum*, perhaps, is not sufficient to have maintained the naval war with England, 72,000 land forces, besides all the other ordinary charges of their Government, whereof the Church is there a part.

To conclude, it seems from the premisses, that all France doth not raise above thrice as much from the public charge as Holland and Zealand alone do.

The difference of Interest between Holland and France.

5. Interest of money in France is £7 per cent.; but in Holland scarcely half so much.

6. The countries of Holland and Zealand consisting, as it were, of islands guarded with the sea, shipping, and marshes, is defensible at one-fourth of the charge that a plain open country is, and where the seat of war may be, both summer and winter: whereas in the others, little can be done but in the summer only.

The superlucration between France and Holland.

7. But above all the particulars hitherto considered, that of Superlucration [*the national capitalizing of wealth, by savings out of income, through thrift, industry, and economy of power*] ought chiefly to be taken in. For if a Prince have ever so many subjects, and his country be ever so good: yet if either through sloth or extravagant expenses, or oppression and injustice, whatever is gained shall be spent as fast as gotten; that State must be accounted poor.

Wherefore let it be considered, how much, or how many times rather, Holland and Zealand are now above what they were a hundred years ago: which we must also do of France. Now if France hath scarce doubled its wealth and power, and that the other have decupled theirs; I shall give the preference to the latter even though the nine-tenths increased by the one, should not exceed the one-half gained by the other; because one has a store for nine years, the other but for one.

To conclude, upon the whole, it seems that though France be in People to Holland and Zealand as 13 to 1; and in quantity of good Land, as 80 to 1; yet is it not 13 times richer and stronger, much less 80 times: nor much above thrice. Which was to be proved.

The causes of the difference between France and Holland.

Having thus despatched the Two first branches of the First principal Conclusion: it follows to shew that this Difference of Improvement in wealth and strength arises from the situation, trade, and policy of the places respectively: and in particular from *conveniences for shipping and water carriage.*

Many writing on this subject, do so magnify the Hollanders as if they were more, and all other nations less, than men, as to matters of trade and policy; making them angels, and others fools, brutes, and sots as those particulars: whereas, I take the Foundation of their achievements to lie originally in *the Situation of the country*; whereby, they do things inimitable by others, and have advantages whereof others are incapable.

The reasons why rich land is better than coarse land, though of the same rent; and consequently why Holland is better than France.

First. The soil of Holland and Zealand is low land, rich and fertile; whereby it is able to feed many men: and so, as that men may live near each other, for their mutual assistance in trade.

I say that a 1,000 acres that can feed 1,000 souls, are better than 10,000 acres of no more effect; for the following reasons:

1. Suppose some great fabric were in building by a 1,000 men: shall not much more Time be spared, if they lived all upon 1,000 acres, than if they were forced to live upon ten times as large a scope of land.
2. The charge of the Cure of their souls and the Ministry would be far greater in one case than in the other: as also of Mutual Defence, in case of invasion, and even of thieves and robbers. Moreover the charge of Administration of Justice would be much easier, where witnesses and parties may be easily summoned, attendance less expensive, when men's actions would be better known, when wrongs and injuries could not be covered as in thin peopled places they are.

   Lastly, those who live in solitary places, must be their own soldiers, divines, physicians, and lawyers; and must have their houses stored with necessary provisions, like a ship going upon a long voyage, to the great waste and needless expense of such provisions.

The value of this First convenience to the Dutch, I reckon or estimate to be about £100,000 *per annum.*

Secondly, Holland is a level country, so as, in any part

thereof, a windmill may be set up; and by its being moist and vaporous, there is always wind stirring over it: by which advantage, the labour of many thousand hands is saved, forasmuch as a mill, made by one man in half a year, will do as much labour as four men for five years together.

The advantages from the level, and windmills, of Holland.

This advantage is greater or less, where employment or ease of labour is so: but in Holland it is eminently great, and the worth of this convenience is nearly £150,000.

Thirdly, there is much more to be gained by Manufacture than Husbandry; and by Merchandise than Manufacture. But Holland and Zealand being seated at the mouths of three long great rivers passing through rich countries, do keep all the inhabitants upon the sides of those rivers but as husbandmen; whilst they themselves are the manufactors [*manufacturers*] of their commodities: and do dispense them into all parts of the world, making returns for the same, at what prices almost they please themselves. And, in short, they keep the Keys of Trade of those countries, through which the said rivers pass.

The advantages of Holland, from manufacture and commerce. The situation of Holland and Zealand upon the mouths of three great rivers.

The value of this Third conveniency, I suppose to be £200,000.

Fourthly, in Holland and Zealand, there is scarcely any place of work or business one mile distant from a navigable water: and the charge of water carriage is generally but one-fifteenth or one-twentieth part of land carriage. Wherefore, if there be as much trade there as in France, then the Hollanders can outsell the French fourteen-fifteenths of all the expense of all travelling, postage, and carriage whatsoever: which even in England I take to be £300,000 *per annum*, where the very postage of letters costs the people perhaps £50,000 *per annum*, though farmed at much less; and all other labour of horses and porters at least six times as much.

Nearness to navigable waters.

The value of this conveniency, I estimate to be above £300,000 *per annum*.

Fifthly, the defensibleness of the country by reason of its situation in the sea, upon islands and in the marshes, impassable ground diked and trenched; especially considering how that place is aimed at, for its wealth.

The defensibleness of Holland.

I say, the charge of defending that country is easier than if it were a plain champion, at least £200,000 *per annum.*

Harbouring of shipping at small expense.

Sixthly, Holland is so considerable for keeping ships in harbour, with small expense of men and ground tackle, that it saves *per annum* £200,000 of what must be spent in France.

Now, if all these natural advantages do amount to above £1,000,000 *per annum* profits: and that the Trade of all Europe, nay, of the Whole World with which our Europeans do trade, is not about £45,000,000 *per annum*, and if one-thirtieth of the Value be one-seventh of the Profit, it is plain that the Hollander may command and govern the whole trade.

Advantages from fishing.

Seventhly, those who have their situation thus towards the sea, and abound with fish at home; and having also the command of shipping, have by consequence the fishing trade; whereof that of herring alone brings more yearly profit to the Hollanders, than the trade of the West Indies to Spain, or of the East to themselves: as many have affirmed: being, as the same say, *viis et modis*, of above £3,000,000 *per annum* profit.

Advantages by naval provisions.

Eighthly, it is not to be doubted, but that those who have the trade of shipping and fishing, will secure themselves of the trade of timber for ships, boats, masts, and caske; of hemp for cordage, sails, and nets; of salt, of iron; as also of pitch, tar, rosin, brimstone, oil, and tallow, as necessary appurtenances to shipping and fishing.

Fitness for universal trade.

Ninthly, those who predominate in shipping and fishing, have more occasions than others, to frequent all parts of the world, and to observe what is wanting or redundant everywhere, and what each people can do, and what they desire; and consequently to be the Factors and Carriers for the Whole World in Trade. Upon which ground, they bring all native commodities to be manufactured at home; and carry the same back, even to that country in which they grew.

All which we see. For do they not work the sugars of the West Indies? the timber and iron of the Baltic? the hemp of Russia? the lead, tin, and wool of England? the quicksilver and silk of Italy? the yarns and dyeing stuffs of Turkey?

To be short. In all the ancient States and Empires, those who had the shipping, had the wealth. And if 2 *per cent.* in the price of commodities be, perhaps, 20 *per cent.* in the gain; it is manifest that they who can, in £45,000,000, undersell others, by £1,000,000 [*i.e., nearly 2 per cent.*], upon account of natural and intrinsic advantages only, may easily have the Trade of the World, without such angelical wits and judgements as some attribute to the Hollanders.

Having thus done with their *Situation*, I now come to their *Trade*.

It is commonly seen that each country flourisheth in the manufacture of its own native commodities, viz., England, for woollen manufacture; France, for paper; Luic land, for iron ware; Portugal, for confectures [*confectionary*]; Italy, for silks. Upon which principle, it follows that Holland and Zealand must flourish most in the trade of shipping, and so become Carriers and Factors of the Whole World of Trade.

Artificial advantages of Trade.

Now the advantages of the Shipping Trade are as followeth, viz.:

Husbandmen, seamen, soldiers, artisans, and merchants are the very Pillars of any Commonwealth: all the other great professions do rise out of the infirmities and miscarriages of these. Now the seaman is three of these four. For every Seaman of industry and ingenuity, is not only a Navigator, but a Merchant, and also a Soldier; not because he hath often occasion to fight and handle arms, but because he is familiarized with hardship and hazards extending to life and limbs. For training and drilling is a small part of soldiery in respect of this last-mentioned qualification: the one being quickly and presently learned; the other, not without many years' most painful experience. Wherefore to have the occasion of abounding in Seamen is a vast conveniency.

Husbandmen, seamen, soldiers, artisans, and merchants are the very Pillars of a Common-wealth; and a Seaman is three of them.

2. The husbandmen of England earns but about 4s. a week; but the seamen have as good as 12s. in wages, victuals, and as it were housing, with other accommodations: so as a seaman is in effect three husbandmen.

A Seaman equivalent to three Husbandmen.

Wherefore there is little ploughing and sowing of corn in Holland and Zealand, or breeding of young cattle: but their land is improved by building houses, ships, engines, dykes, wharfs, gardens of pleasure, extraordinary flowers and fruits; for dairy and feeding of cattle, for rape, flax, madder, &c.—the foundations of several advantageous manufactures.

3. Whereas the employment of other men is confined to their own country, that of seamen is free to the whole world; so as where Trade may, as they call it, be dead, here or there, now and then, it is certain that somewhere or other in the world, Trade is always quick enough, and provisions are always plentiful. The benefit whereof, those who command the shipping enjoy, and they only.

4. The great and ultimate effect of trade is not wealth at large; but particularly abundance of silver, gold, and jewels; which are not perishable, nor so mutable as other commodities, but are wealth at all times, and all places: whereas abundance of wine, corn, fowls, flesh, &c., are riches but *hic et nunc*. So as the raising of such commodities, and the following of such trade which does store the country with gold, silver, jewels, &c., is profitable before others.

Silver, gold, and jewels are Universal Wealth.

But the labour of seamen and freight of ships are always of the nature of an *exported* commodity: the overplus whereof, above what is imported, brings home money, &c.

5. Those who have the command of the sea trade, may work at easier freight with more profit than others at greater. For as cloth must be cheaper made when one cards, another spins, another weaves, another draws, another dresses, another presses and packs; than when all the operations above mentioned are clumsily performed by the same hand: so those who command the trade of shipping, can build long slight ships for carrying masts, fir timber, boards, balks [*beams or rafters*], &c.; and short ones for lead, iron, stones, &c.; one sort of vessels to trade at ports where they need never lie aground, others where they must jump upon the sand twice every twelve hours: one sort of vessels and way of manning, in time of peace and for cheap gross [*bulky*] goods, another for war and precious commodities; one sort of vessels for the turbulent sea,

Reasons why the Hollanders sail for less freight.

another for inland waters and rivers; one sort of vessels and rigging where haste is requisite for the maidenhead [*first sales*] of a market, another where one-third or one-fourth of the time makes no matter; one sort of masting and rigging for long voyages, another for coasting; one sort of vessels for fishing, another for trade; one sort for war for this or that country, another for burden only. Some for oars, some for poles, some for sails, and some for draught by men or horses. Some for the northern navigations amongst ice; and some for the South, against worms, &c.

And this I take to be the chief of several reasons, why the Hollanders can go at less freight than their neighbours, viz., because they can afford a particular sort of vessels for each particular trade.

I have shewn how *Situation* hath given them shipping, and how *Shipping* hath given them, in effect, all other trade; and how Foreign Traffic must give them as much Manufactures as they can manage themselves: and as for the overplus, make the rest of the world but as workmen to their shops.

It now remains to shew the effects of their *Policy* superstructed upon these Natural Advantages, and not, as some think, upon the excess of their understandings. The Policy of Holland.

I have omitted to mention, the Hollanders were, one hundred years since, a poor and oppressed people living in a country naturally cold, moist, and unpleasant; and were withal persecuted for their heterodoxy in religion.

From hence it necessarily followed, that this people must labour hard, and set all hands to work; rich and poor, old and young must study the Art of Number, Weight, and Measure, must fare hard, provide for impotents and orphans out of hope to make profit by their labours; must punish the lazy by labour, and not by crippling them. I say, all these particulars (said to be the subtle excogitations of the Hollanders) seem to me but what could not almost have been otherwise.

Liberty of Conscience, *Registry of Conveyances*, *small Customs* [import duties], *Banks*, *Lumbards* [pawnbrokers] and *Law Merchant* rise all from the same spring, and tend to the same sea. As for *Lowness of Interest*, it is also a necessary effect of all the premisses, and not the fruit of their contrivance.

Wherefore we shall only shew in particular the efficacy of each; and first of *Liberty of Conscience.*

Undermasting of ships.

But before I enter upon these, I shall mention a practice almost forgotten, whether it referreth to *Trade* or *Policy* is not material; which is the Hollanders' under-masting and sailing such of their shipping as carry cheap and gross [*bulky*] goods, and whose sale doth not depend much upon the season.

It is to be noted, that of two equal and like vessels, if one spreads 1,600 yards of like canvas, and the other 2,500, their speed is but as Four to Five: so as one brings home the same timber in four days as the other will in five. Now if we consider that although those ships be but four or five days under sail, that they are perhaps thirty upon the voyage: so as one is but one-thirtieth part longer upon the whole voyage than the other, though one-fifth longer under sail. Now if masts, yards, rigging, cables, and anchors do all depend upon the quantity and extent of the sails, and consequently hands also: it follows that the one vessel goes at one-third less Charge, losing but one-thirtieth of the Time and of what depends there upon.

Liberty of Conscience, and the Reasons thereof in Holland.

I now come to the first *Policy* of the Dutch, viz., *Liberty of Conscience*: which I conceive, they grant upon these grounds; but keeping up always a force to maintain the common peace.

1. They themselves broke with Spain to avoid the imposition of the Clergy.
2. Dissenters of this kind are, for the most part, thinking, sober, and patient men; and such as believe that labour and industry is their duty towards GOD: how erroneous soever their opinions be.
3. These people believing in the Justice of GOD; and seeing the most licentious persons to enjoy most of the world and its best things, will never venture to be of the same religion and profession with voluptuaries and men of extreme wealth and power, whom they think to have their portion in this world.
4. They cannot but know That no man can believe what himself pleases: and to force men to say they believe,

what they do not, is vain, absurd, and without honour to GOD.

5. The Hollanders knowing themselves not to be an infallible church, and that others had the same *Scriptures* for guides as themselves, and withal the same Interest to save their souls, do not think fit to make this matter their business; no more than to take bonds of the seamen they employ, not to cast away their own ships and lives.
6. The Hollanders observe that, in France and Spain, especially the latter, the Churchmen [*Clergy*] are about 100 to 1 to what they use or need; the principal care of whom, is to preserve Uniformity: and this they take to be a superfluous charge.
7. They observe where most endeavours have been used to keep Uniformity, there Heterodoxy hath most abounded.
8. They believe that if one-fourth of the people were heterodox, and that if that whole quarter should (by miracle) be removed; that, within a small time, one-fourth of the remainder would again become heterodox, some way or other: it being natural for men to differ in opinion in matters above Sense and Reason; and for those who have less Wealth, to think they have the more Wit and Understanding, especially of the Things of GOD, which they think chiefly belong to the poor.
9. They think the case of the primitive Christians, as it is represented in the *Acts of the Apostles*, looks like that of the present Dissenters: I mean, externally.

The trade of any country is chiefly managed by the Heterodox party.

Moreover, it is to be observed that Trade doth not, as some think, best flourish under popular Governments: but rather that Trade is most vigourously carried on, in every State and Government, by the heterodox part of the same; and such as profess opinions different from what are publicly established. That is to say, in India, where the Mahometan religion is authorized; there the Banyans are the most considerable merchants. In the Turkish Empire, the Jews and Christians. At Venice, Naples, Leghorn, Genoa, and Lisbon; Jews and non-Papist merchant-strangers. But to be short, in that part of Europe where the Roman Catholic religion now hath, or lately hath had establishment, there three-quarters of the whole trade is in the hands of such as have separated from that Church: that is to say, the inhabitants of England, Scotland, and Ireland, as also those of the United Provinces, with Denmark, Sweden, and Norway, together with the subjects of the German Protestant Princes and the Hanse Towns, do, at this day, possess three-quarters of the Trade of the World. And even in France itself; the Huguenots are, proportionably, far the greatest traders.

Nor is it to be denied, but that in Ireland, where the said Roman religion is not authorized: there, the professors thereof have a great part of the trade.

From whence it follows, that Trade is not fixed to any species of Religion, as such: but rather, as before hath been said, to the heterodox part of the whole: the truth whereof appears also, in all the particular towns of greatest trade in England.

Nor do I find reason to believe, that the Roman Catholic seamen in the whole world, are sufficient to man effectually a Fleet equal to what the King of England now hath: but the non-Papist seamen can do above thrice as much. Wherefore he, whom this latter party doth affectionately own to be their head, cannot probably be wronged in his sea concernments by the other.

All the Papists' seamen of Europe are scarce sufficient to man the King of England's Fleet.

From whence it follows, that for the Advancement of Trade, if that be a sufficient reason, indulgence must be granted in Matters of Opinion: though licentious actings, as even in Holland, be restrained by force.

The second *Policy*, or help to trade used by the Hollanders, is *the securing the Titles to Lands and Houses*. For although lands and houses may be called *terra firma et res immobilis*; yet the title unto them is no more certain than it pleases the Lawyers and Authority to make them. Wherefore the Hollanders do, by Registries and other ways of assurance, make the title as immoveable as the lands. For there can be no encouragement to industry, where there is no assurance of what shall be gotten by it; and where, by fraud and corruption, one man may take away, with ease and by a trick, and in a moment, what another has gotten by many years' extreme labour and pains.

Firm Titles to Lands and Houses.

There hath been much discourse about the introducing

of Registries into England. The Lawyers, for the most part, object against it, alleging that titles of land in England are sufficiently secure already. Wherefore omitting the considerations of small and oblique reasons *pro et contra*; it were good that enquiry were made from the Officers of several Courts, to what sum or value, purchasers have been damnified [*robbed*], for this last ten years, by such fraudulent conveyances as Registries would have prevented: the tenth part whereof, at a medium, is the annual loss which the people sustain for want of them. And then, computation is to be made of the annual Charge of Registering such extraordinary conveyances as would secure the title of lands. Now by comparing these two sums, the question so much agitated may be determined: though some think that, though few are actually damnified [*damaged*], yet that all are hindered by fear, and deterred from dealing.

Of the introducing of Registries into England.

Their third *Policy* is their *Bank*: the use whereof is to increase Money, or rather to make a small sum equivalent in trade to a greater.

The Banks of Holland.

For the effecting whereof, these things are to be considered—

1. How much money will drive the Trade of the nation.
2. How much current money there is actually in the nation.
3. How much money will serve to make all payments of under £50 (or any other more convenient sum) throughout the year.
4. For what sum, the Keepers of the Bank are unquestionable security.

If all these four particulars be well known, then it may also be known, how much of the ready money above mentioned may be safely and profitably lodged in the Bank, and to how much ready current money the said deposited money is equivalent.

As for example, suppose £100,000 will drive the Trade of the nation.

And suppose there be but £60,000 of ready money in the same.

Suppose also that £20,000 will drive on, and answer all payments of under £50.

In this case £40,000 of the £60,000 being put into the Bank, will be equivalent to £80,000: which £80,000, and £20,000 kept out of the Bank, do make up £100,000, that is to say, enough to drive the trade, as was proposed.

Where, note, that the Bank Keepers must be responsible for double the sum intrusted with them; and must have power to levy upon the General [*the nation at large, or the body of shareholders*] what they happen to lose unto particular men.

Upon which grounds, the Bank may freely make use of the received £40,000: whereby the said sum, with the like sum in credit, makes £80,000; and with the £20,000 reserved, are £100,000.

I might here add many more particulars: but being the same as have already been noted by others, I shall conclude with adding one observation; which I take to be of consequence, viz.:

That the Hollanders do rid their hands of two trades which are of greatest turmoil and danger; and yet of least profit.

The Hollanders are seldom husbandmen or foot soldiers.

The first, whereof, is that of a common and private soldier. For such they can hire from England, Scotland, and Germany, to venture their lives for sixpence a day; whilst they themselves safely and quietly follow such trades, whereby the meanest of them gain six times as much. And withal, by this entertainment of such strangers for soldiers, their country becomes more and more peopled: forasmuch as the children of such strangers are Hollanders, and take to trades; whilst new strangers are admitted *ad infinitum*. Besides, these soldiers, at convenient intervals, do at least as much work as is equivalent to what they spend.

And consequently, by this way of employing of strangers for soldiers, they people the country and save their own persons from danger and misery, without any real expense; effecting by this method what others have in vain attempted by Laws for Naturalizing of strangers; as if men could be charmed to transplant themselves from their own native, into a foreign country, merely by words, and for the bare leave of being called by a new name. In Ireland, Laws of Naturalization have had little effect to bring in aliens; and it is no wonder, since Englishmen will not go thither, without they may have the pay of soldiers, or some other advantage amounting to maintenance.

Having intimated the way by which the Hollanders do increase their people; I shall here digress to set down the way of computing the value of every head, one with another: and that by the instance of people in England, viz.:

Suppose the people of England be 6,000,000 in number; that their expense at £7 per head, be £42,000,000. Suppose also that the rent of the lands be £8,000,000; and the yearly profit of all personal estate be £8,000,000 more. It must needs follow, that the labour of the people must have supplied the remaining £26,000,000. The which multiplied by 20 (the mass of mankind being worth twenty years' purchase as well as land), makes £520,000,000, as the value of the whole people: which number divided by 6,000,000 makes above £80 sterling to be the value of each head of man, woman, and child; and of adult persons, twice as much. From whence, we may learn to compute the loss we have sustained by the Plague, by the slaughter of men in war, and by the sending them abroad into the service of foreign Princes.

The method of computing the value of Men and People.

The other trade of which the Hollanders have rid their hands, is the old patriarchal trade of being cow-keepers; and in a great measure, of that which concerns the ploughing and sowing of corn: having put that employment upon the Danes and Polanders [*Poles*]; from whom they have their young cattle and corn.

Now here we may take notice, that as trades and curious Arts increase, so the trade of husbandry will decrease; or else the wages of husbandmen must rise, and consequently the rents of lands must fall.

For proof whereof, I dare affirm that, if all the husbandmen of England, who now earn but 8*d*. a day [=2*s*. *now*] or thereabouts, could become tradesmen [*mechanics*] and earn 16*d*. a day [=4*s*. *now*] (which is no great wages, 2*s*. and 2*s*. 6*d*. [=6*s*. *and* 7*s*. 6*d*. *now*] being usually given); that then, it would be the advantage of England to throw up their husbandry, and to make no use of their lands, but for grass, horses, milch cows, gardens, and orchards, &c. Which, if it be so, and if Trade and Manufacture have increased in England, that is to say, if a greater part of the people apply themselves to those faculties than there did heretofore; and if the price of corn be no greater now than when husbandmen were more numerous and tradesmen fewer; it follows from that single reason, though others may be added, that rents of land must fall. As for example, suppose the price of wheat be 5*s.* or 60*d.* the bushel. Now, if the rent of the land whereon it grows, be the Third Sheaf: then of the 60*d.*, 20*d.* is for the land, and 40*d.* for the husbandman. But if the husbandman's wages should rise one-eighth part, or from 8*d.* to 9*d.* *per diem*, then the husbandman's share in the bushel of wheat rises from 40*d.* to 45*d.*; and, consequently, the rent of the land must fall from 20*d.* to 15*d.* For we suppose the price of the wheat still remains the same, especially since we cannot raise it: for if we did attempt it, corn would be brought in to us, as into Holland, from foreign parts, where the state of husbandry was not changed.

Reasons why rents must fall.

And thus I have done with the First principal Conclusion, that *a small territory and even a few people, may by Situation, Trade, and Policy, be made equivalent to a greater; and that convenience for shipping and water carriage do most eminently and fundamentally conduce thereunto.*

CHAPTER II.

That some kind of taxes and public levies may rather increase, than diminish the wealth of the kingdom.

IF THE money or other effects levied from the people by way of tax, were destroyed and annihilated; then it is clear that such levies would diminish the Common Wealth. Or if the same were exported out of the kingdom, without any return at all; then the case would be also the same or worse.

What shifting of money from hand [to hand] is profitable or not.

But if what is levied as aforesaid be only transferred from one hand to another; then we are only to consider, Whether the said money or commodities are taken from an improving hand, and given to an ill husband; or *vice versâ*?

As, for example, suppose that money, by way of tax, be taken from one who spendeth the same in superfluous eating and drinking, and delivered to another who employeth the same in improving of land, in fishing, in working of mines, in manufacture, &c.; it is manifest that such tax is an advantage to the State whereof the said different persons are members.

Nay, if money be taken from him, who spendeth the same, as aforesaid, upon eating and drinking, or any other perishing commodity; and the same be transferred to one that bestoweth it on Clothes: I say, that, even in this case, the Common Wealth hath some little advantage; because clothes do not altogether perish so soon as meat and drinks. But if the same be spent in Furniture of Houses, the advantage is yet a little more; if in Building of Houses, yet more; if in Improving of Lands, working of mines, fishing, &c., yet more: but, most of all, in bringing gold and silver into the country, because those things are not only not perishable; but are esteemed for wealth at all times and everywhere. Whereas other commodities which are perishable, and whose value depends upon the fashion, or which are contingently scarce and plentiful, are Wealth but *pro hic et nunc;* as shall be elsewhere said.

In the next place, if the people of any country, who have not already a full employment, should be enjoined or taxed to work upon such commodities as are imported from abroad: I say, that such a tax also doth improve the Common Wealth.

Taxing of new works, a benefit to the Common Wealth.

Moreover, if persons who live by begging, cheating, stealing, gaming, borrowing without intention of restoring; who, by those ways, do get from the credulous and careless, more than is sufficient for the subsistence of such persons; I say, that although the State should have no present employment for such persons, and consequently should be forced to bear the whole charge of their livelihood: yet it were more for the public profit, to give

The taxing of Idlers.

all such persons a regular and competent allowance by public tax, than to suffer them to spend extravagantly at the only charge of careless, credulous, and good-natured people; and to expose the Common Wealth to the loss of so many able men, whose lives are taken away for the crimes which ill discipline doth occasion.

On the contrary, if the stocks [*capital*] of laborious and ingenious men, who are not only beautifying the country where they live, by elegant diet, apparel, furniture, housing, pleasant gardens, orchards, and public edifices, &c.; but are also increasing the gold, silver, and jewels of the country by trade and arms: I say, if the stock of these men should be diminished by a tax, and transferred to such as do nothing at all but eat and drink, sing, play, and dance; nay, to such as study the metaphysics or other needless speculation, or else employ themselves in any other way which produces no *material* thing, or things of *real* use and value in the Common Wealth—in this case, I say the Wealth of the Public will be diminished; otherwise than as such exercises are recreations and refreshments of the mind, and which, being moderately used, do gratify and dispose men to what is in itself more considerable.

Wherefore upon the whole matter, to know whether a tax will do good or harm, the state of the people and their employments must be well known, that is to say:

A Judgement of what taxes are advantageous.

What part of the people are unfit for labour by their infancy or impotency; and also what part are exempt from the same by reason of their wealth, function, or dignities, or by reason of their charge and employments otherwise than in governing, directing, and preserving those who are appointed to Labour and Arts?

2. In the next place, computation must be made, What part of those who are fit for Labour and Arts as aforesaid, are able to perform the work of the Nation, in its present state and measure?

3. It is to be considered, Whether the remainder can make all, or any part of those commodities which are imported from abroad? which of them? and how much in particular? The remainder of which sort of people, if any be, may, safely, and without possible prejudice to the

Common Wealth, be employed in Arts and exercises of pleasure and ornament: the greatest whereof, is the improvement of natural knowledge [*natural science*].

Having thus, in general, illustrated this point; which, I think, needs no other proof but illustration: I come next to intimate that no part of Europe hath paid so much, by way of tax and public contribution, as Holland and Zealand, for this last hundred years; and yet no country hath, in the same time, increased its wealth comparably to them. And it is manifest that they have followed the general considerations above mentioned, for they tax meats and drinks most heavily of all, to restrain the excessive expense of those things which twenty-four hours doth, as to the use of man, wholly annihilate; and they are more favourable to commodities of greater duration.

Nor do they tax according to what men gain, but in extraordinary cases: but always according to what men spend; and, most of all, according to what they spend needlessly, and without prospect of return.

Upon which grounds, their Customs upon goods imported and exported are generally low; as if they intended by them, only to keep an account of their Foreign Trade; and to retaliate upon their neighbouring States, the prejudices done them, by their prohibitions and impositions.

It is further to be observed, that, since the year 1636, the taxes and public levies made in England, Scotland, and Ireland, have been prodigiously greater than at any time heretofore; and yet the said kingdoms have increased in their wealth and strength for these last forty years [1637–1677, *therefore this Essay was written about* 1677], as shall hereafter be shown.

It is probable that Holland and England are grown richer under taxes.

It is said, that the King of France, at present, doth levy the Fifth Part of his people's wealth; and yet great ostentation is made of the present riches and strength of that Kingdom.

The difference of Princes' revenues.

Now, great care must be had in distinguishing between the wealth of the People, and that of an Absolute Monarch, who taketh from the people, where, when, and in what proportion he pleaseth.

Moreover, the subjects of two monarchs may be equally rich; and yet one monarch may be double as rich as the other, viz.: if one take the tenth part of the peoples' substance to his own dispose [*disposal*]; and the other but the twentieth.

Nay, the monarch of a poorer people may appear more splendid and gracious than that of a richer: which, perhaps, may be somewhat the case of France, as shall be examined.

As an instance and application of what has been said, I conceive that in Ireland, wherein are about 1,200,000 people, and nearly 300,000 smokes or hearths, it were more profitable for the King that each Head paid 2*s*. [=6*s*. *now*] worth of flax, than that each Smoke should pay 2*s*. in silver. And that for the following reasons:

That Ireland may be more advantageously taxed by a Pole in flax.

Ireland being under-peopled, and land and cattle being very cheap; there being everywhere store of fish and fowl; the ground yield excellent roots (and particularly that bread-like root, Potatoes); and withal they being able to perform their husbandry with such harness and tackle as each man can make with his own hands; and living in such houses as almost every man can build; and every housewife being a spinner and dyer of wool and yarn: they can live and subsist after their present fashion, without the use of gold and silver money; and can supply themselves with the necessaries above mentioned, without labouring two hours *per diem*.

Now, it hath been found that, by reason of insolvencies arising rather from the uselessness, than want, of money among these poor people; that from 300,000 hearths, which should have yielded £30,000 *per annum*, not £15,000 of money could be levied. Whereas it is easily imagined that four or five persons, dwelling in that cottage which hath but one smoke, could easily have planted a ground plot, of about forty feet square, with flax, or the fiftieth part of an acre: for so much ground will bear 8*s*. or 10*s*. worth of that commodity, and the rent of so much ground, in few places amounts to a penny *per annum*. Nor is there any skill requisite to this practice, wherewith the country is not already familiar.

Now as for a market for the flax, there is imported into Holland itself, over and above what that country produces, as much flax as is there sold for between £160,000 and £200,000; and into England and Ireland is imported [*from Holland*] as much linen cloth made of flax, and there spent [*used*] as is worth above half a million of money. As shall be shewn hereafter.

Wherefore, having shewn that silver money is useless to the poor people of Ireland; that half the hearth money could not be raised by reason thereof; that the people are not a fifth part employed; that the people and land of Ireland are competently qualified for flax; that one pennyworth of land produces 10*s*. worth of the same; and that there is market enough, and enough for £100,000 worth: I conceive my Proposition sufficiently proved; at least, to set forwards and promote a practice, which both the present Law and Interest of the country doth require. Especially, since if all the flax so produced should yield nothing, yet there is nothing lost; the same time having been worse spent before.

Upon the same grounds, the like tax of 2*s*. per head may be raised with the like advantage upon the people of England, which will amount to £600,000 *per annum*; to be paid in Flax manufactured into all sorts of Linens, threads, tapes, and laces; which we now receive from France, Flanders, Holland, and Germany: the value whereof doth far exceed the sum last mentioned, as hath appeared by the examination of particulars.

Duties upon redundant commodities may be a harmless tax.

It is observed by clothiers and others, who employ great numbers of poor people, that when corn is extremely plentiful, that the labour of the poor is proportionably dear; and scarcely to be had at all: so licentious are they who labour only to eat, or rather to drink.

Wherefore, when so many acres sown with corn, as do usually produce a sufficient store for the nation, shall produce perhaps double to what is expected, or necessary; it seems not unreasonable that this common blessing of GOD should be applied to the common good of all people, represented by their Sovereign; much rather than that the same should be abused by the vile and brutish part of mankind, to the prejudice of the Common Wealth: and consequently that such surplusage of corn should be sent to public storehouses; from thence to be disposed of, to the best advantage of the public.

Now, if the corn spent in England, at 5*s*. [=15*s*. *now*] per bushel of wheat, and 2*s*. 6*d*. of barley, be worth £10,000,000 *communibus annis*; it follows that in years of great plenty, when the grains are one-third part cheaper, that a vast advantage might accrue to the Common Wealth, which is now spent in overfeeding of the people in quantity or quality, and so indisposing them to their usual labour.

The like may be said of Sugar, Tobacco, and Pepper, which custom hath now made necessary to all sorts of people; and which the overplanting of them, hath made unreasonably cheap. I say, it is not absurd that the Public should be advantaged by this extraordinary plenty.

That an excise should be laid upon Currants also is not unreasonable: not only for this, but also for other reasons.

Of the tax by a Grand Militia, and by two other sorts of armies.

The way of the present Militia, or Trained Bands, is a gentle tax upon the country: because it is only a few days' labour in the year, of a few men in respect to the whole; using their own goods, that is, their own arms.

Now, if there be 3,000,000 of males in England, there be about 200,000 of them who are between the age of sixteen and thirty, unmarried persons, and who live by their labour and service: for of so many, or thereabouts, the present Militia consists.

Now, if 150,000 of these were armed and trained as Foot, and 50,000 as Horse (Horse being of special advantage in islands), the said forces at land, with 30,000 men at sea, would, by GOD's ordinary blessing, defend this nation, being an island, against any force in view.

But the Charge of arming, disciplining, and rendezvousing all these men, twice or thrice a year, would be a very gentle tax levied by the people themselves, and paid to themselves.

Moreover, if out of the said number, one-third part were selected, of such as are more than ordinarily fit and disposed for war, to be exercised and rendezvoused fourteen or fifteen times *per annum*; the charge thereof, being but a fortnight's pay, would also be a very gentle tax.

Lastly, if out of this last-mentioned number, one-third again should be selected; making about 16,000 Foot and nearly 6,000 Horse to be exercised and rendezvoused forty days in the year: I say, that the Charge of all these three Militias, allowing the latter six weeks' pay *per annum*, would not cost above £120,000 *per annum*; which I take to be an easy burden for so great a benefit.

Forasmuch as the present Navy of England requires 36,000 men to man it; and for that the English Trade of Shipping requires about 48,000 men to manage it also: it follow that to perform both well, there ought to be about 72,000 men (and not 84,000) competently qualified for these services. For want whereof, we see that it is a long while before a Royal Navy can be manned: which till it be, it is of no effectual use, but lies at charge. And we see likewise, upon these occasions, that merchants are put to great straights and inconveniences, and do pay excessive rates for the carrying on their trade.

For supplying the Navy and Merchants, with seamen.

Now if 24,000 able-bodied tradesmen [*artisans*] were, by 6,000 of them *per annum*, brought up and fitted for sea service; and for their encouragement allowed 20*s*. [=£3 *now*] *per annum* for every year they had been at sea, even when they stay at home, not exceeding £6 for those who have served six years or upward; it follows that about £72,000, at the *medium* of £3 per man, would salariate the whole number of 24,000.

And so, forasmuch as half the seamen which manage the merchants' trade, are supposed to be always in harbour, and are about 24,000 men; the said half together with the Auxiliaries last mentioned, would, upon all emergencies, man out the whole Royal Navy with 36,000, and leave to the Merchants 12,000 of the abler Auxiliaries to perform their business in harbour till others come home from sea. And thus 36,000, 24,000, and 12,000 make the 72,000 above mentioned.

I say that more than this sum of £72,000 is fruitlessly spent and overpaid by the Merchants, whensoever a great fleet is to be fitted out.

Now these, whom I call Auxiliary Seamen, are such as have another trade besides, wherewith to maintain themselves when they are not employed at sea: and the charge of maintaining them, though £72,000 *per annum*, I take to be little or nothing, for the reasons above mentioned, and consequently an easy tax to the people, because levied by, and paid to themselves.

As we propounded that Ireland should be taxed with flax; England, by linen and other manufactures of the same; I conceive that Scotland also might be taxed as much [*i.e.*, £30,000], to be paid in herrings, as Ireland in flax.

A herring tax upon Scotland.

Now the three taxes, viz., of Flax, Linen, and Herrings; and the maintenance of the triple Militia, and of the Auxiliary Seamen above mentioned, do, all five of them together, amount to £1,000,000 of money. The raising whereof is not a million spent, but gain unto the Common Wealth; unless it can be made to appear that, by reason of all or any of them, the exportation of woollen manufactures, lead, and tin are lessened; or of such commodities as our own East and West India trade do produce: forasmuch as I conceive that the Exportation of these last-mentioned commodities is the Touchstone whereby the wealth of England is tried, and the Pulse whereby the health of the Kingdom may be discerned.

CHAPTER III.

That France cannot, by reason of natural and perpetual impediments, be more powerful at sea than the English or Hollanders now are, or may be.

POWER at sea consists chiefly of Men able to fight at sea; and that, in such shipping as is most proper for the seas wherein they serve: and those are, in these Northern seas, ships from between 300 to 1,300 tons; and of those, such as draw much water, and have a deep latch [*hold*] in the sea, in order to keep a good wind, and not fall to leeward, a matter of vast advantage in sea service.

The qualities of ships fit for the defence of England.

Wherefore it is to be examined, Whether the King of France hath ports in the Northern seas (where he hath most occasion for his fleets of war, in any contests with England), able to receive the vessels above mentioned, in all weathers, both in winter and summer season?

For if the King of France would bring to sea an equal number of fighting men with England and Holland, in small floaty leeward vessels, he would certainly be of the weaker side. For a vessel of 1,000 tons, manned with 500 men, fighting with five vessels of 200 tons, each manned with 100 men apiece, shall, in common reason, have the better, offensively and defensively: forasmuch as the great ship can carry such ordnance as can reach the small ones at a far greater distance than those can reach, or at least hurt the other; and can batter and sink at a distance, when small ones can scarce pierce.

Moreover, it is more difficult for men, out of a small vessel to enter a tall ship; than for men from a higher place to leap down into a lower: nor is small shot [*musketry*] so effectual upon a tall ship, as *vice versâ*.

And as for vessels drawing much water, and consequently keeping good wind; they can take or leave leeward vessels at pleasure, and secure themselves from being boarded by them. Moreover the windward ship has a fairer mark at a leeward ship, than *vice versâ*; and can place her shot upon such parts of the leeward vessel, as upon the next tack will be under water.

Now then, the King of France having no ports able to receive large windward vessels, between Dunkirk and Ushant: what other ships he can bring into those seas will not be considerable.

As for the wide ocean, which his harbours of Brest and Charente do look into: it affordeth it him no advantage upon an enemy; there being so great a latitude of engaging or not, even when the parties are in sight of each other.

Wherefore, although the King of France were immensely rich, and could build what ships he pleased, both for number and quality: yet if he have not ports to receive and shelter that sort and size of shipping which is fit for his purpose, the said riches will, in this case, be fruitless, and a mere expense without any return or profit.

Some will say that other nations cannot build so good ships as the English. I do indeed hope they cannot. But because it seems too possible that they may, sooner or later, by practice and experience, I shall not make use of that argument: having bound myself to shew that the impediments of France, as to this purpose, are natural and perpetual.

Ships and guns do not fight of themselves; but by men, who act and manage them: wherefore it is more material to shew, That the King of France neither hath, nor can have men sufficient to man a fleet of equal strength to that of the King of England, viz.:

The King of England's Navy consists of about 70,000 tons

of shipping, which requires 36,000 men to man it. These men being supposed to be divided into eight parts, I conceive that one-eighth part must be persons of great experience and reputation in sea service: another eighth part must be such as have used the sea, seven years and upwards: half of them, or four-eighths part more, must be such as have used the sea above a twelvemonth, viz., two, three, four, five, or six years: allowing but one quarter of the whole complements to be such as never were at sea at all, or at most but one voyage, or upon one expedition. So that, at a *medium*, I reckon that the whole Fleet must be men of three or four years' growth [*in seamanship*], one with another.

The qualifications of seamen for defence.

FOURNIER, a late judicious writer, making it his business to persuade the world, how considerable the King of France was, or might be, at sea, in the ninety-second and ninety-third pages of his *Hydrography*, saith that "there was one place in Brittany which had furnished the King with 1,400 seamen, and that perhaps the whole sea coast of France might have furnished him with fifteen times as many." Now, supposing his whole allegation were true, yet the said number amounts but to 21,000: all which, if the whole Trade of Shipping in France were quite and clean abandoned, would not, by above a third, man out a Fleet equivalent to that of the King of England. And if the Trade were but barely kept alive, there would not be one-third part of men enough to man the said Fleet.

The number of seamen in France.

But if the Shipping Trade of France be not above a quarter as great as that of England; and that one-third part of the same, namely, the fishing trade to the Banks of Newfoundland, is not peculiar or fixed to the French: then, I say, that if the King of England, having power to press men, cannot, under two or three months' time, man his Fleet; then the King of France, with less than a quarter of the same help, can never do it at all.

For in France, as shall elsewhere be shewn, there are not above 150,000 tons of trading vessels; and consequently not above 15,000 seamen, reckoning a man to 10 tons.

As it has been shewn, that the King of France cannot, at present, man such a Fleet as is above described: we come next to shew, That he never can! being under natural and perpetual impediments, viz.:

1. If there be but 15,000 seamen in all France, to manage its Trade; it is not to be supposed that the said Trade should be extinguished; nor that it should spare above 5,000 of the said 15,000 towards manning the Fleet which requires 35,000.

Now the deficient 30,000 must be supplied, one of these four ways. Either, first, by taking in landsmen; of which sort there must not be above 10,000: since the seamen will never be contented without being the major part. Nor do they heartily wish well to landsmen at all, or rejoice even at those successes of which the landsmen can claim any share: thinking it hard that they themselves, who are bred to miserable, painful, and dangerous employments, and yet profitable to the Common Wealth, should, at a time when booty and purchase is to be gotten, be clogged or hindered by any conjunction with landsmen, or forced to admit those to an equal share with themselves.

The ways whereby the French must increase seamen.

Why Seamen dislike Landsmen.

2. The seamen, which we suppose 20,000, must be had, that is, hired from other nations; which cannot be without tempting them with so much wages as exceeds what is given by merchants: and withal to counterpoise the danger of being hanged by their own Prince, and allowed no quarter if they are taken; the trouble of conveying themselves away, when restraints and prohibitions are upon them; and also the infamy of having been apostates to their own country and cause. I say their wages must be double to what their own Prince gives them; and their assurance must be very great, that they shall not be, at [the] long run, abused or slighted by those that employed them, as "hating the traitor, although they love the treason."

The danger of English seamen, their servng the French.

I say, moreover, that those who will be thus tempted away, must be the basest and lewdest sort of seamen; and such as have not enough of honour and conscience to qualify them for any trust or gallant performance.

3. Another way to increase seamen is to put great num-

bers of landsmen upon ships of war, in order to their being seamen: but this course cannot be effectual, not only for the above-mentioned antipathy between landsmen and seamen; but also because it is seen that men at sea do not apply themselves to labour and practice, without more necessity than happens in over-manned shipping. For where there are fifty men in a vessel that ten can sufficiently navigate, the supernumerary forty will improve little: but where there shall be of ten, but one or two supernumeraries; there necessity will often call upon every man to set his hand to the work, which must be well done, at the peril of their own lives.

How men learn to be good seamen.

Moreover, seamen shifting vessels, almost every six or twelve months, do sometimes sail in small barks, sometimes in middling ships, and sometimes in great vessels of defence; sometimes in lighters, sometimes in hoighs [*hoys*], sometimes in ketches, sometimes in three-masted ships. Sometimes they go to the Southward, sometimes to the Northward; sometimes they coast, sometimes they cross the ocean. By all which variety of service, they do in time complete themselves in every part and circumstance of their faculty. Whereas those who go out for a summer in a man-of-war, have not that variety of practice, nor a direct necessity of doing anything at all.

Besides, it is three or four years, at a *medium*, wherein a seaman must be made; neither can there be less than three seamen, to make a fourth of a landsman. Consequently the 15,000 seamen of France can increase but 5,000 in three or four years: and unless their Trade should increase with their seamen in proportion, the King must be forced to bear the charge of this improvement out of the public Stock [*national Exchequer*], which is intolerable.

So as the question which now remains is, Whether the shipping trade of France is likely to increase?

Whether the shipping trade of France is likely to increase?

Upon which account it is to be considered

That France is sufficiently stored with all kinds of necessaries; as with corn, cattle, wine, salt, linen cloth, paper, silk, fruits, &c.: so as they need little shipping to import more commodities of weight or bulk. Neither is there anything of bulk exported out of France, but wines and salt; the weight whereof is under 100,000 tons *per annum*, yielding not employment to above 25,000 tons of shipping: and these are, for the most part, Dutch and English; who are not only already in possession of the said trade, but also are better fitted to maintain it than the French are, or perhaps ever can be. And that for the following reasons, viz.:

1. Because the French cannot victual so cheap as the English and Dutch, nor sail with so few hands. Reasons why it cannot.
2. The French, for want of good coasts and harbours, cannot keep their ships in port under double the charge that the English and the Hollanders can.
3. By reason of paucity, and distance of their ports one from another, their seamen and tradesmen [*mechanics*] relating to shipping, cannot correspond with and assist one another so easily, cheaply, and advantageously as in other places.

Wherefore, if their shipping trade is not likely to increase within themselves, and much less to increase by their beating out the English and Hollanders from being the Carriers of the World; it follows that their seamen will not be increased by the increase of their said Trade.

Wherefore, and for that they are not likely to be increased by any of the several ways above specified; and for that their ports are not fit to receive ships of burden and quality fit for their purpose, and that by reason by the less fitness of their ports than that of their neighbours'; I conceive that what was propounded hath been competently proved.

The aforenamed FOURNIER, in the ninety-second and ninety-third pages of his *Hydrography*, hath laboured to prove the contrary of all this; unto which I refer the reader: not thinking his arguments of any weight at all, in the present case. Nor, indeed, doth he make his comparisons with the English and Hollanders, but with the Spaniards: who, nor the Grand Signior [*the Turks*] (the latter of whom hath greater advantages to be powerful at sea than the King of France) could ever attain to any illustrious greatness in Naval Power; having often attempted, but never succeeded in the same.

Nor is it easy to believe that the King of England should, for so many years, have continued his Title to the Sovereignty of the Narrow Seas against his neighbours (ambitious enough to have gotten it from him), had not their impediments been Natural and Perpetual, and such as we say do obstruct the King of France.

CHAPTER IV.

That the People and Territories of the King of England are, naturally, nearly as considerable for wealth and strength, as those of France.

Of comparison between the Territories of England and France.

THE Author of *The State of England*, among the many useful truths and observations he hath set down, delivers the proportion between the territories of England and France to be as 30 to 82: the which, if it be true, then England, Scotland, and Ireland, with the islands unto them belonging, will, taken altogether, be nearly as big as France.

Though I ought to take all advantages for proving the paradox in hand: yet I had rather grant that England, Scotland, and Ireland, with the islands before mentioned, together with the planted parts of Newfoundland, New England, New Netherland [*New York*], Virginia, Maryland, Carolina, Jamaica, Bermudas, Barbadoes, and all the rest of the Caribbee Islands, with what the King hath in Asia and Africa, do *not* contain so much territory as France and what planted land [*Canada, &c.*] the King of France hath also in America. And if any man will be heterodox in behalf of the French Interest, I would be contented, against my knowledge and judgement, to allow the King of France's territories to be a Seventh, Sixth, or even a Fifth greater than those of the King of England: believing that both Princes have more land than they do employ to its utmost use.

And here, I beg leave, among the several matters which I intend for serious, to interpose a jocular and perhaps ridiculous digression; and which I indeed desire men to look upon rather as a Dream or reverie than a rational Proposition: the which is, that if all the Moveables and People of Ireland and of the Highlands of Scotland were transported into the rest of Great Britain, that then the King and his subjects would thereby become more rich and strong, both offensively and defensively, than now they are.

A Proposition for quitting Ireland and the Highlands of Scotland.

It is true, I have heard many wise men say, when they were bewailing the vast losses of the English in preventing and suppressing rebellions in Ireland, and considering how little profit hath returned either to the King or subjects of England, for their five hundred years' doing and suffering in that country: I say, I have heard wise men, in such their melancholies, wish "that (the people of Ireland being saved) the island were sunk under water!"

Now it troubles me, that the distemper of my own mind, in this point, carries me to dream that the benefit of those wishes may practically be obtained, without sinking that vast mountainous island under water; which I take to be somewhat difficult: for although Dutch engineers may drain its bogs, yet I know no artists that can sink its mountains. If ingenious and learned men, among whom I reckon Sir THOMAS MORE and DESCARTES, have disputed, That we who think ourselves awake, are or may be really in a dream; and since the greatest absurdities of dreams are but a preposterous and tumultuary contexture of realities: I will crave the umbrage [*example*] of these great men last named; to say something for this wild conception, with submission to the better judgement of all those that can prove themselves awake.

If there were but One man living in England, then the benefit of the whole territory could be but the livelihood of that One man: but if another man were added, the rent or benefit of the same would be double; if two, triple; and so forward, until so many men were planted in it, as the whole territory could afford food unto. For if a man would know what any land is worth, the true and natural question must be, How many men will it feed? How many men are there to be fed?

But to speak more practically. Land of the same quantity and quality in England, is generally worth four or five times as much as in Ireland, and but one-quarter or one-third of what it is worth in Holland: because England is four or five times better peopled than Ireland, and but a quarter so well as Holland.

And, moreover, where the rent is advanced by reason of the multitude of people, there, the number of years' purchase for which an inheritance may be sold is also advanced, though perhaps not in the very same proportion. For 20s. [=£3 *now*] *per annum* in Ireland, may be worth but £8 [=£24 *now*]; and in England, where titles are very sure, above £20 [=£60 *now*]; and in Holland, above £30 [=£90 *now*].

I suppose that in Ireland and the Highlands of Scotland, there may be about 1,800,000 people, or about a Fifth part of what are in all the three Kingdoms [*i.e.*, 9,000,000].

Wherefore the First question will be, Whether England, Wales, and the Lowlands of Scotland cannot afford food (that is to say, corn, fish, flesh, and fowl) to a fifth part more people than are, at present, planted upon it; with the same labour that the said fifth part do now take, where they are? For if so, then what is propounded is naturally possible.

2. It is to be inquired, What the value of the Immoveables, which, upon such removal, must be left behind, are worth? For if they be worth less than the advancement of the price of land in England will amount unto; then the Proposal is to be considered.

3. If the relict [*relinquished*] Lands and the Immoveables left behind upon them, may be sold for money; or if no other nation shall dare meddle with them, without paying well for them; and if the nation who shall be admitted, shall be less able to prejudice and annoy the Transplantees into England, than before: then I conceive that the whole Proposal will be a pleasant and profitable Dream indeed!

That England and the Lowlands of Scotland will feed the people of England, Scotland, and Ireland.

As to the First point, Whether England and the Lowlands of Scotland can maintain a Fifth part more people than they now do, that is to say, 9,000,000 of souls in all?

For answer thereunto, I first say, that the said territories of England and the Lowlands of

Scotland contain about 36,000,000 acres, that is, 4 acres for every head (man, woman, and child): but the United Provinces do not allow above 1½ acres. And England itself, rescinding [*excluding*] Wales, hath but 3 acres to every head; according to the present state of tillage and husbandry.

Now if we consider that England having but 3 acres to a head, as aforesaid, does so abound in victuals as that it maketh laws against the importation of cattle, flesh, and fish from abroad; and that the draining of fens, improving of forests, inclosing of commons, sowing of St. Foyne [*sainfoin*] and clover-grass, be grumbled against by landlords, as the way to depress the price of victuals: then it plainly follows that less than 3 acres, improved as they may be, will serve the turn; and consequently that 4 will suffice abundantly.

I could here set down the very number of acres that would bear bread, drink, and corn, together with flesh, butter, and cheese sufficient to victual 9,000,000 persons, as they are victualled in ships and regular families: but I shall only say in general, that 12,000,000 acres, viz., one-third of 36,000,000 will do it; supposing that roots, fruits, fowls, and fish, and the ordinary profit of lead, tin, and iron mines, and woods, would piece up any defect that may be feared.

As to the Second, I say that the Land and Housing in Ireland and the Highlands of Scotland, at the present market rates, are not worth £13,000,000 [=£39,000,000 *now*] of money: nor would the actual charge of transplantation proposed, amount to £4,000,000 [=£12,000,000 *now*] more.

That the value of all the quitted lands and unmoveable goods and charge of transplantation are not worth above £17,000,000.

So then the question will be, Whether the benefit expected from this Transplantation will exceed £17,000,000 [=£51,000,000 *now*].

To which I say, that the Advantage will probably be nearly four times the last-mentioned sum or about £69,300,000 [=£207,900,000 *now*].

For if the Rent of all England and Wales and the Lowlands of Scotland be about £9,000,000 [=£27,000,000 *now*] *per annum*; and if the Fifth part of the people be superadded unto the present inhabitants of those countries: then the Rent will amount to £10,800,000 [=£32,400,000 *now*]; and the number of years' purchase will rise from 17½ to a fifth part more, which is 21.

So as the Land, which is now worth but £9,000,000 *per annum*, at 17½ years' purchase, making £157,500,000, will then be worth £10,800,000 at 21 years' purchase, viz., £226,800,000 [=£680,400,000 *now*]: which is £69,300,000 [=£207,900,000 *now*] more than it was before.

That those who purchase Ireland shall weaken themselves.

And if any Prince willing to enlarge his territories, will give anything more than £6,500,000, or half the present value, for the said relinquished land; which are estimated to be worth £13,000,000: then the whole profit will be above £75,800,000 [=£227,400,000 *now*]; or above Four times the loss, as the same was above computed.

But if any man shall object that it will be dangerous unto England, that Ireland should be in the hands of any other nation: I answer, in short, that that nation, (whoever shall purchase it) being divided by means of the said purchase, shall not be more able to annoy England than now, in its united condition. Nor is Ireland nearer England, than France and Flanders.

Now if any man shall desire a more clear explanation, How, and by what means, the rents of lands shall rise by this closer cohabitation of people, above described? I answer, that the advantage will arise in transplanting above 1,800,000 people, from the poor and miserable trade of husbandry, to more beneficial handicrafts. For, when the superaddition is made, a very little addition of husbandry to the same lands will produce a fifth part more of food, and consequently the additional hands, earning but 40s. [=£6 *now*] *per annum*, as they may very well do, nay, to £8 [=£24 *now*] *per annum* at some other trade; the superlucration will be above £3,600,000 [=£10,800,000 *now*] *per annum*: which at 20 years' purchase is £70,000,000 [=£210,000,000 *now*].

Moreover, as the inhabitants of cities and towns spend more commodities and make greater consumptions than those who live in wild thin-peopled countries; so when England shall be thicker peopled, in the manner before described, the very same people shall then spend more than when they lived more sordidly and inurbanely; and further asunder, and more out of the sight, observation, and emulation of each other: every man desiring to put on better apparel when he appears in company than when he has no occasion to be seen.

I further add that the charge of the Government (Civil, Military, and Ecclesiastical) would be more cheap, safe, and effectual in this condition of closer cohabitation than otherwise: as not only reason, but the example of the United Provinces doth demonstrate.

But to let this whole digression pass for a mere Dream, I suppose it will serve to prove that in case the King of England's territories should be a little less than those of the King of France, that forasmuch as neither of them is overpeopled, the difference is not material to the question in hand:

That the difference between England's and France's territory is not material.

Wherefore supposing the King of France's advantages to be little or nothing in point of Territory; we come, next, to examine and compare the number of Subjects which each of these monarchs doth govern.

The book called *The State of France* maketh that Kingdom to consist of 27,000 parishes. And another book, written by a substantial author, who professedly enquires into the state of the Church and Churchmen [*Clergy*] of France, sets it down as an extraordinary case, that a parish in France should have 600 souls; where I suppose that the said Author (who hath so well examined the matter) is not of opinion that every parish, one with another, hath above 500. By which reckoning, the whole people of France are about 13,500,000.

Now the people of England, Scotland, and Ireland, with the islands adjoining, by computation from the number of parishes (which commonly have more people in Protestant Churches than in Popish countries), as also from the Hearth Money, Pole Money, and Excise, amount to about 9,500,000.

The King of France hath, in effect, but 13,500,000 of subjects; and the King of England 10,000,000.

The King of France hath 270,000 Churchmen, and the King of England 20,000.

The King of England hath 40,000 seamen; and the King of France, 10,000.

There are in New England, about 16,000 men mustered in arms, and about 24,000 able to bear arms: and consequently about 150,000 in all. And I see no reason why, in all this, and the other Plantations [*Colonies*] of Asia, Africa, and America, there should not be 500,000 in all. But this last, I leave to every man's conjecture.

And consequently, I suppose that the King of England hath about 10,000,000 of subjects *ubivis terrarum orbis*, and the King of France about 13,500,000 as aforesaid.

Although it be very material to know the number of Subjects belonging to each Prince: yet when the question is concerning their Wealth and Strength, it is also material to examine, How many of them do get More than they spend? and How many Less?

In order whereunto, it is to be considered that in the King of England's Dominions, there are not 20,000 Churchmen [*Clergy*]: but in France (as the aforementioned Author of theirs doth aver, who sets down the particular number of each religious Order) there are about 270,000, *viz.*, 250,000 more than we think necessary; that is to say, 250,000 withdrawn out of the World.

Now the said number of adult and able-bodied persons are equivalent to about double the same number of the promiscuous mass of mankind. And the same Author says, that the same Religious Persons do spend, one with another, about 18*d. per diem*, which is triple even, to what a labouring man requires.

Wherefore the said 250,000 Churchmen, living as they do, make the King of France's 13,500,000 to be less than 13,000,000.

Now if Ten men can defend themselves as well in islands as Thirteen can upon the Continent; then the said Ten being not concerned to increase their territory by the invasion of others, are as effectual as Thirteen in point of Strength also.

Wherefore that there are more superlucrators in the English, than in the French Dominions, we say, as followeth:

There be in England, Scotland, Ireland, and the King's other territories, above 40,000 seamen: in France not above a quarter so many, But one seaman earneth as much as two common husbandmen: wherefore this difference in seamen, addeth to the account of the King of England's subjects, is an advantage, equivalent to 60,000 husbandmen.

The multitude of the Clergy does lessen the King of France's people.

The multitude of sea and naval men does increase the King of England's subjects.

There are in England, Scotland, and Ireland, and all other the King of England's territories, 600,000 tons of shipping, worth £4,500,000 [=£13,500,000 *now*] of money: and the Annual Charge of maintaining the shipping of England by new buildings and reparations is about one-third part of the same sum [£1,500,000 =£4,500,000 *now*], which is the wages of 150,000 husbandmen, but is not the wages of above one-third part [*i.e.*, 50,000] of so many artisans as are employed upon shipping of all sorts, viz., shipwrights, caulkers, joiners, carvers, painters, block-makers, rope-makers, mast-makers, smiths of several sorts, flag-makers, compass-makers, brewers, bakers, and all other sorts of victuallers, all sorts of tradesmen [*mechanics*] relating to guns and gunner's stores. Wherefore there being four times more of these artisans in England, &c., than in France, they further add to the account of the King of England's subjects, the equivalent of 80,000 husbandmen more.

The sea-line of England, Scotland, and Ireland, and adjacent islands, is about 3,800 miles, according to which length and the whole contents of acres, the said land would be an oblong or parallelogram figure of 3,800 miles long, and about 24 miles broad: and consequently, every part of England, Scotland, and Ireland is, one with another, but 12 miles from the sea.

The King of England's territories are, in effect, but 12 miles from navigable water: the King of France's 65.

Whereas France, containing but about 1,000 miles of sea-line, is by the like method or computation, about 65 miles from the sea-side; and, considering the paucity of ports in comparison of what are in the King of England's Dominions, as good as 70 miles distant from a port.

Upon which grounds, it is clear that England can be

supplied with all gross and bulky commodities of foreign growth and manufacture, at far cheaper rates than France can be, viz., at about 4s. *per cent.* cheaper: the land carriage for the difference of the distance between England and France from a port being so much, or near thereabouts.

Now to what advantage this conveniency amounteth, upon the importation or exportation of bulky commodities, cannot be less than the labour of 1,000,000 of people: meaning by bulky commodities all sorts of timber, plank, and staves for caske: all iron, lead, stone, bricks, and tiles for building; all corn, salt, and drinks; all flesh and fish; and indeed all other commodities wherein the gain and loss of 4s. *per cent.* is considerable: where note, that the like wines are sold in the inner parts of France for £4 or £5 a tun, which near the ports, yield £7.

The decay of timber in England is no very formidable matter.

Moreover, upon this principle, the decay of timber in England is no very formidable thing, as the rebuilding of London [*after the Fire of* 1666] and of the ships wasted by the Dutch War [1665–7] do clearly manifest.

Nor can there be any want of corn, or other necessary provisions in England; unless the weather hath been universally unseasonable for the growth of the same, which seldom or never happens. For the same causes which make dearth in one place, do often cause plenty in another; wet weather being propitious to high lands, which drowneth the low.

It is observed that the poor in France have generally less wages than in England; and yet their victuals are generally dearer there; which being so, there may be more superlucration in England than in France.

The King of England's subjects spend nearly as much as the King of France's.

Lastly, I offer to the consideration of all those who have travelled through England and France, Whether the plebians of England, for they constitute the bulk of the nation, do not spend a sixth part more than the plebians of France? And if so, it is necessary that they must first get it: and consequently that 10,000,000 of the King of England's subjects are equivalent to 12,000,000 of the King of France;

and, upon the whole matter, to the 13,000,000 at which the French nation was estimated.

It will here be objected that the splendour and magnificences of the King of France appearing greater than those of England, the wealth of France must be proportionably greater than that of England. But that doth not follow, forasmuch as the apparent greatness of the King doth depend upon the *quota pars* of the people's wealth which he levieth from them. For supposing the people to be equally rich, if one of the sovereigns levy a Fifth part and the other a Fifteenth; the one seems actually thrice as rich as the other: whereas, potentially, they are but equal.

The greater splendour of the King of France no certain argument of the greater wealth of his people.

Having thus discoursed of the Territory, People, Superlucration, and Defensibleness of both Dominions; and in some measure of their Trade so far as we had occasion to mention ships, shipping, and nearness to ports: we come, next, to enlarge a little further upon the Trade of each.

Comparison of the foreign Trade of England and France.

Some have estimated that there are not above 300,000,000 people in the whole world. Whether that be so, or not, is not very material to be known: but I have fair grounds to conjecture, and would be glad to know it more certainly, that there are not above 80,000,000 with whom the English and Dutch have commerce; no Europeans that I know of, trading directly or indirectly, where they do not. So that the Commercial World, or World of Trade, consisteth of about 80,000,000 souls as aforesaid.

And I further estimate that the value of all commodities yearly exchanged amongst them doth not exceed the value of £45,000,000 [=£135,000,000 *now*].

Now the Wealth of every nation consisting chiefly in the share which they have in the Foreign Trade with the whole Commercial World, rather than in the Domestic trade of ordinary meat, drink, and clothes, &c., which bring in little gold, silver, jewels, and other Universal

Wealth: we are to consider, Whether the subjects of the King of England, head for head, have not a greater share [in the Foreign Trade] than those of France?

To which purpose it hath been considered that the manufactures of wool yearly exported out of England into several parts of the world, viz.: all sorts of cloth, serges, stuffs, cottons, bayes, sayes, frieze, perpetuanas; as also stockings, caps, rugs, &c., exported out of England, Scotland, and Ireland, do amount unto £5,000,000 [=£15,000,000 *now*].

The value of lead, tin, and coals, to be £500,000 [=£1,500,000 *now*].

The value of all clothes, household stuff, &c., carried into America [*i.e., the English Colonies there*], £200,000 [=£600,000 *now*].

The value of silver and gold taken [*in the way of trade*] from the Spaniards, £60,000 [=£180,000 *now*].

The value of sugar, indigo, tobacco, cotton, and cocoa, brought from the southward parts of America, £600,000 [=£1,800,000 *now*].

The value of the fish, pipe staves, masts, beaver, &c., brought from New England and the northern parts of America, £200,000 [=£600,000 *now*].

The value of the wool, butter, hides, tallow, beef, herrings, pilchards, and salmon exported out of Ireland, £800,000 [=£2,400,000 *now*].

The value of the coals, salt, linen, yarn, herrings, pilchards, salmon, linen cloth, and yarn brought out of Scotland and Ireland, £500,000 [=£1,500,000 *now*].

The value of saltpetre, pepper, calicoes, diamonds, drugs, and silks brought out of the East Indies (above what was spent in England), £800,000 [= £2,400,000 *now*].

The value of the slaves brought out of Africa, to serve in our America Plantations, £20,000[=£60,000 *now*].

Which with the Freight of English shipping trading into foreign parts, being above £1,500,000 [=£4,500,000 *now*], makes in all £10,180,000 [=£30,540,000 *now*].

Which computation is sufficiently justified by the Customs of the three Kingdoms, whose intrinsic value is thought to be nearly £1,000,000 [=£3,000,000 *now*] *per annum*, viz.:

£600,000	[=£1,800,000 *now*]	payable to the King.
£100,000	[= £300,000 *now*]	for the charges of collecting, &c.
£200,000	[= £600,000 *now*]	smuckled [*smuggled*] by the merchants; and
£100,000	[= £300,000 *now*]	gained by the Farmers.
£1,000,000		

according to common opinion and men's sayings.

And this agrees also with that proportion or part of the whole Trade of the World, which I have estimated the subjects of the King of England to be possessed of, viz., of about £10,000,000 of £45,000,000.

But the value of the French commodities brought into England, notwithstanding some current estimates, is not above £1,200,000 [=£3,600,000 *now*] *per annum*; and the value of all they export into all the world besides, not above three or four times as much: which computation also agreeth well enough with the account we have of the Customs of France.

So as France not exporting above Half the value of what England doth; and for that all the commodities of France—except wines, brandy, paper; and the *first* patterns and fashions of clothes and furniture (of which France is the mint)—are imitable by the English; and having withal more people than England: it follows that the people of England, &c., have, head for head, Thrice as much Foreign Trade as the people of France, and about Two parts out of Nine of the Trade of the whole Commercial World: and about Two parts in Seven of all the Shipping.

Notwithstanding all which, it is not to be denied, that the King and some Great Men of France appear more rich and splendid than those of the like Quality in England: all which arises rather from the nature of their Government, than from the intrinsic and natural causes of wealth and power.

CHAPTER V.

That the impediments of England's greatness are but contingent and removeable.

THE first Impediment of England's greatness is that the territories thereunto belonging, are too far asunder, and divided by the sea into many several islands and countries; and, I may say, into so many Kingdoms and several Governments, viz.:

The disunion of the Territories of England is an impediment of its greatness.

There be three distinct Legislative Powers in England, Scotland, Ireland; the which instead of uniting together, do oftèn cross one another's Interest, putting bars and impediments upon one another's trades, not only as if they were foreigners to each other, but sometimes as enemies.

The different Legislatures, another impediment.

2. The islands of Jersey and Guernsey, and the Isle of Man are under jurisdictions different from those, either of England, Scotland, or Ireland.

3. The Government of New England, both Civil and Ecclesiastical, doth so differ from that of His Majesty's other Dominions, that it is hard to say, what may be the consequence of it.

The Colonies belonging to England, a diminution to the Empire.

And the Government of the other Plantations doth also differ very much from any of the rest; although there be not, naturally, substantial reasons, from the situation, trade, and condition of the people, why there should be such differences.

From all which, it comes to pass that small divided remote Governments, being seldom able to defend themselves, the burden of protecting of them all, must lie upon the Chief Kingdom, England: and so all the smaller kingdoms and dominions, instead of being additions, are really diminutions.

But the same is remedied by making Two such Grand Councils as may equally represent the whole Empire: one to be chosen by the King, the other by the People.

The wealth of a King is threefold. One is the Wealth of his subjects. The second is the *Quota pars* of his subjects' wealth, given him for the public defence, honour, and ornament of the people, and to manage such undertaking for the common good, as no one, or a few private men are sufficient for. The third sort is the *Quota* of the last-mentioned *Quota pars*, which the King may dispose of, as his own personal inclination and discretion shall direct him, without account.

Now it is most manifest, that the afore-mentioned distances and differences of kingdoms and jurisdictions are great impediments to all the said several sorts of wealth, as may be seen in the following particulars.

First, in case of war with foreign nations, England commonly beareth the whole burden and charge: whereby many in England are utterly undone.

Secondly, England sometimes prohibiting the commodities of Ireland and Scotland (as, of late, it did the cattle, flesh, and fish of Ireland), did not only make food, and consequently labour, dearer in England: but also hath forced the people of Ireland to fetch those commodities from France, Holland, and other places, which before were sold them from England; to the great prejudice of both nations.

Thirdly, it occasions an unnecessary trouble and charge in collecting of Customs upon commodities passing between the several nations.

Fourthly, it is a damage to our Barbadoes and other American trades, that the goods which might pass thence immediately to several parts of the world, and to be sold at moderate rates; must first come into England, and there pay duties: and afterwards, if at all, pass into those countries, whither they might have gone immediately.

Fifthly, the islands of Jersey and Guernsey are protected at the charge of England: nevertheless the labour and industry of that people, which is very great, redounds most to the profit of the French.

Sixthly, in New England, there are vast numbers of able-bodied Englishmen employed chiefly in husbandry; and in the meanest part of it, which is breeding of cattle: whereas Ireland would have contained all those persons, and, at worst, would have afforded them lands on better terms than they have them in America, if not some other better trade withal than now they can have.

Seventhly, the inhabitants of the other Plantations although they do indeed plant commodities which will not grow so well in England; yet grasping at more land than will suffice to produce the said exotics in a sufficient quantity to serve the whole World, they do therein but distract and confound the effect of their own endeavours.

Eighthly, there is no doubt that the same people far and widely dispersed, must spend more upon their Government and protection, than the same living compactly, and when they have no occasion to depend upon the wind, weather, and all the accidents of the sea.

The different understanding of Prerogative, and Privileges of Parliament; of Law and Equity; Civil and Ecclesiastical [Jurisdictions]; the supreme Legislature of Ireland, &c.

A second impediment to the greatness of England is the different understanding of several material points, viz., of the King's Prerogative, Privileges of Parliament, the obscure differences between Law and Equity, as also between Civil and Ecclesiastical Jurisdictions, doubts whether the Kingdom of England hath power over the Kingdom of Ireland: besides the wonderful paradox, that Englishmen lawfully sent to suppress rebellions in Ireland, should, after having effected the same, be as it were disfranchised, and lose that Interest in the Legislative Power which they had in England; and pay Customs as foreigners for all they spend in Ireland, whither they were sent for the honour and benefit of England.

Want of natural Union, for want of mixture and transplantation.

The third impediment is, that Ireland being a conquered country, and containing not the Tenth part as many Irish natives as there are English in both kingdoms; that natural and firm Union is not made between the two peoples by transplantations and proportionable mixture, so as there may be but a Tenth part of the Irish in Ireland, and the same proportion in England: whereby the necessity of maintaining an army in Ireland at the expense of the quarter of all the rents of that kingdom may be taken away.

The unequal inconvenient method of taxing.

The fourth impediment is, that taxes in England are not levied upon the Expense, but upon the whole Estate; not upon Lands, Stock, and Labour, but chiefly upon land alone: and that not by any equal and indifferent standard, but the casual predominancy of Parties and factions. And moreover that these taxes are not levied with the least trouble and charge, but are let out to Farmers; who also let them from one to another, without explicit knowledge of what they do: but so as in conclusion, the poor people pay twice as much as the King receives.

The fifth impediment is the inequality of shires, dioceses, parishes, church-livings, and other precincts; as also [of] the Representation of the people in Parliament: all which do hinder the operations of Authority in the same manner as a wheel irregularly made and excentrically hung, neither moves so easily, nor performs its work so truly, as if the same were duly framed and poised.

Inequality of shires, dioceses, parishes, Members[hips] of Parliament, &c.

Sixthly, as to whether it be an impediment that the Power of Making War, and Raising Money be not in the same hand? much may be said. But I leave it to those who may more properly meddle with fundamental laws.

None of these impediments are natural: but have arisen, as the irregularity of buildings do, by being built a part at one time and a part at another; and by the changing of the state of things from what they were at the respective times when the practices we complain of were first admitted; and perhaps are but the warpings of time from the rectitude of the first institution.

As these impediments are contingent, so they are also removable.

For may not the land of superfluous territories be sold, and the people, with their movables, brought away? May not the English in the American Plantations, who plant tobacco, sugar, &c., compute what land will serve their turn, and then contract their habitation to that proportion, both for quantity and quality? As for the people of New England, I can but wish they were transplanted into Old England or Ireland, according to Proposals of their own, made within these twenty years [1657–1677]; although they were allowed more Liberty of Conscience than they allow one another.

May not the Three Kingdoms be United into One, and equally represented in Parliament? May not the several species [*races*] of the King's subjects be equally mixed in their habitations? Might not the parishes and other precincts be better equalized? Might not Jurisdictions and other pretences [*claims*] to Power be determined and ascertained? Might not the taxes be equally applotted, and directly applied to their ultimate use? Might not Dissenters in religion be indulged; they paying for a competent force to keep the public peace?

I humbly venture to say all these things may be done, if it be so thought fit by the Sovereign Power; because the like hath often been done already, at several places and times.

CHAPTER VI.

That the power and wealth of England hath increased this last forty years.

IT IS not much to be doubted but that the TERRITORIES under the King's dominion have increased: forasmuch as New Engand, Virginia, Barbadoes, and Jamaica, Tangier, and Bombay, have, since that time, been either added to His Majesty's territories, or improved from a desert condition, to abound with people, buildings, shipping, and the production of many useful commodities.

Many territories have been added to England within about forty years; and many improvements made.

And as for the land of England, Scotland, and Ireland, as it is not less in quantity than it was forty years ago, so it is manifest that, by reason of the draining of the fens, watering of dry grounds, improving of forests and commons, making of heathy and barren grounds to bear sainfoin and clo ver grass, [a]meliorating and multiplying several sorts of fruit and garden stuff, making some rivers navigable, &c.; I say, it is manifest that the land in its present condition is able to bear more provisions and commodities than it was forty years ago.

Secondly, although the PEOPLE of England, Scotland, and Ireland, which have extraordinarily perished, by the Plague and Sword, within these last forty years, do amount to about 300,000 above what [would] have died in the ordinary way: yet the ordinary increase by generation of 10,000,000, which doubles in 200 years, as hath been shewn by the Observators upon the Bills of Mortality, may, in forty years, which is a fifth part of the same time, have increased one-fifth part of the whole number, or 2,000,000.

Where note by the way, that the accession of Negroes to the American Plantations, being all men of great labour and little expense, is not inconsiderable. Besides, it is hoped that New England (where few or no women are barren, and most have many children; and where people live long and healthfully) hath produced an increase of as many people as were destroyed in the late tumults in Ireland.

As for HOUSING, the streets of London itself speaks it. I conceive it is double in value in that city to what it was forty years since. And for Housing in the country, it has increased at Newcastle, Yarmouth, Norwich, Exeter, Portsmouth, Cowes; Dublin, Kinsale, Londonderry and Coleraine in Ireland, far beyond the proportion of what I can learn has been dilapidated in other places. For in Ireland, where the ruin was greatest, the Housing, taking all together, is now more valuable than forty years ago. Nor is this to be doubted: since Housing is now more splendid than in those days; and the number of dwellers is increased by nearly one-fifth part; as in the last paragraph is set forth.

The Housing of London doubled in value.

As for SHIPPING, His Majesty's Navy is now triple or quadruple to what it was forty years since, and before the *Sovereign* was built.

The Shipping is very much increased; with the reasons thereof.

The shipping trading to Newcastle, which is now 80,000 tons, could not be then above a quarter of that quantity.

1. Because the City of London is doubled.
2. Because the use of coals is also at least doubled: because they were heretofore seldom used in chambers as now they are; nor were there so many bricks burned [*baked*] with them, as of late; nor did the country on both sides the Thames make use of them as now.

Besides, there are employed in Guinea [*i.e., the slave dealing*] and American trade, above 40,000 tons of shipping *per annum*; which trade in those days was inconsiderable.

The quantity of wines was not nearly so much as now, and, to be short, the Customs upon imported and exported commodities did not then yield a third part of the present value: which shews that not only Shipping, but Trade itself hath increased somewhat near that proportion.

As to MONEY, the interest thereof was, within these fifty years, at £10 *per cent.*; forty years ago, at £8; and now, at £6: no thanks to any laws which have been made to that purpose! forasmuch as those who can give good security, may now have it at less. But the natural fall of interest is the effect of the increase of money.

Interest of money abated nearly half.

Moreover if *rented* lands and houses have increased, and if trade hath increased also: it is certain that money, which payeth those rents and driveth on trade, must have increased also.

Money and Public Revenue increased.

Lastly, I leave it to the consideration of all observers, whether the number and splendour of Coaches, Equipage, and Household Furniture hath not increased since that time: to say nothing of the Postage of Letters, which has increased from One to Twenty; which argues the increase of business and negotiation.

I might add that His Majesty's Revenue is nearly tripled; and therefore the means to pay, and bear the same, have increased also.

CHAPTER VII.

That One-Tenth part of the Whole Expense of the King of England's subjects is sufficient to maintain 100,000 *Foot*, 40,000 *Horse, and* 40,000 *seamen at sea; and to defray all other charges of the Government, both ordinary and extraordinary, if the same were regularly taxed and raised.*

TO CLEAR this point, we are to find out, What is the middle expense of each head in the King's Dominions, between the highest and the lowest? To which I say, it is not probably less than the expense of a Labourer, who earneth about 8*d.* [=2*s. now*] a day. For the wages of such a man is 4*s.* [=12*s. now*] per week *without* victuals, or 2*s.* [=6*s. now*] *with* them: where the value of his victuals is 2*s.* [=6*s. now*] or £5 4*s.* [=£15 12*s. now*] *per annum.*

An Estimate of the Medium of Expense of each head in England.

Now the value of clothes cannot be less than the wages given to the poorest maidservant in the country; which is 30*s.* [=£4 10*s. now*] *per annum.* Nor can the charge of all other necessaries be less than 6*s.* [=18*s. now*] *per annum* more.

Wherefore the whole charge is £7 [=£21 *now*].

It is not likely that this Discourse will fall into the hands of any that live at £7 *per annum*: and therefore such [*i.e.*, *as read it*] will wonder at this supposition. But if they consider how much the number of the poor and their children is greater than that of the rich; although the personal expense of some rich men should be twenty times more than that of a labourer: yet the expense of the labourer above mentioned may well enough stand for the Standard of the expense of the whole mass of mankind.

Now if the expense of each man, one with another, be £7 *per annum*, and if the number of the King's subjects be 10,000,000; then the tenth part of the whole expense will be £7,000,000 [=£21,000,000 *now*].

But about £5,000,000, or a very little more, will amount to one year's pay for 100,000 Foot, 40,000 Horse, and 40,000 men at sea: winter and summer; which can rarely be necessary!

And the ordinary Charge of Government, in times of deep and serene peace, was not about £600,000 [*or* £1,800,000 *now*] *per annum*.

Where a people thrive, there the Income is greater than the Expense; and consequently the tenth part of the expense is not a tenth part of the income. Now for men to pay a tenth of their expense in a time of the greatest exigency (for such it must be, when so great forces are requisite) can be no hardship, much less a deplorable condition. For to bear a tenth part, a man need spend but a twentieth part less, and labour a twentieth part more (or half an hour *per diem* extraordinary); both of which, within common experience, are very tolerable: there being very few in England who do not eat by a twentieth part more than does them good; and what misery were it, instead of wearing cloth of 20*s*. per yard, to be contented with that of 19*s*., few men having skill enough to discern the difference.

Memorandum. That all this while I suppose that all of these 10,000,000 of people are obedient to their Sovereign, and within the reach of his power: for as things are otherwise, so the calculation must be varied.

CHAPTER VIII.

That there are spare hands enough, among the King of England's subjects, to earn £2,000,000 per annum *more than they now do; and that there are also employments ready, proper, and sufficient for that purpose.*

TO PROVE this point, we must inquire, How much all the people could earn, if they were disposed or necessitated to labour, and, had work whereupon to employ themselves? and compare that sum with that of the total Expense above mentioned; deducting the rents and profits of land and stock [*capital*], which, properly speaking, saveth so much labour.

Now the proceeds of the said lands and stock in the Countries [*counties*] is about Three parts of Seven of the whole expense. So as where the expense is £70,000,000 the rent of the land, and the profit of all personal estate, interest of money, &c., must be about £30,000,000 [=£90,000,000 *now*], and consequently the value of the Labour, £40,000,000 [=£120,000,000 *now*], that is £4 [=£12 *now*] per head.

But it is to be noted that about a Quarter of the mass of mankind are children, male and female, under seven years old: from whom little labour is to be expected.

It is also to be noted that about another Tenth part of the whole people are such as, by reason of their great estates, titles, dignities, Offices and Professions, are exempt from that kind of labour we now speak of: their business being, or ought to be, to govern, regulate, and direct the labours and actions of others.

So that of 10,000,000, there may be about 6,500,000 which, if need require, might actually labour.

And of these, some might earn 3*s.* [=9*s. now*] a week, some 5*s.* [=15*s. now*], and some 7*s.* [=21*s.*]: that is, all of them: might earn 5*s.* per week, at a medium, one with another; or at least £10 [=£30 *now*] *per annum*, allowing for sickness and other accidents. Whereby the whole might earn £65,000,000 [=£195,000,000 *now*] *per annum*: that is £25,000,000 [=£75,000,000 *now*] more than the expense.

The Author of *The State of England* says that the children

of Norwich, between six and sixteen years old, do earn £12,000 [=£36,000 *now*] *per annum* more than they spend. Now forasmuch as the people of Norwich are a three-hundredth part of all the people of England [*i.e.*, 20,000], as appears by the accounts of the Hearth Money; and about a five-hundredth part of all the King's subjects throughout the world, it follows that all his Majesty's subjects between six and sixteen years old, might earn £5,000,000 [=£15,000,000 *now*] *per annum* more than they spend.

Again, forasmuch as the number of the people above sixteen years old, is double the number of those between six and sixteen; and that each of the men can earn double to each of the children: it is plain that if the men and children everywhere, did do as they do at Norwich, they might earn £25,000,000 [=£75,000,000 *now*] *per annum* more than they spend. Which Estimate grounded upon matter of fact and experience, agrees with the former.

Although, as hath been proved, the people of England do thrive; and that it is possible they might superlucrate £25,000,000 *per annum*; yet it is manifest that they do not; nor £23,000,000, which is less by the £2,000,000 herein meant.

For if they did superlucrate £23,000,000, then in about five or six years' time, the whole Stock and Personal Estate of the nation would be doubled: which I wish were true; but find no manner of reason to believe.

Wherefore if they can superlucrate £25,000,000; but do not actually superlucrate £23,000,000, nor £20,000,000, nor £10,000,000, nor perhaps £5,000,000: I have proved what was propounded, viz., that there are spare hands among the King's subjects to earn £2,000,000 more than they do.

But to speak a little more particularly concerning this matter. It is to be noted that since the Fire of London, there was earned, in four years [1666–1670] by tradesmen [*artisans*] relating to building only, the sum of £4,000,000 [=£12,000,000 *now*], viz., £1,000,000 *per annum*: without lessening any other sort of work, labour or manufacture, which was usually done in any other four years before the said occasion.

But if the tradesmen relating to building only, and such of them only as wrought in and about London, could do

£1,000,000 worth of work extraordinary; I think that from thence, and from what hath been said before, all the rest of the spare hands might very well double the same: which is as much as was propounded.

Now if there were spare hands to superlucrate millions upon millions, they signify nothing, unless there were employment for them; and may as well follow their pleasures and speculations, as labour to no purpose. Therefore the more material point is to prove that there is £2,000,000 worth of work to be done; which at present, the King's subjects do neglect.

For the proof of this, there needs little more to be done, than to compute.

1. How much money is paid by the King of England's subjects, to foreigners for freights of shipping?
2. How much the Hollanders gain by their fishing trade practised upon our seas?
3. What is the value of all the commodities imported into and spent in England: which might, by diligence, be produced and manufactured here.

To make short of this matter, upon perusal of the most authentic accounts relating to these several particulars, I affirm that the same amounteth to above £5,000,000 [=£15,000,000 *now*]: whereas I propounded but £2,000,000.

For a further proof whereof, Mr. SAMUEL FORTRY, in his ingenious Discourse of Trade [1673] exhibits the particulars [*details*]: wherein it appears that the goods imported out of France only, amount yearly to £2,600,000 [=£7,800,000 *now*]. And I affirm that the wine, paper, cork, rosin, capers, and a few other commodities which England cannot produce, do not amount to one-fifth part of the said sum.

From whence it follows, that, if Mr. FORTRY hath not erred, the £2,000,000 here mentioned, may arise from France alone; and consequently £5,000,000 or £6,000,000 from all three heads last above specified.

CHAPTER IX.

That there is sufficient Money to drive the Trade of the nation.

SINCE His Majesty's happy Restoration, it was thought fit to call in, and new coin, the money which was made in the times of Usurpation [*Commonwealth*]. Now it was observed, by the general consent of Cashiers [*Goldsmiths or money changers*], that the said money, being by frequent revolutions [*circulations*] well mixed with old, was about a Seventh part thereof; and that the said [*Commonwealth*] money being called in, was about £800,000; and consequently the whole [*coinage was about*] £5,600,000. Whereby it is probable, that, some allowance being given for hoarded money, the whole Cash of England was then about £6,000,000: which I conceive is sufficient to drive the Trade of England: not doubting but the rest of His Majesty's Dominions have the like means to do the same respectively.

If there be 6,000,000 souls in England, and that each spendeth £7 *per annum*, then the whole expense is £42,000,000 or about £800,000 per week: and consequently if every man did pay his expense weekly, and that the money could circulate within the compass of a week, then less than £1,000,000 would answer the ends proposed.

But forasmuch as the rents of the lands in England, which are paid half yearly, are £8,000,000 [=£24,000,000 *now*] *per annum*; there must be £4,000,000 [*in coin; Bank of England notes and cheques not having yet been invented*] to pay them.

And forasmuch as the rents of the Housing of England, paid quarterly, are worth about £4,000,000 [=£12,000,000 *now*] *per annum*; there needs but £1,000,000 to pay the said rents.

Wherefore £6,000,000 being enough to make good the three sorts of circulations above mentioned: I conceive what was proposed, is competently proved: at least, until something better be held forth to the contrary.

CHAPTER X.

That the King of England's subjects have Stock [capital] *competent and convenient to drive the Trade of the whole Commercial World.*

NOw for the further encouragement of Trade, as we have shewn that there is money enough in England to manage the affairs thereof, so we shall now offer to consideration, Whether there be not a competent and convenient Stock to drive the Trade of the whole Commercial World?

To which purpose, it is to be remembered that all the Commodities yearly exported out of every part of the last-mentioned World, may be bought for £45,000,000; and that the Shipping employed in the same World are not worth above £15,000,000 more, and consequently that £60,000,000 [=£180,000,000 *now*] at most would drive the whole Trade above mentioned, without any trust at all.

But forasmuch as the growers of commodities do commonly trust them to such merchants or factors as are worth but such part of the full value of their commodities as may possibly be lost upon the sale of them; whereas gain is rather to be expected: it follows that less than a Stock of £60,000,000; nay, less than half that sum is sufficient to drive the Trade above mentioned. It being well known that any tradesman of good reputation, worth £500, will be trusted with above £1,000 worth of commodities.

Wherefore less than £30,000,000 will suffice for the said purpose: of which sum, the Coin, Shipping, and Stock already in the Trade, do at least make one-half.

And it hath been shewn [*at p.* 23] how, by the policy of a Bank [*of which not one existed in England at the time this was written*], any sum of money may be equivalent in Trade unto nearly double the same: by all which it seems that, even at present, much is not wanting to perform what is propounded.

But suppose £20,000,000 or more were wanting, it is not improbable that since the generality of Gentlemen, and some Noblemen do put their younger sons to merchandise, they will see it reasonable, as they increase in the number of merchants, so to increase the magnitude of Trade, and consequently to increase Stock. Which may effectually be done by inbanking £20,000,000 worth of land (not being above a Sixth or Seventh of the whole territory of England) that is to say, by making a *Fond* [*fund*] of such value to be security for all commodities bought and sold upon the account of the Universal Trade here mentioned [40 *years after this was written, the Landed Interest somewhat attempted this suggestion, in the foundation of the South Sea Company*].

And thus, it having appeared that England having in it, as much land like Holland and Zealand, as the said two Provinces do themselves contain; with abundance of other land, not inconvenient for trade; and that there are spare hands enough, to earn many millions of money more than they now do; and that there is employment to earn several millions, even from the consumption of England itself: it follows from thence, and from what hath been said in the last paragraph about enlarging of Stock, both of money and land, that it is not impossible, nay, a very feasible matter for the King of England's subjects to gain the Universal Trade of the whole Commercial World.

Nor is it unseasonable to intimate this matter. Forasmuch as the younger brothers of the good families of England cannot otherwise be provided for, so as to live according to their birth and breeding.

For if the Lands of England are worth £8,000,000 *per annum*, there be, at a medium, about 10,000 families of about £800 [£=2,400, *now*] *per annum*: in each of which, one with another, we may suppose there is a younger brother, whom less than £200 or £300 [=£600 or £900 *now*] *per annum*, will not maintain suitable to his relations.

Now I say that neither the Offices at Court, nor Commands in our ordinary army and navy, nor Church preferments, nor the usual gains by the Profession of the Law or of Physic, nor the employments under Noblemen and Prelates, will, all of them put together, furnish livelihoods of above £300 *per annum* to 3,000 of the said 10,000 younger brothers: wherefore it remains that Trade alone must supply the rest.

But if the said 7,000 Gentlemen be applied to Trade, without increasing of Trade; or if we hope to increase Trade, without increasing of Stock (which, for ought appears, is only to be done by imbanking a due proportion of Lands and Money); we must necessarily be disappointed.

Where note, that selling of lands to foreigners for gold and silver, would enlarge the Stock of the Kingdom: whereas doing the same between one another, doth effect nothing. For he that turneth all his land into money, disposes himself for trade; and he that parteth with his money for land, doth the contrary: but to sell land to foreigners, increaseth both money and people, and consequently trade.

Wherefore it is to be thought that when the laws denying strangers to purchase, and not permitting them to trade without paying extraordinary duties, were made; that then the public state of things and Interest of the nation were far different from what they now are.

Having handled these Ten principal Conclusions, I might go on with others *ad infinitum*. But what hath been already said, I look upon as sufficient, for to shew what I mean by Political Arithmetic: and to shew

1. The uses of knowing the True State of the People, Land, Stock, Trade, &c.
2. That the King's subjects are not in so bad a condition as discontented men would make them.
3. The great effect of Unity, Industry, and Obedience in order to the common safety and each man's peculiar happiness.

FINIS.

An
Appeal
to
Honour and Justice,
though it be of
his worst Enemies.

By DANIEL DE FOE.

Being
a true Account of his Conduct
in Public Affairs.

JEREM. xviii. 18.
Come, and let us smite him with the tongue, *and let us not give heed to any of his words.*

LONDON:
Printed for J. BAKER, at the *Black Boy*, in
Paternoster row. 1715.

An Appeal to Honour and Justice, &c.

I HOPE the Time is come at last, when the voice of Moderate Principles may be heard. Hitherto, the noise has been so great, and the prejudices and passions of men so strong, that it had been but in vain to offer at any argument, or for any man to talk of giving a reason for his actions. And this alone has been the cause why, when other men (who, I think, have less to say in their own defence) are appealing to the public, and struggling to defend themselves; I, alone, have been silent, under the infinite clamours and reproaches, causeless curses, unusual threatenings, and the most unjust and injurious treatment in the world.

I hear much of people's calling out to Punish the Guilty! but very few are concerned to Clear the Innocent! I hope some will be inclined to judge impartially; and have yet reserved so much of the Christian as to believe, and at least to hope, that a rational creature cannot abandon himself so as to act without some reason: and are willing not only to have me defend myself; but to be able to answer for me, where they hear me causelessly insulted by others, and therefore are willing to have such just Arguments put into their mouths, as the cause will bear.

As for those who are prepossessed, and according to the modern justice of Parties are resolved to be so, let them go! I am not arguing with them, *but against them*! They act so contrary to Justice, to Reason, to Religion, so contrary to the rules of Christians and of good manners, that they are not to be argued with, but to be exposed or entirely neglected. I have a receipt against all the uneasiness which it may be supposed to give me; and that is, to contemn slander, and to think it not worth the least concern. Neither should I think it worth while to give any answer to it, if it were not on some other accounts, of which I shall speak as I go on.

If any man ask me, Why I am in such haste to publish this matter at this time? among many other good reasons which I could give, these are some:

1. I think I have long enough been made *fabula vulgi*, and borne the weight of general slander; and I should be wanting to truth, to my family, and to myself, if I did not give a fair and true state of my conduct, for impartial men to judge of, when I am no more in being, to answer for myself.
2. By the hints of mortality, and by the infirmities of a Life of Sorrow and Fatigue, I have reason to think that I am not a great way off from, if not very near to, the great Ocean of Eternity; and the time may not be long ere I embark on the last voyage. Wherefore I think, I should even accounts with this world, before I go: that no actions (*slanders*) may lie against my heirs, executors, administrators, and assigns, to disturb them in the peaceable possession of their father's inheritance (*character*).
3. I fear (GOD grant I have not a second sight in it!) that this lucid interval of Temper and Moderation which shines, though dimly too, upon us at this time, will be but of short continuance: and that some men (who know not how to use the advantage, GOD has put into their hands) with moderation, will push (in spite of the best Prince of the world) at such extravagant things, and act with such an intemperate forwardness, as will revive the Heats and Animosities, which wise and good men were in hopes should be allayed by the happy Accession of the King [GEORGE I.] to the throne.

It is, and ever was, my opinion that Moderation is the only virtue by which the peace and tranquility of this nation can be preserved. Even the King himself (I believe His Majesty will allow me that freedom!) can only be happy in the enjoyment of the crown by a Moderate Administration. If His Majesty should be obliged, contrary to his known disposition, to join with intemperate counsels; if it does not lessen his security, I am persuaded it will lessen his satisfaction! It cannot be pleasant or agreeable, and, I think, it cannot be safe to any just Prince to rule over a divided people, split into incensed and exasperated Parties. Though a skilful mariner may have courage to master a tempest, and goes fearless through a storm; yet he can never be said to delight in the danger! A fresh fair gale and a quiet sea are the pleasure of his voyage: and we have a saying worth notice, to them that are otherwise minded, *Qui amat periculum periibat in illo.*

To attain at the happy Calm, which, as I say, is the safety of Britain, is the question which should now move us all: and he would merit to be called the Nation's Physician that could prescribe the specific for it. I think I may be allowed to say, a *Conquest of Parties* will never do it! a *Balance of Parties* MAY! Some are for the former. They talk high of punishments! letting blood! revenging treatment they have met with! and the like. If they, not knowing what spirit they are of, think this the course to be taken, let them try their hands! I shall give them up for lost! and look for their downfall from that time. For the ruin of all such tempers slumbereth not!

It is many years that I have professed myself an enemy to all Precipitations in Public Administrations; and often I have attempted to shew that Hot Counsels have ever been destructive to those who have made use of them. Indeed, they have not always been a disadvantage to the nation. As in King JAMES II.'s reign: where, as I have often said in print, his precipitation was the safety of us all; and if he had proceeded temperately and politicly, we had been undone. *Fœlix quem faciunt.* But these things have been spoken, when your ferment has been too high for anything to be heard. Whether you will hear it now or not, I know not! and therefore it was that I said, I fear the present Cessation of Party Arms will not hold long.

These are some of the reasons, why I think this is a proper

juncture for me to give some account of myself and of my past conduct to the world; and that I may do this as effectually as I can (being, perhaps, never more to speak from the Press), I shall, as concisely as I can, give an Abridgement of my own History, during the few unhappy years I have employed myself, or been employed in Public in the World.

Misfortunes in business having unhinged me from matters of trade, it was about the year 1694, that I was invited (by some merchants with whom I had corresponded abroad, and some also at home) to settle at Cadiz in Spain; and that, with offers of very good commissions: but Providence, which had other work for me to do, placed a secret aversion in my mind to quitting England upon any account; and made me refuse the best offers of that kind, to be concerned with some Eminent Persons at home, in proposing Ways and Means to the Government, for raising money to supply the occasions of the war then newly begun.

Some time after this, I was (without the least application of mine, and being then seventy miles from London) sent for, to be Accountant to the "Commissioners of the Glass Duty": in which service I continued, to the determination of their commission [in 1699].

During this time [*or rather somewhat later, on 1st August* 1700], there came out a vile, abhorred pamphlet, in very ill verse, written by one Mr. TUTCHIN, called *The Foreigners*: in which the Author (who he was, I then knew not!) fell personally upon the King himself, and then upon the Dutch nation; and after having reproached His Majesty with crimes that his worst enemy could not think of without horror, he sums up all in the odious name of "Foreigner!"

This filled me with a kind of rage against the book; and gave birth to a trifle which I never could hope should have met with so general an acceptation as it did. I mean *The True Born Englishman* [*which appeared in January*, 1701].

How this poem was the occasion of my being known to His Majesty [*WILLIAM III.*]; how I was afterwards received by him; how employed; and how (above my capacity of deserving) rewarded; is no part of this present Case: and is only mentioned here, as I take all occasions to do, for the expressing of the honour I ever preserved for the immortal and glorious memory of that greatest and best of Princes; whom it was my honour and advantage to call Master as well as Sovereign! whose goodness to me I never forgot, neither can forget! whose memory I never patiently heard abused, nor ever can do so! and who, had he lived, would never have suffered me to be treated, as I have been in the World!

But Heaven, for our sins, removed him, in judgement. How far the treatment he met with from the nation he came to save, and whose deliverance he finished, was admitted by Heaven to be a means of his death; I desire to forget, for their sakes, who are guilty. And if this calls any of it to mind, it is mentioned to move them to treat him better who is now, with like principles of goodness and clemency, appointed by GOD and the Constitution, to be their Sovereign: lest He that protects righteous Princes, avenge the injuries they receive from an ungrateful people! by giving them up to the confusions, their madness leads them to.

And in their just acclamations at the happy Accession of His present Majesty [*GEORGE I.*] to the throne, I cannot but advise them to look back, and call to mind, Who it was, that first guided them to the Family of HANOVER, and to pass by all the Popish branches of ORLEANS and SAVOY? recognizing the just authority of Parliament, in the undoubted Right of Limiting the Succession, and establishing that glorious Maxim of our Settlement, viz., *That it is inconsistent with the Constitution of this Protestant Kingdom to be governed by a Popish Prince.* I say, let them call to mind, Who it was that guided their thoughts first to the Protestant race of our own Kings, in the House of HANOVER? and that it is to King WILLIAM, next to Heaven itself, to whom we owe the enjoying of a Protestant King at this time.

I need not go back to the particulars of His Majesty's conduct in that affair, his journey in person to the country of Hanover, and the Court of Zell, his particular management of the affair afterwards at home, perfecting the design by naming the illustrious Family to the nation, and bringing about a Parliamentary Settlement to effect it; entailing thereby the Crown in so effectual a manner, as we see has been sufficient to prevent the worst designs of our Jacobite people in behalf of the Pretender. A Settlement, together with the subsequent *Acts* which followed it, and the Union with Scotland which made it unalterable, that gave a complete satisfaction to those who knew and understood it; and removed those terrible apprehensions of the Pretender (which some entertained) from the minds of others, who were yet as zealous against him as it was possible for any to be. Upon this Settlement, as I shall shew presently, I grounded my opinion, which I often expressed, *viz., That I did not see it possible, the Jacobites could ever set up their Idol here!* and I think my opinion abundantly justified in the consequences: of which by-and-by.

This digression, as a debt to the glorious memory of King WILLIAM, I could not in justice omit: and as the reign of His present Majesty is esteemed happy, and looked upon as a blessing from heaven by us; it will most necessarily lead us to bless the memory of King WILLIAM, to whom we owe so much of it. How easily could His Majesty have led us to other branches, whose relation to the Crown might have had large pretences? What Prince but would have submitted to have educated a successor of their race in the Protestant Religion, for the sake of such a Crown! But the King, who had our happiness in view, and saw as far into it as any human sight could penetrate; who knew we were not to be governed by inexperienced youths; that the Protestant Religion was not to be established by Political Converts; and that Princes under French influence or instructed in French politics, were not proper Instruments to preserve the Liberties of Britain: fixed his eyes upon the Family which now possesses the Crown, as not only having an undoubted relation to it by blood, but as being, first and principally, zealous and powerful assertors of the Protestant Religion and Interest against Popery; and, secondly, stored with a visible succession of worthy and promising branches, who appeared equal to the weight of Government, qualified to fill a Throne, and guide a Nation, which (without any reflection) are not famed to be the most easy to rule in the world.

Whether the consequence has been a credit to King WILLIAM's judgement, I need not say. I am not writing panegyrics here, but doing justice to the memory of the King my Master, who I have had the honour very often to hear express himself with great satisfaction in having brought the Settlement of the Succession to so good an issue: and to repeat His Majesty's own words, "That he knew no Prince in Europe so fit to be King of England, as the Elector of Hanover." I am persuaded, without any flattery, that if it should not every way answer the expectations His Majesty had of it, the fault will be our own! GOD grant the King to have more comfort of his Crown, than we suffered King WILLIAM to have!

The King being dead, and the Queen [*ANNE*] proclaimed; the Hot Men of that side (as Hot Men of all sides do) thinking the game in their own hands, and all other people under their feet—began to run out into all those mad extremes, and precipitate themselves into such measures, as, according to the fate of all intemperate counsels, ended in their own confusion, and threw them at last out of the saddle.

The Queen (who, though willing to favour the High Church party, did not thereby design the ruin of those she did not employ) was soon alarmed at their wild conduct, and turned them out: adhering to the moderate counsels of those who better understood, or more faithfully pursued Her Majesty's and their country's Interest.

In this turn, fell "Sir EDWARD SEYMOUR's Party"; for so the High Men were then called: and to this turn, we owe the conversion of several other Great Men; who became Whigs upon that occasion, which it is known they were not before. Which conversion begat that unkind distinction of "Old Whig" and "Modern Whig"; which some of the former were, with very little justice, pleased to run up afterwards to an extreme very pernicious to both.

But I am gone too far in this part. I return to my own story. In the interval of these things, and during the heat of the first fury of High Flying; I fell a sacrifice for writing against the rage and madness of that High Party, and in the service of the Dissenters. What justice I met with! and above all, what mercy! are too well known to need a repetition.

This Introduction is made that it may bring me to what has been the *Foundation* of all my further concern in Public Affairs: and will produce a sufficient reason for my adhering to those, whose obligations upon me were too strong to be resisted; even when many things were done by them, which I could not approve. And for this reason it is, that I think it is necessary to distinguish how far I did or did not adhere to, or join in or with the Persons or Conduct of the late Government [*i.e., of Lord* OXFORD'*s Administration*, 1710–1714]: and those who are willing to judge with impartiality and charity, will see reason to use me more tenderly in their thoughts, when they weigh the particulars.

I will make no reflections upon the treatment I met with from the people *I suffered for*! or how I was abandoned, *even in my sufferings*, at the same time that they acknowledged the service it had been to their cause.

But I must mention it, to let you know, that while I lay friendless and distressed in the prison of Newgate, my family ruined, and myself without hope of deliverance; a message was brought [*in May*, 1704] me from a Person of Honour [*ROBERT HARLEY, afterwards Lord OXFORD*], with whom, till that time, I had never had the least acquaintance or knowledge of, other than by fame, or by sight as we know Men of Quality by seeing them on public occasions. I gave no present [*immediate*] answer to the person who brought it, having not duly weighed the import of the message: which was by word of mouth thus, "Pray ask that Gentleman, what I can do for him?"

But in return to this kind and generous message, I immediately took my pen and ink, and wrote the story of the blind man in the Gospel who followed our Saviour, and to whom our blessed LORD put the question, "What wilt thou, that I should do unto thee?" who, as if he had made it strange that such a question should be asked; or as if he had said, "Lord! dost thou see that I am blind! and yet asketh me what thou shalt do for me? My answer is plain in my misery, 'Lord! that I may receive my sight!'"

I needed not to make the application: and from this time, although I lay four months [*May–August*, 1704] in prison after this, and heard no more of it; yet from this time, as I learned afterwards, this Noble Person made it his business to have my Case represented to Her Majesty, and methods taken for my deliverance.

I mention this part, because I am no more to forget the Obligation upon me to the Queen, than to my First Benefactor.

When Her Majesty came to have the truth of the case laid before her, I soon felt the effects of her royal goodness and compassion. And first, Her Majesty declared "that she left all that matter to a certain person [*DANIEL FINCH, Earl of NOTTINGHAM*], and did not think he would have used me in such a manner."

Perhaps these words may seem imaginary to some, and the speaking of them to be of no value; and so they would have been, if they had not been followed with further and more convincing proofs of what they imported: which were these. That Her Majesty was pleased particularly to inquire into my circumstances and family; and by my Lord Treasurer GODOLPHIN, to send a considerable supply to my wife and family; and to send to me in the prison, money to pay my fine, and the expenses of my discharge. Whether this be a just *Foundation*, let my enemies judge!

Here is the *Foundation* on which I built my first Sense of Duty to Her Majesty's *person*; and the indelible bond of gratitude to my First Benefactor.

Gratitude and Fidelity are inseparable from an honest man! but to be thus obliged by a stranger, by a Man of Quality and Honour; and after that, by the Sovereign under whose Administration I was suffering: let any one put himself in my stead! and examine upon what principles I could ever act against either such a Queen, or such a Benefactor! And what must have my own heart reproached me with! what blushes must have covered my face, when I had looked in and called myself ungrateful to Him that saved me thus from distress! or to Her that fetched me out of the dungeon, and gave my family relief! Let any man who knows what principles are, what engagements of honour and gratitude are, make this case his own! and say, What I could have done less, or more, than I have done?

I must go on a little with the detail of the Obligation; and then I shall descend to relate, What I have done, and What I have not done, in this case.

Being delivered from the distress I was in; Her Majesty, who was not satisfied to do me good by a single act of her bounty, had the goodness to think of taking me into her Service: and I had the honour to be employed in several honourable though secret services, by the interposition of my First Benefactor, who then appeared as a member in the Public Administration [*ROBERT HARLEY had succeeded Lord NOTTINGHAM, as Secretary of State, on May* 18, 1704].

I had the happiness to discharge myself in all these trusts so much to the satisfaction of those who employed me, though oftentimes with difficulty and danger: that my Lord Treasurer GODOLPHIN (whose memory I have always honoured) was pleased to continue his favour to me, and to do me all good offices with Her Majesty—even after an unhappy breach had separated him from my First Benefactor. The particulars of which [favour] it may not be improper to relate; and as it is not an injustice to any, so I hope it will not be offensive.

When, upon that fatal breach [*February* 15, 1708], the Secretary of State [*HARLEY*] was dismissed from the Service; I looked upon myself as lost! it being a general rule in such cases, when a Great Officer falls, that all who came in by his Interest, fall with him. And resolving never to abandon the fortunes of the Man to whom I owed so much of my own; I quitted the usual applications which I had made to my Lord Treasurer.

But my generous benefactor, when he understood it, frankly told me, "That I should, by no means, do so! for," said he, in the most engaging terms, "my Lord Treasurer will employ you in nothing but what is for the Public Service, and agreeable to your own sentiments of things: and, besides, it is the Queen you are serving! who has been very good to you. Pray apply yourself as you used to do! I shall not take it ill from you in the least."

Upon this, I went to wait on my Lord Treasurer, who received me with great freedom, and told me smiling, "He had not seen me a long while."

I told his Lordship very frankly the occasion. "That the unhappy breach that had fallen out had made me doubtful whether I should be acceptable to his Lordship, that I knew it was usual when Great Persons fall, that all who were in their Interest fell with them; that his Lordship knew the obligations I was under, and that I could not but fear my Interest in his Lordship was lessened on that account."

"Not at all, Mr. DE FOE!" replied his Lordship, "I always think a man honest, till I find to the contrary."

Upon this, I attended his Lordship as usual: and being resolved to remove all possible ground of suspicion that I kept any secret correspondence [with him], I never visited, nor wrote to, or in any way corresponded with, my Principal Benefactor [*i.e.*, *HARLEY*] for above three years [1708 *to* 1711]; which he so well knew the reason of, and so well approved that punctual behaviour in me; that he never took it ill from me at all.

In consequence of this reception [? *in* 1708], my Lord GODOLPHIN had the goodness, not only to introduce me, for the second time, to Her Majesty and to the honour of kissing her hand, but obtained for me the continuance of an appointment which Her Majesty had been pleased to make me in consideration of a former special service I had done [*in a foreign country*, *see pp.* 83, 100], and in which I had run as much risk of my life as a Grenadier upon the Counterscarp: which appointment however was first obtained for me, at the intercession of my said First Benefactor [*HARLEY*], and is all owing to that intercession and Her Majesty's bounty.

Upon this second introduction, Her Majesty was pleased to tell me, with a goodness peculiar to herself, that she "had such satisfaction in my former services, that she had appointed me for another affair, which was something nice [*delicate or difficult*], and that my Lord Treasurer, should tell me the rest."

And so I withdrew.

The next day, his Lordship, having commanded me to attend, told me that "he must send me into Scotland," and gave me but three days to prepare myself.

Accordingly, I went to Scotland: where neither my business, nor the manner of my discharging it, is material to this Tract; nor will it be ever any part of my character that I reveal what should be concealed. And yet my errand was such as was far from being unfit for a Sovereign to direct, or an honest man to perform: and the service I did on that occasion, as it is not unknown to the greatest man [*the*

Duke of SHREWSBURY] now in the nation, under the King and the Prince [of WALES]; so, I dare say, His Grace was never displeased with the part I had in it, and I hope will not forget it.

These things I mention, upon this account and no other; viz., to state *the Obligation I have been in, all along, to Her Majesty personally; and to my First Benefactor principally*: by which I say, I *think* I was at least obliged not to act against them; even in those things which I might not approve.

Whether I have acted with them further than I ought, shall be spoken to by itself.

Having said thus much of the Obligations laid on me, and the Persons by whom; I have only this to add, that I think no man will say, a subject could be under *greater* bonds to his Prince, or a private person to a Minister of State: and I shall ever preserve this principle, that *An honest man cannot be ungrateful to his benefactor!*

But let no man run away, now, with the notion that I am now intending to plead the Obligation that was upon me from Her Majesty or from any other person, to justify my doing anything that is not otherwise to be justified in itself. Nothing would be more injurious, than such a construction; and therefore I capitulate [*stipulate*] for so much justice as to explain myself by this declaration, viz.

That I only speak of these obligations *as binding me to a Negative conduct: not to fly in the face of, or concern myself in disputes with, those to whom I was under such obligations; although I might not, in my judgement, join in many things that were done.*

No Obligation could excuse me in calling evil, good; or good, evil: but I am of the opinion that I might justly think myself obliged to defend what I thought was to be defended, and *to be silent in anything which I might think was not.*

If this is a crime, I must plead "Guilty!" and give in the History of my Obligation above mentioned, as an extenuation, at least, if not a justification of my conduct.

Suppose a man's father was guilty of several things unlawful and unjustifiable; a man may heartily detest the unjustifiable thing, and yet it ought not to be expected that he should expose his father! I think the case on my side, exactly the same. Nor can the duty to a parent be more strongly obliging, than the Obligation laid on me. But I must allow the case on the other side, not the same.

And this brings me to the Affirmative, and to inquire, What the matters of fact are? what I have done, or have not done, on account of these Obligations which I have been under?

It is a general suggestion, and is affirmed with such assurance that they tell me, "It is in vain to contradict it!" that *I have been employed by the Earl of O*[XFOR]*D, the late Lord Treasurer, in the late disputes about Public Affairs, to write for him*, or to put it into their own particulars, *have written by his direction, taken the materials from him, been dictated to or instructed by him, or by other persons from him, by his order*, and the like; and that *I have received a pension, or salary, or payment from his Lordship for such services as these.*

If I could put it into words that would more fully express the meaning of these people, I profess I would do it.

One would think it was impossible, but that since these things have been so confidently affirmed, some evidence might be produced! some facts might appear! some one body or other might be found, that could speak of certain knowledge! To say "things have been carried too closely to be discovered," is saying *nothing*! for, then, they must own that "it is *not* discovered": and how, then, can they affirm it as they do, with such an assurance as nothing ought to be affirmed by honest men, unless they were able to prove it?

To speak, then, to the fact. Were the reproach upon me only in this particular, I should not mention it. I should not think it a reproach to be directed by a man to whom the Queen had at that time entrusted the Administration of the Government. But as it is a reproach upon his Lordship, Justice requires that I do right in this case.

The thing is true, or false. I would recommend it to those who would be called honest men, to consider but one thing, viz. What if it should *not* be true! Can they justify the injury done to that Person, or to any person concerned? If it cannot be proved, if no vestiges appear to ground it upon; how can they charge men upon rumours and reports, and join to run men's characters down by the stream of clamour.

Sed quo rapit impetus undæ.

In answer to the charge, I bear witness to posterity, that *every part of it is false and forged*! and I do solemnly protest, in the fear and presence of HIM that shall judge us all, both the slanderers and the slandered, that *I have not received any instructions, directions, orders,* or let them call it what they will! *of that kind, for the writing of any part of what I have written; or any materials for the putting together, for the forming any book or pamphlet whatsoever, from the said Earl of O*[XFOR]*D, late Lord Treasurer; or from any person, by his order or direction, since the time that the late Earl of G*[ODOLPHI]*N was Lord Treasurer* [August 10, 1710]. *Neither did I ever shew, or cause to be shewn to his Lordship, for his approbation, correction, alteration, or for any other cause, any book, paper, or pamphlet which I have written and published, before the same was printed, worked off at the press, and published.*

If any man can detect me of the least prevarication in this, or in any part of it, I desire him to do it, by all means! and I challenge all the world to do it! And if they cannot, then I *appeal*, as in my title, *to the honour and justice of my worst enemies*, to know, upon what foundation of truth or conscience, they can affirm these things; and for what it is, that I bear these reproaches?

In all my writing, I never capitulated [*stipulated*] for my liberty to speak according to my own judgement of things. I ever had that liberty allowed me! nor was I ever imposed upon to write this way or that, against my judgement, by any person whatsoever.

I come now, historically, to the point of time, when my Lord GODOLPHIN was dismissed from his employment; and the late unhappy division broke out at Court.

I waited on my Lord, the day he was displaced [*August* 10, 1710]; and humbly asked his Lordship's direction, What course I should take?

His Lordship's answer was, that "He had the same good will to assist me; but not the same power"; that "I was the Queen's servant; and that all he had done for me, was by Her Majesty's special and particular direction"; and that "Whoever should succeed him, it was not material to me; he 'supposed I should be employed in nothing relating to the present differences.' My business was to wait till I saw things settled; and then apply myself to the Ministers of State, to receive Her Majesty's commands from them."

It occurred to me immediately, as a Principle for my conduct, that it was not material to me [*DEFOE being practically one of the permanent Civil Servants of the Crown*] what Ministers Her Majesty was pleased to employ. My duty was to go along with every Ministry, *so far as they did not break in upon the Constitution, and the Laws and Liberties of my country*; my part being only the duty of a subject, viz., to submit to all lawful commands, and to enter into no service which was not justifiable by the Laws.

To all which I have exactly obliged [*conformed*] myself.

By this, I was providentially cast back upon my Original Benefactor [*ROBERT HARLEY*], who, according to his wonted goodness, was pleased to lay my case before Her Majesty; and thereby I preserved my interest in Her Majesty's favour, but without any engagement of service [*i.e., he was not employed on any special secret mission*].

As for consideration, pension, gratification, or reward; I declare to all the world! I have had none! except only that old appointment which Her Majesty was pleased to make me in the days of the Ministry of my Lord GODOLPHIN; of which I have spoken already [*pp.* 79, 100], and which was for services done in a foreign country, some years before.

Neither have I been employed, or directed, or ordered by my Lord T[reasure]r [*Lord OXFORD*] aforesaid, to do, or not to do, anything in the affairs of the unhappy differences [*between Lords OXFORD and BOLINGBROKE*] which have so long perplexed us; and for which I have suffered so many, and such unjust reproaches.

I come next to enter into the Matters of Fact, and what it is I have done, or not done; which may justify the treatment I have met with.

And first, for the Negative part. What I have *not* done.

The first thing in the unhappy breaches which have fallen out, is the heaping up scandal upon the persons and conduct of Men of Honour, on one side as well as on the other: those unworthy methods, of falling upon one another by personal calumny and reproach.

This I have often, in print, complained of as an unchristian, ungenerous, and unjustifiable practice. Not a word can be found in all I have written, reflecting on the persons or conduct of any of the former Ministry [*i.e., Lord* GODOLPHIN'*s*]. I served Her Majesty under their Administration. They acted honourably and justly in every transaction in which I had the honour to be concerned with them: and I never published or said anything dishonourable of any of them in my life; nor can the worst enemy I have, produce any such thing against me.

I always regretted the Change [*i.e., of Ministry in August,* 1710]; and looked upon it as a great disaster to the nation in general. I am sure it was so to me in particular; and the divisions and feuds among parties which followed that Change, were doubtless a disaster to us all.

The next thing which followed the Change was the Peace [*i.e., the Peace of Utrecht on April* 11, 1713].

No man can say that ever I once said in my life, that "I approved of the Peace." I wrote a public Paper at that time [1713], and there it remains upon record against me. I printed it openly, and that so plainly, as others durst not do, that "I did not like the Peace; neither that which was made, nor that which was, before, a making" [*the Negotiations at Gertruydenburg in* 1710]; that "I thought the Protestant Interest was not taken care of, in either." That "the Peace I was for, was such as should neither have given the Spanish Monarchy to the House of BOURBON, nor [to] the House of AUSTRIA; but that this bone of contention should have been broken to pieces: that it should not have been dangerous to Europe on any account:" and that "the Protestant Powers (Britain and the States [*Holland*]) should have so strengthened and fortified their Interest by sharing the commerce and strength of Spain, as should have made them no more afraid either of France, or the Emperor; so that the Protestant Interest should have been superior to all the Powers of Europe, and been in no more danger of exorbitant power, whether French or Austrian."

This was the Peace I argued for, pursuant to the design

of King WILLIAM in the Treaty of Partition; and pursuant to that *Article* in the Grand Alliance, which was directed by the same glorious hand, at the beginning of this last war [1702–1713 *A.D.*], that *all we should conquer in the Spanish West Indies should be our own.*

This was, with a true design that England and Holland should have turned their naval power, which was eminently superior to that of France, to the conquest of the Spanish West Indies: by which the channel of trade and return of bullion, which now enrich the enemies of both, had been ours; and as the Wealth, so the Strength of the World had been in Protestant hands. Spain, whoever had it, must then have been dependent upon us. The House of BOURBON would have found it so poor, without us, as to be scarce worth fighting for: and the people so averse to them, for want of their commerce, as not to make it ever likely France could keep it.

This was the Foundation I ever acted upon with relation to the Peace.

It is true, that when it was made, and could not be otherwise, I thought our business was to make the best of it, and rather to inquire what improvements were to be made of it, than to be continually exclaiming at those who made it: and where the objection lies against this part, I cannot yet see!

While I spoke of things in this manner, I bore infinite reproaches from clamouring pens, of "being in the French Interest! being hired and bribed to defend a bad Peace!" and the like: and most of this was upon a supposition of my writing, or being the author of [an] abundance of pamphlets which came out every day; and which I had no hand in.

And, indeed, as I shall observe again, by-and-by, this was one of the greatest pieces of injustice that could be done me, and which I labour still under without any redress; that, whenever any piece comes out which is not liked, I am immediately charged with being the author! and, very often, the first knowledge I have had of a book's being published, has been from seeing myself abused for being the author of it, in some other pamphlet published in answer to it.

Finding myself treated in this manner, I declined writing at all; and, for a great part of a year [*i.e. in* 1712], never set pen to paper, except in the public Paper called the *Review*.

After this, I was long absent in the north of England, and observing the insolence of the Jacobite party, and how they insinuated fine things into the heads of the common people, of the Right and Claim of the Pretender, and of the Great Things he would do for us, if he was to come in; of his being to turn a Protestant; of his being resolved to maintain our liberties, support our funds, give liberty to Dissenters, and the like: and finding that the people began to be deluded, and that the Jacobites gained ground among them, by these insinuations, I thought it the best service I could do the Protestant Interest, and the best way to open the people's eyes to the advantages of the Protestant Succession, if I took some course effectually to alarm the people with what they really ought to expect, if the Pretender should come to be King. And this made me set pen to paper again [*in* 1712].

And this brings me to the Affirmative part, or to What really *I have done?* and in this, I am sorry to say, I have one of the foulest, most unjust, and unchristian clamours to complain of, that any man has suffered, I believe, since the days of the tyranny of JAMES II.

In order to detect the influence of Jacobite emissaries, as above; the first thing I wrote, was a small tract, called, *A seasonable Caution.* [The full title is, *A seasonable Warning and Caution against the Insinuations of Papists and Jacobites in favour of the Pretender. Being a Letter from an Englishman at the Court of Hanover.* 24 *pp.* Published in 1712.] A book sincerely written to open the eyes of the poor ignorant country people, and to warn them against the subtle insinuations of the emissaries of the Pretender. And that it might be effectual to that purpose, I prevailed with several of my friends, to give them away among the poor people all over England, especially in the North: and several thousands were actually given away, the price being reduced so low, that the bare expense of Paper and Press was only preserved; that every one might be convinced that nothing of gain was designed, but a sincere endeavour to do a public good, and assist to keep the people entirely in the Interest of the Protestant Succession.

Next to this, and with the same sincere design, I wrote two pamphlets; one entituled, *What if the Pretender should come?* [The full title is *And what if the Pretender should come? Or some considerations of the Advantages and real Consequences of the Pretender's possessing the Crown of Great Britain.* 44 *pp.* Published March 26, 1713.] The other, *Reasons against the Succession of the House of Hanover.* [The full title is, *Reasons against the Succession of the House of Hanover; with an Inquiry how far the Abdication of King JAMES, supposing it to be legal, ought to affect the Person of the Pretender.* 48 *pp.* Published February 21, 1713.] Nothing can be more plain, than that the titles of these books were Amusements [*innocent deceptions*], in order to put the books into the hands of those people whom the Jacobites had deluded, and to bring the books to be read by them.

Previous to what I shall further say of these books, I must observe that all these books met with so general a reception and approbation among those who were most sincere for the Protestant Succession, that they sent them all over the Kingdom, and recommended them to the people's reading, as excellent and useful pieces; insomuch that about seven editions of them were printed, and they were reprinted in other places: and I do protest, had His present Majesty, then Elector of Hanover, given me £1,000 [£2,500 *now*], to have written for the Interest of his Succession, and to expose and render the Interest of the Pretender odious and ridiculous, I could have done nothing more effectual to those purposes than those books were.

And that I may make my worst enemies (to whom this is a fair *Appeal*) judges of this, I must take leave, by-and-by, to repeat some of the expressions in those books, which were direct, and need no explication; and which, I think, no man that was in the Interest of the Pretender, nay, which no man but one who was entirely in the Interest of the Hanover Succession could write.

Nothing can be severer in the fate of a man, than to act so between two Parties, that Both Sides should be provoked against him!

It is certain, the Jacobites cursed those tracts and the author; and when they came to read them, being deluded by the titles *according to the design*, they threw them by, with the greatest indignation imaginable! Had the Pretender ever come to the throne, I could have expected nothing but

Death! and all the ignominy and reproach that the most inveterate enemy of his person and claim could be supposed to suffer!

On the other hand, I leave it to any considering man to judge what a surprise it must be to me, to meet with all the public clamour that Informers could invent, as "being guilty of writing *against* the Hanover Succession," and "as having written several pamphlets *in favour* of the Pretender."

No man, in this nation, ever had a more riveted aversion to the Pretender, and to all the family, he *pretended* to come of, than I! A man that had been in arms, under the Duke of MONMOUTH, against the cruelty and arbitrary government of his pretended father! that, for twenty years, had, to my utmost, opposed him [*King JAMES*], and his party, after his abdication! that had served King WILLIAM, to his satisfaction! and the Friends of the Revolution, after his death, at all hazards and upon all occasions! that had suffered and been ruined under the Administration of the Highflyers and Jacobites, of whom some are, at this day, *counterfeit Whigs*! It could not be! The nature of the thing could, by no means, allow it! It must be monstrous! And that the wonder may cease, I shall take leave to quote some of the expressions out of these books; of which, the *worst enemy I have in the world*, is left to judge whether they are in favour of the Pretender or not? But of this, in its place.

For these books, I was prosecuted, taken into custody, and obliged to give £800 bail.

I do not, in the least, object here against, or design to reflect upon the proceedings of the Judges which were subsequent to this. I acknowledged then, and now acknowledge again, that, upon the Information given, there was a sufficient ground for all they did; and my unhappy entering upon my own *Vindication* in print, while the case was before their Lordships in a judicial way, was an error which I neither understood, and which I did not foresee. And therefore, although I had great reason to reflect upon the Informers, yet I was wrong in making that Defence in the manner and time I then made it; and which, when I found, I made no scruple afterwards to petition the Judges, and to acknowledge that they had just ground to resent it: upon which Petition and Acknowledgement, their Lordships were pleased, with particular marks of goodness, to release me; and not take the advantage of an error of ignorance, as if it had been considered and premeditated.

But against the Informers; I think I have great reason to complain: and against the injustice of those writers, who, in many pamphlets, charged me with writing for the Pretender; and the Government, with pardoning an author who wrote for the Pretender. And indeed, the justice of those men can be in nothing more clearly stated, than in this case of mine; where the charge, in their printed papers and public discourse, was brought, not that themselves believed me guilty of the crime, but because it was necessary to blacken the Man! that a general reproach might serve for an answer to whatever he should say, that was not for their turn. So that it was the Person, not the Crime, they fell upon! and they may justly be said to persecute *for the sake of persecution*! as will thus appear.

This matter making some noise, people began to inquire into it; and to ask "What DE FOE was prosecuted for? seeing the books were manifestly written against the Pretender, and for the Interest of the House of Hanover!" And my friends expostulated freely with some of the men who appeared in it; who answered, with more truth than honesty, that "they knew this book [*Reasons against, &c.*] had nothing in it, and that it was meant another way: but that DE FOE had disobliged them in other things; and they were resolved to take the advantage they had, both to punish and expose him!"

They were no inconsiderable people who said this; and had the case come to a trial, I had provided good evidence to prove the words. This is the Christianity and Justice by which I have been treated! and this Injustice is the thing that I complain of!

Now as this was a plot of a few men to see if they could brand me in the world for a Jacobite, and persuade rash and ignorant people that I was turned about for the Pretender: I think they might as easily have proved me to be a Mahometan! Therefore, I say this obliges me to state that matter as it really stands, that impartial men may judge whether those books were written *for* or *against* the Pretender.

And this cannot be better done than by the account of what followed after the first Information; which, in few words, is thus:

Upon the several days appointed, I appeared at the Queen's Bench bar, to discharge my bail; and, at last, had an Indictment for high crimes and misdemeanours exhibited against me [*June*, 1713] by Her Majesty's Attorney-General [*Sir EDWARD NORTHEY*]; which, as I was informed, contained 200 sheets of paper. What the substance of the indictment was, I shall not mention here! neither could I enter upon it, having *never seen the particulars*.

But I was told that "I should be brought to trial, the very next Term."

I was not ignorant that, in such cases, it is easy to make *any* book, a libel; and that the Jury must have found the matter of fact in the indictment, viz., that I *had* written such books: and then what might have followed, I knew not.

Wherefore I thought it was my only way to cast myself on the clemency of Her Majesty, whose goodness I had had so much experience of, many ways; representing in my Petition, that "*I was far from the least intention to favour the Interest of the Pretender; but that the books were all written with a sincere design to promote the Interest of the House of Hanover; and humbly laid before Her Majesty (as I do now before the rest of the world) the books themselves, to plead in my behalf:*" representing further that "*I was maliciously informed against, by those who were willing to put a construction upon the expressions different from my true meaning; and therefore flying to Her Majesty's goodness and clemency, I entreated her gracious Pardon!*"

It was not only the native disposition of Her Majesty to acts of clemency and goodness that obtained me this Pardon; but, as I was informed, Her Majesty was pleased to express in the Council: "She saw nothing but private pique in the first prosecution." And therefore I think I cannot give a better and clearer vindication of myself than what is contained in the Preamble to the *Pardon* which Her Majesty was pleased to grant me: and I must be allowed to say to those who are still willing to object, that I think what satisfied Her Majesty might be sufficient to satisfy them. And I can answer them, that this *Pardon* was not granted without Her Majesty's being specially and particularly acquainted with the things alleged in the *Petition*; the books being looked into, to find the expressions quoted in the *Petition*.

The Preamble to the Patent for a *Pardon*, as far as relates to the matters of fact, runs thus:

WHEREAS, in the Term of Holy Trinity [June, 1713] *last past, Our Attorney-General did exhibit an Information in Our Court of Queen's Bench at Westminster, against DANIEL DE FOE, late of London, Gentleman, for writing, printing, and publishing, and causing to be written, printed and published, three Libels :*

The one intituled, Reasons against the Succession of the House of Hanover; with an Inquiry how far the Abdication of King JAMES, supposing it to be legal, ought to affect the Person of the Pretender.

One other intituled, And what if the Pretender should come? Or some considerations of the Advantages and real Consequences of the Pretender's possessing the Crown of Great Britain.

And one other intituled, An Answer to a Question that nobody thinks of, viz., What if the Queen should die? [44 pp. Published in April, 1713.]

And whereas the said DANIEL DE FOE hath, by his humble Petition, *represented to us, that he, with a sincere design to propagate the Interest of the Hanover Succession, and to animate the people against the designs of the Pretender whom he always looked upon as an enemy to our sacred Person and Government, did publish the said pamphlets. In all which books, although the titles seemed to look as if written in favour of the Pretender, and several expressions (as in all ironical writing it must be) may be wrested against the true design of the whole, and turned to a meaning quite different from the intention of the author: yet the Petitioner humbly assures us, in the solemnest manner, that his true and only design in all the said books, was, by an ironical discourse of recommending the Pretender, in the strongest and most forcible manner, to expose his designs and the ruinous consequences of his succeeding therein :*

Which, as the Petitioner humbly represents, will appear to Our Satisfaction, by the books themselves, where the following expressions are very plain, viz., that the Pretender is recommended,

As a person proper to amass the English Liberties into his own Sovereignty, to supply them with the Privileges of wearing Wooden Shoes; *easing them of the trouble of choosing Parliaments, and the Nobility and Gentry of the hazard and expense of winter journeys, by* governing them, in that more righteous Method of his Absolute Will; *and enforcing the Laws* by a glorious Standing Army; *paying all the nation's debts at once* by stopping the Funds, and shutting up the Exchequer; *easing and quieting their differences in religion, by* bringing them to the Union of Popery or leaving them at liberty to have no religion at all.

That these were some of the very expressions in the said books which the Petitioner sincerely designed to expose and oppose, as far as in him lies, the Interest of the Pretender, and with no other intention.

Nevertheless the Petitioner, to his great surprise, has been misrepresented; and his said books misconstrued, as if written in favour of the Pretender, and the Petitioner is now under prosecution for the same; which prosecution, if further carried on, will be the utter ruin of the Petitioner and his family. Wherefore the Petitioner, humbly assuring us of the innocence of his design as aforesaid, flies to Our clemency, and most humbly prays Our most gracious and free pardon; We, taking the premisses, and the circumstances aforesaid, into Our royal consideration, are graciously pleased [to extend our royal mercy to the Petitioner.

Our Will and Pleasure therefore is, that you prepare a bill for Our royal signature, to pass Our great seal, containing Our gracious and free Pardon unto him, the said DANIEL DE FOE, *of the offences aforementioned, and of all indictments, convictions, pains, penalties, and forfeitures incurred thereby: and you are to insert therein, all such apt and beneficial clauses as you shall judge requisite to make this our intended Pardon more full, valid, and effectual; and for so doing, this shall be your Warrant.*

Given at Our Castle at Windsor, the 20th day of November, 1713, *in the twelfth year of Our reign,*

By Her Majesty's Command,

BOLINGBROKE.]

Let any indifferent man judge whether I was not treated with peculiar malice in this matter; who was, notwithstanding this, reproached in the daily public prints, with having written treasonable books in behalf of the Pretender: nay, and in some of those books as before, the Queen herself was reproached! with "having granted her pardon to an author who wrote for the Pretender."

I think I might with much more justice say, I was the first man that ever was obliged to seek a *Pardon* for writing for the Hanover Succession; and the first man that these people ever sought to ruin for writing against the Pretender: for if ever a book was sincerely designed to further and propagate the affection and zeal of the nation against the Pretender; nay, and was made use of (and that with success too) for that purpose, these books were so. And I ask no more favour of the World to determine the opinion of honest men for or against me, than what is drawn constructively from these books. Let one word, either written or spoken by me, either published or not published, be produced, that was in the least disrespectful to the Protestant Succession, or to any branch of the Family of Hanover, or that can be judged to be favourable to the Interest or Person of the Pretender; and I will be willing to wave Her Majesty's *Pardon*, and render myself to public justice, to be punished for it, as I should well deserve.

I freely and openly challenge the worst of my enemies to charge me with any discourse, conversation, or behaviour in my whole life, which had the least word in it injurious to the Protestant Succession, unbecoming or disrespectful to any of the persons of the Royal Family of Hanover, or the least favourable word of the person, the designs, or friends of the Pretender. If they can do it, let them stand forth and speak! No doubt but they may be heard! And I, for my part, will relinquish all pleas, *Pardons*, and defences, and cast myself into the hands of Justice.

Nay, to go further: I defy them to prove that I ever kept company, or had any society, friendship, or conversation with any Jacobite! so averse have I been to the Interest, and to the people, that I have studiously avoided their company upon all occasions.

As nothing in the world has been more my aversion than the society of Jacobites, so nothing can be a greater misfortune to me than to be accused, and publicly reproached with what is, of all things in the world, most abhorred by me: and that which had made it the more afflicting is, that this charge arises from those very things which I did, with the sincerest design, to manifest the contrary.

But such is my present fate, that I am to submit to it: which I do with meekness and calmness, as to a judgement from heaven; and am practising that duty, which I have studied long ago, of "forgiving my enemies," and "praying for them that despitefully use me."

Having given this brief history of the *Pardon* &c., I hope the impartial part of the world will grant me, that, being thus graciously delivered, *a second time*, from the cruelty of my implacable enemies, and the ruin of a cruel and unjust prosecution; and that, by the mere clemency and goodness of the Queen, my Obligation to Her Majesty's goodness was far from being made less than it was before.

I have now run through the history of my Obligation to Her Majesty, and to the Person of my Benefactor aforesaid. I shall state everything that followed this, with all the clearness I can; and leave myself liable to as little cavil as I may. For I see myself assaulted by a sort of people who will do me no justice. I hear a great noise made of "punishing those that are guilty!"; but, as I said before, not one word of "clearing those that are innocent!" And I must say, in this part, they treat me not only as if I were no Christian, but as if they themselves were not Christians. They will neither prove the charge, nor hear the defence; which is the unjustest thing in the world.

I foresee what will be alleged to the clause of my Obligation &c., to Great Persons: and I resolve to give my adversaries all the advantage they can desire, by acknowledging beforehand that "no Obligation to the Queen or to any Benefactor can justify any man's acting against the Interest of his country! against his principles! his conscience! and his former profession!"

I think this will anticipate all that can be said upon that head: and it will then remain to state the fact, as I am, or am not chargeable with it; which I shall do as clearly as possible in few words.

It is none of my work to enter into the conduct of the Queen, or of the Ministry, in this case. The question is not What they have done, but What I have done?

And though I am very far from thinking of them [*i.e.*, *Lord* OXFORD'*s Ministry*] as some other people think: yet, for the sake of the present argument, I am to give them all up! and suppose (though not granting) that all which is suggested of them by the worst temper, the most censorious writer, the most scandalous pamphlet or lampoon, should be true; and I will go through some of the particulars, as I meet with them in public.

I. That *they made a scandalous Peace, unjustly broke the Alliance, betrayed the Confederates, and sold us all to the French.* GOD forbid it should be all truth, in the manner that we see it in print: but that, I say, is none of my business!

But what hand had I in all this? I never wrote one word for the Peace *before* it was made; or to justify it *after* it was made. Let them produce it, if they can!

Nay, in a *Review* upon that subject, while it was making, I printed it, in plainer words than other men durst speak at that time, that "I did not like the Peace; nor did I like any Peace that was a making since that the Partition; and that the Protestant Interest was not taken care of, either in that, or the Treaty of Gertruydenburg before it."

It is true, that I did say, "That since the Peace was made, and we could not help it, that it was our business and our duty to make the best of it, to make the utmost advantage of it by commerce, navigation, and all kinds of improvement that we could." And this I say still! and I must think it is more our duty to do so, than the exclamations against the thing itself; which it is not in our power to retrieve. That is all, the worst enemy I have can charge me with.

After the Peace was made, and the Dutch and the Emperor stood out; I gave my opinion of what I foresaw would necessarily be the consequence of that difference, viz., that it would inevitably involve these Nations in a war with one or other of them. Any one who was master of common sense in the public affairs might see, that the standing out of the Dutch could have no other event.

For if the Confederates had conquered the French, they

would certainly have fallen upon us, by way of resentment: and there was no doubt but the same counsels that led us to make a Peace, would oblige us to maintain it, by preventing too great impressions upon [*i.e., the annihilation of*] the French.

On the other hand, I alleged that should the French prevail against the Dutch, unless he stopped at such limitations of conquest as the Treaty obliged him to do, we must have been under the same necessity to renew the war against France. And for this reason, seeing we *had* made a Peace, we were *obliged* to bring the rest of the Confederates into it! and to bring the French to give them all such terms as they ought to be satisfied with.

This way of arguing was either so little understood, or so much maligned that I suffered innumerable reproaches in print, for having written for a war with the Dutch: which was neither in the expression, nor ever in my imagination. But I pass by these injuries as small and trifling, compared to others I suffered under.

However, one thing I must say of the Peace. Let it be good or ill in itself, I cannot but think we have all reason to rejoice in behalf of His present Majesty, that, at his accession to the Crown, he found the nation in peace; and had the hands of the King of France tied by a Peace, so as not to be able, without the most infamous breach of *Articles*, to offer the least disturbance to his taking a quiet and leisurely possession, or so much as to countenance those that would. Not but that I believe, if the war had been at the height, we should have been able to have preserved the Crown for His present Majesty, its only rightful Lord: but I will not say, it should have been so easy, so bloodless, so undisputed as now: and all the difference must be acknowledged [*attributed*] to the Peace. And this is all the good I ever yet said of the Peace.

I come next to the general clamour of *the Ministry being for the Pretender*. I must speak my sentiments solemnly and plainly, as I always did in that matter, viz., that, "If it were so, I did not see it! Nor did I ever see reason to believe it!" This I am sure of, that if it were so, I never took one step in that kind of service, nor did I ever hear one word spoken by any one of the Ministry that I had the honour to know or converse with, that favoured the Pretender: but I have had the honour to hear them all protest that there was no design to oppose the Succession of Hanover in the least.

It may be objected to me, that "they might be in the Interest of the Pretender, for all that!"

It is true, they might; but that is nothing to me! I am not vindicating their conduct, but my own! As I never was employed in anything that way, so I do still protest I do not believe it was ever in their design; and I have many reasons to confirm my thoughts in that case, which are not material to the present case.

But be that as it will, it is enough to me, that I acted *nothing* in such Interest; neither did I ever sin against the Protestant Succession of Hanover in thought, word, or deed: and if the Ministry did, I did not see it, or so much as suspect them of it!

It was a disaster to the Ministry, to be driven to the necessity of taking that Set of Men by the hand; who, nobody can deny, were in that Interest. But as the former Ministry answered, when they were charged with a design to overthrow the Church, because they favoured, joined with, and were united to the Dissenters; I say, they answered that "they made use of the Dissenters, but granted them nothing" (*which, by the way, was too true!*): so these gentlemen answer, that "it is true, they made use of the Jacobites; but did nothing for them!"

But this, by-the-by. Necessity is pleaded by both Parties for doing things, which neither side can justify. I wish both sides would for ever avoid the necessity of doing evil: for certainly it is *the worst plea in the world!* and generally made use of, for the worst things.

I have often lamented the disaster which I saw employing Jacobites was to the late Ministry; and certainly it gave the greatest handle to the enemies of the Ministry to fix that universal reproach upon them, of being in the Interest of the Pretender: but there was no medium. The Whigs refused to shew them a safe retreat, or to give them the least opportunity to take any other measures, but at the risk of their own destruction: and they ventured upon that course, in hopes of being able to stand alone at last, without help of either the one or the other; in which, no doubt, they were mistaken.

However, in this part, as I was always assured, and have good reason still to believe, that Her Majesty was steady in the Interest of the House of Hanover; and that nothing was ever offered me or required of me to the prejudice of that Interest: on what ground can I be reproached with the secret reserved design of any; if they have such designs (as I still verily believe they had not)?

I see there are some men who would fain persuade the World, that every man that was in the Interest of the late Ministry, or employed by the late Government, or that served the late Queen, was for the Pretender!

GOD forbid this should be true! and I think there needs very little to be said in answer to it. I can answer for myself, that it is notoriously false! and I think the easy and uninterrupted accession of His Majesty to the Crown contradicts it.

I see no end which such a suggestion aims at, but to leave an odium on all that had any duty or regard to Her late Majesty.

A subject is not always master of his Sovereign's measures, nor always to examine what Persons or Parties the Prince he serves, employs; so be it that they break not in upon the Constitution, that they govern according to Law, and that he is employed in no illegal act, or has nothing desired of him inconsistent with the Laws and Liberties of his country. If this be not right, then a servant of the King is in a worse case than a servant to any private person.

In all these things, I have not erred: neither have I acted or done anything in the whole course of my life, either in the service of Her Majesty, or of her Ministry, that any one can say has the least deviation from the strictest regard to the Protestant Succession, and to the Laws and Liberties of my country.

I never saw an arbitrary action offered at, a law dispensed with, Justice denyed, or Oppression set up, either by Queen or Ministry, in any branch of the Administration wherein I had the least concern.

If I have sinned against the Whigs, it has all been *negatively*, viz., that I have not joined in the loud exclamations against the Queen, and against the Ministry, and against their measures.

And if this be my crime, my plea is twofold.

1. I did not really see cause for their carrying their complaints to that violent degree.
2. What I did see, what (as before) I lamented and was sorry for, and could not join with or approve; as *joining with Jacobites*, the *Peace*, &c.: my OBLIGATION is my plea for my silence.

I have all the good thoughts of the person, and good wishes for the prosperity of my Benefactor [*HARLEY*, *Lord OXFORD*], that charity, that gratitude can inspire me with. I ever believed him to have the true Interest of the Protestant Religion, and of his country in his view: if it should be otherwise, I should be very sorry!

And I must repeat it again that he always left me so entirely to my own judgement in everything I did, that he never prescribed to me what I should write or should not write, in my life: neither did he ever concern himself to dictate to, or restrain me in any kind; nor did he see any one tract that I ever wrote before it was printed. So that all the notion of my writing by his direction is as much a slander upon *him*, as it is possible anything of that kind can be. And if I have written anything which is offensive, unjust, or untrue, I must do that justice to declare, he has had no hand in it: the crime is my own.

As the reproach of his directing me to write, is a slander upon the Person I am speaking of; so that of my receiving pensions and payments from him, for writing, is a slander upon *me*: and I speak it with the greatest sincerity, seriousness, and solemnity that it is possible for a Christian man to speak, that, except the appointment I mentioned before, which Her Majesty was pleased to make me formerly, and which I received during the time of my Lord GODOLPHIN's Ministry, *I have not received of the late Lord Treasurer, or of any one else by his order, knowledge, or direction, one farthing, or the value of a farthing, during his whole Administration*: nor has all the Interest I have been supposed to have in his Lordship been able to procure me the arrears due to me [*for the dangerous service abroad, see p.* 83] in the time of the other Ministry, So help me God!

I am under no necessity of making this declaration. The services I did, and for which Her Majesty was pleased to make me a small allowance, are known to the greatest men in the present Administration; and some of them were then of the opinion, and I hope are so still, that I was not unworthy of Her Majesty's favour. The effect of those services, however small, are enjoyed by those Great Persons and by the whole nation, to this day: and I had the honour once, to be told that "They should never be forgotten!" [*See pp.* 79, 83.]

It is a misfortune that no man can avoid, to forfeit for his deference to the person and services of his Queen, to whom he was inexpressibly obliged. And if I am fallen under the displeasure of the present Government, for anything I ever did in obedience to Her Majesty in the past; I may say it is my disaster, but I can never say it is my fault.

This brings me again to that other Oppression which, as I said [*p.* 85], I suffer under; and which I think is of a kind that no man ever suffered under so much as myself: and this is, to have every libel, every pamphlet, be it ever so foolish, so malicious, so unmannerly, or so dangerous, laid at my door, and be called publicly by my name.

It has been in vain for me to struggle with this injury. It has been in vain for me to protest, to declare solemnly. Nay, if I would have *sworn*, that I had no hand in such a book or paper! never saw it! never read it! and the like; it was the same thing.

My name has been hackneyed about the street by the hawkers, and about the coffee-houses by the politicians; at such a rate, as no patience would bear!

One man will swear to the style! another to this or that expression! another to the way of printing! and all so *positive*, that it is to no purpose to oppose it.

I published once, to stop this way of using me, that I would print nothing but what I set my name to: and I held to it, for a year or two: but it was all one, I had the same treatment!

I now have resolved, for some time, to write *nothing at all:* and yet I find it the same thing!

Two books lately published [*the first two of the three Parts of the* Secret History of the White Staff, *published in October* 1714] being called mine; for no other reason that I know of, than that, at the request of the printer, I revised two sheets [32 *pp.*] of them at the press; and that they seemed to be written in favour of a certain Person [*HARLEY, Lord OXFORD*]: which Person also, as I have been assured, had no hand in them, or any knowledge of them till they were published in print.

This is a Flail which I have no fence against! but to complain of the injustice of it: and that is but *the shortest way* to be treated with more injustice.

There is a mighty charge against me for being Author and Publisher of a Paper called the *Mercator* [*or Commerce revived* from 26th May, 1713, to 20th July, 1714]. I will state the fact first, and then speak to the subject.

It is true that, being desired to give my opinion in the affair of the commerce of France, I did (as I often had done in print, many years before) declare that "It was my opinion we ought to have Open [*Free*] Trade with France; because I did believe we might have the advantage by such a trade": and of this opinion, I am still.

What Part I had in the *Mercator* is well known: and, would men answer with argument and not with personal abuses, I would at any time, defend every part of the *Mercator* which was of my doing. But to say the *Mercator* was mine, is false! I neither was the Author [*Editor*] of it, had the property [*proprietorship*] of it, the printing of it, or the profit by it. I have never had any payment or reward for writing any part of it; nor had I the power to put what I would into it.

Yet the whole clamour fell upon me, because they knew not who else to load with it. And when they came to answer; the method was, instead of argument, to threaten, and reflect upon me! reproach me with private circumstances and misfortunes! and give language which no Christian ought to give! and which no Gentleman ought to take!

I thought any Englishman had the liberty to speak his

opinion in such things: for this had nothing to do with the Public [*State Affairs*]. The press was open to me, as well as to others; and how or when I lost my English liberty of speaking my mind, I know not! neither how my speaking my opinion without fee or reward, could authorize them to call me "villain!" "rascal!" "traitor!" and such opprobrious names.

It was ever my opinion, as it is so still, that were our wool kept from France, and our manufactures spread in France upon reasonable duties; all the improvement which the French have made in woollen manufactures would decay, and in the end be little worth: and consequently the hurt they could do us by them, would be of little moment.

It was my opinion, and is so still, that the 9th *Article* of the *Treaty of Commerce* was calculated for the advantage of our trade (let who will, make it, that is nothing to me!) My reasons are, because it tied up the French to open the door to our manufactures, at a certain duty of importation, there; and left the Parliament of Britain at liberty, to shut theirs out, by as high duties as they pleased, here: there being no limitation upon us, as to duties on French goods, but *that other nations should pay the same*.

While the French were thus bound, and the British free; I always thought we must be in a condition to trade to advantage, or it must be our own fault.

That was my opinion, and is so still. And I would venture to maintain it against any man upon a public stage, before a jury of fifty merchants; and venture my life upon the cause, if I were assured of fair play in the dispute.

But that it was my opinion that we might carry on a trade with France to our great advantage, and that we ought, for that reason, to trade with them, appears in the 3rd, 4th, 5th, and 6th Volumes of the *Review* [*issued between Jan.* 1, 1706, *and May* 23, 1710; *the earlier ones*], above nine [*or rather seven*] years before the *Mercator* [*which commenced on May* 26, 1713] was thought of. It was not thought criminal to say so then! How it comes to be "villainous" to say so now, GOD knows! I can give no account of it. I am still of the same opinion, and shall never be brought to say otherwise, unless I see the state of trade so altered as to alter my opinion; and if ever I do, I will be able to give good reasons for it.

The answer to these things, whether mine or not, was all pointed at me: and the arguments were generally in the terms of "Villain!" "Rascal!" "Miscreant!" "Liar!" "Bankrupt!" "Fellow!" "Hireling!" "Turncoat!" &c. What the arguments were bettered by these methods, that I leave to others to judge of!

Also most of those things in the *Mercator*, for which I had such usage, were such as I was not the author of!

I do grant, had all the books which have been called by my name, been written by me, I must, of necessity, have exasperated every side; and, perhaps, have deserved it. But I have the greatest injustice imaginable in this treatment, as I have [also] in the perverting [of] the design, of what really I have written.

To sum up therefore my Complaint in few words:

I was from my first entering into the knowledge of Public Matters, and have ever been to this day, a sincere lover of the Constitution of my country, zealous for Liberty and the Protestant Interest; but a constant follower of Moderate Principles, a vigorous opposer of Hot Measures of *all* Parties. I never once changed my opinion, my principles, or my Party: and let what will be said of changing sides, this I maintain, that I never once deviated from the Revolution Principles, nor from the doctrine of Liberty and Property on which they were founded.

I own I could never be convinced of the great danger of the Pretender, in the time of the late Ministry; nor can I be now convinced of the great danger of the Church under this Ministry. I believe the cries of the one were politically made use of, then, to serve other designs; and I plainly see the like use, made of the other now. I spoke my mind freely then, and I have done the like now, in a small tract to that purpose, not yet made public, and which if I live to publish, I will publicly own; as I purpose to do everything I write, that my friends may know when I am abused, and they imposed on.

It has been the disaster of all Parties in this nation to be Very Hot in their turn; and as often as they have been so, I have differed with them all! and ever must and shall do so!

I will repeat some of the occasions on the Whigs' side; because from that quarter, the accusation of my Turning About comes.

The first time I had the misfortune to differ with my friends, was about the year 1683, when the Turks were besieging Vienna; and the Whigs in England, generally speaking, were for the Turks taking it: which I (having read the history of the cruelty and perfidious dealings of the Turks in their wars, and how they had rooted out the name of the Christian religion in above threescore and ten kingdoms) could by no means agree with; and though then but a young man, and a younger author, I opposed it and wrote against it, which was taken very unkindly indeed.

The next time I differed with my friends, was when King JAMES was wheedling the Dissenters, to take off the Penal Laws and the Test: which I could by no means come into.

And as, in the first, I used to say, I had rather the Popish House of Austria should ruin the Protestants in Hungary, than the infidel House of Ottoman should ruin both Protestant and Papist, by overrunning Germany; so, in the other, I told the Dissenters I had rather the Church of England should pull our clothes off, by fines and forfeitures; than the Papists should fall both upon the Church and the Dissenters, and pull our skins off by fire and faggot!

The next difference I had with good men was about the scandalous practice of Occasional Conformity: in which I had the misfortune to make many honest men angry; rather because I had the better of the argument, than because they disliked what I said.

And now I have lived to see the Dissenters themselves very quiet, if not very well pleased with an Act of Parliament to prevent it. Their friends indeed laid it on. They would be friends indeed, if they would talk of taking it off again.

Again, I had a breach with honest men for their maltreating King WILLIAM.

Of which, I say nothing: because I think they are now opening their eyes, and making what amends they can to his memory.

The fifth difference I had with them, was about the *Treaty of Partition*, in which many honest men were mistaken; and in which, I told them plainly then, that "they would, at last, end the war upon worse terms."

And so it is my opinion they would have done, though the Treaty of Gertruydenburg had taken place.

The sixth time I differed with them was when the Old Whigs fell on the Modern Whigs; and when the Duke of MARLBOROUGH and my Lord GODOLPHIN were used by the *Observator* in a manner worse, I confess, for the time it lasted, than ever they were used since: nay, though it were by ABEL and the *Examiner*! But the success failed. In this dispute, my Lord GODOLPHIN did me the honour to tell me, "I had served him, and His Grace also, both faithfully and successfully."

But his Lordship is dead [*in* 1712], and I have now no testimony of it but what is to be found in the *Observator*, where I am plentifully abused for being an enemy to my country, by acting in the Interest of my Lord GODOLPHIN and the Duke of MARLBOROUGH. What weathercock *can* turn with such tempers as these!

I am now in the seventh breach with them, and my crime now is, that I will not believe and say the same things of the Queen and the late Treasurer [*Lord OXFORD*], which I could not believe before, of my Lord GODOLPHIN and the Duke of MARLBOROUGH; and which, in truth, I cannot believe, and therefore could not say it of either of them: and which, if I had believed, yet I ought not to have been the man that should have said it; for the reasons aforesaid [*pp.* 76, 78].

In such turns of Tempers and Times, a man must be tenfold a Vicar of Bray, or it is impossible but he must, one time or out, be out with everybody.

This is my present condition; and for this, I am reviled with having abandoned my principles, turned Jacobite, and and what not. GOD judge between me and these men!

Would they come to any particulars with me, what real guilt I may have, I would freely acknowledge! and if they would produce any evidence of the bribes, the pensions, and the rewards I have taken; I would declare honestly, whether they were true or not.

If they would give me a list of the books, which they charge me with; and the reasons why they lay them at my door; I would acknowledge any mistake, own what I have done, and let them know what I have *not* done!

But these men neither shew mercy, nor leave place for repentance! in which they act not only unlike their Maker, but contrary to His express commands.

It is true, good men have been used thus in former times: and all the comfort I have is, that these men have not the Last Judgement in their hands! if they had, dreadful would be the case of those who oppose them. But that Day will shew many men, and things also, in a different state from what they may now appear in: some that now appear clear and fair, will then be seen to be black and foul; and some that are now thought black and foul, will then be approved and accepted. And thither, I cheerfully appeal; concluding this Part in the words of the prophet: "I heard the defaming of many! Fear on every side. Report," say they, "and we will report it!" All my familiars watched for my halting, saying, "Peradventure, he will be enticed, and we shall prevail against him; and we shall take our revenge on him" (Jeremiah xx. 10).

Mr. [MATTHEW] POOLE's *Annotations* [1683–5], has the following remarks on these lines; which I think are so much to that Part of my case which is to follow, that I could not omit them. His words are these:

"*The prophet*," says he, "*here rendereth a reason why he thought of giving over his Work as a prophet: his ears were continually filled with the obloquies and reproaches of such as reproached him; and besides, he was afraid on all hands, there were so many traps laid for him, so many devices devised against him. They did not only take advantages against him; but sought advantages, and invited others to raise stories of him. Not only strangers: but those that he might have expected the greatest kindness from; those that pretended most courteously: they watch*," says he, "*for opportunities to do me mischief, and lay in wait for my halting; desiring nothing more than that I might be enticed to speak, or do something* [in] *which they might find matter of a colourable accusation, that so they might satisfy their malice upon me. This hath always been the genius of wicked men. JOB and DAVID both made complaints much like this.*"

These are Mr. POOLE's words.

And this leads me to several particulars, in which my case may, without any arrogance, be likened to that of the sacred prophet; excepting only the vast disparity of the persons.

No sooner was the Queen dead, and the King (as right required) proclaimed; but the rage of men increased upon me to that degree, that the threats and insults I received, were such as I am not able to express! If I offered to say a word in favour of the present Settlement it was called "fawning! and turning round again!" On the other hand, though I have meddled, neither one way or other, nor written one book since the Queen's death; yet a great many things are called by my name, and I bear, every day, all the reproaches whch all the Answerers of those books cast, as well upon the subject as the authors.

I have not seen or spoken to my Lord of OXFORD, since the King's landing [*September* 18, 1714]; nor received the least message, order, or writing from his Lordship, or in any other way, corresponded with him: yet he bears the reproach of my writing in his defence; and I, the rage of men for doing it! I cannot say it is no affliction to me, to be thus used; though my being entirely clear of the facts is a true support to me.

I am unconcerned at the rage and clamour of Party men: but I cannot be unconcerned to hear men, whom I think are good men and true Christians, prepossessed and mistaken about me. However, I cannot doubt but, sometime or other, it will please GOD to open such men's eyes. A constant, steady adhering to personal Virtue and to public Peace, which (I thank GOD! I can appeal to Him!) has always been my practice, will, *at last*, restore me to the opinion of sober and impartial men; and that is all I desire.

What it will do with those who are resolutely partial and unjust I cannot say; neither is that much my concern. But I cannot forbear giving one example of the hard treatment I receive; which has happened, even while I am writing this tract.

I have six children. I have educated them as well as my circumstances will permit; and so, as I hope, shall recommend them to better usage than their father meets with in the World. I am not indebted one shilling in the world, for any part of their education, or for anything else belonging to bringing them up. Yet the Author of the *Flying Post* published lately that "I never paid for the education of any of my children."

If any man in Britain has a shilling to demand of me, for any part of their education, or anything belonging to them: let him come for it!

But these men care not what injurious things they write, nor what they say, whether truth or not; if it may but raise a reproach on me, though it were to be my ruin.

I may well appeal to the *Honour and Justice of my worst enemies* in such cases as this.

Conscia meus recti famas medidacia ridet.

CONCLUSION

BY THE PUBLISHER.

WHILE this was at the Press, and the copy [manuscript] *thus far finished; the author was seized with a violent fit of apoplexy; whereby he was disabled finishing what he designed in his further defence. And continuing now, for above six weeks, in a weak and languishing condition; neither able to go on, nor likely to recover (at least in any short time): his friends thought it not fit to delay the publication of this any longer. If he recovers, he may be able to finish what he began. If not, it is the opinion of most that know him, that the treatment which he here complains of, and some others that he would have spoken of, have been the apparent cause of his disaster.*

FINIS.

THE

The True Born *Englishman.*

A

SATYR.

"*Statuimus pacem, et securitatem, et concordiam judicium et justitiam inter Anglos et Normannos, Francos, et Britones Walliæ et Cornubiæ, Pictos et Scotos Albaniæ; similiter inter Francos et Insulanos, provincias et patrias, quæ pertinent ad coronam nostrum; et inter omnes nobis subjectos firmiter et inviolabiliter observari.*" —*Charta* Regis WILHELMI Conquisitoris *de Pacis Publica*, cap. I.

Printed in the Year MDCCI.

[*The Title page of this piece is apparently that of the first edition; but the text given is the revised one of* 1703. *In the* Preface *to which*, DEFOE *thus writes.*

No Author is now capable of preserving the purity of his style, no, nor the native product of his thought to Posterity: since, after the first edition of his Work has shewn itself, and perhaps sinks in a few hands, piratic Printers or hackney Abridgers fill the World; the first, with spurious and incorrect copies, and the latter with imperfect and absurd representations, both in fact, style, and design.

It is in vain to exclaim at the villainy of these practices, while no law is left to punish them.

The Press groans under the unhappy burden, and yet is in a strait between two mischiefs:

1. The tyranny of a Licenser. This, in all Ages, has been a method so ill, so arbitrary, and so subjected to bribery and Parties, that the Government has thought fit, in justice to the Learned Part of the World, not to suffer it: since it has always been shutting up the Press to one side, and opening it to the other; which, as Affairs are in England often changing, has, in its turn, been oppressive to both.
2. The unbridled liberty of invading each other's property. And this is the evil the Press now cries for help in.

To let it go on thus, will, in time, discourage all manner of Learning; and authors will never set heartily about anything, when twenty years' study shall immediately be sacrificed to the profit of a piratical printer, who not only ruins the author, but abuses the Work.

I shall trouble myself only to give some instances of this in my own case.

As to the abusing the Copy, the *True Born Englishman* is a remarkable example. By which, the Author, though in it he eyed no profit, had he been to enjoy the profit of his own labour, had gained above a £1,000 [=£2,000 *now*]. A book, that besides Nine Editions of the Author, has been Twelve times printed by other hands: some of which, have been sold for a Penny; others, for Twopence; and others, for Sixpence. The Author's Edition being fairly printed, and on good paper, could not be sold under a Shilling. 80,000 of the small ones have been sold in the streets for Twopence, or at a Penny: and the Author, thus abused and discouraged, had no remedy but patience.

And yet he had received no mortification at this, had his Copy [*manuscript*] been transmitted fairly to the World. But the monstrous abuses of that kind are hardly credible. Twenty, fifty, and in some places sixty lines were left out in a place: others were turned, spoiled, and so intolerably mangled, that the parent of the brat could not know his own child.

This is the thing complained of, and which I wait with patience, and not without hopes, to see rectified.

A true Collection, &c. Vol. II. *Preface.*]

["*Statuimus pacem, et securitatem, et concordiam judicium et justitiam inter Anglos et Normannos, Francos, et Britones Walliæ et Cornubiæ, Pictos et Scotos Albaniæ; similiter inter Francos et Insulanos, provincias et patrias, quæ pertinent ad coronam nostrum; et inter omnes nobis subjectos, firmiter et inviolabiliter observari.*" —*Charta* Regis WILHELMI Conquisitoris *de Pacis Publica*, cap. 1.

An Explanatory Preface.

IT IS not that I see any reason to alter my opinion in anything I have writ[ten], which occasions this *Epistle*; but I find it necessary, for the satisfaction of some Persons of Honour, as well as of Wit, to pass a short Explication upon it, and tell the World what I mean; or rather, what I do not mean in some things, wherein I find I am liable to be misunderstood.

I confess myself something surprised, to hear that I am taxed with bewraying my own nest, and abusing our nation by discovering the meanness of our Original, in order to make the English contemptible abroad and at home. In which, I think they are mistaken. For why should not our neighbours be as good as we to derive from?

And I must add, that had we been an unmixed nation, I am of opinion it had been to our disadvantage. For, to go no further, we have three nations about us, as clear from mixtures of blood as any in the world; and I know not which of them I could wish ourselves to be like: I mean the Scots, the Welsh, and the Irish. And if I were to write a Reverse to the Satyr [*satire*], I would examine all the nations of Europe, and prove, That those nations which are most mixed are the best; and have least of barbarism and brutality among them. And abundance of reasons might be given for it, too long to bring into a *Preface*.

But I give this hint, to let the World know that I am far from thinking it is a Satyr upon the English Nation, to tell them they are derived from all the nations under heaven, that is, from several nations. Nor is it meant to undervalue the original of English; for we see no reason to like them worse, being the relicts of Romans, Danes, Saxons, and Normans, than we should have done if they had remained Britains, that is, if they had been all Welshmen.

But the intent of the Satyr is to point at the vanity of those who talk of their antiquity; and value themselves upon their pedigree, their ancient families, and being *True Born*: whereas it is impossible we should be *True Born*; and, if we could, we should have lost by the bargain.

These sort of people, who call themselves *True Born*; and tell long stories of their families; and, like a nobleman of Venice, think a foreigner ought not to walk on the same side of the street with them; are owned to be meant in this Satyr. What they would infer from their long original, I know not: nor is it easy to make out, whether they are the better or the worse for their ancestors.

Our English nation may value themselves for their Wit, Wealth, and Courage; and I believe few nations will dispute it with them: but for long originals, and ancient *true born* families of English; I would advise them to waive the discourse!

A *True English man* is one that deserves a character, and I have nowhere lessened him, that I know of: but as for a *True Born* English man, I confess I do not understand him!

From hence I only infer, That an English man, of all men, ought not to despise foreigners as such; and I think the inference is just, since what They are to-day, We were yesterday; and To-morrow, they will be like us.

If foreigners misbehave in their several stations and employments, I have nothing to do with that! The laws are open to punish them equally with natives, and let them have no favour! But when I see the Town full of lampoons and invectives against Dutchmen, *only* because they are foreigners; and the King [*WILLIAM III.*] reproached and insulted by insolent pedants and ballad-making poets, for employing foreigners, and for being a foreigner himself: I confess myself moved by it to remind our nation of their own original; thereby to let them see what a banter is put upon ourselves in it; since speaking of Englishmen *ab origine*, we are really *all Foreigners ourselves*!

I could go on to prove it is also impolitic in us to discourage foreigners; since it is easy to make it appear that the multitudes of foreign nations who have taken sanctuary here, have been the greatest additions to the wealth and strength of the nation: the essential whereof is in the *number* of its inhabitants. Nor would this nation ever have arrived to the degree of wealth and glory it now boasts of, if the addition of foreign nations, both as to manufactures and arms, had not been helpful to it. This is so plain, that he who is ignorant of it is too dull to be talked with.

The Satyr therefore, I must allow to be just, till I am otherwise convinced. Because nothing can be more ridiculous than to hear our people boast of that antiquity; which, if it had been true, would have left us in so much worse a condition than we are now. Whereas we ought rather to boast among our neighbours, that we are part of themselves, of the same original as they but bettered by our climate; and, like our language and manufactures, derived from them, but improved by us to a perfection greater than they can pretend to. This we might have valued ourselves upon without vanity.

But to disown our descent from them, to talk big of our ancient families and long originals, and to stand at a distance from foreigners like the Enthusiast in religion, with a "Stand off! I am more holy than thou!" this is a thing so ridiculous in a nation derived from foreigners as we are, that I could not but attack them as I have done.

And whereas I am threatened to be called to a public account for this freedom, and the Publisher of this has been "newspapered" into gaol already for it: though I see nothing in it for which the Government can be displeased; yet if, at the same time, those people who, with an unlimited arrogance in print, every day affront the King, prescribe [to] the Parliament, and lampoon the Government, may be either punished or restrained; I am content to stand or fall by the Public Justice of my native country, which I am not sensible that I have anywhere injured.

Nor would I be misunderstood concerning the Clergy, with whom if I have taken any license more than becomes a Satyr, I question not but those Gentlemen, who are Men of Letters as well as men of so much candour as to allow me a loose [*liberty*] at the crimes of the guilty; without thinking the whole Profession lashed, who are innocent. I profess to have very mean thoughts of those Gentlemen, who have deserted their own principles, and exposed even their morals as well as loyalty; but not at all to think it affects any but such as are concerned in the fact.

Nor would I be misrepresented as to the ingratitude of the English to the King and his friends; as if I meant the English as a Nation, are so.

The contrary is so apparent, that I would hope it should not be suggested of me. And therefore when I have brought in *BRITANNIA* speaking of the King, I suppose her to be the representative or mouth of the Nation as a body.

But if I say we are full of such who daily affront the King and abuse his friends, who print scurrilous pamphlets, virulent lampoons, and reproachful public banters against both the King's person and his Government: I say nothing but what is too true. And that the Satyr is directed as such, I freely own; and cannot say but I should think it very hard to be censured for this Satyr, while such remains unquestioned and tacitly approved. That I can mean none but these, is plain from these few lines, page 27 [*p.* 143].

Ye Heavens, regard! Almighty JOVE, look down
And view thy injured Monarch on the throne!
On their ungrateful heads, due vengeance take,
Who sought his Aid, and then his Part forsake!

If I have fallen rudely upon our vices, I hope none but the vicious will be angry.

As for writing for Interest, I disown it! I have neither Place, nor Pension, nor Prospect; nor seek none, nor will have none!

If matter of fact justifies the truth of the crimes, the Satyr is just. As to the poetic liberties, I hope the crime is pardonable! I am content to be stoned, provided none will attack me but the innocent!

If my countrymen would take the hint, and grow better natured from my "ill-natured poem," as some call it; I would say this of it; that though it is far from the best Satyr that ever was written, it would do the most good that ever Satyr did.

And yet I am ready to ask pardon of some Gentlemen too, who, though they are Englishmen, have good nature enough to see themselves reproved, and can hear it. These are

Gentlemen in a true sense, that can bear to be told of their *faux pas,* and not abuse the Reprover. To such, I must say this is no Satyr. They are exceptions to the general rule: and I value my performance from their generous approbation more than I can from any opinion I have of its worth.

The hasty errors of my Verse, I made my excuse for before: and since the time I have been upon it, has been but little, and my leisure less; I have all along strove rather to make the Thoughts explicit than the Poem correct. However, I have mended some faults in this edition [1703]; and the rest must be placed to my account.

As to *Answers,* Banters, *True English Billingsgate*; I will expect them till nobody will buy, and then the shop will be shut.

Had I written it for the gain of the Press, I should have been concerned at its being printed again and again, by Pirates as they called them, and Paragraph-Men: but would they but do it justice, and print it true, according to the Copy; they are welcome to sell it for a penny, if they please.

Their Pence indeed are the End of their works. I will engage, if nobody will buy, nobody will write! and not a Patriot Poet of them all now, will, in defence of his native country (which I have abused, they say), print an *Answer* to it, and give it about, for GOD's sake!]

THE PREFACE.

[D. Defoe.
Jan. 1701.]

The End of Satyr is Reformation: and the Author though he doubts the work of conversion is at a general stop, has put his hand to the plow.

I expect a storm of ill language from the fury of the Town, and especially from those whose English *talent it is to rail. And without being taken for a conjurer, I may venture to foretell that I shall be cavilled at about my* mean style, rough verse, *and* incorrect language*; things, I might indeed have taken more care in. But the book is printed, and though I see some faults, it is too late to mend them. And this is all I think needful to say to them.*

Possibly somebody may take me for a Dutchman, in which they are mistaken. But I am one that would be glad to see Englishmen behave themselves better to strangers, and to Governors also; that one might not be reproached in foreign countries, for belonging to a "nation that wants manners."

I assure you, Gentlemen, strangers use us better abroad; and we can give no reason but our ill-nature for the contrary here.

Methinks, an Englishman, who is so proud of being called "a good fellow," should be civil: whereas it cannot be denied but we are, in many cases, and particularly to strangers, the churlishest people alive.

As to vices, who can dispute our intemperance, whilst an honest drunken man *is a character in a man's praise? All our Reformations are banters, and will be so until our Magistrates and Gentry reform themselves by way of example. Then, and not till then, they may be expected to punish others without blushing.*

As to our Ingratitude, I desire to be understood of that particular people, who pretending to be Protestants, have all along endeavoured to reduce the Liberties and Religion of this nation into the hands of King JAMES and his Popish powers; together with such who enjoy the peace and protection of the present Government, and yet abuse and affront the King who procured it, and openly profess their uneasiness under him. These, by whatever names or titles they are dignified or distinguished, are the people aimed at. Nor do I disown but that it is so much the temper of an Englishman to abuse his benefactor, that I could be glad to see it rectified.

They who think I have been guilty of any error in exposing the crimes of my own countrymen to themselves, may, among many honest instances of the like nature, find the same thing in Mr. COWLEY, in his Imitation of the second Olympic Ode of PINDAR. His words are these:

But in this thankless World, the Givers
    Are envied even by the Receivers:
'Tis now the cheap and frugal fashion,
Rather to hide, than pay an obligation.
    Nay, 'tis much worse than so!
    It now an Artifice doth grow,
    Wrongs and Outrages to do;
Lest men should think we Owe.

THE INTRODUCTION.

SPEAK, Satyr! For there 's none can tell like thee!
Whether 'tis Folly, Pride, or Knavery
That makes this discontented land appear
Less happy now in Times of Peace, than War?
Why civil feuds disturb the nation more
Than all our bloody wars have done before?

Fools out of favour, grudge at Knaves in Place:
And men are always honest in disgrace.
The Court preferments make men knaves, in course;
But they which would be in them, would be worse!
'Tis not at Foreigners that we repine,
Would Foreigners their perquisites resign!
The Great Contention 's plainly to be seen,
To get some men put Out, and some put In.
For this, our S[enator]s make long harangues,
And floored M[ember]s whet their polished tongues.
Statesmen are always sick of one disease,
And a good Pension gives them present ease:
That 's the specific makes them all content
With any King and any Government.
Good patriots at Court Abuses rail,
And all the nation's grievances bewail;
But when the Sovereign Balsam 's once applied,
The zealot never fails to change his Side;
And when he must the Golden Key resign,
The Railing Spirit comes about again!

Who shall this bubbled nation disabuse,
While they, their own felicities refuse?
Who at the wars, have made such mighty pother;
And now are falling out with one another!
With needless fears, the jealous nation fill,
And always have been saved *against their will*!
Who fifty millions sterling have disbursed
To be at peace, and too much plenty cursed!
Who their Old Monarch eagerly undo,
And yet uneasily obey the New!

Search, Satyr! search! a deep incision make!
The poison 's strong, the antidote 's too weak!
'Tis Pointed Truth must manage this dispute;
And downright English, Englishmen confute!
Whet thy just anger at the nation's pride;
And with keen phrase repel the vicious tide!
To Englishmen, their own beginnings shew,
And ask them, "Why they slight their neighbours so?"

Go back to elder Times and Ages past,
And nations into long oblivion cast;
To old BRITANNIA's youthful days retire,
And there for the *True Born Englishmen* inquire!
BRITANNIA freely will disown the name;
And hardly knows herself, from whence they came.
Wonders that They, of all men, should pretend
To birth and blood, and for a Name contend!
Go back to causes, where our follies dwell,
And fetch the dark Original from hell!
Speak, Satyr! for there 's none like thee, can tell.

The *True Born* Englishman.

PART I.

WHEREVER GOD erects a House of Prayer,
The Devil always builds a Chapel there;
And 'twill be found, upon examination,
The latter has the largest congregation.
For ever since he first debauched the mind,
He made a perfect conquest of mankind.
With Uniformity of *Service*, he
Reigns with a general aristocracy.
No Nonconforming Sects disturb his reign;
For of his yoke, there 's very few complain!
He knows the Genius and the inclination,
And matches proper sins for every nation.
He needs no Standing Army Government,
He always rules us by our own consent!
His laws are easy, and his gentle sway
Makes it exceeding pleasant to obey.
The list of his Vicegerents and Commanders
Outdoes your CÆSARS or your ALEXANDERS:
They never fail of his infernal aid,
And he 's as certain ne'er to be betrayed.
Through all the world, they spread his vast command,
And Death's eternal empire is maintained.

They rule so politicly and so well,
As if there were Lords Justices of Hell!
Duly divided, to debauch mankind,
And plant infernal dictates in their mind.

PRIDE, the first Peer, and President of Hell;
To his share, Spain, the largest province, fell.
The subtle Prince thought fittest to bestow
On these, the golden mines of Mexico,
With all the silver mountains of Peru;
Wealth which, in wise hands, would the World undo!
Because he knew their Genius to be such,
Too lazy and too haughty to be rich.
So proud a people, so above their fate,
That if reduced to beg, they'll beg in State!
Lavish of money, to be counted brave;
And proudly starve, because they scorn to save.
Never was nation in the World before,
So very rich, and yet so very poor.

LUST chose the torrid zone of Italy,
Where swelling veins o'erflow with livid streams,
With heat impregnate from Vesuvian flames,
Whose flowing sulphur forms infernal lakes;
And human body, of the soil partakes.
There Nature ever burns with hot desires,
Fanned with luxuriant air from subterranean fires.
Here undisturbed, in floods of scalding lust,
The infernal King reigns with infernal gust.

DRUNKENNESS, the darling favourite of hell,
Chose Germany to rule; and rules so well!
No subjects more obsequiously obey!
None please so well, or are so pleased as they!
The cunning Artist manages so well,
He lets them bow to heaven, and drink to hell.

If but to wine and him, they homage pay,
He cares not to what deity they pray!
What God they worship most! or in what way!
Whether by LUTHER, CALVIN, or by Rome,
They sail for heaven: by wine, he steers them home!

Ungoverned PASSION settled first in France,
Where mankind lives in haste, and thrives by chance:
A dancing nation, fickle and untrue!
Have oft undone themselves, and others too;
Prompt, the infernal dictates to obey;
And in hell's favour, none more great than they!

The Pagan World, he blindly leads away,
And personally rules, with arbitrary sway.
The mask thrown off, *Plain Devil* his title stands:
And what elsewhere, he Tempts; he, here Commands!
There, with full gust, the ambition of his mind
Governs, as he, of old, in heaven designed!
Worshipped as God, his paynim altars smoke,
Embued with blood of those that him invoke.

The rest, by Deputies, he rules as well,
And plants the distant colonies of hell:
By them, his secret power, he well maintains,
And binds the World in his infernal chains.

By zeal, the Irish; and the Rush by folly:
Fury, the Dane; the Swede, by melancholy.
By stupid ignorance, the Muscovite:
The Chinese, by a child of hell called Wit.
Wealth makes the Persian too effeminate;
And Poverty, the Tartars desperate.
The Turks and Moors, by MAHOMET he subdues;
And GOD has given him leave to rule the Jews.
Rage rules the Portuguese; and fraud, the Scotch;
Revenge, the Pole; and avarice, the Dutch.

Satyr, be kind! and draw a silent veil!
Thy native England's vices to conceal.
Or if that task 's impossible to do,
At least be just, and shew her virtues too!
Too great, the first! alas, the last too few!

England unknown as yet, unpeopled lay.
Happy had she remained so to this day,
And not to every nation been a prey!
Her open harbours and her fertile plains
(The merchants' glory these, and those, the swains'),
To every barbarous nation have betrayed her!
Who conquer her as oft as they invade her.
So Beauty, guarded but by Innocence!
That ruins her, which should be her defence.

INGRATITUDE, a devil of black renown,
Possessed her very early for his own:
An ugly, surly, sullen, selfish spirit,
Who SATAN's worst perfections does inherit.
Second to him in malice and in force,
All Devil without, and all within him worse.

He made her first born race to be so rude,
And suffered her to be so oft subdued.
By several crowds of wandering thieves o'errun,
Often unpeopled, and as oft undone:
While every nation, that her powers reduced,
Their language and manners soon infused.
From whose mixed relics our compounded Breed
By spurious generation does succeed:
Making a Race uncertain and uneven,
Derived from all the nations under heaven!

The Romans first, with JULIUS CÆSAR came,
Including all the nations of that name,
Gauls, Greeks, and Lombards, and by computation,
Auxiliaries or slaves, of every nation.
With HENGIST, Saxons; Danes with SUENO came;
In search of plunder, not in search of fame.
Scots, Picts, and Irish from the Hibernian shore;
And Conquering WILLIAM brought the Normans o'er.

All these, their barbarous offspring left behind;
The dregs of armies, they, of all mankind:
Blended with Britains who before were here,
Of whom the Welsh have blest the character.

From this amphibious ill-born mob began
That vain ill-natured thing, an *Englishman*.
The customs, surnames, languages, and manners
Of all these nations are their own explainers:
Whose relics are so lasting and so strong,
They have left a Shibboleth upon our tongue,
By which, with easy search, you may distinguish
Your Roman-Saxon-Danish-Norman English.

The great invading * Norman let us know
What conquerors in after Times might do!
To every * musketeer, he brought to Town,
He gave the lands which never were his own.
When first, the English crown he did obtain;
He did not send his Dutchmen home again!
No re-assumption in his reign was known;
DAVENANT might there have let his book alone!
No Parliament, his army could disband;
He raised no money, for he paid in land!
He gave his Legions their eternal Station,
And made them all freeholders of the nation!

* WILLIAM the Conqueror.

* Or Archer.

He cantoned out the country to his men,
And every soldier was a denizen!
The rascals thus enriched, he called them, Lords!
To please their upstart pride with new made words:
And *Domesday Book*, his tyranny records.

And here begins our ancient pedigree
That so exalts our poor Nobility!
'Tis that from some French trooper they derive,
Who with the Norman Bastard did arrive.
The trophies of the families appear:
Some shew the sword, the bow, and some the spear,
Which their Great Ancestor, forsooth! did wear.
These in the Heralds' *Register* remain,
Their noble *mean* extraction to explain.
Yet who the hero was, no man can tell!
Whether a drummer, or a Colonel?
The silent record blushes to reveal
Their undescended dark Original!

But grant the best! How came the change to pass,
A *True Born Englishman*, of *Norman* race?
A Turkish horse can shew more history
To prove his well-descended family!
Conquest, as by the * Moderns 'tis exprest,
May give a title to the lands possests:
But that the longest sword should be so civil,
To make a Frenchman, *English*; that 's the Devil!

*Dr. SHERLOCK *de Facto.*

These are the heroes who despise the Dutch,
And rail at new-come foreigners so much!
Forgetting that themselves are all derived
From the most scoundrel race that ever lived!
A horrid crowd of rambling thieves and drones,
Who ransacked kingdoms, and dispeopled towns!
The Pict and painted Britain, treacherous Scot;

By hunger, theft, and rapine hither brought!
Norwegian pirates, buccaneering Dane,
Whose red-haired offspring everywhere remain;
Who, joined with Norman French, compound the breed
From whence your *True Born Englishmen* proceed!

And lest, by length of time it be pretended,
The climate may this modern breed have mended;
Wise Providence, to keep us where we are,
Mixes us daily, with exceeding care!
We have been Europe's Sink! the Jakes where she
Voids all her offal outcast progeny.
From our Fifth HENRY's time, the strolling bands
Of banished fugitives from neighbouring lands,
Have here a certain sanctuary found:
The eternal refuge of the vagabond!
Where, in but half a common Age of time,
Borrowing new blood and manners from the clime,
Proudly they learn all mankind to contemn,
And all their race are *True Born Englishmen*!

Dutch, Walloons, Flemings, Irishmen, and Scots,
Vaudois and Valtolines and Huguenots,
In good Queen BESS's charitable reign,
Supplied us with three hundred thousand men.
Religion (God, we thank Thee!) sent them hither,
Priests, Protestants, the Devil and all together!
Of all professions, and of every trade,
All that were persecuted or afraid;
Whether for debt, or other crimes they fled,
DAVID at Hackilah was still their head.

The offspring of this miscellaneous crowd
Had not their new plantations long enjoyed,
But they grew Englishmen, and raised their votes
At foreign shoals of interloping Scots.

The Royal* Branch, from Pict land did succeed, * King JAMES I.
With troops of Scots, and scabs from North-by-Tweed.
The seven first years of his pacific reign
Made him and half his nation, Englishmen.
Scots from the northern frozen banks of Tay,
With packs and plods came Whigging all away;
Thick as the locusts which in Egypt swarmed,
With pride and hungry hopes completely armed:
With native truth, diseases, and no money,
Plundered our Canaan of the milk and honey.
Here they grew quickly Lords and Gentlemen,
And all their race are *True Born Englishmen*!

The Civil Wars, the common purgative
Which always use to make the nation thrive,
Made way for all the strolling congregation
Which thronged in pious C[HARLE]S' Restoration.
The Royal Refugee our breed restores
With foreign Courtiers, and with foreign whores;
And carefully repeopled us again
Throughout his lazy, long, lascivious reign,
With such a blest and *True Born English* fry
As such illustrates our Nobility.
A gratitude which will so black appear,
As future Ages must abhor to hear;
When they look back on all that crimson flood,
Which streamed in LINDSEY's and CARNARVON's blood,
Bold STAFFORD, CAMBRIDGE, CAPEL, LUCAS, LISLE,
Who crowned in death, his father's funeral pile:
The loss of whom, in order to supply,
With *True Born English* bred Nobility,
Six bastard Dukes survive his luscious reign,
The labours of the Italian CASTLEMAINE,
French PORTSMOUTH, Tabby Scot, and Cambrian;
Besides the numerous bright and virgin throng
Whose female glories shade them from my Song.

This offspring, if one Age they multiply,
May half the House, with *English* Peers supply!
There, with true English pride, they may contemn
SCHOMBERG and PORTLAND, new made Noblemen.

French cooks, Scotch pedlars, and Italian whores
Were all made Lords, or Lords' progenitors.
Beggars and bastards by this new creation,
Much multiplied the P[eera]ge of the nation:
Who will be all, ere one short Age runs o'er,
As *True Born* Lords as those we had before.

Then to recruit the Commons he prepares,
And heal the latent breaches of the Wars.
The pious purpose better to advance,
He invites the banished Protestants of France.
Hither, for GOD's sake, and their own, they fled:
Some for religion came, and some for bread.
Two hundred thousand pair of Wooden Shoes,
Who (God be thanked!) had nothing left to lose,
To Heaven's great praise, did for religion fly;
To make us starve our poor, in charity.
In every port, they plant their fruitful train,
To get a race of *True Born Englishmen*:
Whose children will, when riper years they see,
Be as ill-natured and as proud as we!
Call themselves English! foreigners despise!
Be surly like us all, and just as wise!

Thus from a mixture of all kinds, began
That heterogeneous thing, an *Englishman*.
In eager rapes, and furious lust begot,
Betwixt a painted Britain and a Scot;
Whose gendering offspring quickly learned to bow,
And yoke the heifers to the Roman plow.

From whence a mongrel half-breed race there came
With neither name or nation, speech or fame.
In whose hot veins, new mixtures quickly ran,
Infused betwixt a Saxon and a Dane.
This nauseous brood directly did contain
The well-extracted blood of *Englishmen.*

Which medley cantoned in a Heptarchy,
A rhapsody of nations to supply;
Among themselves maintained eternal wars,
And still the Ladies loved the Conquerors.

The western Angles, all the rest subdued;
A bloody nation barbarous and rude:
Who by the tenure of the sword, possesst
One part of Britain; and subdued the rest.
And as great things denominate the small,
The conquering Part gave title to the Whole.
The Scot, Pict, Britain, Roman, Dane submit,
And with the English-Saxon all unite:
And these the mixture have so close pursued,
The very Name and Memory 's subdued!
No Roman now, no Britain does remain!
(Wales strove to separate, but strove in vain)
The silent nations undistinguished fall!
And *Englishman* 's the common Name for all.
Fate jumbled them together, God knows how!
Whate'er they were, they 're *True Born English* now!

The wonder which remains, is at our Pride,
To value that which all wise men deride;
For *Englishmen* to boast of Generation,
Cancels their knowledge, and lampoons the nation!

A *True Born Englishman* 's a contradiction!
In speech, an irony! in fact, a fiction!

A banter made to be a test of fools!
Which those that use it, justly ridicules.
A metaphor invented to express
A man akin to all the Universe!

For as the Scots, as learned men have said,
Throughout the world their wandering seed have spread;
So open-handed England, 'tis believed,
Has all the gleanings of the world received.

Some think, of England 'twas, our Saviour meant;
The Gospel should, to all the world be sent:
Since, when the blessed sound did hither reach,
They to all nations might be said to preach.

'Tis well that Virtue gives Nobility;
How shall we else the Want of Birth and Blood supply?
Since scarce one Family is left alive,
Which does not from some foreigner derive.
Of sixty thousand English Gentlemen
Whose Names and Arms in *Registers* remain;
We challenge all our Heralds to declare
Ten Families which English Saxons are!

France justly boasts the ancient noble line
Of BOURBON, MONTMORENCY, and LORRAINE.
The Germans too their House of AUSTRIA shew,
And Holland their invincible NASSAU:
Lines which in heraldry were ancient grown,
Before the name of Englishman was known.
Even Scotland too, her elder glory shews!
Her GORDONS, HAMILTONS, and her MONROES;
DOUGLAS, MACKAYS, and GRAHAMS, names well known
Long before ancient England knew her own.

But England, modern to the last degree,
Borrows or makes her own Nobility;
And yet she boldly boasts of pedigree!
Repines that foreigners are put upon her,
And talks of her antiquity and honour!
Her S[ACKVIL]LES, S[AVI]LES, C[ECI]LS, DELA[ME]RES,
M[OHU]NS and M[ONTAG]UES, D[URA]S, and V[EE]RES;
Not one have English names, yet all are English Peers!
Your HOUBLONS, PAPILLONS, and LETHULIERS
Pass now for *True Born English* Knights and Squires,
And make good Senate Members, or Lord Mayors,
Wealth (howsoever got) in England, makes
Lords, of mechanics! Gentlemen, of rakes!
Antiquity and Birth are needless here.
'Tis Impudence and Money make a P[ee]r!

Innumerable City Knights we know,
From Bluecoat Hospitals and Bridewell flow!
Draymen and porters fill the City Chair;
And footboys, Magisterial purple wear!
Fate has but very small distinction set
Betwixt the "Counter" and the Coronet.
Tarpaulin L[or]ds, Pages of high renown,
Rise up by poor men's valour, not their own!
Great Families, of yesterday, we shew;
And Lords, whose parents were, the Lord knows who!

PART II.

THE Breed 's described. Now, Satyr, if you
 can,
Their Temper shew! for "manners make
 the man."
Fierce as the Britain, as the Roman brave;
And less inclined to conquer than to save:
Eager to fight, and lavish of their blood,
And equally of Fear and Forecast void.
The Pict has made them sour, the Dane, morose;
False from the Scot, and from the Norman worse.
What honesty they have, the Saxons gave them;
And that, now they grow old, begins to leave them!
The climate makes them terrible and bold,
And English beef their courage does uphold:
No danger can their daring spirit pall,
Always provided that their belly 's full.

In close intrigues, their faculty 's but weak;
For generally, whate'er they know, they speak;
And often their own counsels undermine
By mere infirmity, without design:
From whence, the Learned say, it does proceed,
That English treasons never can succeed.
For they 're so open-hearted, you may know
Their own most secret thoughts, and others' too.

The Labouring Poor, in spite of double pay,
Are saucy, mutinous, and beggarly.
So lavish of their money and their time,
That Want of Forecast is the nation's crime.
Good drunken company is their delight,
And what they get by day, they spend by night.
Dull Thinking seldom does their heads engage;
But drink their Youth away, and hurry on old Age.
Empty of all good husbandry and sense,
And void of manners most when void of pence;
Their strong aversion to Behaviour 's such,
They always talk too little or too much.
So dull, they never take the pains to Think,
And seldom are good-natured but in drink.
In English Ale their dear enjoyment lies,
For which, they 'll starve themselves and families!
An Englishmen will fairly drink as much
As will maintain two families of Dutch.
Subjecting all their labour to the pots;
The greatest artists are the greatest sots.

The Country Poor do, by example, live:
The Gentry lead them, and the Clergy drive.
What may we not, from such examples hope?
The landlord is their God, the priest their Pope!
A drunken Clergy, and a swearing Bench,
Have given the Reformation such a drench,
As wise men think, there is some cause to doubt
Will purge Good Manners and Religion out!

Nor do the poor alone their liquor prize;
The Sages join in this great sacrifice!
The learnèd men, who study ARISTOTLE,
Correct him with an explanation bottle;

Praise EPICURUS rather than LYSANDER,
And *ARISTIPPUS more than ALEXANDER.
The Doctors, too, their GALEN here resign,
And generally prescribe specific wine.
The Graduate's study 's grown an easier task,
While for the urinal, they toss the flask.
The Surgeon's Art grows plainer every hour,
And wine 's the balm which, into wounds they pour.

* The drunkard's name for Canary.

Poets, long since, Parnassus have forsaken,
And say the ancient bards were all mistaken.
APOLLO 's lately abdicate and fled,
And good King BACCHUS governs in his stead.
He does the chaos of the head refine;
And Atom-Thoughts jump into Words by wine.
The inspiration 's of a finer nature,
As wine must needs excel Parnassus water.

Statesmen, their weighty politics refine;
And soldiers raise their courages, by wine.
CECILIA gives her choristers their choice,
And lets them all drink wine to clear their voice.

Some think the Clergy first found out the way,
And wine 's the only Spirit, by which they pray:
But others, less profane than such, agree
It clears the lungs, and helps the memory.
And therefore all of them Divinely think,
Instead of study, 'tis as well to drink.

And here I would be very glad to know,
Whether our Asgilites may drink or no?
Th' enlightened fumes of wine would certainly
Assist them much when they begin to fly;
Or, if a fiery chariot should appear,
Inflamed by wine, they 'd have the less to fear!

Even the Gods themselves, as mortals say,
Were they on earth, would be as drunk as they.
Nectar would be no more celestial drink;
They 'd all take wine, to teach them how to think.
But English drunkards, gods and men outdo!
Drink their estates away, and senses too.
COLON 's in debt, and if his friends should fail
To help him out, must die at last in gaol.
His wealthy uncle sent a hundred nobles
To pay his trifles off, and rid him of his troubles.
But COLON, like a *True Born Englishman*,
Drank all the money out in bright champagne;
And COLON does in custody remain.
Drunkenness has been the darling of the realm,
E'er since a drunken Pilot* had the helm. [* CHARLES II.]

In their Religion, they are so uneven,
That each man goes his own by-way to heaven;
Tenacious of mistakes to that degree,
That every man pursues it separately;
And fancies none can find the Way but he.
So shy of one another they are grown;
As if they strove to get to heaven alone.
Rigid and zealous, positive and grave,
And every grace but Charity, they have.
This makes them so ill-natured and uncivil,
That all men think an *Englishman* the Devil.

Surly to strangers, froward to their friend,
Submit to Love with a reluctant mind;
Resolved to be ungrateful and unkind.
If, by necessity, reduced to ask,
The Giver has the difficultest task:
For what 's bestowed, they awkwardly receive;
And always take less freely than they give.

The Obligation is their highest grief,
And never love, where they accept relief.
So sullen in their sorrows, that 'tis known
They 'll rather die than their afflictions own:
And if relieved, it is too often true,
That they 'll abuse their benefactors too.
For in distress, their haughty stomach 's such,
They hate to see themselves obliged too much.
Seldom contented, often in the wrong;
Hard to be pleased at all, and never long.

If your mistakes, their ill opinion gain;
No merit can their favour re-obtain!
And if they 're not vindictive in their fury,
'Tis their unconstant temper does secure ye!
Their brain 's so cool, their passion seldom burns;
For all 's condensed before the flame returns:
The fermentation 's of so weak a matter,
The humid damps the fume, and runs it all to water.
So though the inclination may be strong,
They 're pleased by fits, and never angry long.

Then if Good Nature shews some slender proof;
They never think they have reward enough:
But like our Modern Quakers of the Town,
Expect your manners, and return you none.

Friendship, th' abstracted Union of the Mind,
Which all men seek, but very few can find.
Of all the nations in the universe
None talk on 't more, or understand it less!
For if it does their Property annoy;
Their Property, their friendship will destroy!

As you discourse them, you shall hear them tell
All things in which they think they do excel;

No panegyric needs their praise record:
An Englishman ne'er wants his own good word!
His long discourses generally appear
Prologued with his own wondrous Character.
But first t' illustrate his own good name,
He never fails his neighbour to defame!
And yet he really designs no wrong:
His malice goes no further than his tongue.
But pleased to tattle, he delights to rail,
To satisfy the lechery of a tale.
His own dear praises close the ample speech;
Tells you, how wise he is, that is, how rich!
For Wealth is Wisdom! He that's rich is wise!
And all men learned, poverty despise!
His generosity comes next. And then,
Concludes that he 's a *True Born Englishman*!
And they, 'tis known, are generous and free,
Forgetting, and forgiving injury.
Which may be true, thus rightly understood,
"Forgiving ill turns, and forgetting good."

Cheerful in labour, when they have undertook it;
But out of humour, when they 're out of pocket.
But if their belly, and their pocket 's full,
They may be phlegmatic, but never dull.
And if a bottle does their brain refine,
It makes their Wit as sparkling as their wine.

As for the general vices which we find
They 're guilty of, in common with mankind,
Satyr, forbear! and silently endure!
We must conceal the crimes we cannot cure.

Nor shall my Verse, the brighter sex defame,
For English Beauty will preserve her name!
Beyond dispute, agreeable and fair,

And modester than other nations are.
For when the vice prevails, the great temptation
Is want of money more than inclination.
In general, this only is allowed:
They 're something noisy, and a little proud.

An Englishman is gentlest in command;
Obedience is a stranger in the land:
Hardly subjected to the Magistrate,
For Englishmen do all subjection hate.
Humblest when rich, but peevish when they 're poor;
And think whate'er they have, they merit more.

The meanest English plowman studies law,
And keeps thereby the Magistrates in awe;
Will boldly tell them, what they ought to do,
And sometimes punish their omission too.

Their Liberty and Property 's so dear;
They scorn their Laws or Governors to fear!
So bugbeared with the name of Slavery,
They can't submit to their own liberty!
Restraint from Ill is freedom to the wise,
But Englishmen do all restraint despise!
Slaves to the liquor, drudges to the pots;
The mob are Statesmen, and their Statesmen sots.

Their Governors, they count such dangerous things,
That 'tis their custom to affront their Kings.
So jealous of the Power their Kings possessed,
They suffered neither Power nor Kings to rest:
The bad, with force, they eagerly subdue;
The good, with constant clamours they pursue.
And did King JESUS reign, they'd murmur too!
A discontented nation, and by far

Harder to rule in times of peace than war.
Easily set together by the ears,
And full of careless jealousies and fears;
Apt to revolt, and willing to rebel,
And never are contented when they're well.
No Government could ever please them long,
Could tie their hands, or rectify their tongue!
In this, to ancient Israel well compared,
Eternal murmurs are among them heard.

It was but lately, that they were oppressed,
Their Rights invaded, and their Laws suppressed;
When, nicely tender of their liberty,
Lord! what a noise they made of Slavery!
In daily tumults shewed their discontent,
Lampooned their King, and mocked his Government;
And if in arms they did not first appear,
'Twas want of force, and not for want of fear.
In humbler tones than English used to do,
At foreign hands, for foreign aid they sue!

WILLIAM, the great Successor of NASSAU,
Their prayers heard, and their oppressions saw;
He saw and saved them! GOD and him, they praised;
To this, their thanks; to that, their trophies raised.
But glutted with their own felicities,
They soon their new Deliverer despise!
Say all their prayers back! their joy disown!
Unsing their thanks! and pull their trophies down!
Their harps of praise are on the willows hung,
For Englishmen are ne'er contented long.

The Reverend Clergy too (and who'd ha' thought
That they, who had such Non-Resistance taught,
Should e'er to arms against their Prince be brought!
Who up to heaven did Regal Power advance,

Subjecting English Laws to Modes of France,
Twisting Religion so with Loyalty,
As one could never live, and t'other die:)
And yet, no sooner did their Prince design
Their glebes and perquisites to undermine;
But (all their Passive Doctrines laid aside)
The Clergy, their own principles denied!
Unpreached their Non-Resisting cant, and prayed
To heaven, for help; and to the Dutch, for aid!
The Church chimed all their doctrines back again!
And Pulpit Champions did the Cause maintain!
Flew in the face of all their former zeal,
And Non-Resistance did at once repeal!

The Rabbis say, "It would be too prolix
To tie Religion up to Politics!
The Church's safety is *suprema lex*."
And so, by a new Figure of their own,
Their former doctrines all at once disown:
As laws *post facto*, in the Parliament,
In urgent cases have obtained assent;
But are as dangerous precedents laid by,
Made lawful only by necessity.

The Reverend Fathers then in arms appear,
And Men of GOD become the Men of War!
The nation, fired by them, to arms apply!
Assault their Antichristian Monarchy!
To their due channel, all our laws restore;
And made things what they should have been before.
But when they came to fill the Vacant Throne,
And the pale Priests looked back on what they 'd done;
How English Liberty began to thrive,
And Church of England Loyalty outlive!
How all their persecuting days were done,
And their Deliverer placed upon the throne!

The Priests, as Priests are wont to do, turned tail!
They 're *Englishmen*! and Nature will prevail.
Now, they deplore the ruins they have made,
And murmur for the Master they betrayed.
Excuse those crimes, they could not make him mend;
And suffer for the Cause they can't defend.
Pretend they 'd not have carried things so high,
And Proto-martyrs make for Popery.
"Had the Prince done," as they designed the thing,
"Had set the Clergy up, to rule the King;
Taken a donative for coming hither,
And so had left their King and them together:
We had," say they, "been now a happy nation!"
No doubt, we 'd seen a blessed Reformation!
For wise men say, "'Tis as dangerous a thing,
A Ruling Priesthood as a Priest-rid King!"
And of all plagues, with which mankind are curst,
Ecclesiastic Tyranny 's the worst.

If all our former grievances were feigned;
King JAMES has been abused! and we trepanned!
Bugbeared with Popery and Power Despotic!
Tyrannic Government! and Leagues exotic!
The Revolution 's a "Fanatic" Plot!
W[ILLIAM], a tyrant, and K[ing] J[AMES] was not!
A factious army and a poisoned nation
Unjustly forced King JAMES's Abdication!

But if he did, the subjects' rights invade;
Then he was punished only, not betrayed!
And punishing of Kings is no such crime,
But Englishmen have done it, many a time!

When Kings, the Sword of Justice first lay down;
They are no Kings, though they possess the Crown!
Titles are shadows! Crowns are empty things!

The Good of Subjects is the End of Kings!
To guide in war, and to protect in peace.
Where Tyrants once commence, the Kings do cease!
For Arbitrary Power 's so strange a thing,
It makes the Tyrant, and unmakes the King.
If Kings by foreign priests and armies reign,
And Lawless Power, against their oaths maintain,
Then subjects must have reason to complain.
If oaths must bind us, when our Kings do ill;
To call in foreign aid is to rebel!
By force to circumscribe our lawful Prince,
Is wilful treason in the largest sense!
And they who once rebel, most certainly,
Their GOD, their King, and former oaths defy!
If we allow no maladministration
Could cancel the allegiance of the nation;
Let all our learned Sons of LEVI try
This Ecclesiastic riddle to untie!
How they could make a step to call the Prince,
And yet pretend to Oaths and innocence?

By the first *Address*, they made beyond the sea,
They 're perjured in the most intense degree!
And without scruple, for the time to come,
May swear to all the Kings in Christendom!
And, truly, did our Kings consider all,
They 'd never let the Clergy swear at all!
Their politic allegiance they 'd refuse!
For whores and Priests will never want excuse.

But if the "Mutual Contract" was dissolved,
The doubt 's explained, the difficulty solved.
That Kings when they descend to tyranny,
Dissolve the Bond, and leave the subject free!
The Government 's ungirt! when Justice dies;

And Constitutions are nonentities.
The nation 's all a mob! There 's no such thing
As Lords or Commons, Parliament or King!
A great promiscuous crowd, the Hydra lies,
Till Laws revive, and Mutual Contract ties.

A Chaos free to choose, for their own share,
What Case of Government they please to wear.
If to a King, they do the reins commit,
All men are bound in conscience to submit;
But then that King must, by his oath, assent
To *Postulatas* of the Government:
Which if he breaks, he cuts off the entail,
And Power retreats to its Original.

This Doctrine has the sanction of assent,
From Nature's universal Parliament;
The Voice of Nations and the Course of Things
Allow that Laws superior are to Kings.
None but delinquents would have Justice cease,
Knaves rail at Laws, as soldiers rail at peace!
For Justice is the End of Government,
As Reason is the Test of Argument.

No man was ever yet so void of sense
As to debate the Right of Self-Defence:
A principle so grafted in the mind,
With Nature born, and does like Nature bind.
Twisted with Reason, and with Nature too,
As neither one, nor t'other can undo.

Nor can this Right be less, when national?
Reasons which govern one, should govern all.
Whate'er the dialect of Courts may tell,
He that his Right demands, can ne'er rebel!

Which Right, if 'tis by Governors denied,
May be procured by force, or foreign aid.
For "Tyranny!" 's a nation's Term of Grief;
As folks cry "Fire!" to hasten in relief:
And when the hated word is heard about,
All men should come to help the people out.

Thus England cried. BRITANNIA's voice was heard,
And great NASSAU to rescue her appeared.
Called by the universal voice of Fate,
GOD's and the People's Legal Magistrate.

Ye Heavens, regard! Almighty JOVE, look down
And view thy injured Monarch on the throne!
On their ungrateful hands the vengeance take,
Who sought his Aid, and then his Side forsake!
Witness, ye Powers! It was our Call alone,
Which now our Pride makes us ashamed to own!
BRITANNIA's troubles fetched him from afar,
To court the dreadful casualties of war:
But where requital *never* can be made,
Acknowledgment 's a tribute seldom paid!

He dwelt in bright MARIA's circling arms,
Defended by the magic of her charms
From foreign fears, and from domestic harms.
Ambition found no fuel for her fire;
He had what GOD could give, or man desire.
Till Pity roused him from his soft repose,
His life to unseen hazards to expose.
Till Pity moved him in our Cause t'appear.
Pity, that word which now we hate to hear!
But English Gratitude is always such,
To hate the hand which does oblige too much.

BRITANNIA's cries gave birth to his intent,
And hardly gained his unforeseen assent;
His boding thoughts foretold him, he should find
The people fickle, selfish, and unkind:
Which thought did to his royal heart appear
More dreadful than the dangers of the war;
For nothing grates a generous mind so soon,
As base returns for hearty service done.

Satyr, be silent! awfully prepare
BRITANNIA's Song and WILLIAM's praise to hear!
Stand by, and let her cheerfully rehearse
Her grateful vows in her immortal verse!
Loud Fame's eternal trumpet, let her sound!
Listen, ye distant poles, and endless round!
May the strong blast the welcome news convey
As far as sound can reach, or spirit can fly!
To neighbouring worlds, if such there be, relate
Our Hero's fame, for theirs to imitate!
To distant worlds of spirits, let her rehearse!
For spirits, without the help of voice converse.
May angels hear the gladsome news on high,
Mix with their everlasting symphony!
And hell itself stand in suspense, to know
Whether it be the Fatal Blast or no?

BRITANNIA.

THE Fame of Virtue 'tis, for which I sound;
And Heroes, with immortal Triumphs crowned!
Fame built on solid Virtue, swifter flies
Than morning light can spread my Eastern skies!
The gathering air returns the doubling sound,
And loud repeating thunders force it round!

Echoes return from caverns of the deep:
Old Chaos dreams on 't in eternal sleep!
Time hands it forward to its latest urn;
From whence it never, never shall return!
Nothing is heard so far, or lasts so long;
'Tis heard by every ear, and spoke by every tongue!

My Hero, with the sails of honour furled,
Rises like the Great Genius of the world.
By Fate and Fame wisely prepared to be
The Soul of War, and Life of Victory.
He spreads the Wings of Virtue on the throne,
And every Wind of Glory fans them on.
Immortal trophies dwell upon his brow,
Fresh as the garlands he has won but now.

By different steps, the high ascent he gains;
And differently that high ascent maintains.
Princes for Pride and Lust of Rule make war,
And struggle for the name of Conqueror.
Some fight for Fame, and some for Victory;
He fights to save, and conquers to set free.

Then seek no phrase, his titles to conceal;
And hide with words, what actions must reveal!
No parallel from Hebrew stories take!
Of Godlike Kings, my similies to make.
No borrowed names conceal my living theme,
But names and things directly I proclaim!
His honest Merit does his glory raise:
Whom that exalts, let no man fear to praise!

Of such a subject no man need be shy;
Virtue 's above the reach of flattery.
He needs no character but his own fame,
Nor any flattering titles but his name.
WILLIAM 's the name that 's spoke by ev'ry tongue;
WILLIAM 's the darling subject of my Song!
Listen, ye virgins, to the charming sound,
And in eternal dances hand it round!
Your early offerings to this altar bring,
Make him at once a lover and a King!
May he submit to none, but to your arms;
Nor ever be subdued but by your charms!
May your soft thought for him be all sublime,
And every tender vow be made for him!
May he be first in every morning thought,
And Heaven ne'er hear a prayer, where he 's left out!
May every omen, every boding dream
Be fortunate, by mentioning his name!
May this one charm, infernal powers affright,
And guard you from the terrors of the night!
May every cheerful glass, as it goes down
To WILLIAM's health, be cordial to your own!

Let every Song be chorused with his name,
And Music pay her tribute to his fame!
Let every poet tune his artful verse;
And in immortal strains his deeds rehearse!
And may APOLLO never more inspire
The disobedient bard with his seraphic fire!
May all my sons their grateful homage pay!
His praises sing, and for his safety pray!

Satyr, return to our unthankful isle,
Secured by Heaven's regard, and WILLIAM's toil!
To both ungrateful, and to both untrue;
Rebels to GOD, and to Good Nature too!

If e'er this Nation be distressed again;
To whomsoe'er they cry, they'll cry in vain!
To Heaven, they cannot have the face to look,
Or if they should, it would but Heaven provoke!
To hope for help from Man would be too much;
Mankind would always tell them of the Dutch!
How they came here our freedoms to maintain;
Were paid! and cursed! and hurried home again!
How by their aid, we first dissolved our fears;
And then our helpers damned for "Foreigners!"
'Tis not our English temper to do better!
For *Englishmen* think every man their debtor.

'Tis worth observing, that we ne'er complained
Of Foreigners, nor of the wealth they gained;
Till all their services were at an end!
Wise men affirm, "It is the English way,
Never to grumble till they come to pay;
And then, they always think, their temper 's such,
The work 's too little, and the pay too much!"

As frighted patients, when they want a cure,
Bid any price, and any pain endure!
But when the doctor's remedies appear;
The cure's too easy, and the price too dear!

Great PORTLAND ne'er was bantered when he strove
For Us, his Master's kindest thoughts to move!
We ne'er lampooned his conduct when employed,
King JAMES's secret counsels to divide!

Then, we caressed him as the only Man
Which could the doubtful Oracle explain!
The only HUSHAI able to repel
The dark designs of our ACHITOPHEL!
Compared his Master's courage, to his Sense;
The ablest Statesman, and the bravest Prince!
Ten years in English service he appeared,
And gained his Master's and the World's regard:
But 'tis not England's custom to reward!
The wars are over. England needs him not!
Now he 's a Dutchman, and the Lord knows what!

SCHOMBERG, the ablest soldier of his Age,
With great NASSAU did in our cause engage:
Both joined for England's rescue and defence,
The greatest Captain and the greatest Prince!
With what applause, his stories did we tell!
Stories which Europe's volumes largely swell.
We counted him an Army in our aid;
Where he commanded, no man was afraid!
His actions with a constant Conquest shine,
From Villa Vitiosa to the Rhine!
France, Flanders, Germany, his fame confess;
And all the World was fond of him, but Us!
Our turn first served, we grudged him the command:
Witness the grateful temper of the land!

We blame the K[ing] that he relies too much
On strangers, Germans, Huguenots, and Dutch;
And seldom would his great Affairs of State
To English Councillors communicate.
The fact might very well be answered thus.
He has so often been betrayed by us,
He must have been a madman to rely
On English Gentlemen's fidelity!

For laying other arguments aside;
This thought might mortify our English pride,
That Foreigners have faithfully obeyed him!
And none but English have e'er betrayed him.
They have our ships and merchants bought and sold,
And bartered English blood for foreign gold!
First, to the French, they sold the Turkey Fleet;
And injured TALMARSH next, at Camaret!
The King himself is sheltered for their snares,
Not by his merit, but the crown he wears.
Experience tell us, 'tis the English way,
Their benefactors always to betray!

And lest examples should be too remote,
A modern Magistrate, of famous note,
Shall give you his own history, by rote.
I'll make it out, deny it he that can!
His Worship is a *True Born Englishman*,
In all the latitude that empty word
By modern acceptation 's understood.
The Parish Books, his great descent record;
And now, he hopes ere long to be a Lord!
And truly, as things go, it would be pity
But such as he, should represent the City!
While robbery, for burnt offering he brings;
And gives to GOD, what he has stolen from Kings.
Great monuments of charity he raises,
And good St. Magnus whistles out his praises.
To City gaols, he grants a Jubilee,
And hires "Huzzas" from his own mobile.

Lately he wore the Golden Chain, and Gown;
With which equipped, he thus harangued the Town,

His fine speech, &c.

"With clouted iron shoes, and sheepskin breeches,
More rags than manners, and more dirt than riches;
From driving cows and calves to Leyton Market,
While of my greatness, there appeared no spark yet:
Behold I come! to let you see the pride
With which exalted beggars always ride!

"Born to the needful labours of the plough;
The cart whip graced me, as the chain does now!
Nature and Fate, in doubt what course to take,
Whether I should a Lord or ploughboy make,
Kindly at last resolved, they would promote me,
And first a Knave, and then a Knight they vote me.
What Fate appointed, Nature did prepare;
And furnished me, with an exceeding care
To fit me, for what they designed to have me:
And every gift but Honesty, they gave me.

"And thus equipped, to this proud town I came,
In quest of bread, and not in quest of fame:
Blind to my future Fate, a humble boy;
Free from the guilt and glory I enjoy.
The hopes which my ambition entertained,
Were in the name of Foot Boy all contained.
The greatest heights from small beginnings rise:
The gods were great on earth, before they reached the skies.

"B[ACK]WELL (the generous temper of whose mind
Was always to be bountiful inclined),
Whether by his ill fate or fancy led,
First took me up, and furnish me with bread.

The little services, he put me to,
Seemed labours rather than they were truly so;
But always my advancement he designed,
For 'twas his very nature to be kind.
Large was his soul, his temper ever free,
The best of masters and of men to me.
And I (who was before decreed by Fate,
To be made infamous as well as great),
With an obsequious diligence obeyed him,
Till trusted with his All; and then betrayed him!

"All his past kindness, I trampled on;
Ruined his fortunes, to erect my own!
So vipers in the bosom bred, begin
To hiss at that hand first which took them in.
With eager treachery, I his fall pursued,
And my first Trophies were Ingratitude.

"Ingratitude, the worst of human guilt,
The basest action mankind can commit!
Which (like the sin against the HOLY GHOST)
Has least of honour, and of guilt the most.
Distinguished from all other crimes by this,
That 'tis a crime which no man will confess!
That sin alone, which should not be forgiven
On earth, although perhaps it may in heaven.

"Thus my first benefactor I o'erthrew;
And how should I be, to a second true?
The Public Trust came next into my care,
And I to use them scurvily prepare;
My needy Sovereign Lord I played upon,
And lent him many of thousand of his own:
For which great interests I took care to charge,
And so my ill-got wealth become so large!

"My predecessor, JUDAS, was a fool,
Fitter to have been whipt and sent to school,
Than sell a Saviour! Had I been at hand,
His Master had been so cheap trapanned!
I would ha' made the eager Jews ha' found,
For Thirty pieces, Thirty Thousand pound!

"My cousin *Ziba*, of immortal fame
(*Ziba* and I shall never want a name!),
First Born of treason, nobly did advance
His Master's fall, for his inheritance.
By whose keen arts, old DAVID first began
To break his sacred oath to JONATHAN.
The good old King 'tis thought was very loth
To break his Word, and therefore broke his Oath!
Ziba 's a traitor of some Quality;
Yet *Ziba* might ha' been informed by me!
Had I been there, he ne'er had been content
With half the estate, nor half the Government!

"In our late Revolution, 'twas thought strange,
That I, of all mankind, should like the change!
But they who wondered at it, never knew
That, in it, I did my old game pursue;
Nor had they heard of Twenty thousand Pound,
Which ne'er was lost, yet never could be found!

"Thus all things in their turn, to sale I bring,
GOD and my Master first; and then the King!
Till by successful villainies made bold,
I thought to turn the nation into gold:
And so to forg[er]y my hand I bent,
Not doubting I could gull the Government:
But that was ruffled by the Parliament!
And if I 'scaped the unhappy tree to climb,
'Twas want of Law, and not for want of Crime.

"By my * Old Friend, who printed in my face
A needful competence of English brass,
Having more business yet for me to do,
And loth to lose his trusty servant so,
Managed the matter with such art and skill,
As saved his hero, and threw out the b[i]ll.

* The Devil.

"And now, I am graced with unexpected honours;
For which, I'll certainly abuse the donors!
Knighted, and made a Tribune of the people,
Whose Laws and properties I'm like to keep well!
The *Custos Rotulorum* of the City
And Captain of the Guards of their *banditti.*
Surrounded by my Catchpoles, I declare
Against the needy debtor, open war.
I hang poor thieves for stealing of your pelf;
And suffer none to rob you, but myself!

"The King commanded me to help reform ye!
And how I'll do it, Miss shall inform ye!
I keep the best Seraglio in the nation,
And hope in time to bring it into fashion.
Am not I a Magistrate for Reformation!
For this my praise is sung by every bard,
For which Bridewell would be a just reward!
In print my panegyrics fill the street,
And hired gaol-birds, their huzzas repeat.
Some charity 's contrived to make a shew:
Have taught the needy rabble to do so!
Whose empty noise is a mechanic fame,
Since for Sir BEELZEBUB, they 'd do the same!"

The Conclusion.

THEN let us boast of ancestors no more!
Or deeds of heroes done in days of yore;
In latent records of the Ages past,
Behind the rear of Time, in long Oblivion placed!
For if our Virtues must in lines descend,
The merit with the families would end;
And intermixtures would most fatal grow,
For Vice would be hereditary too!
The tainted blood would of necessity,
In voluntary wickedness convey!

Vice, like ill-nature, for an Age or two,
May seem a generation to pursue:
But Virtue seldom does regard the breed,
Fools do the Wise, and wise men Fools succeed.
What is it to us, what ancestors we had?
If good, what better? or what worse, if bad?
Examples are for imitation set,
Yet all men follow Virtue with regret!

Could but our ancestors retrieve their fate,
And see their offspring thus degenerate;
How we contend for birth and names unknown,
And build on their past actions, not our own:
They 'd cancel records, and their tombs deface,
And openly disown the vile degenerate race!
For fame of Families is all a cheat!
'TIS PERSONAL VIRTUE ONLY MAKES US GREAT!

THE HISTORY OF THE Kentish PETITION.

LONDON, Printed in the Year, 1701.

THE PREFACE.

'TWOULD be hard to suspect him of errors in fact, who writes the Story of Yesterday. A Historian of Three Weeks must certainly be just, for had he never so much mind to lie, it would be nonsense to expect the World could be imposed upon. Everybody's memory would be a living witness against him, and the effect would only be to expose himself.

Authors of Histories generally apologise for their Quotations, place their industry in the search after Truth, and excuse themselves by asserting the faithfulness of their Collections. The Author of the following sheets is not afraid to let the World know that he is so sure everything related in this Account is literally and positively true, that he challenges all the Wit and Malice the World abounds with, to confute the most trifling circumstance.

If aggravations are omitted, and some very ill-natured passages let go without observations, those persons who were guilty of them, may observe that we have more good nature than they have manners: and they ought to acknowledge it, since a great many rudenesses, both against the King himself and the Gentlemen concerned, have escaped their scurrilous mouths, which are not here animadverted upon.

And lest the World should think this presumptive, and that the accusation is only a surmise; we will query, What they think of that kind remark of Mr. J. H[O]W[E], finding the King's Letter *to the House, and the* Kentish Petition *to come both on a day, and the substance to be the same, that "the King, the Dutch, and the Kentish men were all in a plot against the House of Commons!"*

I could have swelled this Pamphlet to a large Volume, if I should pretend to collect all the Billingsgate language of a certain House full of men, against the King, the Lords, and the Gentlemen of Kent; but it is a fitter subject for a Satyr than a History. They have abused the nation, and now are become a Banter to themselves; and I leave them to consider of it, and reform!

I assure the World, I am no Kentish man; nor was my hand to the Petition*; though, had I been acquainted with it, I would have gone a hundred miles to have signed it, and a hundred more to have had the opportunity of serving my Country at the expense of an unjust confinement for it.*

It may be fairly concluded, I am no Warwickshire man neither, with a Petition *in my pocket, brought a hundred miles, and afraid to deliver it.*

Nor [*is*] *my name Sir* ROBERT CLAYTON *: by which you may know I did not promise the Members, who were then in fear enough, to use my Interest to stifle a City* Petition.

Nor is my name LEGION. *I wish it were! for I should have been glad to be capable of speaking so much truth, and so much to the purpose, as is contained in that unanswerable Paper* [LEGION'S Memorial, *see pp.* 179-186].

But I am an unconcerned Spectator, and have been an exact Observer of every passage, have been an Eye and Ear-Witness of every most minute article, and am sure that everything related is exactly true, as the causes of it all are scandalous and burdensome to the nation.

As to the Gentlemen of the House of Commons, I shall not pretend to enter into their character, because I care not to enter into captivity! nor come into the clutches of that worst of brutes, *their Sergeant!*

Literally speaking, no Member of the House of Commons can *be a Jacobite, because they have taken the oaths to King* WILLIAM.

But this may be observed, that the Jacobites in England are generally the only people who approve of their proceedings, and applaud their measures. And it is observable that at Paris, at St. Germains, the general compliment of a Health in all English company is à la santé [de] Monsieur JACK HOW[E]! *the truth of which, there are not a few very good Gentlemen in Town can attest, from whence I think I may draw this Observation, that either he is a Jacobite, or the Jacobites are a very good-natured people.*

Noscitur ex socio qui non dignoscitur ex se.

The following pages contain an exact History of the Kentish Petition, *and of the treatment the Gentlemen who presented it, met with both from the House, the Sergeant, and at last, from their ountry.*

The best way to come to a conclusion, whether the Gentlemen Petitioners were well or ill used, is to review the matter of fact? All panegyrics and encomiums came short of the natural reflections which flow from a True Account of that proceeding: and the whole is collected in this form, that all the World may judge by a true light, and not be imposed upon by partial and imperfect Relations.

THE

HISTORY

OF THE

Kentish

PETITION.

ON THE 29th of April, 1701, the Quarter Sessions for the County of Kent, began at Maidstone: where WILLIAM COLEPEPER of Hollingbourne, Esq., was chosen Chairman, though he was then absent; and, with an unusual respect, the Bench of Justices proceeded to do business, and kept the Chair for him for several hours, till he came.

The people of the County of Kent, as well as in most parts of the Kingdom, had expressed great dissatisfaction at the slow proceedings of the Parliament; and that the King was not assisted, nor the Protestants abroad considered: and the country people began to say to one another, in their language, that "they had sowed their corn, and the French were a-coming to reap it!"

And from hence it is allowed to proceed that, during the sitting of the Sessions, several of the principal freeholders of the County applied themselves to the Chairman aforesaid, and told him, "It was their desire that the Bench should consider the making of some application to the Parliament, to acquaint them of the apprehensions of the people."

The Chairman replied, "It was the proper work of the Grand Jury to present the grievances of the Country"; and therefore he referred them to the said Grand Jury, who were then sitting.

The Grand Jury being applied to, accepted the proposal; and addressing to the said Mr. COLEPEPER, the Chairman, acquainted him that they had approved of such a motion made as before, and desired that the Bench would join with them.

The Chairman told them, he would acquaint the Justices of it; which he did: and they immediately approved of it also, and desired the said W. COLEPEPER, Esq., their Chairman, to draw a *Petition.*

Mr. COLEPEPER withdrew to compose it, and having drawn a *Petition,* it was read and approved: and immediately ordered to be carried to the Grand Jury, being twenty-one in number, who all unanimously signed it, and brought it into Court, desiring all the Gentlemen on the Bench would do the same.

Whereupon the Chairman and twenty-three of the Justices signed it; and the freeholders of the County crowded in so fast, that the parchment was filled up in less than five hours' time: and many thousands of hands might have been had to it, if the Justices had not declined it, refusing to add any more rolls of parchment; as insisting more upon the merits of the *Petition,* than the number of the subscribers.

By all which, it appears how foolish and groundless their pretences are, who would suggest that the *Petition* was a private thing, transacted by a few people; whereas it is plain, it was the Act and Deed of the whole Country.

The words of the *Petition* are, as follows.

To the Knights, Citizens, and Burgesses in Parliament assembled.

The humble Petition of the Gentlemen, Justices of the Peace, Grand Jury, and other freeholders, at the General Quarter Sessions of the Peace holden at Maidstone, the 29th of April, in the 13th year of the reign of our Sovereign Lord, King WILLIAM *III., over England, &c.*

WE, THE *Gentlemen, Justices of the Peace, Grand Jury, and other freeholders, at the General Quarter Sessions at Maidstone, in Kent, deeply concerned at the dangerous estate of this Kingdom and of all Europe, and considering that the fate of us and our posterity depends on the wisdom of our Representatives in Parliament, think ourselves bound in duty, humbly to lay before this Honourable House, the consequences in this conjuncture of your speedy resolution and most sincere endeavour to answer the Great Trust reposed in you by your country.*

And in regard that, from the experience of all ages, it is manifest no nation can be great and happy without Union; We hope that no pretence whatsoever shall be able to create a misunderstanding among ourselves, or the least distrust of His Majesty, whose great actions for this nation are written in the hearts of his subjects, and can never, without the blackest ingratitude, be forgotten.

We most humbly implore this Honourable House, to have regard to the Voice of the People! that our religion and safety may be effectually provided for, that your Loyal Addresses may be turned into Bills of Supply, and that His most sacred Majesty (whose propitious and unblemished reign over us, We pray GOD long to continue!) may be enabled powerfully to assist his Allies, before it be too late.

And your Petitioners shall ever pray &c.

Signed by all the Deputy Lieutenants there present, above twenty Justices of the Peace, and all the Grand Jury, and other freeholders then there.

As soon as the *Petition* was signed, and there was no more room for any hands [*signatures*], it was delivered by the Grand Jury to the aforesaid WILLIAM COLEPEPER, Esq., Chairman of the Session; and he was desired to present it, in their names, to the Parliament: which, at their request, he promised to do. And the rest of the Gentlemen, viz., THOMAS COLEPEPER, Esq., JUSTINIAN CHAMPNEYS, Esq., DAVID POLEHILL, Esq., and WILLIAM HAMILTON, Esq., offered themselves to go with him.

On Tuesday, the 6th of May, they came to Town, with the *Petition*; and the next day, they went up to the House, and applied themselves to Sir THOMAS HALES, in order to desire him to present it to the House: he being one of the Representatives of the County of Kent.

Sir THOMAS read the *Petition*, and telling them it was too late to present it that day, it being after twelve a clock, desired they would let him shew it [to] Mr. PELHAM of Sussex.

Mr. COLEPEPER told him, he was willing enough Mr. PELHAM should see the *Petition*, not doubting he would be a friend to it: but that he was unwilling to part with it, being entrusted with it by his Country; adding that he "should make but an indifferent figure in the County, if the *Petition* should be got out of his hands, and lost."

Whereupon, Sir THOMAS HALES passed his word and honour, that he would not shew it to any person whatever, but to Mr. PELHAM; and that he would return it immediately. But his word and honour so solemnly pledged, were as easily forgotten. For having got the *Petition*, he carried it into the House, where he stayed an hour and a half; and then returning, he gave it to the Gentlemen, and told them he had shewn it to Sir EDWARD SEYMOUR and several others.

This perfidious action [towards] that very part of the nation which he represented, deserves some special notice; and there is no question but the people will remember it for him, and shew their resentment on proper occasions.

Mr. COLEPEPER, in the name of the rest, gave him an answer suitable to the action; and sufficient to let him know their surprise at so ungentleman-like usage: viz., that "he had broke his word, and served his Country very ill!"

But this being neither place nor season for further debates, Sir THOMAS HALES appointed to meet them in the evening: and then, after making them wait two hours beyond his time, he adjourned them till next morning, in the Court of Requests; where he told them absolutely, that he "would not deliver the *Petition*."

Here it is very observable, that, at the very time Sir THOMAS HALES came out of the House, and returned the *Petition* in the manner above mentioned, Mr. MEREDITH, the other Representative for the Country, came to them, and told them "their *Petition* had been exposed in the House, and that Mr. How[E] was then making a speech against it."

The Gentlemen finding themselves thus betrayed by Sir THOMAS HALES, consulted together about finding another more proper person to deliver the *Petition*; and resolved to apply themselves to Mr. MEREDITH, the other Member for the County of Kent. Mr. MEREDITH having agreed to deliver it, in case Sir THOMAS HALES should refuse, had appointed to meet them, with several other Gentlemen, Members of the House, in order to consult about the matter of the *Petition*, and the manner of delivering it.

In the morning [*Wednesday*, *7th May*, 1701], the House being met; Mr. MEREDITH came out, and told them that "the House was in such a ferment, that none of the Gentlemen durst appear for it, nor come to them; and he doubted [*feared*] would not venture so much as to speak a word in the House for the *Petition*."

Nor were these all the discouragements the Gentlemen met with, in their presenting the *Petition*: but several Members of the House pretending respect, and others that were really their friends and in concern for them, came out of the House to them, and endeavoured to persuade them, not to expose themselves to the fury of the House, by delivering the *Petition*. Telling them, that Mr. HOW[E] in particular had said, that, "if there were one hundred thousand hands to the *Petition*, they should be all made examples of!" and Sir EDWARD SEYMOUR added that "the whole County should be double taxed; and the estates of those who presented it, should be confiscated to the use of the War."

Although these menaces, together with the almost omnipotent power of the House of Commons, had circumstances enough in them to shake the resolution of a whole County; yet they had not the effects here which were expected. For the Gentlemen, far from being terrified at all this, unanimously declared their resolution to discharge the trust placed in them by their Country, and to present it to the House.

Mr. WILLIAM COLEPEPER, in particular, alluding to the words of LUTHER, to those who dissuaded him from going to the city of Worms, told them that, "if every tile upon the Chapel of * St. Stephen's were a devil, he would present the *Petition*!" And all of them declared that, "if one of the Gentlemen would not do their Country so much service, as to present their grievances to the Parliament in a legal *Petition*; they would knock at the door of the House, and deliver it themselves!"

* The House that the Commons sit in, was formerly St. Stephen's Chapel.

Mr. MEREDITH finding the Gentlemen so resolute, did consent to carry in the *Petition*; which he performed with great discretion and fidelity.

The *Petition* being thus delivered, the Gentlemen attended. For Mr. Speaker [*ROBERT HARLEY*] further to intimidate them, had let fall some speeches, that "it was the usage of the House, when a *Petition* was brought in, the persons who presented it, ought to be ready without, to justify the matter of their *Petition*."

And the Gentlemen, seeing no reason to be ashamed of theirs in particular, resolved to bide the utmost which their and the nation's enemies could do to them.

Having waited almost half an hour, they were called in to the Bar of the House; where (Mr. Speaker, treating them in his usual haughty tone) this short dialogue passed between them:

Speaker. (*Holding up the* Petition *by one corner.*) Gentlemen, is this your *Petition*?

Gentlemen. (*Bowing very respectfully.*) Yes, Mr. Speaker.

Speaker. And, Gentlemen, you own this *Petition*?

Gentlemen. Yes, Mr. Speaker.

Speaker. And, Gentlemen, your Hands are to this *Petition*?

Gentlemen. Yes, Mr. Speaker.

Speaker. (*Turning to one of the Clerks.*) Carry it to them, and see if they will own their Hands! (*Which they severally did.*)

Speaker. Withdraw, and expect the Order of the House!

Whereupon they withdrew, and attended in the Lobby.

And now began the second attack, upon the[ir] resolution: for the Members, who came out, represented with all the terror imaginable, the fury of the House. Imprisonment and the ruin of their fortunes and families was the least they had to expect; Impeachments, Laws *ex post facto*, tacking them to Money Bills; and all arbitrary methods which any arbitrary Parliament have ever made use of to ruin those who have felt their magnipotent indignation, were laid before them.

When some, who pretented pity for the misfortune of so many worthy Gentlemen, came out of the House, and told them, "they had yet a lucky moment left them, by an immediate submission, to fly to the clemency of the House!" that "they were sent out by Sir EDWARD SEYMOUR and the rest of the Gentlemen on that side, to let them know that Mr. How[E] was now speaking, and would continue so for some time, to give them opportunity to recollect themselves, and by a timely acknowledgement to save themselves from ruin :

The Gentlemen being at a loss to know in what particular they could have given the House such offence, and being well assured they were in the protection of the Law, and had not acted anything but what the known Constitution of the Realm expressly allowed, remained still unshaken; and boldly replied "They had nothing to say, but what was in their *Petition*!"

But being further pressed by Sir THEOPHILUS OGLETHORP and several other Gentlemen; and because they would not shew any disrespect to the House, or seem to slight their displeasure; they considered of an Answer to be given to the proposal of Submission.

•And because whatever Answer they gave, might be misrepresented to the House; [if] delivered by word of mouth; they resolved to put it into writing, and having consulted a while, they agreed to send in this civil Answer.

We are humbly of opinion that it is our Right to petition this honourable House, according to the Statute of 13 *CAR. II. As to the matter of our* Petition*; we declare that we intend nothing offensive to this honourable House.*

This writing being shewn to Sir THEOPHILUS OGLETHORP and several other Members, then began to smile, and imagined their point gained; and told the Gentlemen, "they were glad they begun to be sensible of their danger, and that if they would but add one word more, namely, that *they were sorry for what they had done*, they would undertake [*guarantee*] for the clemency of the House."

Thus they unanimously refused: one of the Gentlemen, with some heat replying, "We will have no *sorry*!"

Here the Members, or conspirators rather, would have had them put it, that they did it *through inadvertency*.

This they also refused, declaring they did it, at the request of their Country, maturely and deliberately; were justified in doing it, by the Laws of the land, and they would never recede from it.

So they delivered the Paper to Sir THOMAS HALES; but

whether he delivered it to the House or not, he never had the civility to inform them.

The debate in the House held five hours. After which, notice was given them by the Messengers, that the House had voted the *Petition scandalous, insolent, and seditious* (*vide* the *Votes*), *tending to destroy, &c.*; and ordered them to be taken into custody for the same.

Upon which, the Gentlemen went, and immediately surrendered themselves to the Sergeant, though the *Warrant* was not made out for some hours after.

The Sergeant only asked, Where he should come to them, at dinner? which was agreed to be at the *Castle* Tavern, in Fleet street.

Where they dined, on Thursday, Friday, and Saturday; and were hitherto very civilly treated of his Officers. They were accompanied by great numbers of citizens and Gentlemen of the first Quality, and not a few of the Nobility. The Officers were seldom with them, went errands for them; and oftentimes were all absent together. So that there was no colour of reason for the Sergeant to say he feared a rescue. For they had all the opportunities they could desire, if they had had the least design to escape: and it was never heard of, that they who could escape when they pleased, would expose their friends to the hazard of a rescue.

On Friday [*9th May*], in the evening, Mr. Sergeant begun to treat with them; and representing his absolute power, let them know that he had an unbounded liberty of using them at discretion: that he could confine them at pleasure, put them in dungeons, lay them under ground, keep them apart, remove them daily, and keep all people from them by making them "close prisoners."

He thereby gave them to understand that he expected a consideration suitable to his civility. Upon this, the Gentlemen offered him One Hundred Guineas: half in hand, and the other, when they should be discharged; though it should be the next day.

The Sergeant neither accepted nor refused the offer, nor expressed any dislike, as if he thought it too little: but appointed to come to them, the next day.

Saturday [10*th May*], in the evening, Mr. THOMAS COLEPEPER, having notice that his Lady was much frighted at his confinement, desired leave of the Messenger in whose custody he was, to let him go down to Maidstone, upon his parole to return by Monday night: which the Messenger tacitly granted.

The rest of the Gentlemen being met at the tavern, expecting the Sergeant according to appointment, and having waited till ten a clock; instead of coming himself, he sends orders to the Messengers to separate the Gentlemen, and confine them in several prisons, that very night. Which orders, the Officers executed as rudely as the Sergeant could desire; saving that they obtained the civility from the Officers to be confined two in a place, and two in another; but were hurried away with such unmannerly indecency, that they would not permit them to send for their night-gowns and necessaries.

In this manner, Mr. WILLIAM COLEPEPER and Mr. JUSTINIAN CHAMPNEYS were carried to MYAT the Messenger's house, in Fox Court, in Holborn: where they had this hard choice proposed to them, at their entrance, Whether they would lodge in the Cellar or the Garret? And choosing the latter, they were thrust into a little hole on the top of the house: where they had all the inconveniences of the nasty prison, as base lodging, foul sheets, little covering, and a cold room; by which means, they both took such cold as they have not yet recovered from.

But Mr. Sergeant, lest they should not be ill-treated enough, coming, the next morning, to Mr. MYAT's house, was in a great rage at him, and drawing his sword, cut him over the head, for "using the Gentlemen so civilly," as he called it.

Afterwards, coming up into the garret, where Mr. COLEPEPER and Mr. JUSTINIAN CHAMPNEYS were lodged: they asked him, "What Order he had, for using them thus?"

He replied, "He had an Order from those who committed them."

Being asked again, "If there was any such Vote passed in the House?"

He said, "No, but he had an Order."

Mr. COLEPEPER replied, "If it be not a Vote of the

House, pray how is it an Order? Have the Majority of the House, one by one, come to you, and given you directions to use us thus barbarously?"

He replied "Yes, they had!" For which scandalous reflection, if false, his masters the Members of the House of Commons are exceedingly obliged to him.

Mr. COLEPEPER told him, he believed he should live to see him hanged.

And so they parted.

All this while, Mr. POLEHILL and Mr. HAMILTON were put into a cellar, without the favour of having their choice; and had so vile a lodging, that they could scarcely breathe.

They were likewise, in their turn, bullied by Mr. Sergeant, the next day.

When they asked him, to shew the copy of their Commitment: he denied it.

Mr. POLEHILL, in particular, replied, "They asked him nothing but what, by Law, he ought to grant."

He rudely replied, "He cared not a farthing for them, nor the Law neither!" And so left them.

Which refusal of his, he may hear of again, perhaps, in a way of legal application.

On Tuesday [13*th May*], he gave the House notice, that the younger Mr. COLEPEPER had made his escape; though he had a letter from him, that he would be in Town that very day. And at the same time, he made a complaint that the other Gentlemen behaved themselves so disorderly, that he apprehended a rescue: though the Gentlemen, to avoid any suspicion, had voluntarily surrendered their swords to the Messengers, without being required so to do.

This complaint to the House was the Gentlemen's deliverance, and the Sergeant's disappointment; though not in kindness to them neither. For ordering them to the Gatehouse, as a more ignominious confinement, the Sergeant lost the extravagant fees which he designed to extort from them; and the humanity of Captain TAYLOR, the Keeper of the Gatehouse, made their restraint easy to them.

For this Keeper used them like Gentlemen, and the reputation he has obtained by his civility will be as lasting as the infamy of the Sergeant: the one leaves a grateful acknowledgement in the mouths of all men, and will always be spoken of to his advantage; and the other nauseous, like the person, is dishonourable both to his memory and to the House that employed him.

On Wednesday [14*th May*], THOMAS COLEPEPER, Esq., the younger brother, who had been in Kent, and who was just come up according to his promise, rendered himself to the Speaker, and desired to be sent to his brethren.

Mr. Sergeant, who thought to make himself amends upon him, laboured to have him continued in his custody: and had not that Party in the House thought the Gatehouse a greater punishment, possibly it had been so. But therein, that infallible House were deceived! and he was delivered from the hands of a villain, by his enemies themselves: who thought they had mortified him the more; to the infinite regret of the Sergeant, and the general satisfaction of his fellow-sufferers.

The same morning [14*th May*] that Mr. COLEPEPER surrendered himself, *The LEGION Paper* [*see pp*. 179-186], as it was called, was sent to the House. It was said, it was delivered to the Speaker by a woman. But I have been informed since, that it was a mistake: and that it was delivered by the very person [*DANIEL DEFOE*] who wrote it, guarded with about sixteen Gentlemen of Quality; who, if any notice had been taken of him, were ready to have carried him off by force.

It was reported that Mr. THOMAS COLEPEPER brought it out of Kent, and that all the Country [*County*] were at his heels, to make it good: though it was really no such thing, and that Gentleman declared he knew nothing at all of it.

But be it as it will, that Paper struck such a terror into the Party in the House, that, from that time, there was not a word ever spoken in the House, of proceeding against the Kentish Petitioners; and the Members of that Party began to drop off, and get into the country: for their Management began to be so disliked over the whole nation, that their own fears dictated to them, they had run things too far.

The clashings with the Upper House about the trial of the four Peers they had impeached; and the miserable shifts they were driven to by the Lords, to avoid trying them, served but to make them more uneasy, and to hasten the despatch of the money bills, in order to the Prorogation, which was on the 23rd of June, 1701.

By the Prorogation, the Kentish Gentlemen were discharged: but to shew their respect to the civility of Captain TAYLOR their Keeper, they continued to lodge with him, till they went into the country.

The first honour done to them, on account of their sufferings, was their being invited to a noble entertainment at Mercers Hall in Cheapside, at the charge of the citizens of London: where above two hundred Gentlemen dined with them, together with several noble Lords and Members of Parliament.

Thursday, the 2nd of July [1701], they set out for Kent. The citizens had offered to accompany them out of Town: but they declined it, desiring to go privately. And those who pretend to charge them with affecting popularity; would do well to remember, that they were fain to send their coaches empty out of Town, and go by water to meet them, to avoid the respect which the citizens would have shewn them.

But there was no shunning the Appearance of the Country; who shewed their value for the Gentlemen and the Cause for which they had suffered, in all possible terms of respect and affection.

The first instance of this, was at Blackheath, where Mr. DAVID POLEHILL, one of the Gentlemen, was to separate from the rest; his road lying near Bromley, to his house at Ottford in Kent.

He was met at Blackheath by above 500 Horse: who received him into the midst of them, and surrounded his coach, with such shouts and joy, as sufficiently testified their respect for him, and their satisfaction at his return among them.

Nor can I omit, that having, to satisfy my curiosity, drank among, and discoursed with some of that party, while they were waiting for Mr. POLEHILL; I [*DANIEL DEFOE*] never heard of any Gentleman more universally beloved by the Country, or more particularly distinguished for the modesty and Temper: and I believe I may affirm, that it would be hard to find any Gentleman so near the City of London, who could have had such an Appearance of his own tenants and neighbours, to congratulate his deliverance.

Mr. POLEHILL being come to the corner of the Park wall on Blackheath, stopped to take leave of his brethren; and giving them a loud huzza, wished them a good journey, and proceeded to Ottford.

All possible demonstrations of joy concluded the day: and it has not been known that the Country ever expressed more satisfaction since the Coronation of King WILLIAM, than at the return of this Gentleman.

The rest of the Gentlemen proceeded to Rochester, where they were met by such a body of Horse, that the principal inns of the town could not entertain them: some of whom had come twenty miles to meet them.

The Mayor of Rochester paid his respect to them, and complained that he had no notice given him of their coming: otherwise he would have met them out of the town, with a good body of Horse.

Here they rested, to refresh themselves and their horses.

And about six a clock, they set forward for Maidstone.

The people of Maidstone, though it was market day, could not have patience to wait at that place where they generally go to meet the Judges; but a great many horsemen met them on the Downs, and on the top of Boxley Hill, four miles from the town.

At Sandlin, about two miles from the town, the Gentlemen of the neighbourhood met them with their coaches; and an innumerable multitude of people, on horseback and on foot, shouting and bidding them welcome.

After a short stay here, to receive the compliments of the Gentlemen; they proceeded, the Gentlemen's coaches falling into the rear, to the Park, the seat of the Lady TAYLOR, who is married to Mr. THOMAS COLEPEPER; where they were welcomed by the said Lady, the old Lady COLEPEPER, the mother of the Gentleman, and several Ladies of Quality: the people shouting all the while "A Colepeper!" "A Colepeper!"; and the poor strewing the ways with greens and flowers.

And thus they proceeded into the town, with such universal acclamations of the people as the like was never seen in that Country, since the Restoration of King CHARLES the Second.

The night concluded with a great bonfire, and the Healths of all the Gentlemen drank round it: to the great mortification of the Jacobites, of whom there are but very few in those parts; and to the general satisfaction of the Country.

Nor was this the only Appearance. For at Beartsted, about three miles further, the Country was assembled, the bells rung, and several hundreds of people continued together all night, with extraordinary joy, expecting that the elder Mr. COLEPEPER, Mr. CHAMPNEYS, and Mr. HAMILTON would have continued their journey to Hollingbourne, the ancient seat of the Family of the COLEPEPERS.

But the extraordinary reception they found at Maidstone had detained them so long, that it was too late to go on. So they lay at Maidstone that night.

And the next day, abundance of Gentlemen and Country people came particularly to pay their respects to them, and to bid them welcome into the Country.

And at the time of the Assizes, lately held at Maidstone, the Grand Jury consisting of very eminent Gentlemen and freeholders of the Country, whereof twelve were Justices of the Peace, went in a body to the Gentlemen, and publicly gave them thanks for their fidelity to the Country in delivering their *Petition* to the Parliament.

In all these expressions of the Country joy at the return of these honest Gentlemen; it might be enquired, What they said of the Parliament? because it is so natural to curse with one hand, when we bless with the other, that it might be rationally expected. It is true, the Country, being justly disobliged at the ill-usage of these Gentlemen, did not spare their reflections. But I choose to pass it over: because it is not Parliaments in general, but the Conspirators and Jacobite Party in a Parliament, that are at present the Nation's burthen, and from whom, she groans to be delivered.

THE CONCLUSION.

HAD this Nation listened to the Calls of their own Reason, and to the Voice of Things; all this confusion of counsels had been prevented! Had the People of England chosen men of honesty and of peaceable principles, men of candour, disengaged from Interest and design, that had nothing before them but the benefit of their Country, the safety of Religion, and the Interest of Europe, all this had been avoided! They never would have imprisoned five honest Gentlemen, for coming to them, with the sense of their Country, in a peaceable Petition*! They would never have had the occasion to repent of their refusing to hearken to the Voice of the People!*

But it is too late to look back! The Nation has had the misfortune to choose them! and our Peace and Liberty, and the Protestant Interest in Europe are too much in their hands.

All the advice I can pretend to give to my fellow-slaves and countrymen, is that they would not be backward to let the Gentlemen know, that the Nation is sensible they are not doing their duty: and withal, that to impose upon the Rights and Liberties of the English Nation has always been fatal to the persons of those who have attempted it; and their examples stand as buoys and marks to warn Posterity of the hidden dangers they have fallen into.

It has been fatal to Favourites, to Judges, to Lords, and to Kings; and will certainly be so, even to Parliaments, if they descend to abuse the People they represent.

The imprisoning these five Gentlemen had neither Reason, Law, Pretence, nor Policy in it.

It had no Reason in it, because they had offended against no law, either of reason, or the nature of the thing.

It had no Law in it, because they had no legal power to commit any but their own Members.

And I am of the opinion, they are convinced there was no Policy in it: for there is seldom much policy in doing that publicly, which we know we shall be ashamed of.

The not proceeding against them afterward, shewed they were either ashamed or afraid. Had they been in the right, there could be no reason to fear; and if in the wrong, they had all the reason in the World to be ashamed.

To commit five Gentlemen to custody, for petitioning them to do, what they really knew they ought to have done; it was the most preposterous thing in Nature! To punish for humbly petitioning *! it is nonsense in itself!*

GOD himself permits the meanest and most despicable of his creatures to remind Him, as we may say, of their wants, and petition for his aid. The most contemptible beggar is permitted to be importunate for relief; and though the Law is against him, we are not affronted at it. But to resent the representation of their Country, and imprison Gentlemen who, at the request of the freeholders of a County, came, under the express protection of an Act *of Parliament, to deliver a Petition: it was the most ridiculous inconsistent action that ever Parliament of England was guilty of: and, with submission, I think the best action the same House can do, at their next meeting, is to Vote that it should be razed out of their* Journals, *and never be made a precedent for the time to come. Upon which condition, and no other, the Nation ought to forgive them.*

The Act *of* 13 CAR. II. *to assert the Right of the Subject's Petitioning, is a sufficient authority for any one to quote: and those that pretend to call this an illegal act, must first trample down the authority of that* Act *of Parliament.*

Let this Act *justify me, in saying, that to imprison Englishmen for petitioning is Illegal, and a dishonour to English Parliaments.*

But say the lame excusers of this eccentric Motion of this House, "This was a factious thing contrived by a few private insignificant people of no value; and the matter of it is saucy and impertinent."

First, had it been a Petition *of the meanest and most inconsiderable person in England, and that single by himself, provided he were a freeholder of England, he had Legal Right to speak his mind. For that same reason from whence the Commons in Parliament claim a Freedom of Speech, gives every Commoner a Freedom to speak to the House; since every freeholder has an equal concern in their Debates, and equal power in deputing them to sit there.*

But because this Right unlimited, might be multitudinous and uneasy, therefore the method, how he shall do it, is circumscribed for decency's sake, that it shall be done by Petition*; and that* Petition *shall be presented* so *and* so, *and by* such a number, *and no more.*

But that it should not be lawful to petition, *no tribunal, no Court, no Collective or Representative Body of men in the World ever refused it! Nay, the Inquisition of Spain does not forbid it! the Divan of the Turks allows it! and I believe, if* SATAN *himself kept his Court in public, he would not prohibit it.*

But besides this, the fact is not true. As for it being contrived by a few people, let the Impartial Relation here given, answer that ridiculous untruth: unless you will account the County of Kent a few; for certainly eleven parts of twelve in the whole County, and now of the whole Kingdom, approve of it.

Nor has the reproach upon the Persons presenting it more of truth; unless Gentlemen of ancient and illustrious Families, whose ancestors have been known, for several Ages, to be Men of Honour and estates, allied to several of the Nobility, and now known and valued by the whole County, both for their considerable fortunes as well as personal merit: unless, I say, such men are to be accounted private and inconsiderable, the charge cannot be true. To such I shall only say, that the ancestors of these Gentlemen were Members of ancient Parliaments, and of such Parlia-

ments as would have been ashamed of committing such an absurdity as to imprison the freeholders of England for a peaceable Petition.

As to the matter of the Petition, *and which some people say was a banter, the* turning their Loyal Addresses into Bills of Supply. *The Gentlemen ought to have had liberty to explain themselves: which, if they had done, I am of opinion that it would have been to this purpose, that " they thought it was proper* the House should speedily supply the King so with money, as that he might be enabled to defend our Protestant neighbours from the encroachment of France; and not to lose their time in addressing the King in matters of less moment."

I shall conclude with this short animadversion, by way of remark; and let all men judge of the justness of the Observation.

That as this was the First time that ever the English nation petitioned to be taxed; so this was the First Parliament that ever addressed the King to take care of himself, and [to] *defend himself against his people.*

SOME book-learned fools pretend to find a flaw
In our late Senate *Votes* for want of Law,
And insolently saw the Men of Kent
Were rudely handled by the Parliament:
Knowledge of Things would teach them every hour
That Law is but a heathen word for Power.
Might, Right, Force, Justice, Equity
Are terms synonymous, and must agree!
For who shall e'er the argument confute,
Where Power prevails, and no man dares dispute?
Nature has left this tincture in the blood,
That all men would be Tyrants, if they could!
Not Kings alone, not Ecclesiastic pride;
But Parliaments! and all mankind beside.
All men, like PHÆTON, would command the reins,
'Tis only Want of Power that restrains!
Then why should we think strange the Parliament
The People's late *Petitions* should resent?
'Tis fatal to Tyrannic Power, when they
Who should be ruined, grumble to obey!
And Tyrants never can complete their reign,
So long as injured subjects *dare* complain!
If they do not, their *first* Address withstand;
What now they supplicate, they 'll soon command!
By first suppressing *early* discontent;
They aimed, the Consequences to prevent!
For well they knew, that should the Nation try
To ask *once more*, they durst not *twice* deny!
England has this own fate peculiar to her;
Never to want a Party to undo her!
The Court, the King, the Church, the Parliament
Alternately pursue the same intent,

Under the specious name of Liberty,
The passive injured People to betray.
And it has always been the People's fate,
To see their own mistakes, when 'twas too late;
Senseless of danger, sleepy and secure,
Till their distempers grew too strong to cure:
Till they 're embraced by the approaching grave,
And none but JOVE and miracles can save.
  In vain, bold heroes venture to redeem
A People willinger to sink than swim!
If there 's a BRUTUS in the Nation found,
That dare Patrician Usurpation wound;
He 's sure to find an ignominious grave,
And perish by the People he would save!
  Such are by Virtue signalised in vain!
We 'll own the Merit, but abuse the Men.
MARIUS saved Rome, and was by Rome despised;
And many a RUSSELL we have sacrificed!
Then who for English Freedom would appear,
Where lives of patriots are never dear!
And streams of generous blood flow unregarded there.

  Posterity will be ashamed to own
The actions we, their ancestors have done,
When they, for ancient precedents enquire,
And to the *Journals* of this Age retire,
To see One Tyrant banished from his home,
To set Five Hundred Traitors in his room!
They 'll blush to find the Head beneath the Tail,
And Representing Treachery prevail.
They 'll be amazed to see, there were but *Five*
Whose Courage could their Liberty survive!
While we, that durst Illegal Power dethrone,
Should basely be enslaved by Tyrants of our own.

FINIS.

DANIEL DEFOE.

[*LEGION's Memorial.*]

[A copy of the original secretly printed 4*pp.* 4to, in the British Museum ; Press mark, 1093 b 35.]

MR. S[*PEAKE*]*R*,

THIS *enclosed* Memorial, *you are charged with ! in the behalf of many thousands of the good People of England.*

There is neither Popish, Jacobite, Seditious, Court, or Party Interest concerned in it ; but Honesty and Truth.

You are commanded by Two Hundred Thousand Englishmen, to deliver it to the H[*ous*]*e of* C[ommon]s, *and to inform them that it is no banter, but serious truth ; and a serious regard to it is expected. Nothing but Justice, and their Duty is required : and it is required by them who have both a right to require, and power to compel, viz., the People of England.*

We would have come to the House strong enough to oblige them to hear us ; but we have avoided any tumults : not desiring to embroil, but to save our native country.

If you refuse to communicate it to them, you will find cause in a short time to repent it !

To R[OBER]T H[ARLE]Y Esq., S[peake]r to the H[ous]e of C[ommon]s. These

The Memorial.

To the K[night]s, C[ommon]s, and B[aron]s in P[arliamen]t assembled.

A Memorial

From the Gentlemen, freeholders, and inhabitants of the counties of ———, in the behalf of themselves, and many thousands of the good People of England.

GENTLEMEN,

IT WERE to be wished you were men of that Temper, and possessed of so much honour as to bear with the Truth, though it be against you: especially from Us who have so much right to tell it you: but since even Petitions to you from your Masters, for such are the people who choose you, are so haughtily received, as with the committing the authors to illegal custody; you must give Us leave to give you this fair notice of your Misbehaviour without exposing our names.

If you think fit to rectify your errors, you will do well! and possibly may hear no more of Us: but if not, assure yourselves the nation will not long hide their resentments.

And though there is no stated Proceeding to bring you to your duty, yet the great law of Reason says, and all nations allow that whatever Power is above Law, it is burdensome and tyrannical; and may be reduced by *extrajudicial* methods. You are not above the People's resentments! They that made you Members, may reduce you to the same rank from whence they chose you, and may give you a taste of their abused kindness, in terms you may not be pleased with.

When the People of England assembled in Convention, presented the Crown to His present Majesty; they annexed a *Declaration of the Rights of the People*, in which was expressed what was Illegal and Arbitrary in the former reign, and what was claimed, as of Right, to be done by succeeding Kings of England.

In like manner, here follows, Gentlemen, a short Abridgement of the Nation's grievances, and of your illegal and unwarrantable practices; and a Claim of Right, which we make in the name of our Selves and such of the good People of England as are justly alarmed at your proceedings.

I. To raise Funds for money, and declare by borrowing clauses that whosoever advances money on those Funds, shall be reimbursed out of the next *Aids*, if the Funds fall short; and then [to] give subsequent Funds, without transferring the deficiency of the former, is a horrible cheat on the Subject who lent the money, a breach of Public Faith, and destructive to the honour and credit of Parliaments.

II. To imprison men who are not your own Members, by no proceedings but a Vote of your House, and to continue them in custody *sine die*, is Illegal, a notorious breach of the Liberty of the People, setting up a Dispensing Power in the House of Commons which your fathers never pretended to, bidding defiance to the *Habeas Corpus Act* which is the bulwark of personal liberty, destructive of the Laws, and betraying the Trust reposed in you. *The King, at the same time, being obliged to ask you leave, to continue in custody the horrid assassinators of his person.*

III. Committing to custody those Gentlemen, who, at the command of the People, whose servants you are, and in a peaceable way, put you in mind of your duty, is Illegal and injurious, destructive of the Subject's liberty of Petitioning for redress of grievances; which has, by all Parliaments before you, been acknowledged to be their undoubted Right.

IV. Voting a Petition from the Gentlemen of Kent *insolent*, is ridiculous and impertinent; because the freeholders of England are your superiors; and is a contradiction in itself, a contempt of the English Freedom, and contrary to the nature of Parliamentary Power.

V. Voting people *guilty of bribery and ill-practices*, and committing them as aforesaid, without bail; and then, upon submission, and kneeling to your House, discharging them, exacting exorbitant fees by your Officers, is Illegal; betraying the Justice of the Nation, selling the Liberty of the Subject, encouraging the extortion and villany of Gaolers and Officers, and discontinuing the legal prosecutions of offenders in the ordinary course of Law.

VI. Prosecuting the crime of bribery in some, to serve a Party; and then [to] proceed no further, though proof lay before you, is partial and unjust, and a scandal upon the honour of Parliaments.

VII. Voting the *Treaty of Partition* "fatal to Europe, because it gave so much of the Spanish dominions to the French," and not concerning yourselves to prevent their taking possession of it all; deserting the Dutch, when the French are at their doors, till it be almost too late to help them: is unjust to our Treaties, and unkind to our Confederates, dishonourable to the English nation, and shew you very negligent of the safety of England and of our Protestant neighbours.

VIII. Ordering immediate hearings to trifling Petitions, to please Parties at elections; and postponing the petition of a widow for the blood of her murdered daughter without giving it a reading; is an illegal delay of justice, dishonourable to the public Justice of the nation.

IX. Addressing the King, to displace his friends upon bare surmises, before a legal trial, or an *Article* proved, is Illegal, inverting the Law, and making Execution go before Judgement: contrary to the true sense of the Law, which esteems every man a good man till something appears to the contrary.

X. Delaying proceedings upon Capital Impeachments, to blast the reputation of the persons, without proving the fact, is Illegal and oppressive, destructive of the Liberty of Englishmen, a delay of Justice and a reproach to Parliaments.

XI. Suffering saucy and indecent reproaches upon His Majesty's person to be publicly made in your House; particularly by that Impudent Scandal of Parliaments, J[OH]N H[o]W[E], without shewing such resentments as you ought to do. The said J[OH]N H[o]W[E] saying openly that "His Majesty had made a felonious Treaty, to rob his neighbours," insinuating that the *Partition* Treaty (which was every way as just as blowing up one man's house to save another's) "was a combination of the King to rob the Crown of Spain of its due." This is to make a Billingsgate of the House, and setting up to bully your Sovereign; contrary to the intent and meaning of the Freedom of Speech, which you claim as a right; is scandalous to Parliaments; undutiful and unmannerly, and a reproach to the whole nation.

XII. Your S[peake]r exacting the exorbitant rate of £10 *per diem* for the *V[ote]s*, and giving the Printer encouragement to raise it on the People, by selling them at 4*d*. a sheet, is an illegal and arbitrary exaction, dishonourable to the House, and burdensome to the People.

XIII. Neglecting still to pay the nation's debts, compounding for interest, and postponing Petitions, is Illegal, dishonourable, and destructive of the Public Faith.

XIV. Publicly neglecting the great work of Reformation of Manners, though often pressed to it by the King, to the great dishonour of GOD, and encouragement of vice; is a neglect of your Duty, and an abuse of the Trust reposed in you by GOD, His Majesty, and the People.

XV. Being scandalously vicious yourselves, both in your morals and religion, lewd in life and erroneous in doctrine, having public blasphemers and impudent deniers of the Divinity of our Saviour among you; and suffering them unreproved and unpunished to the infinite regret of all good Christians, and the just abhorrence of the whole nation.

WHEREFORE, in the said prospect of the impending ruin of our native country; while Parliaments, which ought to be the security and defence of our Laws and Constitution, betray their Trust, and abuse the people whom they should protect; and no other way being left us but that Force which we are very loth to make use of: that Posterity may know we did not insensibly fall under the tyranny of a prevailing Party; We do hereby

Claim and Declare,

1. That it is the undoubted Right of the People of England, in case their Representatives in Parliament do not proceed according to their Duty, and the People's Interest; to inform of their dislike, disown their actions, and to direct them to such things as they think fit, either by Petition, Address, Proposal, Memorial, or any other peaceable way.

2. That the House of Commons, separately, and otherwise than by *Bill* legally passed into an *Act*, have no Legal Power to suspend or dispense with the Laws of the land; any more than the King has, by his Prerogative.

3. That the House of Commons have no Legal Power to imprison any person, or commit them to the custody of Serjeants or otherwise, their only Members excepted; but ought to address the King, to cause any person, on good grounds, to be apprehended: which person, so apprehended, ought to have the benefit of the *Habeas Corpus Act*; and be fairly brought to trial by due course of Law.

4. That if the House of Commons, in breach of the Laws

and Liberties of the people, do betray the Trust reposed in them; and act negligently or arbitrarily and illegally: it is the undoubted Right of the People of England to call them to an account for the same; and by Convention, Assembly, or Force, may proceed against them, as traitors and betrayers of their country.

These things we think proper to Declare, as the Unquestioned Right of the People of England, whom you serve.

And in pursuance of that Right; avoiding the ceremony of Petitioning our inferiors (for such you are by your present circumstances, as the person sent is less than the sender): We do publicly Protest against all your foresaid Illegal Actions; and, in the name of our Selves, and of all the good People of England, do

Require and Demand,

1. That all the Public just Debts of the nation be forthwith paid and discharged.

2. That all persons illegally imprisoned as aforesaid, be either immediately discharged, or admitted to bail, as by Law they ought to be: and the Liberty of the Subject recognized and restored.

3. That J[OH]N H[O]W[E] aforesaid, be obliged to ask His Majesty pardon for his vile reflections; or be immediately expelled the House.

4. That the growing power of France be taken into consideration, the Succession of the Emperor to the Crown of Spain supported, our Protestant neighbours protected, as the true Interest of England and the Protestant Religion require.

5. That the French King be obliged to quit Flanders, or that His Majesty be addressed to declare war against him.

6. That suitable Supplies be granted to His Majesty, for the putting all these necessary things in execution; and that

care be taken that such taxes as are raised, may be more equally assessed and collected, and scandalous deficiencies prevented.

7. That the Thanks of the House may be given to those Gentlemen, who so gallantly appeared in the behalf of their country, with the *Kentish Petition*; and have been so scandalously used for it.

Thus, Gentlemen, you have your Duty laid before you! which it is hoped you will think of! But if you continue to neglect it, you may expect to be treated according to the resentments of an injured Nation! For Englishmen are no more to be Slaves to Parliaments, than to a King!

Our name is LEGION, and we are Many.

Postscript.

If you require to have this Memorial signed with our Names; it shall be done, on your first Order: and personally presented *!*

THE SHORTEST-WAY WITH THE DISSENTERS: OR PROPOSALS FOR THE ESTABLISHMENT OF THE CHURCH.

LONDON:
Printed in the Year MDCCII.

[The meaning then of this Paper is, in short, to tell these Gentlemen :

1. That it is nonsense to go round about, and tell us of the crimes of the Dissenters ! to prepare the World to believe they are not fit to live in a human society ; that they are enemies to the Government, and Law ! to the Queen, and the Public Peace, and the like. *The Shortest Way*, and the soonest, would be to tell us plainly that they would have them all hanged, banished, and destroyed.

2. But withal to acquaint these Gentlemen, who fancy the time is come to bring it to pass, that they are mistaken ! For that when the thing they mean is put into plain English, the whole nation replies with the Assyrian Captain, "Is thy servant a dog, that he should do these things ?"

The Gentlemen are mistaken in every particular. It will not go down ! The Queen, the Council, the Parliament are all offended to have it so much as suggested, that such a thing was possible to come into their minds : and not a man but a learned Mercer not far from the corner of Fenchurch street, has been found to approve it.

Thus a poor Author has ventured to have all mankind call him "Villain !" and "Traitor to his country and his friends," for making other people's thoughts speak in his words. . . .

As to expressions which seem to reflect upon persons or nations ; he declares them to be only the Cant of the Non-Juring Party exposed : and thinks it very necessary to let the World know that it is their usual language, with which they treat the late King, the Scotch Union, and the Line of HANOVER.

It is hard, after all, that this should not be perceived by all the Town ! that not one man can see it, either Churchman or Dissenter !

A brief explanation . . . of The Shortest Way. 1703.

I'll prove by the Preachings, Printings, and declared Judgement of several of the most zealous High Party, that however the practice was disowned by the Party upon the unreasonable exposing [of] it, by the book called *The Shortest Way* ; yet that it has all along been their desire, and very often their design. And I appeal for the truth of it, among many instances, to a letter of a known Churchman [*Clergyman*], whose original I have by me, it being written to a person who sent him the book for a present.

SIR,

I received yours, and, enclosed, the book called, The Shortest Way with the Dissenters, *for which I thank you : and, next to the* Holy Bible *and Sacred Comments, I place it as the most valuable thing I can have. I look upon it as the Only Method ! and I pray GOD to put it into the heart of our most gracious Queen, to put what is there proposed in execution.*

Here is the Character of a High Churchman drawn to the life! But when, in a post or two, this Gentleman understood it was written by a Dissenter; in his next, he sends up an invidious Character of a Whig: and what, in his opinion, such a one deserved.

The Dissenters' Answer to the High Church Challenge. Ed. 1702.

A certain Printer, whose practice that way is too well known to need a name, having frequently practised the same thing in particulars [*as to single works*], made the first essay in general [*in a collected edition*], and printed [*about January*, 1703] a spurious and erroneous copy [*text*], of sundry things which he called Mine; and intituled them, *A Collection of the Works of the Author of* The True Born Englishman.

And though the Author was then embroiled with the Government, for one of the Pamphlets [*The Shortest Way*] he collected: yet had this man the face to print among them, the same Pamphlet; presuming so far upon the partiality of the Public Resentment, that he should pass with impunity, for the publishing of that very thing, for which the Author was to be pursued with the utmost severity.

This, as it was a full proof, and most undeniable testimony, that the resentment shewed to the Author was on some other and less justifiable Account than the publishing of that book; so was it a severe Satire, on the ignorance and unwariness of that Ministry, who had not eyes to see their justice plainly exposed, and their general proceedings bantered by a petty printer, in publishing barefaced and in defiance of them, that same book, for which another man stood arraigned, and was to be exposed.

Nor was the Insult to the Government, all the circumstance of guilt in this publication: but the most absurd and ridiculous mistakes in the copies [*texts*] were such as rendered it a double cheat.

First, to the Author; to whom it was a most aggravated theft: first, as it was invading his right; and secondly, as it was done while he was in trouble, and unable to right himself.

Secondly, to the Buyers, to whom it was a most ridiculous banter, and the mere picking of their pockets; the Author having, in his first perusal of it, detected above 350 errors in the printing; marring the Verse, spoiling the sense, and utterly inverting the true intent and meaning.

The Author having expressed himself, though in decent terms, against the foulness of this practice; the Printer (having no plea to the barbarity of the fact) justifies it, and says, "He will do the like by anything an Author prints on his own account [*at his own risk*]; since Authors have no right to employ a printer, unless they have served their time [*apprenticeship*] to a bookseller."

This ridiculous allegation seems to me, to be as if a man's house being on fire, he had no right to get help for the quenching of it, of anybody but the Insurers' firemen.

A true Collection, &c. Vol. II. *Preface.*]

THE SHORTEST-WAY WITH THE DISSENTERS, &c.

SIR ROGER L' ESTRANGE tells us a story in his collection of *Fables*, of the Cock and the Horses. The Cock was gotten to roost in the stable among the horses; and there being no racks or other conveniences for him, it seems, he was forced to roost upon the ground. The horses jostling about for room, and putting the Cock in danger of his life, he gives them this grave advice, "Pray, Gentlefolks! let us stand still! for fear we should tread upon one another!"

There are some people in the World, who, now they are *unperched*, and reduced to an equality with other people, and under strong and very just apprehensions of being further treated as they deserve, begin, with ESOP's Cock, to preach up Peace and Union and the Christian duty of Moderation; forgetting that, when they had the Power in their hands, those Graces were strangers in their gates!

It is now, near fourteen years, [1688–1702], that the glory and peace of the purest and most flourishing Church in the world has been eclipsed, buffeted, and disturbed by a sort of men, whom, GOD in His Providence, has suffered to insult over her, and bring her down. These have been the days of her humiliation and tribulation. She has borne with an invincible patience, the reproach of the wicked: and GOD has at last heard her prayers, and delivered her from the oppression of the stranger.

And now, they find their Day is over! their power gone! and the throne of this nation possessed by a Royal, *English*, true, and ever constant member of, and friend to, the Church of England! Now, they find that they are in danger of the Church of England's just resentments! Now, they cry out, "Peace!" "Union!" "Forbearance!" and "Charity!": as if the Church had not too long harboured her enemies under her wing! and nourished the viperous brood, till they hiss and fly in the face of the Mother that cherished them!

No, Gentlemen! the time of mercy is past! your Day of Grace is over! you should have practised peace, and moderation, and charity, if you expected any yourselves!

We have heard none of this lesson, for fourteen years past! We have been huffed and bullied with your *Act of Toleration*! You have told us, *you* are the Church established by Law, as well as others! have set up your canting Synagogues at our Church doors! and the Church and her members have been loaded with reproaches, with Oaths, Associations, Abjurations, and what not! Where has been the mercy, the forbearance, the charity you have shewn to tender consciences of the Church of England that could not take Oaths *as fast as you made them*? that having sworn allegiance to their lawful and rightful King, could not dispense with that Oath, *their King being still alive*; and swear to your new hodge podge of a Dutch Government? These have been turned out of their Livings, and they and their families left to starve! their estates double taxed to carry on a war they had no hand in, and you got nothing by!

What account can you give of the multitudes you have forced to comply, against their consciences, with your new sophistical Politics, who, like New Converts in France, sin because *they cannot starve*? And now the tables are turned upon you; *you* must not be persecuted! it is not a Christian spirit!

You have butchered one King! deposed another King! and made a Mock King of a third! and yet, you could have the face to expect to be employed and trusted by the fourth! Anybody that did not know the temper of your Party, would stand amazed at the impudence as well as the folly to think of it!

Your management of your Dutch Monarch, who you reduced to a mere King of Cl[ub]s, is enough to give any future Princes such an idea of your principles, as to warn them sufficiently from coming into your clutches; and, GOD be thanked! the Queen is out of your hands! knows you! and will have a care of you!

There is no doubt but the Supreme Authority of a nation has in itself, a Power, and *a right to that Power*, to execute the Laws upon any part of that nation it governs. The execution of the known Laws of the land, and that with but a gentle hand neither, was all that the Fanatical Party of this land have ever called Persecution. This they have magnified to a height, that the sufferings of the Huguenots in France were not to be compared with them. Now to execute the known Laws of a nation upon those who transgress them, after having first been voluntarily consenting to the making of those Laws, can never be called Persecution, but Justice. But Justice is always Violence to the party offending! for every man is innocent in his own eyes.

The first execution of the Laws against Dissenters in England, was in the days of King JAMES I.; and what did it amount to? Truly, the worst they suffered was, at their own request, to let them go to New England, and erect a new colony; and give them great privileges, grants, and suitable powers; keep them under protection, and defend them against all invaders; and receive no taxes or revenue from them!

This was the cruelty of the Church of England! Fatal lenity! It was the ruin of that excellent Prince, King CHARLES I. Had King JAMES sent all the Puritans in England away to the West Indies; we had been a national unmixed Church! the Church of England had been kept undivided and entire!

To requite the lenity of the Father, they take up arms against the Son, conquer, pursue, take, imprison, and at last to death the Anointed of GOD, and destroy the very Being and Nature of Government: setting up a sordid Impostor, who had neither title to govern, nor understanding to manage, but supplied that want, with power, bloody and desperate counsels and craft, without conscience.

Had not King JAMES I. withheld the full execution of the Laws: had he given them strict justice, he had cleared the nation of them! And the consequences had been plain; his son had never been murdered by them, nor the Monarchy overwhelmed. It was too much mercy shewn them that was the ruin of his posterity, and the ruin of the nation's peace. One would think the Dissenters should not have the face to believe, that we are to be wheedled and canted into Peace and Toleration, when they know that they have once requited us with a Civil War, and once with an intolerable and unrighteous Persecution, for our former civility.

Nay, to encourage us to be easy with them, it is apparent

that they never had the upper hand of the Church, but they treated her with all the severity, with all the reproach and contempt as was possible! What Peace and what Mercy did they shew the loyal Gentry of the Church of England, in the time of their triumphant Commonwealth? How did they put all the Gentry of England to ransom, whether they were actually in arms for the King or not! making people compound for their estates, and starve their families! How did they treat the Clergy of the Church of England! sequester the Ministers! devour the patrimony of the Church, and divide the spoil, by sharing the Church lands among their soldiers, and turning her Clergy out to starve! Just such measure as they have meted, should be measured to them again!

Charity and Love is the known doctrine of the Church of England, and it is plain She has put it in practice towards the Dissenters, even beyond what they ought [*deserved*], till She has been wanting to herself, and in effect unkind to her own sons: particularly, in the too much lenity of King JAMES I., mentioned before. Had he so rooted the Puritans from the face of the land, which he had an opportunity early to have done; they had not had the power to vex the Church, as since they have done.

In the days of King CHARLES II., how did the Church reward their bloody doings, with lenity and mercy! Except the barbarous Regicides of the pretended Court of Justice, not a soul suffered, for all the blood in an unnatural war! King CHARLES came in all mercy and love, cherished them, preferred them, employed them, withheld the rigour of the Law; and oftentimes, even against the advice of his Parliament, gave them Liberty of Conscience: and how did they requite him? With the villanous contrivance to depose and murder him and his successor, at the Rye [House] Plot!

King JAMES [II.], as if mercy was the inherent quality of the Family, began his reign with unusual favour to them. Nor could their joining with the Duke of MONMOUTH against him, move him to do himself justice upon them. But that mistaken Prince, thinking to win them by gentleness and love, proclaimed a Universal Liberty to them! and rather discountenanced the Church of England than them! How they requited him, all the World knows!

The late reign [*WILLIAM III.*] is too fresh in the memory

of all the World to need a comment. How under pretence of joining with the Church in redressing some grievances, they pushed things to that extremity, in conjunction with some mistaken Gentlemen, as to *depose* the late King: as if the grievance of the Nation could not have been redressed but by the absolute ruin of the Prince!

Here is an instance of their Temper, their Peace, and Charity!

To what height they carried themselves during the reign of a King of their own! how they crope [*creeped*] into all Places of Trust and Profit! how they insinuated themselves into the favour of the King, and were at first preferred to the highest Places in the nation! how they engrossed the Ministry! and, above all, how pitifully they managed! is too plain to need any remarks.

But particularly, their Mercy and Charity, the spirit of Union, they tell us so much of, has been remarkable in Scotland. If any man would see the spirit of a Dissenter, let him look into Scotland! There, they made entire conquest of the Church! trampled down the sacred Orders and suppressed the Episcopal Government, with an absolute, and, as they supposed, irretrievable victory! though it is possible, *they may find themselves mistaken*!

Now it would be a very proper question to ask their impudent advocate, the *Observator*, "Pray how much mercy and favour did the members of the Episcopal Church find in Scotland, from the Scotch Presbyterian Government? and I shall undertake for the Church of England, that the Dissenters shall still receive as much here, though they deserve but little.

In a small treatise of *The Sufferings of the Episcopal Clergy in Scotland*, it will appear what usage they met with! How they not only lost their Livings; but, in several places, were plundered and abused in their persons! the Ministers that could not conform, were turned out, with numerous families and no maintenance, and hardly charity enough left to relieve them with a bit of bread. The cruelties of the Party were innumerable, and are not to be attempted in this short Piece.

And now, to prevent the distant cloud which they perceive to hang over their heads from England, with a true Presbyterian policy, they put it for a Union of Nations! that England might unite their Church with the Kirk of Scotland,

and their Assembly of Scotch canting Long-Cloaks in our Convocation. What might have been, if our Fanatic Whiggish Statesmen continued, GOD only knows! but we hope we are out of fear of that now.

It is alleged by some of the faction, and they have begun to bully us with it, that "if we won't unite with them, they will not settle the Crown with us again; but when Her Majesty dies, will choose a King for themselves!"

If they won't we must make them! and it is not the first time we have let them know that we are able! The Crowns of these Kingdoms have not so far disowned the Right of Succession, but they may retrieve it again; and if Scotland thinks to come off from a Successive to an Elective State of Government; England has not promised, not to assist the Right Heir, and put him into possession, without any regards to their ridiculous *Settlements*.

THESE are the Gentlemen! these, their ways of treating the Church, both at home and abroad!

Now let us examine the Reasons they pretend to give, why we should be favourable to them? why we should continue and tolerate them among us?

First. *They are very numerous*, they say. *They are a great part of the nation, and we cannot suppress them!*

To this, may be answered,

First. They are not so numerous as the Protestants in France: and yet the French King effectually cleared the nation of them, at once; and we don't find he misses them at home!

But I am not of the opinion, they are so numerous as is pretended. Their Party is more numerous than their Persons; and those mistaken people of the Church who are misled and deluded by their wheedling artifices to join with them, make their Party the greater: but those will open their eyes when the Government shall set heartily about the Work, and come off from them, as some animals, which they say, always desert a house when it is likely to fall.

Secondly. The more numerous, the more dangerous; and therefore the more need to suppress them! and GOD has suffered us to bear them as goads in our sides, for not utterly extinguishing them long ago.

Thirdly. If we are to allow them, only because we cannot suppress them; then it ought to be tried, Whether we can or not? And I am of opinion, it is easy to be done! and could prescribe Ways and Means, if it were proper: but I doubt not the Government will find effectual methods for the rooting of the contagion from the face of this land.

Another argument they use, which is this. *That this is a time of war, and we have need to unite against the common enemy.*

We answer, This common enemy had been no enemy, if they had not made him so! He was quiet, in peace, and no way disturbed and encroached upon us; and we know no reason we had to quarrel with him.

But further. We make no question but we are able to deal with this common enemy without their help: but why must we unite with them, because of the enemy? Will they go over to the enemy, if we do not prevent it, by a Union with them? We are very well contented [that] they should! and make no question, we shall be ready to deal with them and the common enemy too; and better without them than with them! Besides, if we have a common enemy, there is the more need to be secure against our private enemies! If there is one common enemy, we have the less need to have an enemy in our bowels!

It was a great argument some people used against suppressing the Old Money, that "it was a time of war, and it was too great a risque [*risk*] for the nation to run! If we should not master it, we should be undone!" And yet the sequel proved the hazard was not so great, but it might be mastered, and the success [*i.e., of the new coinage*] was answerable. The suppressing the Dissenters is not a harder work! nor a work of less necessity to the Public! We can never enjoy a settled uninterrupted union and tranquility in this nation, till the spirit of Whiggism, Faction, and Schism is melted down like the Old Money!

To talk of difficulty is to frighten ourselves with Chimeras and notions of a powerful Party, which are indeed a Party without power. Difficulties often appear greater at a distance than when they are searched into with judgement, and distinguished from the vapours and shadows that attend them.

We are not to be frightened with it! This Age is wiser than that, by all our own experience, and theirs too! King CHARLES I. had early suppressed this Party, if he had taken more deliberate measures! In short, it is not worth arguing, to talk of their arms. Their MONMOUTHS, and SHAFTESBURYS, and ARGYLES are gone! Their Dutch Sanctuary is at an end! Heaven has made way for their destruction! and if we do not close with the Divine occasion, we are to blame ourselves! and may hereafter remember, that we had, once, an opportunity to serve the Church of England, by extirpating her implacable enemies; and having let slip the Minute that Heaven presented, may experimentally complain, *Post est Occasio CALVO*!

Here are some popular Objections in the way.

As First, *The Queen has promised them, to continue them in their tolerated Liberty; and has told us* She will be a religious observer of her word.

What Her Majesty will do, we cannot help! but what, as the Head of the Church, she ought to do, is another case. Her Majesty has promised to protect and defend the Church of England, and if she cannot effectually do that, without the destruction of the Dissenters; she must, of course, dispense with one promise to comply with another!

But to answer this cavil more effectually. Her Majesty did never promise to maintain the Toleration to the destruction of the Church; but it was upon supposition that it may be compatible with the well-being and safety of the Church, which she had declared she would take especial care of. Now if these two Interests clash, it is plain Her Majesty's intentions are to uphold, protect, defend, and establish the Church! and this, we conceive is impossible [*that is, while maintaining the Toleration*].

Perhaps it may be said, *That the Church is in no immediate danger from the Dissenters; and therefore it is time enough.*

But this is a weak answer. For first. If the danger be real, the distance of it is no argument against, but rather a spur to quicken us to Prevention, lest it be too late hereafter.

And secondly. Here is the opportunity, and the only one perhaps, that ever the Church had to secure herself, and destroy her enemies.

The Representatives of the Nation have now an opportunity! The Time is come, which all good men have wished for! that the Gentlemen of England may serve the Church of England, now they are protected and encouraged by a Church of England Queen!

What will you do for your Sister in the day that she shall be spoken for ?

If ever you will establish the best Christian Church in the World?

If ever you will suppress the Spirit of Enthusiasm?

If ever you will free the nation from the viperous brood that have so long sucked the blood of their Mother?

If ever you will leave your Posterity free from faction and rebellion, this is the time! This is the time to pull up this heretical Weed of Sedition, that has so long disturbed the Peace of the Church, and poisoned the good corn!

But, says another hot and cold Objector, *This is renewing Fire and Faggot! reviving the* Act, De heretico comburendo *! This will be cruelty in its nature! and barbarous to all the World!*

I answer, It is cruelty to kill a snake or a toad in cold blood, but the poison of their nature makes it a charity to our neighbours, to destroy those creatures! not for any personal injury received, but for prevention; not for the evil they have done, but the evil they may do! Serpents, toads, vipers, &c., are noxious to the body, and poison the sensitive life: these poison the soul! corrupt our posterity! ensnare our children! destroy the vitals of our happiness, our future felicity! and contaminate the whole mass!

Shall any Law be given to such wild creatures! Some beasts are for sport, and the huntsmen give them the advantages of ground: but some are knocked on the head, by all possible ways of violence and surprise!

I do not prescribe Fire and Faggot! but as SCIPIO said of Carthage, *Delenda est Carthago!* They are to be rooted out of this nation, if ever we will live in peace! serve GOD! or enjoy our own! As for the manner, I leave it to those hands, who have a Right to execute GOD's Justice on the Nation's and the Church's enemies.

But if we must be frighted from this Justice, under the[se] specious pretences, and odious sense of cruelty; nothing will be effected! It will be more barbarous to our own children and dear posterity, when they shall reproach their fathers, as we ours, and tell us [!]," You had an Opportunity to root out this cursed race from the World, under the favour and protection of a True Church of England Queen! and out of your foolish pity, you spared them: because, forsooth, you would not be cruel! And now our Church is suppressed and persecuted, our Religion trampled under foot, our estates plundered; our persons imprisoned, and dragged to gaols, gibbets, and scaffolds! Your sparing this Amalekite race is our destruction! Your mercy to them, proves cruelty to your poor posterity!"

How just will such reflections be, when our posterity shall fall under the merciless clutches of this uncharitable Generation! when our Church shall be swallowed up in Schism, Faction, Enthusiasm, and Confusion! when our Government shall be devolved upon Foreigners, and our Monarchy dwindled into a Republic!

It would be more rational for us, if we must spare this Generation, to summon our own to a general massacre: and as we have brought them into the World free, to send them out so; and not betray them to destruction by our supine negligence, and then cry "It is mercy!"

MOSES was a merciful meek man; and yet with what fury did he run through the camp, and cut the throats of three and thirty thousand of his dear Israelites that were fallen into idolatry. What was the reason? It was mercy to the rest, to make these examples! to prevent the destruction of the whole army.

How many millions of future souls, [shall] we save from infection and delusion, if the present race of Poisoned Spirits were purged from the face of the land!

It is vain to trifle in this matter! The light foolish handling of them by mulcts, fines, &c.; 'tis their glory and their advantage! If the Gallows instead of the Counter, and the galleys instead of the fines; were the reward of going to a conventicle, to preach or hear, there would not be so many sufferers! The spirit of martyrdom is over! They that will go to church to be chosen Sheriffs and Mayors, would go to forty churches, rather than be hanged!

If one severe Law were made, and punctually executed, that *Whoever was found at a Conventicle should be banished the nation, and the Preacher be hanged*; we should soon see an end of the tale! They would all come to church again, and one Age [*generation*] would make us all One again!

To talk of Five Shillings a month for not coming to the Sacrament, and One Shilling per week, for not coming to Church: this is such a way of converting people as was never known! This is selling them a liberty to transgress, for so much money!

If it be not a crime, why don't we give them full license? and if it be, no price ought to compound for the committing of it! for that is selling a liberty to people to sin against GOD and the Government!

If it be a crime of the highest consequence, both against the peace and welfare of the nation, the Glory of GOD, the good of the Church, and the happiness of the soul: let us rank it among capital offences! and let it receive a punishment in proportion to it!

We hang men for trifles, and banish them for things not worth naming; but that an offence against GOD and the Church, against the welfare of the World, and the dignity of Religion shall be bought off for FIVE SHILLINGS: this is such a shame to a Christian Government, that it is with regret I transmit it to posterity.

If men sin against GOD, affront His ordinances, rebel against His Church, and disobey the precepts of their superiors; let them suffer, as such capital crimes deserve! so will Religion flourish, and this divided nation be once again united.

And yet the title of *barbarous* and *cruel* will soon be taken off from this Law too. I am not supposing that all the Dissenters in England should be hanged or banished. But as in case of rebellions and insurrections, if a few of the ringleaders suffer, the multitude are dismissed; so a few obstinate people being made examples, there is no doubt but the severity of the Law would find a stop in the compliance of the multitude.

To make the reasonableness of this matter out of question, and more unanswerably plain, let us examine for what it is, that this nation is divided into Parties and factions? and let us see how they can justify a Separation? or we of the Church of England can justify our bearing the insults and inconveniences of the Party.

One of their leading Pastors, and a man of as much learning as most among them, in his *Answer* to a Pamphlet entituled *An Enquiry into the Occasional Conformity*, hath these words, *p.* 27: "Do the Religion of the Church and the Meeting Houses make two religions? Wherein do they differ? The Substance of the same Religion is common to them both, and the Modes and Accidents are the things in which only they differ." *P.* 28: "Thirty-nine *Articles* are given us for the Summary of our Religion: thirty-six contain the Substance of it, wherein we agree; three are additional Appendices, about which we have some differences."

Now, if as, by their own acknowledgement, the Church of England is a true Church; and the difference is only in a few "Modes and Accidents": why should we expect that they will suffer the gallows and galleys, corporal punishment and banishment, for these trifles? There is no question, but they will be wiser! Even their own principles won't bear them out in it!

They will certainly comply with the Laws, and with Reason! And though, at the first, severity may seem hard, the next Age will feel nothing of it! the contagion will be rooted out. The disease being cured, there will be no need of the operation! But if they should venture to transgress, and fall into the pit; all the World must condemn their obstinacy, as being without ground from their own principles.

Thus the pretence of cruelty will be taken off, and the Party actual suppressed; and the disquiets they have so often brought upon the Nation, prevented.

Their numbers and their wealth make them haughty; and that is so far from being an argument to persuade us to forbear them, that it is a warning to us, without any more delay, to reconcile them to the Unity of the Church, or remove them from us.

At present, Heaven be praised! they are not so formidable as they have been, and it is our own fault if ever we suffer them to be so! Providence and the Church of England seem to join in this particular, that now, the Destroyers of the Nation's Peace may be overturned! and to this end, the present opportunity seems to put into our hands.

To this end, Her present Majesty seems reserved to enjoy the Crown, that the Ecclesiastic as well as Civil Rights of the Nation may be restored by her hand.

To this end, the face of affairs has received such a turn in the process of a few months as never has been before. The leading men of the Nation, the universal cry of the People, the unanimous request of the Clergy agree in this, that the Deliverance of our Church is at hand!

For this end, has Providence given such a Parliament! such a Convocation! such a Gentry! and such a Queen! as we never had before.

And what may be the consequences of a neglect of such opportunities? The Succession of the Crown has but a dark prospect! Another Dutch turn may make the hopes of it ridiculous, and the practice impossible! Be the House of our future Princes ever so well inclined, they will be Foreigners! Many years will be spent in suiting the Genius of Strangers to this Crown, and the Interests of the Nation! and how many Ages it may be, before the English throne be filled with so much zeal and candour, so much tenderness and hearty affection to the Church, as we see it now covered with, who can imagine?

It is high time, then, for the friends of the Church of England to think of building up and establishing her in such a manner, that she may be no more invaded by Foreigners, nor divided by factions, schisms, and error.

If this could be done by gentle and easy methods, I should be glad! but the wound is corroded, the vitals begin to mortify, and nothing but amputation of members can complete the cure! All the ways of tenderness and compassion, all persuasive arguments have been made use of in vain!

The humour of the Dissenters has so increased among the people, that they hold the Church in defiance! and the House of GOD is an abomination among them! Nay, they have brought up their posterity in such prepossessed aversion to our Holy Religion, that the ignorant mob think we are all idolators and worshippers of BAAL! and account it a sin to come within the walls of our churches! The primitive Christians were not more shy of a heathen temple, or of meat offered to idols; nor the Jews, of swine's flesh, than some of our Dissenters are of the church and the *Divine Service* solemnized therein.

The Obstinacy must be rooted out, with the profession of it! While the Generation are left at liberty daily to affront GOD Almighty, and dishonour His holy worship; we are wanting in our duty to GOD, and to our Mother the Church of England,

How can we answer it to GOD! to the Church! and to our posterity; to leave them entangled with Fanaticism! Error, and Obstinacy, in the bowels of the nation? to leave them an enemy in their streets, that, in time, may involve them in the same crimes, and endanger the utter extirpation of the Religion of the Nation!

What is the difference betwixt this, and being subject to the power of the Church of Rome? from whence we have reformed. If one be an extreme to the one hand, and one on another: it is equally destructive to the Truth to have errors settled among us, let them be of what nature they will! Both are enemies of our Church, and of our peace! and why should it not be as criminal to admit an Enthusiast as a Jesuit? why should the Papist with his Seven Sacraments be worse than the Quaker with no Sacraments at all? Why should Religious Houses be more intolerable than Meeting Houses?

Alas, the Church of England! What with Popery on one hand, and Schismatics on the other, how has She been crucified between two thieves. NOW, LET US CRUCIFY THE THIEVES!

Let her foundations be established upon the destruction of her enemies! The doors of Mercy being always open to the returning part of the deluded people, let the obstinate be ruled with the rod of iron!

Let all true sons of so holy and oppressed a Mother, exasperated by her afflictions, harden their hearts against those who have oppressed her!

And may GOD Almighty put it into the hearts of all the friends of Truth, to lift up a Standard against Pride and ANTICHRIST! that the Posterity of the Sons of Error may be rooted out from the face of this land, for ever!

FINIS.

A HYMN TO THE PILLORY.

LONDON:
Printed in the Year, MDCCIII.

[*London*, *July* 31 [1703]. On [Thursday] the 29th instant, DANIEL FOE *alias DE FOE*, stood in the Pillory before the Royal Exchange in Cornhill, as he did yesterday near the Conduit in Cheapside, and this day at Temple Bar; in pursuance of the sentence given against him, at the last Sessions at the Old Bailey, for writing and publishing a seditious libel, intituled *The Shortest Way with the Dissenters*. By which sentence, he is also fined 200 marks, to find sureties for his good behaviour for seven years, and to remain in prison till all be performed.

London Gazette. No. 3936. August 2nd, 1703.

I had purposed to have given a short history here of the several tracts in this *Collection*, and something of the reason of them: but I find it too long for a *Preface*.

The *Hymn to the Pillory* seems most to require it. The Reader is desired to observe that this Poem was the Author's Declaration, even when in the cruel hands of a merciless as well as unjust Ministry, that the treatment he had from them, was unjust, exorbitant, and consequently Illegal.

As this Satyr or Poem (call it which you will!) was written at the very time he was treated in that manner; it was taken for a Defiance of their Illegal Proceedings! and their not thinking fit to prosecute him for it, was a fair concession of Guilt in their former proceedings; since he was in their power, and, as they thought, not likely to come out of it.

It is true some faint shew of resentment was made, and the Author, though then in prison, never declined the test of it: but they began to see themselves in the wrong from the very first exerting of their Cruelty and Treachery upon this Author; and the Interest of the Party sensibly decayed from that very moment of time.

Multitudes of occasions have, since that, served to convince the World, that every word of the book [*The Shortest Way*] he suffered for, was both literally and interpretively, the Sense of the Party pointed at; true in fact, and true in representation: and therefore he cannot but repeat the conclusion as relating to himself, which he has seen made good, even to public satisfaction.

Tell them, The men that placed him there
Are scandals to the Time,
Are at a loss to find his guilt,
And can't commit his crime.

I should enlarge on this subject, but that perhaps the World may, in some proper season, be troubled with a Journal of all the Proceedings, Trials, Treaties, and Debates, upon that head; and the barbarity as well as folly of their conduct be set in a true light to the World.

A true Collection, &c. Vol. II. *Preface.*]

A

HYMN

TO THE

PILLORY.

HAIL! hieroglyphic State Machine,
Contrived to punish Fancy in!
Men, that are men, in thee can feel no pain;
And all thy insignificants disdain!
Contempt, that false new word for Shame,
Is, without crime, an empty name!
A Shadow to amuse mankind;
But never frights the wise or well-fixed mind!
Virtue despises human scorn!
And scandals, Innocence adorn.

Exalted on thy Stool of State,
What prospect do I see of sovereign Fate!
How the inscrutables of Providence,
Differ from our contracted sense!
Here, by the errors of the Town,
The fools look out! the knaves look on!
Persons or Crimes find here the same respect;
And Vice does, Virtue oft correct!
The undistinguished fury of the street,
With mob and malice, mankind greet!
No bias can the rabble draw;
But Dirt throws dirt, without respect to Merit or to Law!

Sometimes, the air of Scandal to maintain,
Villains look from thy lofty Loops in vain!
But who can judge of Crimes, by Punishment?
Where Parties rule, and L[aw] 's subservient.
Justice, with change of Interest learns to bow;
And what was Merit once, is Murder now!
Actions receive their tincture from the Times,
And as they change, are Virtues made, or Crimes.
Thou art the State-Trap of the Law!
But neither canst keep knaves, nor honest men in awe:
These are too hardened in offence,
And those upheld by innocence.

How have thy opening Vacancies received
In every Age, the criminals of State!
And how has Mankind been deceived,
When they distinguish crimes by fate!
Tell us, Great Engine! how to understand
Or reconcile the Justice of the land!
How BASTWICK, PRYNNE, HUNT, HOLLINGSBY, and PYE
(Men of unspotted honesty,
Men that had Learning, Wit, and Sense;
And more than most men have had since)
Could equal title to thee claim,
With OATES and FULLER, men of later fame?
Even the learned SELDEN saw
A prospect of thee, through the law!
He had thy lofty Pinnacles in view;
But so much honour never was thy due!
Had the great SELDEN triumphed on thy stage
(SELDEN, the honour of his Age),
No man would ever shun thee more,
Or grudge to stand where SELDEN stood before.

Thou art no Shame to Truth and Honesty!
Nor is the character of such defaced by thee,
Who suffer by oppressive injury!

Shame, like the exhalations of the sun,
Falls back where first the motion was begun.
And he who, for no crime shall on thy Brows appear,
Bears less reproach than they who placed him there.
But if Contempt is on thy Face entailed,
Disgrace itself shall be ashamed!
Scandal shall blush, that it has not prevailed
To blast the man it has defamed!

Let all that merit equal punishment,
Stand there with him! and we are all content.

There would the famed S[ACHEVERE]LL* stand,
With trumpet of sedition in his hand,
Sounding the first *Crusado* in the land!
He, from of Church of England pulpit first,
All his Dissenting brethren curst!
Doomed them to SATAN for a prey;
And first found out the *Shortest Way*!
With him, the wise Vice-Chancellor of the Press,
Who (though our Printers, licenses defy)
Willing to shew his forwardness,
Bless it with his authority!
He gave the Church's sanction to the Work,
As Popes bless colours for troops which fight the Turk.
Doctors in Scandal, these are grown,
For red-hot Zeal and furious Learning known!
Professors in Reproach! and highly fit
For JUNO's Academy, Billingsgate!
Thou, like a *True Born English* tool,
Hast, from their Composition stole;
And now art like to smart, for being a fool!

* This line shews that the pronunciation, in his own day, of the High Flying Doctor's name was SA-CHEVE-RELL. E. A.

And as of Englishmen, 'twas always meant,
They 're better to improve, than to invent:
Upon their model, thou hast made
A Monster makes the World afraid.

With them, let all the Statesmen stand,
Who guide us with unsteady hand!
Who armies, fleets, and men betray
And ruin all, the *Shortest Way*!
Let all those soldiers stand in sight,
Who 're willing to be paid, and not to fight!
Agents and Colonels, who false musters bring,
To cheat their country first; and then, their King!
Bring all your coward Captains of the fleet!
Lord! what a crowd will there be, when they meet!

They who let POINTI 'scape to Brest!
Who all the gods of Carthagena blest.
Those who betrayed our Turkey Fleet,
Or injured TALMASH sold at Camaret!
Who missed the squadron from Toulon,
And always came too late, or else too soon!
All these are heroes! whose great actions claim
Immortal honours to their dying fame,
And ought not to have been denied
On thy great Counterscarp! to have their valour tried.

Why have not these, upon thy spreading Stage,
Tasted the keener justice of the Age?
If 'tis because their crimes are too remote,
Whom leaden-footed Justice has forgot;
Let 's view the modern scenes of fame,
If Men and Management are not the same?
When fleets go out with money and with men,
Just time enough to venture home again.

Navies prepared to guard the insulted coast;
And convoys settled, when our ships are lost.
Some heroes lately come from sea,
If they were paid their due, should stand with thee!
Papers too should their deeds relate
To prove the justice of their fate.
Their deeds of war, at Port St. Mary's done;
And set the Trophies by them, which they won!
Let OR[MON]D's *Declaration* there appear!
He 'd certainly be pleased to see them there.
Let some good limner represent
The ravished nuns! the plundered town!
The English honour how misspent!
The shameful Coming Back, and little done!

The Vigo men should next appear
To triumph on thy Theatre!
They who, on board the great Galleons had been,
Who robbed the Spaniards first, and then the Queen!
Set up the praises, to their valour due;
How Eighty Sail had beaten Twenty-two!
Two troopers so, and one dragoon
Conquered a Spanish boy at Pampelune!
Yet let them OR[MON]D's conduct own!
Who beat them first on shore, or little had been done!
What unknown spoils from thence are come!
How much was brought away; how little, home!
If all the thieves should on thy Scaffold stand
Who robbed their masters in Command;
The multitude would soon outdo
The City crowds of Lord Mayor's Show!

Upon thy Penitential Stools,
Some people should be placed, for fools!
As some, for instance, who, while they look on,

See others plunder all, and they get none.
Next the Lieutenant General,
To get the Devil, lost the De'il and all:
And he, some little badge should bear
Who ought, in justice, to have hanged them there!
This had his honour more maintained
Than all the spoils at Vigo joined.

Then clap thy wooden Wings for joy,
And greet the Men of Great Employ!
The authors of the Nation's discontent,
And scandal of a Christian Government!
Jobbers and Brokers of the City *Stocks*,
With forty thousand tallies at their backs,
Who make our Banks and Companies obey,
Or sink them all the *Shortest Way*!
The intrinsic value of our Stocks
Is stated in their calculating books,
The imaginary prizes rise and fall
As they command who toss the ball.
Let them upon thy lofty Turrets stand,
With bear-skins on the back, Debentures in the hand!
And write in capitals upon the post,
That here they should remain
Till this enigma they explain:
How Stocks should fall, when Sales surmount the cost;
And rise again when ships are lost.

Great Monster of the Law, exalt thy head!
Appear no more in masquerade!
In homely phrase, express thy discontent!
And move it in the approaching Parliament!
Tell them, how Paper went, instead of Coin;
With interest Eight per cent., and discount Nine!
Of Irish transport debts unpaid,

Bills false endorsed, and long accounts unmade!
And tell them all the Nation hopes to see,
They 'll send the guilty down to thee!
Rather than those that write their history.

Then bring those Justices upon thy bench,
Who vilely break the Laws they should defend;
And upon Equity intrench
By punishing the crimes they will not mend.
Set every vicious Magistrate
Upon thy sumptuous Chariot of State!
There, let them all in triumph ride!
Their purple and their scarlet laid aside.
Such who with oaths and drunk'ness sit
And punish far less crimes than they commit:
These, certainly, deserve to stand,
With Trophies of Authority in either hand.

Upon thy Pulpit, set the drunken Priest,
Who turns the Gospel into a jest!
Let the Fraternity degrade him there,
Lest they, like him appear!
These, let him his *memento mori* preach;
And by example, not by doctrine, teach!

If a poor Author has embraced thy Wood,
Only because he was not understood;
They punish Mankind but by halves,
Till they stand there,
Who false to their own principles appear;
And cannot understand themselves!

Those Nimshites, who with furious zeal drive on
And build up Rome to pull down Babylon,
The real Authors of the *Shortest Way*,
Who for destruction, not conversion pray.

There let these Sons of Strife remain,
Till this Church Riddle they explain!
How at Dissenters they can raise a storm,
But would not have them all conform?
For there, their certain ruin would come in;
And Moderation (which they hate!) begin.
Some Churchmen next would grace thy Pews,
Who talk of Loyalty, they never use:
Passive Obedience well becomes thy Stage,
For both have been the Banter of the Age.
Get them but once within thy reach,
Thou 'lt make them practise, what they used to teach!

Next bring some Lawyers to thy Bar!
By innuendo, they might all stand there.
There let them expiate that guilt,
And pay for all that blood their tongues have spilt;
These are the Mountebanks of State.
Why, by the slight of tongue, can crimes create,
And dress up trifles in the robes of Fate
The Mastiffs of a Government
To worry and run down the innocent!
The Engines of infernal Wit
Covered with cunning and deceit!
SATAN's sublimest attribute they use;
For first they tempt, and then accuse!
No vows or promises can bind their hands:
Submissive Law obedient stands!
When Power concurs, and lawless Force stands by;
He 's lunatic that looks for Honesty!

There sat a man of mighty fame,
Whose actions speak him plainer than his name;
In vain he struggled, he harangued in vain
To bring in "Whipping sentences" again!

And to debauch a milder Government
With *abdicated* kinds of punishments!
No wonder he should Law despise,
Who, JESUS CHRIST himself denies!
His actions only now direct
What we, when he is made a J[udg]e expect.
Set L[OVE]LL next to this Disgrace
With WHITNEY'S horses staring in his face!
There, let his Cup of Penance be kept full!
Till he 's less noisy, insolent, and dull.

When all these heroes have passed o'er thy Stage,
And thou hast been the Satyr of the Age;
Wait then a while, for all those Sons of Fame
Whom Present Power has made too great to name!
Fenced from thy Hands, they Keep our Verse in awe;
Too great for Satyr! too great for Law!
As they, their Commands lay down;
They A L L shall pay their homage to the Cloudy Throne!
And till within thy reach they be,
Exalt them in effigy!

The martyrs of the by-past reign,
For whom new Oaths have been prepared in vain.
SHE[RLOC]K'S disciple, first by him trepanned
He for a k[nave], as they for f[ool]s should stand;
Though some affirm he ought to be excused,
Since to this day, he had refused.
And this was all the frailty of his life,
He d——d his conscience, to oblige his wife!
But spare that Priest, whose tottering conscience kne
That if he took but one, he perjured two;
Bluntly resolved he would not break them both,
And swore, "By God! he'd never take the Oath!"
Hang him! he can't be fit for thee!
For his unusual honesty.

Thou Speaking Trumpet of men's fame,
    Enter in every Court, thy claim !
Demand them all (for they are all thy own)
Who swear to three Kings, but are true to none.
    Turncoats of all sides, are thy due !
And he who once is false is never true,
To-day can swear, to-morrow can abjure ;
For Treachery 's a crime no man can cure.
Such, without scruple, for the Time to come,
May swear to all the Kings in Christendom !
    But he 's a mad man will rely
    Upon their lost fidelity !

They that, in vast employments rob the State,
Let them in thy Embraces, meet their fate !
Let not the millions, they by fraud obtain
Protect them from the scandal, or the pain !
    They who from mean beginnings grow
        To vast estates, but God knows how !
        Who carry untold sums away
    From little Places, with but little pay !
        Who costly palaces erect,
    The thieves that built them to protect :
The gardens, grottoes, fountains, walks, and groves
Where Vice triumphs in pride and lawless love ;
Where mighty luxury and drunk'ness reign,
Profusely spend what they profanely gain !
Tell them, *Mene Tekel* 's on the wall !
Tell them, the nation's money paid for all !

    Advance thy double Front, and show,
And let us both the Crimes and Persons know !
Place them aloft upon thy Throne,

Who slight the nation's business for their own!
Neglect their posts, in spite of double pay;
And run us all in debt the *Shortest Way*!

What need of Satyr to reform the Town,
Or Laws to keep our vices down?
Let them to Thee due homage pay,
This will reform us all the *Shortest Way*!
Let them to Thee, bring all the knaves and fools!
Virtue will guide the rest by rules.
They 'll need no treacherous friends, no breach of faith,
No hired evidence with their infecting breath,
No servants masters to betray,
Or Knights of the Post, who swear for pay!
No injured Author 'll on thy Steps appear;
Not such as *won't* be rogues, but such as *are*!

The first Intent of Laws
Was to correct the Effect, and check the Cause;
And all the Ends of Punishment
Were only future mischiefs to prevent.
But Justice is inverted when
Those Engines of the Law,
Instead of pinching vicious men,
Keep honest ones in awe!
Thy business is, as all men know,
To punish villains, *not to make men so*!

Whenever then, thou art prepared
To prompt that vice, thou should'st reward,
And by the terrors of thy grisly Face

Make men turn rogues to shun disgrace;
The End of thy Creation is destroyed;
Justice expires, of course! and Law 's made void!

What are thy terrors? that, for fear of thee,
Mankind should dare to sink their honesty?
He 's bold to impudence that dares turn knave,
The scandal of thy company to save!
He that will crimes he never knew, confess,
Does, more than if he know those crimes, transgress!
And he that fears thee, more than to be base;
May want a heart, but does not want a face!

hou, like the Devil dost appear,
Blacker than really thou art, by far!
A wild chimeric notion of Reproach;
Too little for a crime, for none too much.
Let none th'indignity resent;
For Crime is all the shame of Punishment!

Thou Bugbear of the Law! stand up and speak!
Thy long misconstrued silence break!
Tell us, Who 'tis, upon thy Ridge stands there,
So full of fault, and yet so void of fear?
And from the Paper in his hat,
Let all mankind be told for what!

Tell them, It was, because he was too bold!
And told those truths which should not have been told!
Extol the Justice of the land;
Who punish what they will not understand!

Tell them, He stands exalted there
For speaking what we would not hear!
And yet he might have been secure,
Had he said less, or would he have said more!

Tell them that, This is his reward,
And worse is yet for him prepared;
Because his foolish virtue was so nice,
As not to sell his friends, according to his friends' advice!
And thus he 's an example made,
To make men, of their honesty afraid;
That for the Time to come, they may
More willingly, their friends betray!

Tell them, The m[en] that placed him here,
Are sc[anda]ls to the Times!
Are at a loss to find his guilt,
And can't commit his crimes!

FINIS.

A

REVIEW

OF THE

Affairs of FRANCE:

AND OF ALL

EUROPE,

As Influenc'd by that NATION:

BEING

Historical Observations on the Public Transactions of the WORLD; Purged from the Errors and Partiality of News-Writers, and Petty Statesmen of all Sides:

WITH AN

Entertaining Part in every Sheet,

BEING

ADVICE from the Scandal[ous] Club, To the Curious Enquirers; in Answer to Letters sent them for that Purpose.

LONDON:

Printed in the Year MDCCV.

Preface to the First Volume of the Review.

WHEN Authors present their Works to the world; like a thief at the gallows, they make a speech to the people.

The Author, indeed, has something like this to say too, "Good people all, take warning by me!" I have studied to inform and to direct the World, and what have I had for my labour?

Profit, the Press would not allow; and therein I am not deceived, for I expected none! But Good Manners and Good Language, I thought I might expect; because I gave no other: and it were but just to treat mankind, as we would be treated by them. But neither has this been paid me, in debt to custom and civility.

How often have my ears, my hands, and my head been to be pulled off! Impotent bullies! that attacked by Truth, and their vices stormed, fill the air with rhodomontades and indecencies; but never shew their faces to the *resentment* Truth had a just cause to entertain for them.

I have passed through clouds of clamour, cavil, ralliery, and objection; and have this satisfaction, that Truth being the design, *Finis coronat*!

I am never forward to value my own performances. "Let another man's mouth praise thee!" said the Wise Man: but I cannot but own myself infinitely pleased, and more than satisfied, that wise men read this Paper with pleasure, own the just observations in it, and have voted it useful.

The first design [*the Review of the Affairs of France, &c.*] I allow is not *yet* pursued, and indeed I must own the field is so large, the design so vast, and the necessary preliminaries so many; that though I cannot yet pass for an old man, I must be so, if I live to go through with it.

This Volume has passed through my descriptions of the French Grandeur, with its influence on the Affairs of Poland, Sweden, and Hungary. What assaults have I met with, from the impatience of the readers; what uneasiness of friends, lest I was turned about to the enemy: I leave to their reading the sheets to discover!

How is this Age unqualified to bear feeling [the] Truth! how unwilling to hear what we do not like, though ever so necessary to know!

And yet if this French Monarchy were not very powerful, vastly strong, its power terrible, its increasing encroaching measures formidable; why do we (and justly too) applaud, extol, congratulate, and dignify the victorious Duke of MARLBOROUGH at such a rate? If it had been a mean and contemptible enemy, how shall we justify the English Army's march [*i.e., to Blenheim*] through so many hazards! the nation's vast charge! the daily just concern in every article of this War! and (as I have frequently hinted) *Why not beat them*, all this while?

They who have made, or may make, an ill use of the true Plan of French Greatness, which I have laid down; must place it to the account of their own corrupted prejudiced thoughts. My design is plain. To tell you the strength of your enemy, that you may fortify yourselves in due proportion; and not go out with your ten thousands against his twenty thousands.

In like manner, I think myself very oddly handled, in the case of the Swedes and the Hungarians. How many complaints of Ambassadors for the one, and of fellow Protestants for the other! And yet, after the whole Story is finished, I have this felicity (than which no author can desire a greater) viz., not one thing I ever affirmed, but was exactly true! not one conjecture have I made, but has appeared to be rational! not one inference drawn, but the consequences [*the events*] have proved [to be] just! and not one thing guessed at, but what has come to pass!

I am now come home to England, and entered a little into our own Affairs. Indeed, I have advanced some things as to Trade, Navies, Seamen, &c., which some may think a little arrogant, because perfectly new. But as I have offered nothing but what I am always ready to make appear practicable, I finish my Apology by saying to the World, "Bring me to the test! and the rest, I leave to time."

In the bringing the Story of France down to the matter of Trade; I confess myself surprisingly drawn into a vast wilderness of a subject; so large, that I know not where it will end. The misfortune of which is, that thinking to have finished it with this Volume, I found myself strangely deceived, and indeed amazed, when I found the Story of it intended to be the end of this Volume ; and hardly enough of it entered upon, to say *it is begun*.

However, the Volume being of necessity to be closed, I am obliged to content myself with taking what is here as an Introduction to the next Volume ; and to give this notice, that the matter of our English Trade appears to be a thing of such consequence to be treated of, so much pretended to, and so little understood, that nothing could be more profitable to the readers, more advantageous to the public Interest of this nation, or more suitable to the greatness of *this* undertaking, than to make an Essay at the Evils, Causes, and Remedies of our general Negoce.

I have been confirmed in my opinion of the consequences and benefit of this Undertaking, by a crowd of entreaties from persons of the best judgement, and some of extraordinary genius in these affairs : whose letters are my authority for this clause, and whose arguments are too forcible for me to resist.

And this is to me, a sufficient Apology for a vast digression from the Affairs of France, which were really in my first design; and to which, my title at first too straightly bound me.

Whoever shall live to see this Undertaking finished, if the Author (or some better pen after him) shall bring 20 or 30 Volumes of this Work on the Stage, it will not look so preposterous, as it seems now, to have one whole Volume to be employed on the most delightful as well as profitable subject of the English Trade.

Things at short distance, look large ! and public patience is generally very short : but when remote, the case alters, and people see the reason of things in themselves. It is this remote prospect of affairs which I have before me. And this makes me not so much regard the uneasiness people shew at the Story being frequently broken abruptly, and running great lengths before it revolves upon itself again : but as Time and the Course of Things will bring all about again, and make the whole to be of a piece with itself ; I am content to wait the approbation of the readers, till such time as the thing itself forces it from the at present impatient readers.

Readers are *strange* judges when they see but *part* of the design. It is a new thing for an Author to lay down his thoughts piece-meal. Importunate cavils assault him every day. They claim to be answered *to-day*! before to-morrow! and are so far from staying till the Story is finished, that they can hardly stay till their letters come to hand; but follow the first with a second! *that* with clamour! and *this* sometimes with threatening scoffs, banters, and raillery!

Thus I am letter-baited by Querists; and I think my trouble in writing civil private answers to teasing and querulous epistles, has been equal to, if not more troublesome than, all the rest of this Work.

Through these difficulties I steer with as much temper and steadiness as I can. I still hope to give satisfaction in the *Conclusion*; and it is this alone, that makes the continuing of the Work tolerable to me. If I cannot, I have made my Essay.

If those that know these things better than I, would bless the World with further instructions, I shall be glad to see them; and very far from interrupting or discouraging them, as these do me.

Let not those Gentlemen who are critics in style, in method, or manner, be angry, that I have never pulled off my cap to them, in humble excuse for my loose way of treating the World as to Language, Expression, and Politeness of Phrase. Matters of this nature differ from most things a man can write. When I am busied writing Essays and Matters of Science, I shall address them for their aid; and take as much care to avoid their displeasure as becomes me: but when I am upon the subject of Trade and the Variety of Casual Story, I think myself a little loose from the Bonds of Cadence and Perfections of Style; and satisfy myself in my study to be explicit, easy, free, and very plain. And for all the rest, *Nec Careo! Nec Curo!*

I had a design to say something on the Entertaining Part of this Paper: but I have so often explained myself on that head, that I shall not trouble the World much about it.

When I first found the Design of this Paper (which had its birth in *tenebris*): I considered it would be a thing very historical, very long; and [even] though it could be much better performed than ever I was likely to do it, this Age had such a natural aversion to a solemn and tedious affair, that however profitable, it would never be diverting, and the World would never read it.

To get over this difficulty, the Secret Hand (I make no doubt) that directed this birth into the World, dictated to make some sort of entertainment or amusement at the end of every Paper, *upon the immediate subject, then on the tongues of the Town*; which innocent diversion would hand on the more weighty and serious part of the Design into the heads and thoughts of those to whom it might be useful.

I take this opportunity to assure the World, that receiving or answering letters of doubts, difficulties, cases, and questions; as it is a work I think myself very meanly qualified for, so it was the remotest thing from my first Design of anything in the World: and I could be heartily glad, if the readers of this Paper would excuse me from it yet. But I see it cannot be, and the World will have it done. I have therefore done my best to oblige them; but as I have not one word to say for my performance that way, so I leave it where I found it, a mere circumstance casually and undesignedly annexed to the Work, and a curiosity; though honestly endeavoured to be complied with.

If the method I have taken in answering Questions has pleased some wiser men more than I expected it would; I confess it is one of the chief reasons why I was induced to continue it.

I have constantly adhered to this rule in all my Answers; and I refer my reader to his observation for the proof, that from the loosest and lightest questions, I endeavour to draw some useful inferences, and, if possible, to introduce something solid, and something solemn in applying it.

The custom of the ancients in writing fables is my very laudable pattern for this: and my firm resolution, in all I write, to exalt Virtue, expose Vice, promote Truth, and help men to Serious Reflection, is my first moving Cause, and last directed End.

If any shall make ill use of, wrest, wrongly interpret, wilfully or otherwise mistake the honest Design of this Work; let such wait for the end! when I doubt not, the Author will be cleared by their own vote; their want of charity will appear, and they be self-condemned till they come to acknowledge their error, and openly to justify

Their humble servant, D. F.

D. F. [*i.e.*, DANIEL FOE. Notice the change of the name into DEFOE, at the end of the next *Preface*, at *p.* 231.]

Preface to the Second Volume of the Review.

THIS Volume of the *Reviews* requires but a short *Preface*: and yet it requires a *Preface* perhaps more than the former [one]; the frequent turning of the Author's design demanding something to be said for it.

In pursuing the subject of Trade, with which this Part began, I really thought to have taken up this whole Volume; and I know a great many people impatiently bear the delay, having great expectations of something very useful as well as diverting on the subject of Trade. I wish their dependence upon me in that case, may be answered to their content.

I have indeed laid a vast Scheme of Trade to discourse upon, and shall, in the next Volume, endeavour to finish it to the best of my capacity: but a word or two to this Volume, by the way.

While I was pursuing the subject of Trade, I received a powerful diversion, from our own Public Affairs. The dissolution of the late Parliament, with some particular transactions of their last session, known by the title of Dangerous Experiments, Tackings, and the like, made a more than usual fermentation in this Kingdom.

I saw with concern, the mighty juncture of a new Election for Members approach. The variety of wheels and engines set on work in the nation, and the furious methods to form Interests on either hand, had put the tempers of men on all sides into an unusual motion, and things seemed acted with so much animosity and Party fury that I confess it gave me terrible apprehensions of the consequences.

I am sorry to say, that the methods on both sides, seemed to me very scandalous; and the low steps our Gentlemen sometimes take to be chosen, merit some Satyr; and perhaps in time may have it! But the inveteracy in the tempers of people at this time, seemed to have something fatal in it; something that deserved not a Satyr, but a sad and serious Application.

Each side strove, with indefatigable pains and exceeding virulence, to set up their own Party. All the slanders, reproaches, and villifying terms possible filled the mouths of one Party against another. If I should say that, in many places, most horrid and villainous practices were set on foot to supplant one another, that the Parties stooped to vile and unbecoming meannesses, and that infinite briberies, forgeries, perjuries, and all manner of debaucheries of the principles and manners of the Electors were attempted; I am told I should say nothing but what might easily be made to appear.

That all sorts of violence, tumults, riots, and breaches of the peace neighbourhood and good manners have been made use of to support Interests, and carry on Elections; the black history of the Election of C[oven]try preparing for the public view, will, I dare say, defend me in advancing.

That this sad scene of affairs, I confess, gave a melancholy view; and I thought I saw this nation running directly upon the steep precipice of General Confusion. In the serious reflecting on this, and how I might, if possible, contribute to the good of my native country, as I thought every honest man was bound to do; I bestowed some thoughts on the serious inquiry, "What was to be done?"

In the short search into the state of the nation, it presently appeared to me that all our pretensions, on either side, were frivolous, but that the breach lay deeper than appeared; that the designs lay in a few, though the whole nation was involved; that King JAMES, the French Power, and a general Turn of Affairs was at the bottom; and the quarrels betwixt Church and Dissenters were only a politic noose, they had hooked the Parties on both sides into, which they diligently carried on to such height as they hoped it would end in a rupture, and then they should open a gap to come in and destroy both.

It presently occurred to my mind, how easily all this might be remedied! how easily this enemy might be disappointed! and that here wants but one thing to heal all this mischief. But one slight matter would make all whole again: and this is included in this one word PARTY-PEACE.

Full satisfied of the certainty of my opinion, I immediately set myself in the *Review* No 19 [of Vol. II. of 17th April, 1705], to exhort, persuade, entreat, and in the most moving terms I was capable of, to prevail on all people in general, to STUDY PEACE.

I thought to have written but that one Paper on this subject, persuading myself the plainness of the argument must be of such force that men's eyes would be opened, and take the useful hint; and there would be no more need to talk about it: and accordingly went on with the old subject of Trade.

But as all my friends, and generally all the men of peace (for, I thank GOD! none but such are my friends!) saw the necessity and usefulness of the subject; they came about me with incessant importunities to go on with it.

I have not vanity enough to own the success of these Papers in this undertaking, not to say what some are pleased to say of it. It is my satisfaction that wise men have owned them useful; and a greater honour I cannot desire.

I have, with an impartial warmth, addressed myself to all sorts of people, on the behalf of Peace: and if I am proud of anything in it, it is that Providence has been pleased to direct things so, that the Public Measures have, in many cases, come up to what I foresaw, was the *only means* of our safety.

If I have said the same thing with our late *Votes*, *Speeches*, and *Proclamations*, in my Observations on the pretended danger of the Church: it is not only an honour to me, that Her Majesty and the Parliament repeat almost my very words; but it is a glorious testimony to the Truth, that it leads all persons that sincerely follow it, to the same conclusions, and often the same expression. And I glory that I have such a voucher to what I said, viz., "That the false clamours of plots against the Church appear to be formed on purpose to conceal real plots against the Church of England." *Review* No. 86. *p.* 341 [of Vol. II. of the 20th September, 1705].

Let none of the well-wishers to Peace be angry that I saw this before them. It is their happiness they see it now! Envy no man!

But I have a most undeniable testimony of the success of this Paper in the great work of National Peace, in the implacable rage and malice of the Hot Party: in which, they witness to the hurt this Paper hath done to their cause; and they have my humble acknowledgement that they can do me and this Labour no greater honour.

It would be endless to me, and tiresome to the Reader, to repeat the threatening letters, the speeches, the opprobrious terms, the Bear-Garden insulting language I have, daily, thrown upon me, in all parts, for persuading men to Peace. If I had been assassinated as often as I have been threatened with pistols, daggers, and swords; I had long ago paid dear for this Undertaking!

But I go naked [*without arms*] and unguarded. These Gentlemen are harmless enemies. They are like Colonel L[ ]'s Sergeant at S[ ]ld; that, while I was there, said not a word to me; but as soon as I was gone, was for doing terrible things to me, when he could find me! Or like Justice S[ ]D of Devonshire, that issued his *Warrant* for me, and caused all the houses in the town to be searched except that he knew I lodged in; and sent to every part of the country [*county*] for me, but that to which he knew I was gone.

I remark nothing, from these passages, so much as the weak grounds these people know they have, for their resentment. Is it possible a man can merit so much ill will for persuading men to Peace? Were it not that their designs being from another place, and of another kind; the heavenly glorious spirit of Peace is particularly hateful and unpleasant to them.

Well, Gentlemen, so the Peace be wrought; let what will become of me, I am unsolicitous! and, blessed be GOD! it *is effectually wrought*! The victory is gained, the battle is over, and I have done!

Why did I solicit to have all cavilling Papers suppressed? Not that we have not the better of the argument in every case; for really the adverse Party have nothing to say! And as I had not begun this Paper but with a prospect of a justifiable necessity; so the work being over, the necessity ceases; and, lo, I return to the matter I was on before; and the writing of and persuading to Peace ends with the Volume, because the thing is obtained. The nation embraces Peace with a universal joy, and there remains now no more occasion to persuade.

How easy, how satisfied, how pleased does all the nation appear! Peace and joy sit on the faces of our people. Not one man that has any regard for, or sense of the Public Good but rejoices at it! How people congratulate one another! and bless the Time! the Queen! the Government! and every instrument of this extraordinary Turn of Affairs!

What glory has this happy conjunction brought to Her Majesty's reign! From this time, the nation will take the date of her new prosperity! and the reign of this Queen, like that of Queen ELIZABETH, will be ranked in history, among those of the most fortunate of the nation! Nor can Posterity do Her Majesty justice, if they do not own that this universal happiness has had its rise in the Court. The Queen has not only the honour, but Her Majesty has been really the Instrument of this peace! and would our wiser Hot Party have given due regard to Her Majesty's exhortations, this peace had been brought to pass a great while sooner.

We have had formerly, a great struggle between Court Party and Country Party; and always saw cause to suspect the former of encroaching on our liberties: but the case is quite contrary here. Her Majesty so espouses the real Interest of her people, and obliges all that depend on her service to do so; that Patriots are our Courtiers, the Prince's favourites are the People's favourites, and our safety is now found in them we used always to be afraid of. Such effects have wise Princes upon their affairs, that *regis ad exemplum*, the Crown shall be the People's Saviour, and the Men of Rights and Privileges become the Men of Oppression and Confusions.

May our sense of this Peace, and of Her Majesty's care of the privileges and properties of subjects continually increase! that the Obligation [*see p.* 77] to such a Princess may sink deep in the minds of these people, and they may follow those exhortations to Union and Peace, which Her Majesty exhorts to encourage, and has had such success in attempting.

This Volume is now ended. Those Gentlemen that think this Work useful enough to deserve binding it, have herewith an Index of the particulars for their convenience.

I shall be very glad our Peace may be so settled that, in future Ages, there may be no occasion to make these Papers further useful. *DE FOE.*

ADVERTISEMENT.

The Gentlemen who were pleased to be Subscribers for the encouragement of this Work, in spite of all the banters and reproaches of the Town; *if they please to send to Mr.* MATTHEWS, *may have the Volume of this past year delivered them* gratis, *printed upon the fine paper.*

Preface to the Third Volume of the Review.

[1706.]

IT HAS been the misfortune of this Paper, among all the other rubs it has had in its way, that the Volumes have been a little too much depending upon one another.

Such has been the Course of the Subject, the length of the Circumstance then on foot, or the absence of the Author, that the Story and the Book have not brought their periods to jump exactly. Thus it was in the last Volume, which broke off in the middle of the great Undertaking which the Author, at the utmost hazard, went through, in pressing this nation to Peace, and warning them against a sort of people, then known by the names of Tackers and Tories.

And thus it is now, when pursuing the same general good of his native country, the Author has embarked in the great affair of the Union of Britain.

I must confess I have sometimes thought it very hard, that having voluntarily, without the least direction, resistance, or encouragement (in spite of all that has been suggested), taken upon me the most necessary work of removing national prejudices against the two most capital blessings of the World, Peace and Union; I should have the disaster to have the nations receive the Doctrine, and damn the Teacher. That even those that have owned the truth of what has been said, and even the seasonableness of saying it, have nevertheless flown in the face of the Instrument: endeavouring to break the poor earthen vessel, by which the rich treasure (viz. the Knowledge of their own Happiness) has been conveyed.

Indeed, I cannot but complain! and should I descend to particulars, it would hardly appear credible that in a Christian, a Protestant, Reformed nation, any man could receive such treatment, as I have done, from even those very people whose consciences and judgements have stooped to the venerable Truth; and owned it has been useful, serviceable, and seasonable.

It would make this *Preface* a History, to relate the

reproaches, the insults, the contempt with which these Papers have been treated, in discourse, writing, and print; even by those that say they are embarked in the same Cause, and pretend to write for the same Public Good.

The charge made against me, of partiality, of bribery, of pensions and payments: a thing, the circumstances, family, and fortunes of a man devoted to his country's peace, clears me of.

If paid, Gentlemen! for writing, if hired, if employed; why still harassed with merciless and malicious men? why pursued to all extremities by Law for old accounts, which you clear other men of, every day? why oppressed, distressed, and driven from his family; and from all his prospects of delivering them or himself? Is this the fate of men employed and hired? Is this the figure, the agents of Courts and Princes make?

Certainly, had I been hired or employed, those people that own the service [*employed me*] would, by this time, have set their servant free from the little and implacable malice of litigious prosecutions, murdering *Warrants*, and men whose mouths are to be stopped by trifles.

Let this suffice, then, to clear me of all the little and scandalous charge, of being hired and employed.

I come next to examine what testimonies I have of this Work being my proper employ. For some of our good friends, whose Censure runs before their Charity, attack me with this. "*Ay, it is true! These things are so: but what has he to do to meddle with it? What has he to do, to examine the conduct of Parliament men, or exhort the People to this or that?*"

Wise Gentlemen, in truth, pray go on with it! "*Sirs, ay, it is true, he did happen to see a house just on fire: but what had he to do to make a noise, wake all the neighbourhood, fright*[*en*] *their children, and like a busy fellow, cry* "Fire!" *in the night! It was none of his neighbourhood! He had ne'er a house there! What business had he to meddle?*"

Or to put it another way. "*Ay, indeed, he did happen to see a parcel of rogues breaking up a Gentleman's house in the night; but what business had he to go and raise the country* [county] *upon them! cry "Thieves!" and "Murder!" and I know not what! and so bring a parcel of poor fellows to the gallows! What business had he with it? It was none of his house!*"

Truly, Gentlemen, this is just the case. I saw a parcel of people caballing together to ruin Property, corrupt the Laws, invade the Government, debauch the People; and in short, enslave and embroil the Nation: and I cried "Fire!" or rather, I cried "Water!" for the fire was begun already. I saw all the nation running into confusions, and directly flying in the face of one another, and cried out "Peace!" I called upon all sorts of people that had any senses, to collect them together and judge for themselves, what they were going to do; and excited them to lay hold of the madmen, and take from them the wicked weapon, the knife; with which they were going to destroy their mother! rip up the bowels of their country! and at last effectually ruin themselves!

And what had I to do with this? Why, yes, Gentlemen, I had the same right as every man that has a footing in his country, or that has a posterity to possess Liberty and claim Right, must have: viz., as far as possible to preserve the Laws, Liberty, and Government of that country to which he belongs. And he that charges me with meddling in what does not concern me, meddles himself with what, it is plain he does not understand.

Well, through all the maltreatment of both friends and enemies, I have hitherto, undiscouraged by the worst circumstances, unrewarded and unsupported, pursued the first design of pressing all people that have any regard for the Interest of Religion, the honour of their country, and the good of posterity, to come to a Temper about Party strifes! to shorten their disputes! encourage calmness! and revive the old Christian principle of *Love to one another*.

I shall not boast here of my success. Let the rage and implacable hatred against me, conceived by the enemies of this healing principle; let the confessions of those who reap the benefit and own the service, though they abandon and despise the Instrument; let these be my witnesses! and these shall testify for me, that I have not been an unprofitable servant to anybody but myself! and of that, I am entirely regardless in this case.

From the same zeal with which I first pursued this blessed subject of Peace, I found myself embarked in the farther extent of it, I mean, THE UNION. If I thought myself obliged, in duty to the Public Interest, to use my utmost endeavour to quiet the minds of enraged Parties; I found myself under a stronger necessity to embark in the same design, between too much enraged Nations.

As to the principle, from which I have acted, I shall leave to the issues of Time, to determine whether it has been sincere or not? Hypocrites only make use of masks and false lights to conceal present reserved designs: Truth and Sincerity only dare appeal to Time and Consequences.

I covet no better testimony of the well-laid design of these Sheets, than that evidence Time and farther light into Truth shall discover!

I saw the Union of the two Kingdoms begun. I saw the principle, on which both sides seemed to act, look with a different face, from what was ever made use of before. All the former treaties looked like Politic Shams, mere Amusements and frauds to draw in and deceive the people: while Commissioners met, little qualified and less inclined to the General Good of the whole.

But now I thought I foresaw the success of the Treaty in the temper, sincerity, and inclinations of the Treaters on both sides. They came together furnished for the work, convinced fully of the advantages on both sides of it, and blessed with sincere intentions to bring it to pass.

When I saw this, I thought it my duty to do my part without doors. And I know no part I could act, in my sphere, so natural, so useful, and so proper to the work, as to attempt to remove the National Prejudices, which both peoples, by the casualty of time, and the errors, industry, and malice of Parties, had too eagerly taken up, and were too tenacious of, one against another.

To this purpose, I wrote two Essays against national prejudices in England [*An Essay at removing National Prejudices against a Union with Scotland.* Part I. published on 4th May, and Part II. on 28th May, 1706], while the Treaty was in agitation there: and four more in Scotland, while it was debating in Scotland by the Parliament there: the contents of all which are repeated in this Paper.

Nor did I think my time or labour ill bestowed to take a long, tedious, and hazardous journey thither; or to expose myself to a thousand insults, scoffs, rabbles, and tumults; to all manner of despiteful and injurious treatment; if possible, to bring the people there to their senses, and free them from the unreasonable prejudices they had entertained against the prosperity of their country.

And having seen the Treaty happily ratified there, with some few amendments, which I hope are not considerable; I thought this a proper period to close this Volume, which had already run beyond its usual bounds: and the next Volume will begin at the Parliament of England entering upon the Treaty; where I hope, it shall meet with better treatment than it has met with in Scotland, and a better reception with the people.

If it shall be my lot to live to see this Treaty finished, I think to venture one Essay at the General and Reciprocal Duties of the two Nations, one to another. In which, I shall endeavour to move England, to engage Scotland with all the acts of kindness and all the advantages which can be desired in reason, in order to plant and cultivate the new relation of the two kingdoms: and on the other hand, to move Scotland to entertain no jealousies, nor be anxious about anything, without great reason and good ground, as the only way to bring about the general peace of both Kingdoms, and settle the doubtful minds of the people on both sides.

This I hope I shall pursue with an equality of arguments on both sides, without partiality or affection to one more than another: and in *that*, shew that the original of my concerning myself in this matter, was merely to be serviceable, if possible, to both Kingdoms, and to the united body in general.

I doubt not, however, but I shall give offence in this too! For there are a people in the world who are not to be pleased with anything! But I shall content myself, in pursuing what is the true end of Union, the flourishing of Peace, and the equalities on every hand, in matters of Advantage, Liberty, Religion, and Trade.

I am very sensible all coalitions without this, will render the Union still imperfect and ineffectual. The Union will never have its full perfection of extent, nor will either nation reap the benefit of it, till it becomes a Union of Affection and a Union of Interest.

This is my business: and let the enemies of GOD and the Nation's Peace be as angry as they please, this is what I shall pursue to the uttermost! This Volume ends with it! the next will begin with it! and those that cry, "It is too long, and it is nothing but what has been heard before!" must bear with the prolixity of the Author, till they please to shorten the occasion.

Whenever they please to lay aside their spirit of division, anger, malice, wrath, strife, &c.; when they leave off raising unnecessary heats about scruples and trifles, merely to divide, not to inform; when National Prejudices on either side cease, and I can see the least prospect of a Calm among the men of cavil and continual objection: I shall be the first that shall cease calling upon them to Peace. But till then, the tautology is in the Crime, not in the Reprover: and I shall not fail to alarm them on all occasions.

Preface to the Fourth Volume of the Review.

[1708.]

I HAVE been so loth to interrupt the discourse of Public Things, that I have run this Volume to an unusual length: but there is a necessity of ending it here.

I shall make no scruple to tell you, I think this Volume the best qualified to inform the readers of the Affair on the north side of Britain; of anything at least that I have written. I was not unsensible, when I entered on the particulars of the Union, that it would cloy the wandering humour of this Age; who hate to dwell upon a thing, though of never so great moment: nay, so eager are they to see novelty, that when they are best pleased with a subject in its beginning, yet they will never have patience to hear it out.

However, I was content to hear the readers of this Paper cry, "It was dull!"; see them throw it by, without reading; and hear them say, "He preaches so long on the Union, because he has nothing else to say." And, in short, all manner of contempt has been thrown upon it, not because the Affair of the Union was not worth recording; nor was it, in itself, useless: but Union! Union! nothing but Union! for four months together, glutted their fancy, and palled the modishness of the Town's humour. And so the poor *Review* lost its faculty of pleasing you.

And now I am to tell you, that I value this Volume for that very thing, for which it lost so much of the common opinion. Nor is this value I put upon it, merely my own. I have the approbation of that valuable Few, whose judgement I have reason to esteem, and with which I am abundantly contented.

The former Volumes pleased the Readers of the Day better than this; and this will please the Readers of Futurity better than they: and thus what I lost in the Shire, I shall find in the Hundred; and I am very well contented.

I am not going about to panegyric upon my own Work in this: but to answer some of the innumerable cavils, which generally attack me in every thing I do. And this is one.

"What does this fellow pretend to!" says a Warm Gentleman, with a band on, at a public coffee-house not far from Newgate street; "he has been in Scotland this twelvemonth, and he pretends to write a Paper in London! What can he say to anything, either in its time, or to any purpose?"

Really, Gentlemen, I was under the inconvenience of distance of place; and suffered some reproach which could not be avoided: particularly when a *Review* was published making some conjectures about the Siege of Toulon; and, in spite of a person's care who pretended to revise it, that very Paper was printed the next post after the news arrived that the siege was raised. But though, by the negligence of the person I depended upon to repair that defect which my distance occasioned, I fell into that misfortune: yet, Gentlemen, the guesses at, and inferences from the affair of Toulon which I, too unhappily, appeared right in, might very well atone for that slip; and does do so, in the eyes of all friendly remarkers.

How I was treated in the affair of that siege; how insulted by *Observators* and *Rehearsers*, for my suggesting you would be balked in that design; how charged with directing the enemy, for telling you what they would do, though some of it was after it was done: I need not remind you of. I reflect on it with this satisfaction, that when the Town saw

I had but made too right a judgement, and their wagers of 70 guineas to receive 100, gave me an opportunity to upbraid their blind conclusions in my turn, and use them as they deserved: I yet forbore it, and shewed them I knew how to receive ill usage without returning it.

And after all this, I must tell you, it is none of the easiest things in the World, to write a Paper to come out three times a week among you; and perhaps be liable to more censure and ill usage also, than other Papers are, and yet, at the same time, reside for sixteen months together, at almost four hundred miles distance from London, and sometimes at more.

The Volume is now ended, and the next begins with a new scene of Affairs. This tells you much of your behaviour to your brethren of North Britain, upon your uniting with them: the next will tell you something of their usage of you, after this Union.

The French have made an Attempt on them [*the attempted invasion of Scotland, by a fleet from Dunkirk, under* FOURBIN, *in March*, 1708]; and we are yet in suspense concerning the issue of that affair. I must own, considering the circumstances of that part of Britain, I have often wondered they had not done it sooner: and had they made but the like shew of an invasion, whether they completed it or not, in the time of the Treaty and Parliament, the last year [1707]; I think I may safely tell you, either the Union had been made with more unanimity, or never made at all.

After all, I am free to say, if the French are disappointed in the present Attempt they are making on that country, the benefit to Scotland will be worth all the fright, expense, and fatigue it has put us to: for it has made a great progress in discovering faces, and turning some people inside out. You have now an opportunity to separate sheep and goats; and to distinguish between dissatisfied Presbyterians and dissatisfied Episcopal Dissenters. How one, though discontented at circumstances, is hearty and stedfast to the Foundation; the other, though openly quiet and seemingly passive, yet is apparently hatching destruction to the Establishment, both Civil and Sacred.

I have given you no *Index* to this Volume, as a thing which the subject of it does not so naturally require.

In my next, I have begun, to make one part of the Work

to contain a kind of History of Fact; I mean as far as relates to the present Affair in Scotland: and though it may look as if I invaded the News-Writer's province, yet I believe the issue will prove it otherwise. Most of what I shall communicate to you, being by Hands they cannot converse with, and on a subject which they cannot acquaint you of.

I should make some apology for the length of this Volume, which I know is some charge to the Collectors of it, but I know no better excuse to make for it, than by assuring you, if I live to finish any more, they shall be of a shorter extent: and to Amend an error, is Confession and Reformation best put together. Your humble servant, *D. F.*

Volumes of this Work on the fine paper, will be ready next Week, to be delivered to those Gentlemen, gratis, *who were pleased to be Subscribers to the Author at his first undertaking* [*it*].

J. MATTHEWS.

Preface to the Fifth Volume of the Review.

[1709.]

THE Fifth Volume having now run a full year, two reasons oblige me to put an end to it.

1. The usual bulk of the book requiring it, and
2. The request of some Gentlemen in Scotland: who have, by their own voluntary subscription encouraged the reprinting it at Edinburgh; and being to begin at this Quarter, have desired that the Volume and their subscription may go on together.

It has been customary to add a *Preface* to every Volume; which, though placed at the beginning, is written, as this is, at the end of the Work.

The great variety, this Work has gone through, gives indeed room for a large *Preface*: but I shall reduce it to a shorter compass than usual.

The Author having been in Scotland, at the time of finishing the Union there [1706—1707]; the last Volume and this are taken up, in many parts of them, with that Affair.

At first, the novelty of the Union took up everybody's thoughts, and the Town was delighted to hear the disputed points, as they went on: but Novelty, this Age's whore, debauching their taste, as soon as they had fed on the Shell of the Union, they were satisfied; and the *Review* entering into the Substance of it—they grew palled and tired.

Like an honest Country Gentleman, who hearing his Minister preach most excellently on the subject of Eternal Blessedness, applauded him up to the skies, for his first sermon. The good man thinking it was useful as well as acceptable, or indeed thinking it would be useful because it was acceptable, went on with the subject. But the Gentleman was observed to sleep all the while.

It happened that a stranger coming to his house, and going to Church with him, was exceedingly taken with the admirable Discourse of the Minister: and praising him to the Gentleman, asked him with freedom, "How he could sleep, while he was upon such a sublime subject, and handled it so admirably well?"

"Why, truly," says he, "I was mightily pleased with it, for the first sermon or two. But I hate a story that is long a telling!"

And indeed, Gentlemen, it is too true in practice. One reason why your Ministers are no more acceptable, and their Preaching no more minded, is this very thing. This *Story of Heaven is so long a telling*, you hate to hear of it! But that by the by.

And just thus it was with the *Review*. The people would take up the Paper, and read two or three lines in it, and find it related to Scotland and the Union, and throw it away. "Union! Union! this fellow can talk of nothing but Union! I think he will never have done with this Union! He is grown mighty dull, of late!"

And yet, Gentlemen, give me leave to tell you, you have hardly learnt to understand the Union all this while. The truth of the case is this. *The story is good*, but *it is too long a telling*. You hate a long story! The palate is glutted. Novelty is the food you lust after: and if the story were of Heaven, you will be cloyed with the length of it.

Now, Gentlemen, the Author takes the liberty to tell you, he knew (though distant) the general dislike, and he knew the disease of your reading appetite. And though, at other times, he has laboured to please you by variety, and diverting subjects: yet he found this Affair so necessary, so useful, and (with some few good judgements) so desirable, that he chose to be called "dull" and "exhausted," he ventured the general censure of the Town Critics, to pursue the subject. And ventures to tell you, that, among those people whose opinion is past any man's contempt, these Two Volumes pass for the most useful of the Five: and I cannot but join my assent to it. The Bookseller [*publisher*] also gives a testimony to the truth of this, by an observation particular to the trade, viz., that of these Two Volumes fewer have been sold in single sheets, but twice the number in Volumes of any of the former.

Nor has it been without its testimony abroad, since the application of the Author, in this volume especially, to the real work of Uniting the Hearts of these two Nations, who have so lately joined Hands, has been received by our brethren of North Britain, as so profitable, so honest, and so needful a Work, that they have desired the reprinting it at Edinburgh, in order to its being seen throughout Scotland, and have voluntarily subscribed a sufficient sum for the expense of it.

Unhappy to you in England, is the inference I draw from hence, viz.:

That it seems, you Gentlemen in England were more solicitous to bring the Scots into a Union, than you are to pursue the vital principles of that Union, now it is made. I mean Union of Affection, and Union of Interests; in which alone, the happiness of both Kingdoms consists.

I must confess, and I speak it to your reproach! the temper you shewed of Uniting, when first you put the wheels to work to form the Union, seemed to me quite different from what you shew, now it is done. As if, your politic ends being answered, you were diligent to *discover* that you did not unite from any true design of General Good, but for your Private Advantage only. Thus you seem now united to Scotland, but not one jot more united to the Scots nation.

And do not call this a slander, Gentlemen! For I can give you but too many instances of it, though I spare you for the present: my desire being to heal, not exasperate.

But this I cannot omit. How have you permitted insolent scribblers to abuse, reproach, and insult the Established

Church of Scotland! slander the very nation! and insult her Judicatories in print! even while the very Parliament of Britain is sitting. And yet the Laws have not been executed in that behalf, nor the Legislative Authority been pleased to give that discouragement to it, that, in case of the Established Church of England being so treated, has frequently been done; and, I believe, would have been done.

I speak not to prompt any private man's persecution. My design is not to punish persons, but to prevent the practice.

But, with all humble deference to the Parliament of Britain now sitting, and whose care and concern the Church of Scotland is, and ought to be, equally with the Church of England; I crave their leave to ask this question.

If the Government and Discipline, if the Doctrine and Worship, if the Judicatories and Authority of the Church of Scotland (which, by the Union, are legally established; and are the care of the whole nation to support) shall be trampled under foot, reproached, slandered and insulted, be libelled and falsely accused in public and in print; without due resentment and legal prosecution: and, at the same, the same liberty with the Church of England is not taken; or if taken, is not allowed, but censured and prosecuted—HOW THEN do the subjects of both Kingdoms enjoy equal privileges? And if you do not permit the subjects of both Kingdoms to enjoy equal privileges; how then is the Union made more and more effectual? as has been frequently proposed to be done in our British Parliament.

I hope there is nothing bolder in this, than may consist with Reason, with Truth, with Justice, and with due Respect.

I may seem by some to reflect in this, on the Parliament's treating a late Paper concerning the *Sacramental Test*: but I have not my eye that way. I doubt not, but when GOD's time is come, when Dissenters are less easy in Compliance, and the Church of England's charity less straitened in Imposition; I doubt not, I say, but even the Church herself will take that yoke from the necks of her brethren, and cast it away, as too unchristian! too near akin to persecution! and too much a prostituting the Sacred to the Profane, to consist either with her reputation, her Interest, or her principles!

We have a great cry here, in matters of Trade, of late, against Monopolies and Exclusive Companies. I wish these

Gentlemen, who are making an Exclusive Company of the Church, and a Monopoly of Religion, would remember that these things are what they themselves will, one day, cast off as a deformity in practice, and a deviation from the great Rule of original Charity. But of this hereafter.

I shall end this *Preface* with this short remark on the Work in general. The title is, *A Review of the State of the British Nation*. I cannot pursue this Title, and make the outside and inside agree, unless I always plainly animadvert upon everything, on either side, which appears inconsistent with you all, as a British Nation: that is, as an united Nation.

I have been a witness to the great Transaction of the Union. I know the warmth with which England pursued it. I know the difficulty with which Scotland complied with it. I acknowledge, it lies upon England, to convince the Scots that when they opposed it, they stood in their own light, and opposed their own Wealth, Freedom, Safety and Prosperity: and this can only be done by endeavouring to assist them in Trade, encouraging them in Improvements, supporting them in their just Liberties, and taking off their ancient chains of bondage.

And if this be omitted, you must expect to be told of it, by this Author, as long as he has a tongue to speak or a hand to write, whether it shall please you, or provoke you.

D. F.

The Preface to the Sixth Volume of the Review.

[1710.]

I AM now come to the conclusion of the Sixth Volume of this Work: though like a teeming woman, I have thought every Volume should be the last. Where it will end now, and when; God only knows! and time only will discover. As for me, I know nothing of it!

This particular Paper, though written at the end of the Work, carries the title of the *Preface*, more because it is placed by the bookseller at the frontispiece, than that it is anything of an Introduction to the

Volume: for it is really written at the close of the whole, and its subject is very particular.

We have had a most distracting turbulent time for the last two months of this year, occasioned by the Prosecution and Defence of a High Flying Clergyman [*Doctor* SACHEVERELL] who has undertaken, in the teeth of the very Parliament, as well as of the Nation, to justify and defend the exploded ridiculous doctrine of Non-Resistance.

This Defence has been carried on with all possible heat, fury, and violence among the Party, and a strong conjunction of Papist, Jacobite, and High-Church madmen has appeared in it, which has made them seem very formidable to the World. Rabbles, tumults, plundering houses, destroying Meeting-houses; insulting Gentlemen in the streets, and honest men in their dwellings, have been the necessary appendices of this Affair.

And, after all, I must own, though the man has been condemned, his Principles censured, and his *Sermon* burnt; yet it has not been without most fatal consequences over the whole nation: as it has revived the heats, feuds, and animosities which were among us, and which, by the blessed example and exhortation of Her Majesty, began to be laid asleep in the nation.

I have been endeavouring to shew you the mischief of these tumults, the bloody designs of the persons that have raised them, and how they have differed from all that went before them. I have given you instances of their most villanous designs, such as rifling the Bank, demolishing the Meeting-houses, and murdering the [Dissenting] Ministers: all which they openly professed to be their design. GOD deliver this Nation from the pernicious effect of the present fermentation, which we are now generally in on all sides!

I have, however, faithfully discharged, what I thought myself obliged to, as a debt to Peace and in duty to the present Constitution, *to speak plainly* in these cases, whatever risk I ran, and at whatever hazard these Truths are to be told. I have not been afraid "to bear my testimony" as some call it, to the Liberties of Britain, against the reviving mischiefs of tyranny: and have, in the midst of all your mobs and rabbles, openly declared Non-Resistance to be damned by Parliament; and English (now British) Liberty to be built upon the Foundation of the *Claim of RIGHT*, and of the Revolution; of which the Protestant Succession, *which sets by, the more immediate heirs*, is the great exemplication. The great King WILLIAM was the Re-edifier of the Building, the collective Body of the People were the great and happy Original, and the Union is the Topstone.

I am none of those that boast of their adventures, and love to tell long stories of the dangers they run. I am not always to be frighted with threatening letters and shams of assassinations. I ever thought those people that talk so much of killing folks, never do it! Though I am none of those you call Fighting Fellows: yet I am none of those that are afraid to see themselves die! and I may, I hope, without being taxed with vanity, profess not to practise Non-Resistance.

I have by me, about fifteen letters, from Gentlemen of more anger than honour, who have faithfully promised me to come and kill me by such and such a day: nay, and some have descended to tell me the very manner. Yet not one of them has been so good as his word.

Once I had the misfortune to come into a room, where five Gentlemen had been killing me a quarter of an hour *in their way*! and yet, to the reproach of their villanous design, as well as of their courage, durst not, all together, own it to a poor naked [*unarmed*] single man that gave them opportunity enough, and whom they had too much in their power. In short, I here give my testimony from my own experience, and I note it for the instruction of the five assassins above, that their Cause is villanous! and that makes the Party cowardly. A man, that has any honour in him, is really put to more difficulty how to speak, than how to act! In the case of murders and assassinations, he is straitened between the extremes of shewing too much courage, or too much fear.

Should I tell the World the repeated cautions given me by friends, not to appear! not to walk the streets! not to shew myself! letters sent me, to bid me remember Sir EDMUNDBURY GODFREY, JOHN TUTCHIN, and the like; I must talk myself up for a mad man that dares go abroad! Should I let you know, how I have been three times beset, and waylaid for the mischief designed, but that still I live; you would wonder what I mean!

For my part, I firmly believe, the villains that insulted

honest SUTHERLAND's house, robbed and frighted his wife, and with naked swords bullied the poor woman, threatening that they would murder her husband whenever they met him! knew well enough he was not at home, and never will meet him when he is.

Wherefore, my brief resolution is this. I, while I live, they may be assured, I shall never desist doing my duty, in exposing the doctrines that oppose GOD and the Revolution; such as Passive Submission to tyrants, and Non-Resistance in cases of oppression; if the gentlemen, being at a loss for arguments, are resolved to better their cause by violence and blood, I leave the issue to GOD's Providence! and must do as well with them as I can.

As to defence, I have had some thoughts to stay at home in the night, and by day to wear a piece of armour on my back. The first, because I am persuaded, these murderers will not do their work by daylight; and the second, because I firmly believe, they will never attempt it so fairly, to my face, as to give occasion of armour anywhere else.

I confess, there may be some reasons for me to apprehend this Wicked Party, and therefore, as, I thank GOD! I am without a disturbing fear, so I am not perfectly secure, or without caution. The reasons are such as these:

That truly assassination and murder is something more suitable to the High-Flying Cause, and has been more in use among their Party, than in other cases, and with other people. It is the Cause of Tyranny, and Tyranny always leads to Blood! Oppression goes hand-in-hand with Violence; and he that would invade my Liberty, will invade my Life, as he has opportunity! And had their rabble got a little more head, we might have come again into the laudable practice of cutting of throats, and cold blood murders—and by the same rule, their downfall being so apparent, this desperate cure may be thought needful to their desperate cause.

But I cannot see, why they should be so exasperated at the poor *Review*, "a sorry despised Author," to use the words of one of their Party, whom nobody gives heed to.

Well, Gentlemen, then let your anger be pointed at some more significant animal, that is more capable to wound you! And do not own this author to be so considerable as to engage your resentment, lest you prove the unanswerable force of what he says, by the concern you are at to suppress him. What will the World say to this way of dealing? You should first answer the argument! that is the best way of murdering the author! To kill him first, is to own you could not answer him. If your doctrine of Non-Resistance will subsist, if it will uphold itself! You have advantage enough; writing against it will be of no force! even the House of Commons must fall before it! for Truth will prevail. But if not, if this Author, and all that open their mouths against it, were to be sacrificed by your impious hands, Truth would never want champions to defend it against this absurd error. And killing the *Review* would be like cutting off the monster's head, when a hundred rise up in the room of it.

Upon these accounts, I go on perfectly easy, as to the present threats I daily meet with from this cowardly and abominable Party. If I am attacked by multitude, I must fall; as ABNER fell, before wicked men. If I am fairly and honourably attacked, I hope I shall fairly resist; for I shall never practise the notion I condemn, and every honest man ought to go prepared for a villain.

This, though it is irksome to me to say, and no man that fights loves to talk of it; yet I thought it proper for me to let you all see, that I have my share of this High-Church Mob. And that whatever may happen to me, the World may know whence it comes.

I might, and ought indeed to speak a word or two to three Gentlemen, besides those mentioned before, who have been pleased personally to threaten my life—with abundance of preambles and justification of themselves about it. What I shall say to them is, I shall demonstrate my being perfectly unconcerned at the matter, by refusing the advice given me, even by their own friends, of binding them to the peace. It seems a little unnatural to me, and what I shall never practise, to go to law with a man for beating me, much less for threatening me: and least of all, when the persons are such harmless creatures as these! Wherefore, all the Answer I shall give them is this, with the utmost contempt of their folly, *The cur that barks is not the cur that bites!*

These things regard particular men, and I know, the

persons will understand me when they read it. I assure you, it is in courtesy to them, that I bury their folly, by concealing their names.

Upon the whole, as I am going on in what I esteem my duty, and for the Public Good, I firmly believe, it will not please GOD to deliver me up to this bloody and ungodly Party; and therefore I go on freely in what is before me, and shall still go on to detect and expose a vicious Clergy, and a bigoted race of the people, in order to reclaim and reform them, or to open the eyes of the good People of Britain, that they may not be imposed upon by them: and whether in this work I meet with Punishment or Praise, Safety or Hazard, Life or Death, *Te Deum Laudamus.*

Your humble servant, D. F.

Preface to the Seventh Volume of the Review.

[1711.]

CONTRARY to many people's hopes, and some expectations; this Work has happily arrived at the end of the Seventh Volume.

When Posterity shall revise the several sheets, and see what Turn of Times have happened! what Parties! what fury! what passions have reigned! how the Author of this Paper has treated them all! and they, him! it may add something to their wonder, how either this Writing has been supported, or the Author left alive to shew his face in the world.

I have sometimes thought it hard, that while I endeavour so manifestly to steer the Middle Channel between all Parties; and press either side to pursue, at least preferably to their private prospects, the Public Interest: I should be maltreated by any! much more, that I should be so, by both Sides!

But so shall it fare with any man that will not run into

the same excess of riot with any People. For my part, I have always thought the only true Fundamental Maxim of Politics that will ever make this nation happy is this, *That the Government ought to be of no Party at all.* Would this Ministry [*Lord* OXFORD'S], or any Ministry that shall succeed them, pursue this principle; they would make themselves immortal! and without it, they will be mere annuals, that die with the return of the season, and must be planted anew. Had the Ministries of the last twenty, nay, I may say of the last fifty years [1661-1711], practised this; we had had no Revolution! no invasions of Liberty! no abdications! no turnings in and turnings out, at least not, in general, once in an Age.

Statesmen are the nation's Guardians. Their business is not to make Sides, divide the nation into Parties, and draw the factions into battle array against one another. Their work ought to be to scatter and disperse Parties, as they would Tumults; and to keep a balance among the interfering Interests of the nation, with the same care as they would the civil Peace.

But Interest and ambition are to a Court, what fevers are to the body. They give a nation no rest, while Putting Out or Putting In is the word. Faction, like the wind and the tide, when they run counter, will ever be heaving and setting, now this way, now that way: and that people or that Government which are subjected to the power of that Motion, shall be sure to have just as much rest as the sea, and no more!

This makes Government change hands, Favourites rise and fall, Favour shift sides, and Parties take their turns in the State as the sailors at the helm, spell and spell. This makes the Ministry and Council, ay, and Parliaments too! to be to-day of one side, and to-morrow of another! and the poor distracted people turn their tales and their coats, and their faces, and their religion so often, that no man knows his neighbour any longer than this or that Party which is uppermost, discovers him.

Nay, such is the influence, or contagion rather, of this mischief, that *all* things partake of the Division of the State. It reaches even to our eating and drinking. This is called "loyal," that "fanatic" liquor; this "Protestant," that

"Popish" cheer; this "High Church" ale, that "Low Church" ale. And you shall not meet with a pack of hounds now, after a hare, but you may hear the huntsmen cry, "Hark, Tory!" to him, "High Church" to another, "Pox of that Whig! He is a mere cur! He always cries it false! He'll ne'er be a staunch hound!"

I remember my grandfather had a huntsman that used the same familiarity with his dogs: and he had his "Round Head" and his "Cavalier," his "Goring" and his "Waller." All the Generals of both armies were hounds in his pack. Till the times turning, the old gentleman was fain to scatter the pack; and make them up of more dog-like surnames.

And where shall we say this will end? Or when shall we have a Ministry with eyes in their heads? I thought long ago, the Variety of Parties that we have seen in this nation had exhausted the Fund of Faction: but hell is deep, and the supply as bottomless as the Pit they flow from. And as long as faction feeds the flame, we shall never want Billingsgate to revile one another with.

In such an Age as this, has the Author of this Paper wrote, for now seven years together. He has cried "Peace!" "Peace!"; but it will not be, till that great Voice that said to the ocean *Peace, be still!* shall speak to the Parties here, with the same commanding voice. That Voice, to whom to command is to cause himself to be obeyed; and to say and to do are the same thing.

It is in vain to oppose the Stream of Parties! when they turn like the first shot of the ebb, they run sharp, and they bear down all before them. An instance of this, we have had in the late elections [*Autumn of* 1710]; the tumults and riots of which were indeed insufferable. And how strange is it to look back upon them? What was the language of the day? "A new Ministry!" "A new Parliament!" "Down with the Whigs!"

Well, all this was done: but what then? "Down with the Dissenters!" "D——n the Presbyterians!" "Confound the Low Church!" "Make peace with France!" and so on, even to bringing in the Pretender. And for a man to tell them of Moderate Measures, of Peace, of Temper, and of Toleration, had been to raise the mob about one's ears.

Often, this Paper took the freedom to tell them, they

would be soberer in time! that when they came to Parliament and Cabinets, and to handle the Management, they would talk another language! that Money was a Low Churchman; Credit, born of Whig parents, and learned to dance at a Whig dancing school; that Government was the Firstborn of Moderation, and took such a fright at the late Civil Wars [1640-1660], that she always fell into fits upon the least fermentation of her blood. I told them, they would all turn Whigs, when they came to *act*.

Well, they laughed at me! scolded at me! cursed me! and *both* Sides used me according to their custom of treating those that dare speak Truth to them.

Yet it was not a month after this, but the Parliament came together [25 *Nov.* 1710], and what then?

Why, then it was, "We will maintain the peace and quiet of the nation, by discouraging tumults and rabbles! We will support the Queen against all her enemies. We will carry on the war against France! We will pay the public debts! We will uphold the Credit! and for our fellow Christians, and fellow subjects, the Dissenters; we will, &c."

"D——n them all!" said a High Flyer, that looked for other things, when he read the Commons' *Address*, "is it all come to this? Why then, we are, but where we were before!"

"Why, where would you be?" said I again. "Did I not tell you this, before?"

And now, gentlemen, what is the consequence. Why the Hot Men, that being akin to old JEHU were for driving the Government off the wheels, found themselves out of breath; and that Government which keeps its due bounds, had made a full stop at her due place, Moderation, and would go no further· immediately, they turn malecontent, drink "October" for a month [*referring to the October Club*], tainted with mob fury—And they set up for themselves!

Now, say I, is a time for the Ministry, if their eyes are open, to fix themselves for ever! if they can but find out the just Proposition, and set upon the exact Medium between all these extremes.

Indeed the Ministry may more properly say, just now, that they are of no Party than ever they could, or any Ministry before them could do. For no Party likes them:

yet no Party finds fault with them, *October* excepted; and *their* complaints will increase the honour of the Ministry, because the substance of them is ridiculous.

If they will exist, let them stand fast *between* the Parties. If they waver, and think by embracing one Party to crush the other, they are gone! I would not give two years' purchase for their *Commissions*! Ministry should be of the Nation's Party! The Ministry, the Government, is a Party by itself; and ought in matters of Parties, to be independent. When they cease to be so, they set the shoe on the head! they set the nation with the bottom upward! and must expect to be mob-ridden till they cease to be a Party at all, but become slaves to the Party they espouse, and fall under the Party they oppose. And this is what has ruined all the Ministries that have been these last twenty years [1691-1711]. "He that hath ears to hear, let him hear!"

This *Review* has subsisted in the Administration of four Ministries, and has, all along, endeavoured to speak plain. Whether it does so now or not, I leave any to judge!

I am now to suppose it drawing towards a period, and the Party that have so long regretted that old branch of English liberty, *Freedom of Speech*, please themselves, with stopping the mouths of the Whigs, by laying a tax upon Public Papers [*the Stamp Act*].

If such a design goes on, it will soon appear, whether it be a proposal to raise money, or a design to crush and suppress the Papers themselves. If it be the first, it may readily answer the end. There being as I have calculated it, above 200,000 single Papers published every week in the nation, a light tax would raise a considerable sum, and yet not check the thing. But if it be a design to suppress these Papers, it will be seen by their laying on such a rate as will disable the printing of them.

For my part, I am perfectly easy. Whatever ends I may be supposed to write for, none will suggest I do it for my private gain; and I shall as readily therefore be silent as any man that writes. Though I prophesy this to the Party, that it will not answer their end! For the stopping of the Press will be the opening of the Mouth; and the diminution of Printing will be the increase of Writing, in which the liberty is tenfold, because no authors can be found out, or punished if they are.

And this made King CHARLES II. (and he understood these things very well) say that the Licenser of the Press did more harm than good; and that if every one was left to print what he would, there would be less treason spread about, and fewer Pasquinades.

And I take upon me to say, that let them stop the Press when they will! what is wanting in pamphlet, will be made up in lampoon!

As to this Work, let it fall when it will! this shall be said of it by friend and foe. It has spoken boldly and plainly to them both; and so it shall continue to do, while it speaks at all! And whether it shall go on, or be put down is of so equal a weight to me, as to my Particular [*private interests*], that no man is less concerned to inquire about it, than myself.

Preface to the Eighth Volume of the Review

[1712.]

I HAVE now finished the 8th Volume of this Work, and as this particular part has been the Subject of as much Clamour and Noise as any of the former, though on a different Account, and from different People; I cannot close it, without giving some account, both of it and myself.

From the beginning of this Undertaking, which I have now carried on almost Ten Years, I have always, according to the best of my Judgment, calculated it for the Support and Defence of TRUTH and LIBERTY; I was not so weak when I began, as not to expect Enemies, and that by speaking plain, both to Persons and Things, I should exasperate many, against both the Work and the Author, and in that Expectation I have not been deceived.

I confess I did not expect, that if the same Truth summoned me to reprove, or differ from the Conduct of the People I was serving, they would treat me as they do for it: I own, I thought, an uninterrupted Fidelity, and steady adhering to an honest Principle for near 40 Years, would have been some Plea in my behalf; and if not that, suffering the Shipwreck of my Fortunes, which were at that time recovering, and by the Bounty of his late Majesty, in a fair way of being restored, suffering all the Indignities, Penalties and Punishments an Enraged Party could inflict upon me, and above three thousand Pounds loss; I say, I thought this might have lodged a little in the Breasts of my Friends, and might have allowed them at least to examine, *before they condemned me*, whether they did me wrong or no.

I thought, that while I had given such Proof, that I could neither be Bribed from the Truth, or Threatened, or Terrified from my Principles, it might, at least, be a Ground for *Impartial Honest Men* to Examine, before they censured me, whether it was true or no, that I had been now Guilty of both.

But I have found all this in vain; and as if forfeiting my Reason as well as my Estate, were a Debt from me to the Party I espoused, I am now hunted with a full cry, Acteon like, by my own Friends, I won't call them Hounds, in spite of protested Innocence; in spite of want of Evidence; against the genuine Sense of what I write; against fair Arguing; against all Modesty and Sense; Condemned by common Clamour, as Writing for Money, Writing for particular Persons, Writing by great Men's Direction, being dictated to, and the like; every title of which, I have the Testimony of my own Conscience, is abominably false, and the Accusers must have the Accusation of their own Consciences, that they do not know it to be true.

I cannot say it has not given me a great deal of disturbance; for an Ungrateful Treatment of a People that I had run all manner of Risk for, and thought I could have died for, cannot but touch a less sensible Temper, than I think, mine to be; but I thank God that Operation is over, and I endeavour to make other Uses of it, than perhaps the People themselves think I do.

First, *I look in*, and upon the narrowest search I can make of my own Thoughts, Desires, and Designs, I find a clear untainted Principle, and consequently an entire calm of Conscience, founded upon the satisfying Sense that I neither am touched with Bribes, guided or influenced by Fear, Favour, Hope, Dependence or Reward, of, upon, or from any Person, or Party under Heaven; and that I have written and do write nothing, but what is my Native, Free, Undirected Opinion and Judgment, and what was so many Years ago, as I think I made unanswerably appear by the very last *Review* of this Volume, where I quoted the very same Thing which I write now, and which was Printed in the 5*th* Volume of this Work, No. 155, in the Year 1709.

Next, *I look up*, and not Examining into His Ways, the Sovereignty of whose Providence I adore: I submit with an entire Resignation to whatever happens to me, as being by the immediate Direction of that Goodness, and for such wise and glorious Ends, as however I may not yet see through, will, at last issue in good, even to me; fully depending, that I shall yet be delivered from the Power of Slander and Reproach, and the Sincerity of my Conduct be yet cleared up to the World; and if not, *Te Deum Laudamus.*

In the third place, *I look back*, on the People who treat me thus, who notwithstanding, *under the Power of their Prejudices*, they fly upon me, with a Fury that I think unchristian and unjust, yet as I doubt not, the Day will still come, when they will be again undeceived in me; I am far from studying their Injury, or doing myself Justice at their Expence, *which I could do with great Advantage:* It is impossible for the Dissenters in this Nation to provoke me to be an Enemy to their Interest; should they fire my House, sacrifice my Family, and assassinate my Life, I would ever requite them with defending their Cause, and standing to the last against all those that should endeavour to weaken or reproach it. But this is, as I think it, a just and righteous Cause, founded upon the great Principle of Truth and Liberty, which I am well assured I shall never abandon, and not that I am insensible of being ill Treated by them, or that I make any court to their Person.

When any Party of Men have a clear View of their own Case, or a right knowledge of their own Interest, he that will serve them, and knows the Way to do it, must be certain not to please them, and must be able to see them revile and reproach him, and use him in the worst manner imaginable, and not be moved, either to return them ill, or refrain doing them good; and this is the true meaning of that Command, which I thank God, I cheerfully obey, *viz.*, *To pray for them that despitefully use me.*

I have not so ill an Opinion of myself, as not to think I merit better Usage from the Dissenters; and I have not so ill an Opinion of the Dissenters, as not to think they will, some time or other, know their Friends from their Enemies better than they do now; nor have I so far forgot my Friends, as not to own a great many of them do already. I remember the Time when the same People treated me in the same manner, upon the Book called *The Shortest Way*, etc., and nothing but suffering for them would ever open their Eyes; He that cleared up my integrity then, can do it again by the same Method, and I leave it to Him; *Ad te quacumque vocas* is my Rule; my Study and Practice is Patience and Resignation, and in this I triumph over all the Indignity, Reproach, Slander and Railery in the World; in this I enjoy in the midst of a Million of Enemies a perfect Peace and Tranquility, and when they misconstruct my Words, pervert the best Meaning, turn every Thing which I say, their own Way; it gives me no other contemplation than this, "How vain is the Opinion of Men, either when they judge well or ill!"

This makes me go on steadily, and regard no Clamour: When I write against a War with the Dutch, they rail and exclaim at me, and say, I write for a War with the Dutch; when I write against erecting an Austrian Tyrant in room of a French, they tell me I write for the French; when I write for putting an End to the War, they tell me I write for a French Peace, and the like.

I have made such Protestations of my receiving no Reward or Direction whatever, in or for this Work, as none but those who are used to prevaricate themselves, can, upon any Foundation that is consistent with Christianity, suspect, and the Circumstances I labour under in the World, are a Corroborating Evidence of the Truth of it; yet without Ground, without Evidence, without any Testimony, but general Notion, they will have it be otherwise; two of their Authors have the Impudence to assert it, *but not one step have they taken to prove it*, nor can they do it, though both openly challenged to do it, and a Hundred Guineas offered upon the Proof of it; thus they give the Lie and the Rascal to themselves without my help, who quietly let them go on their own Way.

My Measures are to the best of my Judgment steady: What I approve I defend, what I dislike I censure, without any Respect of Persons, only endeavouring to give my Reasons and to make it appear, that I approve and dislike upon good and sufficient Grounds; which *being first well assured of*, the Time is yet to come, that I ever refrained to speak my Mind for fear of the Face of Man: If what I have said were false, my Enemies would certainly choose to answer rather than to rail: But as I have Unanswerable Truth on my side, they choose to rail rather than to answer.

I have lived too long, and seen too much, not to know that all these violent Party Feuds are of short Duration, and we see the very Men I now speak of, approve today what they were loudest against but yesterday. In the beginning of the late Changes, we saw those Gentlemen threatening the public credit; and one and all, they resolved to lend no Money to the Government; had they held there, they might indeed have distressed the New Managers in their beginning; but no sooner was a Fund raised *with a little trifling Advantage*, but how were they ready to tread one another to Death to get in their Money! This was a convincing testimony of two things, which, were they rightly considered, might be improved very much to the advantage of the honest People themselves, and as their Enemies do consider them, they are at present a means to represent their Figure in the Nation too much to their disadvantage, viz.: (1) That the Whigs act upon no Foundation of concert with, or confidence in one another, in any thing they do, and that the Remains of a public Spirit, which their Ancestors were guided by, are sunk so low, as to be entirely governed by their private Advantage; (2) That the Moneyed Men among them, upon whom the public Credit has so much seemed to depend, are in as much want of the Funds, as the Funds are of the Moneyed Men, of both which, I say no more here, because I shall have Room to speak at large of 'em hereafter: To return to the unsteadiness of the Temper now reigning among us, I mean among the honest and well-meaning but Hot People, among the Whigs: I farther have observed, that not long since, we saw many of them railing at *a South-Sea Trade*, cursing and wishing Confusion (at a most unchristian Rate) to the Contrivers of it, nay, and some more furious, cursing themselves if ever they came into it; bantering and ridiculing it, and drinking a Health to it in a Cup of Whipped Froth, as a suitable Emblem of its Invalidity. And yet a little Patience, a little waiting, and letting them alone a little, has so changed the Humour, that all the Clamour is sunk, and we find the very same Men are at this Day the only Men that buy up the South-Sea Stock. We found them the same about the Article of Dunkirk; they begin to like it already, and think it very well that we have it in our Hands; thus like crammed Fowls, they must be made Fat against their Stomachs, but they are pleased with the Flesh when they feel it upon their Bones.

It is my disinterested study to serve them, but I confess 'tis not so to please them; I shall never leave off to wish well to their Interest, and can I but serve it they shall have leave to throw Stones at me as long as I live; but this does by no means hinder, but that I may, and ever shall, as the best mark of my Zeal for their Interest, tell them plainly their Mistakes.

This passion I have for their Interest, fills me with Resentment at the Barbarity of the Treatment which the Dissenters have received in the Affair of the *Occasional Bill*, and that from a People they had deserved other Usage from, and in this, as I said before, I do them but Justice: That they themselves are so easy under it, as not only to make no Complaint, but even to say it has done them no harm, is an Evidence of their unconquerable Passion to a particular View, which I believe they will always be disappointed in, since it is evident this has ruined the interest of the Whigs in almost all the Corporations in England, and put them into such a Posture, as never but by Miracle to recover it.

I pity the Delusion of those, who entertain a Notion, that if ever the Low-Church-Men come to the Administration, they will restore the Dissenters; I grant it would be both Just and Generous so to do, but if they will first shew me one Low-Church-Man in the Nation *of any Figure*, that however he may exclaim at the Method does not appear secretly satisfied that it is done, then I'll join in expecting it; but I shall farther shew them the Vanity of these Hopes, in the Consequence of my other Discourses upon this Head.

We need not wonder at the other Mistakes we see some People run into, when they are so intent upon the Party Interest they push at, that they are contented to be the Sacrifice offered up for the Purchase of Human help to carry it on; in all which unchristian course, we have seen them effectually disappointed, and I must own, till I see another Spirit among them, I do not look for their Deliverance.

Their Eyes are now wholly bent upon the War abroad; the considerations that it may be hazardous to the Protestant Succession, threatening of embroiling us with the Dutch, destructive of our General Safety, and many Ways fatal to our Peace at Home, weigh not with them; the growing Interest of the Pretender at home, the Insolence and Encrease of Jacobitism among us, seem to be quite left out of their Thoughts; I shall say no more to them but this, that, I think, if God should give them Deliverance their own Way, they would be undone; and I pray that a Spirit fit for Deliverance may be given them, and then their Eyes will be opened to that Way that shall be best for us all.

To return to my own case, I am a Stoic in whatever may be the Event of Things; I'll do and say what I think is a Debt to Justice and Truth to do and say, without the least regard to Clamour and Reproach; and as I am utterly unconcerned at Human Opinion, the People that throw away their Breath so freely in censuring me, may consider of some better Improvement to make of their Passions, than to waste them on a Man, that is both above and below the reach of them.

I know too much of the World to expect good in it; and I have learnt to value it too little, to be concerned at the Evil; I have gone through a Life of Wonders, and am the Subject of a vast Variety of Providences: I have been fed more by Miracle than Elijah, when the Ravens were his Purveyors; I have some time ago summed up the Scenes of my Life in this Distich.

No Man has tasted differing Fortunes more
And Thirteen Times I have been Rich *and* Poor.

In the School of Affliction I have learnt more Philosophy than at the Academy, and more Divinity than from the Pulpit: In Prison I have learnt to know that Liberty does not consist in open Doors, and the free Egress and Regress of Locomotion. I have seen the rough side of the World as well as the smooth, and have in less than half a Year tasted the difference between the Closet of a King, and the Dungeon of Newgate.

I have suffered deeply for cleaving to Principle; of which Integrity I have lived to say, None but those I suffered for, ever reproached me with it: The immediate Causes of my Suffering have been by being betrayed by those I have trusted, and scorning to betray those that trusted me. To the Honour of English Gratitude I have this remarkable Truth to leave behind me, That I was never so basely betrayed, as by those whose Families I had preserved from starving; nor so basely treated as by those I starved my own Family to preserve. The same Chequer-Work of Fortunes attends me still; the People I have served, and love to serve, cut my throat every day, because I will not cut the throat of those that have served and assisted me. Ingratitude has always been my Aversion, and perhaps for that Reason it is my Exercise.

And now I live under universal Contempt, which Contempt I have learnt to contemn, and have an uninterrupted Joy in my Soul, not at my being contemned, but that no Crime can be laid to my Charge, to make that Contempt my Due.

Fame, a lying Jade, would talk me up for I know not

what of Courage; and they call me a fighting Fellow; I despise the Flattery, I profess to know nothing of it, farther than Truth makes any Man bold; and I acknowledge, that give me but a bad Cause and I am the greatest Coward in the World; Truth inspires Nature, and as in defence of Truth no honest Man can be a Coward, so no Man of Sence can be bold when he is in the wrong: He that is Honest must be Brave, and it is my opinion that a coward cannot be an Honest Man. In defence of Truth, I THINK (pardon me that I dare go no further, for who knows himself?) I say, I think I could dare to Die, but a Child may beat me if I am in the wrong. Guilt gives trembling to the Hands, blushes to the Face, and fills the Heart with Amazement and Terror: I question whether there is much, if any, difference from Bravery and Cowardice, but what is founded in the Principle they are engaged for; and I no more believe any Man is born a Coward, than that he is born a Knave—Truth makes a Man of Courage, and Guilt makes that Man of Courage a Coward.

Early Disasters and frequent turns of my Affairs, as above, have left me incumbered with an insupportable weight of Debt; and the remarkable Compassion of some Creditors, after continued Offers of stripping myself naked, by entire surrenders upon Oath, have never given me more Trouble than they were able, or less than they knew how; by which means most of the Debts I have discharged have cost me 40*s.* in the Pound to pay, and the Creditor half as much to recover.

I have a large Family, a Wife and six Children, who never want what they should enjoy, or spend what they ought to save.

Under all these Circumstances, and many more too long to write, my only Happiness is this; I have always been kept cheerful, easy, and quiet; enjoying a perfect calm of Mind, clearness of Thought, and Satisfaction not to be broken in upon, by whatever may happen to me: If any Man ask me how I arrived to it, I answer him in short, 'By a constant serious Application to the great, solemn and weighty Work of Resignation to the Will of Heaven;' by which, let no Man think I presume; I have endeavoured, and am in a great measure able to say feelingly and effectually the following Lines, which I recommend to the World, not only as the Fruit of my own experience, but for the Practice of all such as know how to value it, and think they need it.

HAPPY, because confirmed above,
And to Heaven's dispose resigned;
I by his Rule, direct my Steps,
And on him stay my Mind.

Upon his various Providence
With Satisfaction rest,
I unexalted can enjoy,
And suffer Undepressed.

Boldly I steer through storms of Life
And Ship-wreck of Estate,
Without Inheritance I 'm rich,
And without Honours Great.

When the world trembles, I 'm unmoved,
When cloudy, I 'm serene:
When Darkness covers all without,
I 'm always bright within.

In Labour I enjoy my Rest,
In weighty Sorrows, Ease!
When Pride and Parties rage with Strife,
I 'm all in Calms and Peace.

In Scarcity, I fear no want;
In Plenty, guard my Mind;
In Prison, I 'm at Liberty,
In Liberty confined.

With steady Foot, and even Pace,
I tread the Milky Way;
I 've Youth without it's Levity,
And Age without decay.

I scorn the Terrors of the World,
And equally her Charms ;
If those affright, or these allure,
I shake her from my Arms.

Often I 've been by Power oppressed,
And with deep Sorrow tried ;
By the same Power I 've been caressed,
And I have both defied.

By my Eternal Guide kept safe,
Through both Extremes I steer,
These could not bribe my Principles,
Or those excite my fear.

The Patriots of the cause I serve,
Those Services contemn ;
Yet move me not, because I serve
The Cause, and not the Men.

Under their Universal Scorn
I 'm cool, and unsurprised ;
Most Humble when I 'm most caressed,
And Cheerful when despised.

The secret Hand to which I look,
Has always kept me true ;
Patience for every Trial I 've had,
And Trial for Patience too.

Though Envy grins, and Slander barks,
And Clamouring Monsters rail ;
They neither can my Passions move,
Or on my Smiles prevail.

My Temper forms the Good, or Ill,
Of every different State ;
I taste the Gall without the Grief,
Without the Snare, the Sweet.

To keep my Passions regular
I 've full Command within ;
I 'm pleased without Impertinence
And Angry without Sin.

Thoughtful without Anxiety
And grieved without Despair,
Cheerful but without Levity,
And cautious without fear.

I 'd Gravity before Grey Hairs,
And now I 'm old I 'm gay ;
Patient in Life, and hope I shall
Without Reluctance DIE.

When fierce Afflictions charge me home,
I see the Secret Hand ;
I cease to pore on Instruments
But always view their End.

If Prosperous Things are made my Lot
And the World speaks me fair,
I 'm always jealous of the Joy,
And guard against the Snare.

Ambition, Malice, Rage and Hate,
Are Strangers to my Soul ;
But Peace and Joy possess the Parts,
And Charity the Whole.

I cannot Envy when I 'm low,
Nor when I 'm high can fear ;
In Wealth I can no more be proud
Than when I 'm Poor despair.

The HONEST PART I fain would act
As Heaven shall Means restore ;
Till then I nurse the Principle,
And Heaven expects no more.

If Rich, my Temper suits my State
If Mean, my Frame supplies:
And I 'm more thankful when I fall
Than others when they rise.

I freely shun Opinion-Fame,
Which Gusts of Parties raise;
I seek the Merit, not the Name,
The Vertue, not the Praise.

From my Low Station I look up
Pity great Men of Crime;
I neither over-rate their Rage
Or Value their Esteem.

My full dependence is above,
I own and eye HIS Power;
I know I must account to Him,
And wait with Joy the Hour.

In vain we talk of Happiness,
In any State below;
There is no calm on Earth, but what
Must from this Fountain flow.

Resigned to Heaven, we may with Joy,
To any State submit;
And in the world of Miseries,
Have Happiness complete.

D. F.

DANIEL DEFOE.

Papers from the REVIEW.

The Prototype and Plan of the Review.

[Supplementary Journal to the *Advice from the Scandal Club* for the month of September, 1704.]

IT HAS been objected to the Author, that this design is not new, and is only a Mimic of HARRY CARE, in his *Weekly Packet of Advice from Rome*, with the [*Popish*] *Courant* at the end of every Paper.

Such gentlemen do not tell us, whether that Work was valuable or not. They neither give their judgement on the design, nor on the performance.

If that was a useful Work, well designed, and more happily performed than this Author will pretend to: then these gentlemen say nothing to our Author's disparagement, since all the Wit of Mankind seems now to be composed but of Imitations, and there "is nothing new under the sun."

If they think that work mean, and the performance dull (which the present scarcity and value of those Collections [*i.e., sets of the* Weekly Packet] plainly contradict); it remains for those gentlemen to tell us where the meannesses are? and where the dulness of that Author appears?

It is true, he had his imperfections: and the fury of the Times, the poverty of circumstances, and the unhappy love of his bottle, reduced him too low, for a man of his capacity. But as in all parts of his design, and the length of his happy performance; he discovered such a spirit, such learning, such strength of reason, and such a sublime fancy; as in which the Author of this cannot esteem himself worthy to carry his books after him: so he shall always value this Undertaking so much the more as it resembles his; and wishes, for the sake of the reader as well as himself, he could come near him in the performance.

Some, we know, have no relish for History, and value therefore only the Entertaining Part of the *Review*: and by such, we have been often solicited to leave off troubling ourselves with the grave puzzling part of the Paper, telling a long story of the Swedes, Hungarians, and the Lord knows what! and bring our Paper to all mirth, pleasantry, and delight. And they promise to furnish us with matter enough.

Others, and as many in number as the former, frequently press us "to leave off jesting and bantering," as they call it; and to pursue the vast work which the title leads to, and which the first sheets promised, viz., *A Review of the Affairs of France.* A subject, say they, truly fruitful, of a vast variety, and suited to an undertaking of the greatest magnitude: and it is a pity it should be clogged with the impertinence and nonsense of the *Scandalous Club.*

And thus we are brought before our own Society both ways.

Now, gentlemen, as this design was not at first undertaken without a full prospect of all this variety of judgements and censures: so in all this, there seems nothing material enough to turn the Author from pursuing his first design—which is, the middle between those two extremities.

It is true, the *History of the Affairs of France,* in all the vast and unobserved parts of its growth and increase, is the *main* and *original* thought: and, if the Author lives to carry it on, it shall be brought, in its due time, to the full period, where Providence shall place it, at the very end of this Work.

But as all men are not Historians, and even many of those that are care but for a little reading at a time; this design was laid to bring such people to read the Story; which, if it had been always serious, and had proceeded too fast, had been too voluminous, too tedious, either for their leisure or inclination. And thus we *wheedle them in* (if it may be allowed that expression) to the Knowledge of the World; who, rather than take more pains, would be content with their ignorance, and search into nothing.

To carry on this honest cheat, and bring people to read with delight; the latter part of this Paper was contrived: every jot as useful in its kind; and, if we may be allowed to judge, by common acceptation, as pleasing.

It cannot but be pleasing to the Author, to find both parts of his design so well approved. And therefore to those, who are not equally pleased with both; he says, "He desires those who like but one Part, to bear with the other; for the sake of those whose judgements approve of what they do not!" Those that like both Parts, need nothing farther to be said to them, than that "He is glad, he is able to please them!" And those who like neither Part, are welcome to let it alone.

DEFOE'S *intention to stop the* Review *with No.* 100; *and how it came to be continued.*

[*Review*, No. 98, Vol. I. *p.* 408. Saturday, 10 February, 1705.]

THE Author of the *Review* having received a letter, signed F. L. containing Proposals for continuing this Work, but hearing no more of it, supposed it a banter. But having since received a letter, signed L. A.; several others signed G. M., O. K., and T. W., containing very kind and honourable Offers for the encouragement of the Work: he thinks himself obliged to the Gentlemen, whether it comes to anything or not; and gives them for answer:

> He has, gratis, without reward, profit, or promise of any advantage, freely written this Paper a whole year. His encouragement has been, to see wise men approve it, and accept it. But as neither can his affairs permit him to spare so much time as is now required, more than at first; nor can the sale of so small a Paper make the Publisher able to allow [*i.e., to him*] what may be encouraging and suitable to the trouble: he therefore concluded to lay it down.

But if those Gentlemen (who are pleased so much to value his performance above its merit, as to press him to the continuing it, and have made these Offers) are in earnest, and will either send him their designed Proposal to Mr. MATTHEWS [*the Publisher*], or give him a meeting: he professes himself willing to oblige them: and will convince them, that he is far from being selfish or unreasonable; and humbly desires their answer before the end of next week.

[*Review*, No. 100, Vol. I. *p.* 413. Saturday 17 February, 1705.]

This being the last *Review* of this Volume, and designed to be so, of this Work; the Author cannot close it without paying the just debt of duty and acknowledgement to those Gentlemen, who, beyond his merit and expectation, have been pleased to receive it with the same candour and on the same foot[ing] on which it was originally designed, Public Usefulness, Entertainment, and Instruction.

For all his errors, meannesses, and mistakes; for all his digressions, comments, and needless remarks; for all his incorrect, rash, and (unhappily!) too plain expression; for his too freely, too frequently, too positively giving his opinion; for all the sallies out of his province, and invasions of the talent of the Learned, either as Divines or Philosophers; for all his really, or supposed wrong notions of things, places, or persons; for all his unpoliteness of style, improprieties and deformities of every sort, whether in diction or conception; for errors of the Press, errors of the pen, or errors of opinion: he humbly asks his readers' pardon, desires they will place them, *with the addition of their charity*, to the account of haste, human frailty, and such other incidents of common infirmity as, he presumes, most of his fellow creatures have, more or less, a share of.

To all those Gentlemen of Honour, sense, and reading, who have, *beyond his ambition*, honoured this Work with their generous approbation, have thought it worth their reading, and worth giving the World the trouble they have had with it; the author returns his most humble acknowledgements: assuring them, he esteems it a full recompense to all his labour, *hitherto bestowed gratis upon the World*; and values himself more in the approbation of a few wise men that can judge with candour and impartiality, than upon any presumption of his own, or than on the unpolished praises of a crowd, who, wanting no ignorance, speak what they hear others say, and judge without understanding.

As for the censuring, partial, and prejudiced part of mankind; who dislike the work for its unhappy despicable Author, and its Author because his judgement and theirs may not agree: it is in vain to capitulate [*stipulate*] with them for civility and fair treatment. The rudeness, the heat, the contempt they treat him with, is the less a concern to him, as he sees it plainly produced by their passion, rather than by their judgement.

The nature, usefulness, and advantage of the design, they

have sometimes been forced to acknowledge; and could like the Work, were it performed by anybody but their humble Servant.

And yet, even to these Gentlemen he has to say, he always endeavoured to give them as little offence as possible. He has avoided making it a Party paper: and considering the numerous insults, assaults, and snares he has met with, to bring him into the article of raillery; he thinks he has said less, on all occasions, than any of the Party writers on the other side would have done in the like case.

When he has engaged with such Gentlemen of a contrary opinion to himself, who have been of temper and manners; he has carefully behaved himself, and to their satisfaction. Though he has not agreed with their opinions; he has defended his own, without offence to their persons, or any breach of decency and behaviour.

He heartily wishes all the Gentlemen on the other side would give him equal occasion to honour them for their charity, temper, and gentlemanlike dealing, as for their learning and virtue; and that when we cannot agree like Brethren, we might fall out like Gentlemen. And he would willingly capitulate with them, and enter into a treaty or Cartel for Exchange of Good Language with them: and to let all our debates be carried by strength of reasoning and argument, solid proofs, matter of fact, and demonstrations; and not by dint of Billingsgate storms of raillery, and showers of ill words, that Frenzy of the Tongue! and Shame of a good Cause!

Among the various questions, the Author has had sent him to answer (a thing altogether foreign to his first design), he had one lately, in the following terms, which he purposely reserved to be answered in this place.

Thus—

Gentlemen,

You have given your opinions freely about several sorts of Religions. Pray what religion is your Society [i.e., Scandalous Club] *of?*

Yours.

The truth is, the Author little thought to make a Public Confession of Faith in his Paper; and though he ought always to be ready to do it, whenever *legally* required; yet he shall take the freedom to reply to this Querist, not so much in the *literal sense* of the words, as in the sense which he presumes the inquirer *would be answered in.*

As to the *literal sense*, of Religion generally understood, he answers directly, *Catholic Christians*!

As to the *meaning* of it, which he understands to be, "What Party do you belong to?" he freely again answers for himself, that which he presumes to be his meaning, *A Protestant Dissenter.*

And to them that like him the worse for it, he desires their patience to read the account he gave of himself, in a letter to a Divine of the C[hurch] of E[ngland] in some debates between them, on a question published in the last *Supplement*, page 2; and he freely appeals to the Gentleman himself, who is absolutely a stranger to him, for the justness of the quotation.

I never miss expressing on all occasions, my hearty wishes that there was no such thing as Faction or Party in the nation.

I own I dissent in some matters from the Established Church. Will you hear my opinion with charity? I am sure you cannot despise such a Dissenter, and I heartily wish there no other.

I dissent from the National Church in nothing doctrinal or essential to salvation. I entertain a sincere universal charity for the Church, and all her Christian members.

I earnestly wish and desire I could conform in all things the Law requires.

I freely and heartily acquiesce in the Government being always in the hands of the Church [i.e., that all Ministers of State should always be Members of the Church of England]: *and if it were entirely in my choice or disposal, would place it there, rather than in any sort of, or in the hands of* all *the Dissenters together.*

I can never be guilty of undermining the Church, or fomenting any faction or rebellion against her: for I would have her hold the reins of Government.

I confess I would have the Church extend her charity and

tenderness to us that cannot conform; not treat us as enemies, condemn us unheard, and punish us not being guilty.

As to those Warm Gentlemen, whom no argument will reach, no courtesy oblige, who will damn the Author and his Work in spite of argument, sense, or manners; let my Lord ROCHESTER answer for us, when, writing of his Poetry, he says,

I slight the rabble! 'Tis enough for me,
If SACKVILLE, SAVILLE, BOYLE, and WYCHERLEY,
Great B——, and S——, and C——, and BUCKINGHAM,
And some few more whom I omit to name,
Approve my verse,
I count your censure, fame!

The Author thinks it convenient to inform the world that this Paper not being able to contain all he thinks needful to say, at the dismiss of this work; there will be two more papers published in course, as the conclusion of the whole.

Also that a Preface and Index shall be prepared to be bound up with the volume; which all those Gentlemen who have made collections [*sets*] of the Paper, will find necessary to have to complete the book.

How the Review *came to be continued.*

[*Review*, No. 101, Vol. I. *p.* 420. Tuesday, 20 Feb., 1705.]

The author of this, having received a very obliging letter, signed, P. G., D. H., L. M., J. B., V. R., B. B., &c., concerning the promoting, supporting, and continuing this Work; the Author, acknowledging the courtesy and kindness of the Gentlemen, desires they will please to give him leave, and direct him where to send them an answer in writing, before he publishes their generous offer.

[See *pp.* 231, 240.]

DANIEL DEFOE.

The Revolution of 1688, *its principles and purposes in a nutshell.*

Daniel Defoe.

The Revolution of 1688, its principles and purposes, in a nutshell.

[Written at the time of the trials of Doctor SACHEVEREL, the High Flying Doctor, in the *Review* Nos. 118 and 119. Vol. VI. Saturday 7th and Tuesday 10th January, 1710.]

With the humblest submission to the opinion of the British Parliament, and yet in a cheerful confidence in their justice, love to their country, and zeal for the public peace: I take leave to address this Paper to the Commons of Britain, assembled at this time in Parliament, as follows.

THE public peace of Britain, Right Honourables! having by the Wonders of Providence, been preserved in the late glorious Revolution; and the religious as well as civil liberties of this island been rescued from the ruinous projects of Popery and Tyranny: it pleased GOD to direct the Commons of England by their Representatives, assembled in Convention in conjunction with the Nobility, to apply themselves to such future Establishments as might effectually secure us from any subsequent relapse into the mischiefs of the former reign.

To this purpose, they presented the Crown, upon the abdication of the late King JAMES (whom Guilt and Fear would not permit to shew his face among us), to their glorious Deliverer, King WILLIAM, and his blessed Consort, Queen MARY then the next Protestant heir in succession: and entailed it on Her present Majesty [*Queen ANNE*] in default of heirs; without any regard to the other issue of King JAMES, then alive or to be born.

By which celebrated action, I humbly conceive, the Convention did the several things following: whether immediately or consequentially, or both, is not material.

1. They effectually secured the Crown in the hands of Protestants; having passed that *never-to-be-forgotten* Vote; which was sent up to the Lords, January 22, 1689.

   That it is inconsistent with the Constitution of this Protestant Nation, to be governed by a Popish Prince.

   Upon which Claim, our Religion is now established; and our religious rights are all founded and secured.

2. They asserted the Rights of the People of England, assembled either in Parliament or Convention, to dispose of the Crown, even in bar of hereditary right; *i.e.*, in Parliament style [*language*] *to limit the Succession of the Crown.*

By which latter article, I humbly suggest, all the pretences of our Princes to an *inherent Divine Right* of blood, and to an *Absolute Unconditioned Obedience* in their subjects; together with that modern delusion of the *Unlawfulness of Resistance or Self-Defence, in cases of Tyranny and Oppression*, were entirely suppressed, declared against, and disowned.

These things (as the *Journals* of our own House will abundantly inform you, and to which I humbly refer) received, at divers times and in various manners, all possible sanction, both in the same assembled Convention when afterwards turned into a Parliament, and in several subsequent Parliaments to this day, in the several *Acts* passed in both Kingdoms, for *Recognition of King WILLIAM and Queen MARY*, for *taking the Association for security of the persons of the King and Queen*, for *further Limitation of the Crown*, for *Settling the Succession*, and, at last, *for Uniting the two Kingdoms*. To all which *Acts*, I humbly refer. Every one of them, either expressly mentioning, or necessarily implying the *Right* of the Parliament *to limit the Succession of their Princes*, and to declare the established conditions of the People's obedience. But all which *Acts*, the absurd doctrines of Passive Obedience and Non-Resistance are, by undeniable consequences, exploded and rejected, as inconsistent with the Constitution of Britain.

Now, may it please this Honourable House to consider,

that, though as this Happy Revolution was established over all gainsayers, and that all opposition to it was crushed, in both Kingdoms, in its beginning: yet it involved the nation in a bloody, expensive, and a tedious war with the King of France; the great Pattern of Tyranny in Europe, and to whom all the abdicated Tyrants of Christendom have fled for succour.

And as this terrible War has continued now above twenty years, with a small interval of an imperfect Peace; and, as is usual in like cases, it has been attended with various [*varying*] successes, especially before the late Series of Wonder [*MARLBOROUGH's victories*] began, in which GOD has signally blessed Her Majesty with an almost uninterrupted success: so the great and powerful enemies of our Peace abroad, were not without their secret friends among us; who, as traitors in the bosom of their native country, have, by all manner of artifice, from time to time endeavoured to weaken the hands of the established Government, to encourage the enemy, and on all occasions assisted them in open invasions or secret treachery, to attempt the Restoration of Slavery and Bondage upon their own country.

This is the prayer of the [above] Petition! this is the present cure for all this popular frenzy! and will do more to establish our Peace, than the whole twenty years' war has done! this will prepare us, either to carry the war on abroad, or to receive peace when GOD shall think fit to trust us with that blessing again!

> That you would be pleased to condemn the *Principle*! It is nothing what ye do with the man [*Doctor SACHEVEREL*].

The Principle is the plague sore that runs upon the nation; and its contagion infects our gentry, infects our clergy, infects our politics; and affects the loyalty, the zeal, and the peace of the whole island.

Passive Obedience, Non-Resistance, and the Divine Right of Hereditary Succession are *inconsistent* with the rights of the British Nation (not to examine the Rights of Nature)! inconsistent with the Constitution of the British Government! inconsistent with the Being and Authority of the British Parliament! and inconsistent with the *declared* essential Foundation of the British Monarchy!

These abhorred notions would destroy the inestimable Privileges of Britain, of which the House of Commons are the glorious conservators! They would subject all our Liberties to the arbitrary lust of a single person! They would expose us to all kinds of tyranny, and subvert the very foundations on which we stand! They would destroy the unquestioned sovereignty of our Laws; which, for so many Ages, have triumphed over the invasions and usurpations of ambitious Princes! They would denude us of the beautiful garment of Liberty, and prostitute the honour of the nation to the mechanicism of Slavery! They would divest GOD Almighty of His praise, in giving His humble creatures *a right to govern themselves*! and they charge Heaven with having *meanly* subjected mankind to the crime, Tyranny! which He himself abhors.

It is to this Honourable House, the whole nation now looks for relief against these invaders.

Honest men hope that *now is the time* when the illegitimate spurious birth of these Monsters in Politics shall be exposed by your voice.

Now is the time, when you shall declare it criminal for any Man to assert that *the subjects of Britain are obliged to an absolute unconditioned Obedience to their Princes*. The contrary being evident by the *Claim of Right* made, in both Kingdoms [*England and Scotland*], when they tendered the Crowns to King WILLIAM and Queen MARY; and in the *Oath of Government* taken by them, at the same time; and which no man, by law, can or dare impeach! and, indeed, ought not to be permitted unpunished, to reproach.

Now is the time, when you shall declare it criminal for any man to assert *the Illegality of Resistance on any pretence whatever &c.*; or, in plain English [against] *The Right of Self-Defence against Oppression and Violence, whether national or personal*.

The contrary of which is evident by the subjects of Britain inviting over the Prince of ORANGE to assert and defend the Liberties of this island, and to resist the invasions of Popery and Tyranny; in which he was honourably joined by the Nobility and Commons assembled at Nottingham: who took arms, *anno* 1688, to resist the Invaders of our Liberties; and were assisted and countenanced by the voices and persons of the Clergy, the Prelates, and Her [present] Majesty in person.

Now is the time, when you shall *again* declare *the Rights of the People of England*, either in Parliament or in Convention assembled, *to limit the Succession of the Crown in bar of hereditary claims; while those claims are attended with other circumstances inconsistent with the Public Safety and the established Laws of the Land.* Since Her Majesty's *Title to the Crown* (as now owned and acknowledged by the whole nation) and the *Succession to the Crown* (as entailed by the *Act of Succession* in England, and the late Union of Britain), are built on the Right of Parliament to limit the Crown, and that Right was recognized by the Revolution.

This is the substance of the Author's humble application, viz.:

That the Sense of the House as to the principles of Passive Obedience, Non-Resistance, and Parliamentary Limitation might be so declared, as that this wicked Party may be no more at liberty to insult the Government, the Queen, and the Parliament; or to disturb the peace, or debauch the loyalty of Her Majesty's subjects.

Daniel Defoe.

The Education of Women.

[*An Essay upon Projects.* Written about 1692, but first printed in 1697.]

I HAVE OFTEN thought of it as one of the most barbarous customs in the world, considering us as a civilized and a Christian country, that we deny the advantages of learning to women. We reproach the sex every day with folly and impertinence; while I am confident, had they the advantages of education equal to us, they would be guilty of less than ourselves.

One would wonder, indeed, how it should happen that women are conversible at all; since they are only beholden to natural parts, for all their knowledge. Their youth is spent to teach them to stitch and sew, or make baubles. They are taught to read, indeed, and perhaps to write their names, or so; and that is the height of a woman's education. And I would but ask any who slight the sex for their understanding, what is a man (a gentleman, I mean) good for, that is taught no more? I need not give instances, or examine the character of a gentleman, with a good estate, or a good family, and with tolerable parts; and examine what figure he makes for want of education.

The soul is placed in the body like a rough diamond; and must be polished, or the lustre of it will never appear. And 'tis manifest, that as the rational soul distinguishes us from brutes; so education carries on the distinction, and makes some less brutish than others. This is too evident to need any demonstration. But why then should women be denied the benefit of instruction? If knowledge and understanding had been useless additions to the sex, GOD Almighty would never have given them capacities; for he made nothing needless. Besides, I would ask such, What they can see in ignorance, that they should think it a necessary ornament to a woman? or how much worse is a wise woman than a fool? or what has the woman done to forfeit the privilege of being taught? Does she plague us with her pride and impertinence? Why did we not let her learn, that she might have had more wit? Shall we upbraid women with folly, when 'tis only the error of this inhuman custom, that hindered them from being made wiser?

The capacities of women are supposed to be greater, and their senses quicker than those of the men; and what they might be capable of being bred to, is plain from some instances of female wit, which this age is not without. Which upbraids us with Injustice, and looks as if we denied women the advantages of education, for fear they should *vie* with the men in their improvements. . . . .

THEY] SHOULD be taught all sorts of breeding suitable both to their genius and quality. And in particular, Music and Dancing; which it would be cruelty to bar the sex of, because they are their darlings. But besides this, they should be taught languages, as particularly French and Italian: and I would venture the injury of giving a woman more tongues than one. They should, as a particular study, be taught all the graces of speech, and all the necessary air of conversation; which our common education is so defective in, that I need not expose it. They should be brought to read books, and especially history; and so to read as to make them understand the world, and be able to know and judge of things when they hear of them.

To such whose genius would lead them to it, I would deny no sort of learning; but the chief thing, in general, is to cultivate the understandings of the sex, that they may be capable of all sorts of conversation; that their parts and judgements being improved, they may be as profitable in their conversation as they are pleasant.

Women, in my observation, have little or no difference in them, but as they are or are not distinguished by education. Tempers, indeed, may in some degree influence them, but the main distinguishing part is their Breeding.

The whole sex are generally quick and sharp. I believe,

I may be allowed to say, generally so: for you rarely see them lumpish and heavy, when they are children; as boys will often be. If a woman be well bred, and taught the proper management of her natural wit; she proves generally very sensible and retentive.

And, without partiality, a woman of sense and manners is the finest and most delicate part of GOD's Creation, the glory of Her Maker, and the great instance of His singular regard to man, His darling creature: to whom He gave the best gift either GOD could bestow or man receive. And 'tis the sordidest piece of folly and ingratitude in the world, to withhold from the sex the due lustre which the advantages of education gives to the natural beauty of their minds.

A woman well bred and well taught, furnished with the additional accomplishments of knowledge and behaviour, is a creature *without comparison.* Her society is the emblem of sublimer enjoyments, her person is angelic, and her conversation heavenly. She is all softness and sweetness, peace, love, wit, and delight. She is every way suitable to the sublimest wish: and the man that has such a one to his portion, has nothing to do but to rejoice in her, and be thankful.

On the other hand, Suppose her to be the *very same* woman, and rob her of the benefit of education, and it follows—

If her temper be good, want of education makes her soft and easy.

Her wit, for want of teaching, makes her impertinent and talkative.

Her knowledge, for want of judgement and experience, makes her fanciful and whimsical.

If her temper be bad, want of breeding makes her worse; and she grows haughty, insolent, and loud.

If she be passionate, want of manners makes her a termagant and a scold, *which is much at one with Lunatic.*

If she be proud, want of discretion (which still is breeding) makes her conceited, fantastic, and ridiculous.

And from these she degenerates to be turbulent, clamorous, noisy, nasty, the devil! . . . .

THE GREAT distinguishing difference, which is seen in the world between men and women, is in their education; and this is manifested by comparing it with the difference between one man or woman, and another.

And herein it is that I take upon me to make such a bold assertion, That all the world are mistaken in their practice about women. For I cannot think that GOD Almighty ever made them so delicate, so glorious creatures; and furnished them with such charms, so agreeable and so delightful to mankind; with souls capable of the same accomplishments with men: and all, to be only Stewards of our Houses, Cooks, and Slaves.

Not that I am for exalting the female government in the least: but, in short, *I would have men take women for companions, and educate them to be fit for it.* A woman of sense and breeding will scorn as much to encroach upon the prerogative of man, as a man of sense will scorn to oppress the weakness of the woman. But if the women's souls were refined and improved by teaching, that word would be lost. To say, the *weakness* of the sex, as to judgement, would be nonsense; for ignorance and folly would be no more to be found among women than men.

I remember a passage, which I heard from a very fine woman. She had wit and capacity enough, an extraordinary shape and face, and a great fortune: but had been cloistered up all her time; and for fear of being stolen, had not had the liberty of being taught the common necessary knowledge of women's affairs. And when she came to converse in the world, her natural wit made her so sensible of the want of education, that she gave this short reflection on herself: "I am ashamed to talk with my very maids," says she, "for I don't know when they do right or wrong. I had more need go to school, than be married."

I need not enlarge on the loss the defect of education is to the sex; nor argue the benefit of the contrary practice. 'Tis a thing will be more easily granted than remedied. This chapter is but an Essay at the thing: and I refer the Practice to those Happy Days (if ever they shall be) when men shall be wise enough to mend it.

LAW

IS A

Bottomless Pit.

Exemplified in the CASE of

The Lord STRUTT, JOHN BULL,

NICHOLAS FROG, and LEWIS BABOON:

Who spent all they had in a Lawsuit.

Printed from a Manuscript found in the Cabinet of the famous Sir HUMPHRY POLESWORTH.

LONDON:

Printed for JOHN MORPHEW, near Stationers' Hall, 1712. Price 3d.

THE CONTENTS.

Law is a Bottomless Pit.

CHAPTER I.

The Occasion of the Lawsuit.

I NEED not tell you the great quarrels that have happened in our neighbourhood, since the death of the late Lord STRUTT [*the late King of Spain, CHARLES II., who died in* 1700], how the Parson [*Cardinal PORTOCARRERO*] and a cunning Attorney got him to settle his estate upon his cousin PHILIP BABOON [*the Duke of ANJOU, afterwards PHILIP V.*], to the great disappointment of his cousin, Esquire SOUTH [*the Archduke CHARLES*]. Some stick not to say, that the Parson and the Attorney forged a Will, for which they were well paid by the Family of the BABOONS [*the House of BOURBON*]. Let that be as it will, it is matter of fact, that the honour and estate have continued ever since in the person of PHILIP BABOON.

You know that the Lord STRUTTS have, for many years, been possessed of a very great landed estate, well conditioned, wooded, watered; with coal, salt, tin, copper, iron, &c., all within themselves: that it has been the misfortune of the Family, to be the property of their stewards, tradesmen, and inferior servants, which has brought great incumbrances upon them; and, at the same time, the not abating of their expensive way of living has forced them to mortage their best manors. It is credibly reported, that the butcher's and baker's bills of a Lord STRUTT that lived two hundred years ago, are not yet paid.

When PHILIP BABOON came first to the possession of the Lord STRUTT's estate, his Tradesmen [*the Allies*], as is usual upon such occasions, waited upon him, to wish him joy, and to bespeak his custom. The two chief were JOHN BULL [*the English*] the clothier, and NIC. FROG [*the Dutch*] the linen draper. They told him, that "the BULLS and the FROGS had served the Lord STRUTTS with drapery ware for many years, that they were honest and fair dealers, that their bills had never been questioned, that the Lord STRUTTS lived generously and never used to dirty their fingers with pen, ink, and counters, that his Lordship might depend upon their honesty, and they would use him as kindly as they had done his predecessors."

The young Lord seemed to take all in good part, and dismissed with a deal of seeming content; assuring them that he did not intend to change any of the honourable maxims of his predecessors.

CHAPTER II.

How BULL and FROG grew jealous, that the Lord STRUTT intended to give all his custom to his grandfather LEWIS BABOON.

IT HAPPENED, unfortunately for the peace of our neighbourhood, that this young Lord had an old cunning rogue, or, as the Scots call it, a "false loon" of a grandfather, that one might justly call a "JACK of all trades." Sometimes you would see him behind his counter selling broadcloth; sometimes, measuring linen; next day he would be dealing in mercery ware. High heads, ribbons, gloves, fans, and lace, he understood to a nicety; CHARLES MATHER could not bubble a young beau better with a toy! nay, he would descend even to the selling of tape, garters, and shoebuckles. When shop was shut up, he would go about the neighbourhood, and earn half a crown by teaching the young men and maids to dance. By these methods he had acquired immense riches, which he used to squander away at back-sword, quarter-staff, and cudgel-play, in which he took great pleasure; and challenged all the country.

You will say it is no wonder if BULL and FROG should be jealous of this fellow.

"It is not impossible," says FROG to BULL, "but this old rogue will take the management of the young Lord's business into his hands; besides, the rascal has good ware, and will serve him as cheap as anybody, in that case. I leave you to judge, what must become of us and our families! we must starve, or turn journeymen to old LEWIS BABOON! therefore, neighbour, I hold it advisable that we write to young Lord STRUTT, to know the bottom of this matter.

CHAPTER III.

A copy of BULL and FROG's letter to Lord STRUTT.

MY LORD,

I SUPPOSE your Lordship knows that the BULLS and the FROGS have served the Lord STRUTTS with all sorts of drapery ware, time out of mind; and whereas we are jealous, not without reason, that your Lordship intends henceforth to buy of your grandsire, old LEWIS BABOON: this is to inform your Lordship, that this proceeding does not suit with the circumstances of our families, who have lived and made a good figure in the World by the generosity of the Lord STRUTTS. Therefore we think fit to acquaint your Lordship, that you must find sufficient security to us, our heirs and assigns, that you will not employ LEWIS BABOON, or else we will take our remedy at law, clap an action upon you of £20,000 for old debts, seize and destrain your goods and chattels; which, considering your Lordship's circumstances, will plunge you into difficulties from which it will not be easy to extricate yourself: therefore we hope when your Lordship has better considered on it, you will comply with the desire of

Your loving friends,

JOHN BULL,
NIC. FROG.

Some of BULL's friends advised him to take gentler methods with the young Lord; but JOHN naturally loved rough play.

It is impossible to express the surprise of the Lord STRUTT, upon the receipt of this letter. He was not flush in "ready" [money], either to go to law or to clear old debts; neither could he find good bail.

He offered to bring matters to a friendly accommodation; and promised, upon his word of honour, that he would not change his drapers: but all to no purpose, for BULL and FROG saw clearly that old LEWIS would have the cheating of him!

CHAPTER IV.

How BULL and FROG went to law with Lord STRUTT about the premisses, and were joined by the rest of the Tradesmen.

ALL endeavours of accommodation between Lord STRUTT and his drapers proved vain. Jealousies increased, and indeed it was rumoured abroad, that the Lord STRUTT had bespoke his new liveries of old LEWIS BABOON.

This coming to Mrs. BULL's ears, when JOHN BULL came home, he found all his family in an uproar. Mrs. BULL [*the late Ministry of Lord GODOLPHIN and the Duke of MARLBOROUGH*], you must know, was very apt to be choleric.

"You sot!" says she, "you loiter about alehouses and taverns! spend your time at billiards, nine-pins or puppet-shows! or flaunt about the streets in your new gilt chariot! never minding me, nor your numerous family. Don't you hear how Lord STRUTT has bespoke his liveries at LEWIS BABOON's shop! Don't you see how that old fox steals away your customers, and turns you out of your business every day; and you sit, like an idle drone, with your hands in your pockets! Fie upon it! Up man! rouse thyself! I'll sell to my shift, before I'll be so used by that knave!"

You must think Mrs. BULL had been pretty well tuned up by FROG; who chimed in with her learned harangue.

No further delay, now! but to Counsel learned in the Law they go! who unaminously assured them of the justice and infallible success of their Lawsuit.

I told you before, that old LEWIS BABOON was a sort of a "JACK of all trades"; which made the Tradesmen jealous, as well as BULL and FROG. They hearing of the quarrel, were glad of an opportunity of joining against old LEWIS BABOON, provided that BULL and FROG would bear the charges of the suit; even lying NED the Chimney-sweeper [*the Duke of SAVOY*], and TOM the Dustman [*the King of PORTUGAL*] put in their claims; and the Cause [*war*] was put into the hands of HUMPHRY HOCUS [*the Duke of MARLBOROUGH*] the Attorney [*the General*].

A *Declaration* was drawn up to shew, that *BULL and FROG had undoubted right by prescription to be drapers to the Lord STRUTTS; that there were several old contracts to that purpose; that LEWIS BABOON had taken up the trade of Clothier and Draper, without serving his time or purchasing his Freedom; that he sold goods, that were not marketable without the stamp; that he himself was more fit for a bully than a tradesman, and went about through all the country fairs, challenging people to fight prizes, wrestling, and cudgel-play.* And abundance more to this purpose.

CHAPTER V.

The true characters of JOHN BULL, NIC. FROG, and HOCUS.

FOR the better understanding of the following History, the reader ought to know, that BULL, in the main, was an honest, plain-dealing fellow, choleric, bold, and of a very unconstant temper. He dreaded not old LEWIS either at back-sword, single falchion, or cudgel-play; but then he was very apt to quarrel with his best friends, especially if they pretended to govern him. If you flattered him, you might lead him like a child! JOHN's temper depended very much upon the air; his spirits rose and fell with the weather-glass. JOHN was quick, and understood his business very well: but no man alive was more careless in looking into his accounts; or more cheated by partners, apprentices, and servants. This was occasioned by his being a boon companion, loving his bottle and his diversion: for, to say truth, no man kept a better house than JOHN, or spent his money more generously. By plain and fair dealing, JOHN had acquired some "plumbs"; and might have kept them, had it not been for this unhappy Lawsuit.

NIC. FROG was a cunning sly whoreson, quite the reverse

of JOHN in many particulars: covetous, frugal, minded domestic affairs: would pine his belly to save his pocket; never lost a farthing by careless servants or bad debtors. He did not care much for any sort of diversions, except tricks of High German artistes and legerdemain. No man exceeded NIC. in these. Yet it must be owned, that NIC. was a fair dealer; and, in that way, had acquired immense riches.

HOCUS [*the Duke of MARLBOROUGH*] was an old cunning Attorney. What he wanted of skill in law, was made by a Clerk which he kept [?], that was the prettiest fellow in the world. He loved money, was smooth-tongued, gave good words, and seldom lost his temper. He was *not* "worse than an Infidel"; for he provided plentifully for his family: but he loved himself better than them all. He had a termagant wife [*the Duchess of MARLBOROUGH*], and, as the neighbours said, "was plaguy henpecked!" He was seldom observed, as some Attorneys will practise, to give his own personal evidence in causes: he rather chose to do it *per test. conduct.* In a word, the man was very well for an Attorney [*General*].

CHAPTER VI.

Of the various success of the Lawsuit.

"LAW is a bottomless pit! It is a cormorant, a harpy that devours everything!"

JOHN BULL was flattered by his lawyers that his suit would not last above a year or two, at most; that before that time he would be in quiet possession of his business; yet ten long years did HOCUS steer his Cause [*the war*] through all the meanders of the Law, and all the Courts: no skill, no address was wanting. And, to say truth, JOHN did not starve the cause. There wanted not "yellow boys" to fee Counsel, hire witnesses, and bribe juries. Lord STRUTT was generally cast, never had one verdict [*victory*] in his favour: and JOHN was promised, that the Next, and the Next, would be the *final Determination.* But, alas, that final Determination and happy conclusion were like an enchanted island: the nearer JOHN came to it, the further it went from him. New trials upon new points still arose! new doubts, new matters to be cleared! In short, lawyers seldom part with so good a cause, till they have got the oyster, and their clients the shell.

JOHN's ready money, book debts, bonds, mortgages, all went into the lawyers' pockets. Then JOHN began to borrow money on *Bank Stock, East India Bonds*: and now and then a farm went to pot.

At last, it was thought a good expedient to set up Squire SOUTH's [*Archduke CHARLES'*] title, to prove the Will forged, and dispossess PHILIP, Lord STRUTT, at once. Here again was a new field for the lawyers! and the Cause grew more intricate than ever. JOHN grew madder and madder. Wherever he met any of Lord STRUTT's servants, he tore off their clothes. Now and then, you would see them come home naked, without shoes, stockings, and linen.

As for old LEWIS BABOON, he was reduced to his last shift, though he had as many as any other. His children were reduced from rich silks to doily stuffs. His servants were in rags and barefooted: instead of good victuals, they now lived upon neck beef and bullock's liver. In short, nobody got much by the matter, but the men of law.

CHAPTER VII.

How JOHN BULL was so mightily pleased with his success, that he was going to leave off his trade, and turn lawyer.

IT IS wisely observed by a great philosopher, that "habit is a second nature." This was verified in the case of JOHN BULL, who, from an honest and plain tradesman, had got such a haunt about the Courts of Justice, and such a jargon of law words, that he concluded himself as able a lawyer as any that pleaded at the bar, or sat on the bench.

He was overheard, one day, talking to himself after this manner. "How capriciously does Fate or Chance dispose of mankind! How seldom is that business allotted to a man for which he is fitted by Nature! It is plain I was intended for a man of law! How did my guardians mistake my genius, in placing me, like a mean slave, behind a counter! Bless me! what immense estates these fellows raise by the Law! besides, it is the profession of a Gentleman. What a pleasure it is to be victorious in a cause! to swagger at the bar! What a fool am I to drudge any more in this woollen trade! for a lawyer I was born, and a lawyer I will be! One is never too old to learn!"

All this while, JOHN had conned over such a catalogue of hard words, as were enough to conjure up the Devil. These he used to bubble indifferently in all companies, especially at coffeehouses; so that his neighbour tradesmen began to shun his company, as a man that was cracked. Instead of the affairs of Blackwall Hall, and price of broad cloth, wool, bayes; he talked of nothing but "Actions upon the Case, Returns, *Capias*, *Alias capias*, Demurrers, *Venire facias*, Replevins, *Supersedeas*, *Certioraris*, Writs of Error, Actions of Trover and Conversion, Trespasses, *Precipes et Dedimus*."

This was matter of jest to the learned in law. However, HOCUS and the rest of the tribe, encouraged JOHN in his fancy; assuring him, that he had a great genius for law; that they questioned not but, in time, he might raise money enough by it, to reimburse him of all his charges; that if he studied, he would undoubtedly arrive to the dignity of a Lord Chief Justice. As for the advice of honest friends and neighbours, JOHN despised it. He looked upon them as fellows of a low genius; poor grovelling mechanics! JOHN reckoned it more honour to have got one favourable verdict, than to have sold a bale of broad cloth.

As for NIC. FROG, to say the truth, he was more prudent: for though he followed his Lawsuit closely, he neglected not his ordinary business; but was both in Court and in his shop at the proper hours.

CHAPTER VIII.

How JOHN discovered that HOCUS had an intrigue with his wife, and what followed thereupon.

JOHN had not run on a madding so long, had it not been for an extravagant wife [*the Administration of Lord GODOLPHIN*], whom HOCUS perceiving JOHN to be fond of, was resolved to win over to his side. It was observed by all the neighbourhood, that HOCUS had dealings with JOHN's wife, that were not so much for his honour: but this was perceived by JOHN a little too late.

She was a luxurious jade, loved splendid equipages, plays, treats, and balls; differing very much from the sober manners of her ancestors, and by no means fit for a tradesman's wife. HOCUS fed her extravagancy, and, what was still more shameful, with JOHN's own money! It is matter of fact, that upon all occasions, she ran out extravagantly on the praise of HOCUS. When JOHN used to be finding fault with his bills, she used to reproach him as ungrateful to his greatest benefactor! one that had taken so much pains in his Lawsuit, and retrieved his Family from the oppression of old LEWIS BABOON.

A good swinging sum of JOHN's readiest cash went towards building of HOCUS's country-house [*the Vote for the building of Blenheim*]. This affair between HOCUS and Mrs. BULL was so open, that all the world were scandalized at it. JOHN was not so clodpated, but at last he took the hint.

The Parson of the parish [*Doctor SACHEVEREL*] preaching one day, a little sharply against adultery [*Resistance to Kings*], Mrs. BULL told her husband, that "he was a very uncivil fellow to use such coarse language before People of Condition;" that "HOCUS was of the same mind, and that they would join, to have him turned out of his living, for using personal reflections."

"How do you mean," says JOHN, "by personal reflections? I hope in God, wife, he did not reflect on you!"

"No, thank God! my reputation is too well established in the world, to receive any hurt from such a foul-mouthed scoundrel as he! His doctrine tends only to make husbands [*Sovereigns*], tyrants; and wives [*Nations*], slaves. Must we be shut up, and husbands left to their liberty? Very pretty, indeed! A wife must never go abroad with a Platonic to see a play or a ball! she must never stir without her husband, nor walk in Spring Gardens with a cousin! I do say, husband! and I will stand by it, that without the innocent freedoms of life, matrimony would be a most intolerable state! and that a wife's virtue ought to be the result of her own reason, and not of her husband's government. For my part, I would scorn a husband that would be jealous!"

All this while, JOHN's blood boiled in his veins. He was

now confirmed in his suspicions. Jade was the best word that JOHN gave her.

Things went from better to worse, until Mrs. BULL aimed a knife at JOHN; though JOHN threw a bottle at her head very brutally indeed. After this, there was nothing but confusion. Bottles, glasses, spoons, plates, knives, forks, and dishes flew about like dust. The result of which was, that Mrs. BULL received a bruise in her right side, of which she died half a year after [*the fall of Lord GODOLPHIN's Administration, about six months after the trial of Doctor SACHEVEREL in March*, 1710].

The bruise imposthumated, and afterwards turned into an ulcer, which made everybody shy to come near her, she smelt so; yet she wanted not the help of many able physicians, who attended very diligently, and did what men of skill could do: but all to no purpose, for her condition was now quite desperate; all regular physicians and her nearest relations having given her over.

CHAPTER IX.

How Signior CAVALLO, an Italian Quack, undertook to cure Mrs. BULL of her ulcer.

THERE is nothing so impossible in Nature, but mountebanks will undertake; nothing so incredible, but they will affirm. Mrs. BULL's condition was looked upon as desperate by all Men of Art. Then Signior CAVALLO [*the Duke of SHREWSBURY*] judged it was high time for him to interpose. He bragged that he had an infallible ointment and plaster, which, being applied to the sore, would cure it in a few days; at the same time, he would give her a pill that would purge off all her bad humours, sweeten her blood, and rectify her disturbed imagination.

In spite of all Signior CAVALLO's applications, the patient grew worse. Every day she stank so, that nobody durst come within a stone's throw of her; except Signior CAVALLO and his wife, whom he sent every day to dress her, she having a very gentle, soft hand. All this while, Signior apprehended no danger.

If one asked him, "How Mrs. BULL did?"

"Better and better!" says Signior CAVALLO; the "parts heal and her constitution mends. If she submits to my Government, she will be abroad in a little time."

Nay, it is reported that he wrote to his friends in the country that "she should dance a jig [*meet the Parliament*] next October, in Westminster Hall! that her illness had been chiefly owing to bad physicians."

At last, Signior, one day, was sent for in great haste, his patient growing worse and worse.

When he came, he affirmed that "it was a gross mistake, that she was never in a fairer way. Bring hither the salve," says he, "and give her a plentiful draught of my cordial!"

As he was applying his ointments, and administering the cordial, the patient gave up the ghost: to the confusion of Signior CAVALLO, and the great joy of BULL and his friends. Signior flang away out of the house in great disorder, and swore there was foul play, for he was sure that his medicines were infallible.

Mrs. BULL having died without any signs of repentance or devotion, the Clergy would hardly allow her Christian burial.

The Relations had once resolved to sue JOHN for murder: but considering better of it, and that such a trial would rip up old sores, and discover things not so much to the reputation of the deceased; they dropped their design.

She left no Will: only there was found in her strong box the following words written on a scrip of paper. "My curse on JOHN BULL and all my posterity, if ever they come to any Composition with my Lord STRUTT!"

There were many epitaphs written upon her. One was as follows:

Here lies JOHN's wife,
Plague of his life!
She spent his wealth!
She wronged his health!
And left him daughters three
As bad as She!

The daughters' names were POLEMIA [*War*], DISCORDIA [*Discord*], and USURIA [*High rate of Interest*].

CHAPTER X.

Of JOHN BULL's second wife, and the good advice that she gave him.

JOHN quickly got the better of his grief, and it being that neither his constitution, nor the affairs of his Family could permit him to live in an unmarried state: he resolved to get him another wife.

A cousin of his last wife was proposed; but he would have no more of that breed! In short, he wedded a sober Country Gentlewoman, of a good family, and plentiful fortune [*Queen ANNE*]: the reverse of the other in her temper. Not but that she loved money, for she was of a saving temper; and applied her fortune to pay JOHN's clamorous debts, that the unfrugal methods of his last wife, and this ruinous Lawsuit had brought him into.

One day, as she had got her husband into a good humour, she talked to him after the following manner: "My Dear! since I have been your wife, I have observed great abuses and disorders in your Family. Your servants are mutinous and quarrelsome, and cheat you most abominably. Your cook-maid is in a combination with your butcher, poulterer, and fishmonger. Your butler purloins your liquor, and your brewer sells you hogwash. Your baker cheats, both in weight and tale [*number*]. Even your milk-woman and your nursery-maid have a fellow feeling. Your tailor, instead of shreds, cabbages [*steals*] whole yards of cloth. Besides, having such long scores, and not going to market for ready money, forces us to take bad ware of the Tradesmen, at their own price. You have not posted your books these ten years. [*Lord GODOLPHIN carrying War Credits over from year to year, during the period of his Administration.*] How is it possible for a man of business to keep his affairs even in the World, at this rate? Pray God, this HOCUS be honest! Would to God, you would look over his bills, and see how matters stand between FROG and you! Prodigious sums are spent in this Lawsuit, and more must be borrowed of scriveners and usurers, at heavy interest. Besides, my Dear! let me beg of you to lay aside that wild project, of leaving your business to turn lawyer: for which, let me tell you, Nature never designed you. Believe me, these rogues do but flatter, that they may pick your pocket!"

JOHN heard all this while, with patience, till she pricked his maggot, and touched him in the tender point. Then, he broke out into a violent passion, "What, I not fit for a lawyer! Let me tell you, my clodpated relations spoilt the greatest genius in the World, when they bred me a mechanic! Lord STRUTT and his old rogue of a grandsire have found, to their cost, that I can manage a Lawsuit as well as any other."

"I do not deny what you say," says Mrs. BULL, "nor do I call in question your parts; but I say it does not suit with your circumstances. You and your predecessors have lived in good reputation among your neighbours by this same clothing trade; and it were madness to leave it off! Besides, there are few that know all the tricks and cheats of these lawyers. Does not your own experience teach you, how they have drawn you on from one Term to another; and how you have danced the round of all the Courts, still flattering you with a final issue: and, for aught I can see, your Cause is not a bit clearer than it was seven years ago."

"I'll be hanged," says JOHN, "if I accept of any Composition from STRUTT, or his Grandfather! I'll rather wheel about the streets an engine to grind knives and scissors! However, I will take your advice, and look over my accounts."

CHAPTER XI.

How JOHN looked over his Attorney's bill.

WHEN JOHN first brought out the bills [*the War Credits*], the surprise of all the Family was unexpressible, at the prodigious dimensions of them. In short, they would have measured with the best bale of cloth in JOHN's shop. Fees to Judges, *puisne* Judges, Clerks, Protonotaries, Philizers, Chirographers, Under Clerks, Proclamators, Counsel, Witnesses, Jurymen, Marshals, Tipstaffs, Cryers, Porters; for enrollings, exemplifications, bails, vouchers, returns, *caveats*, examinations, filings of words, entries, declarations, replications, *recordats*, *nolle prosequis*, *certioraris*, *mittimus*, demurrers, special verdicts, informations, *scire facias*, *supersedeas*, *Habeas Corpus*, coach hire, treating of witnesses, &c.

"Verily," says JOHN, "there are a prodigious number of learned words in this Law; what a pretty science it is!"

"Ay, but husband! you have paid for every syllable and letter of these fine words! Bless me! what immense sums are at the bottom of the account!"

JOHN spent several weeks in looking over his bills, and by comparing and stating his accounts, he discovered that, besides the extravagance of every article, he had been egregiously cheated; that he had paid for Counsel that were never fee-ed, for Writs that were never drawn, for dinners that were never dressed, and journeys that were never made. In short, that HOCUS and FROG had agreed to throw the burden of the Lawsuit upon his shoulders.

CHAPTER XII.

How JOHN grew angry, resolved to accept a Composition; and what methods were practised by the lawyers for keeping him from it.

WELL might the learned DANIEL BURGESS say, that "a Lawsuit is a suit for life!" He that sows his grain upon marble, will have many a hungry belly before harvest. This JOHN felt, by woful experience. JOHN's Cause was a good milch cow; and many a man subsisted his family out of it.

However JOHN began to think it high time to look about him. He had a cousin in the country, one Sir ROGER BOLD [*ROBERT HARLEY, Earl of OXFORD*]; whose predecessors had been bred up to the law, and knew as much of it as anybody; but having left off the profession for some time, they took great pleasure in compounding lawsuits amongst their neighbours: for which, they were the aversion of the Gentlemen of the Long Robe, and at perpetual war with all the country attorneys.

JOHN put his Case in Sir ROGER's hands, desiring him to make the best of it.

The news had no sooner reached the ears of the lawyers, but they were all in an uproar. They brought all the rest of the Tradesmen [*the Allies*] upon JOHN. Squire SOUTH [*Archduke CHARLES*] swore he was betrayed, that he would starve before he compounded. FROG said he was highly wronged. Even NED the Chimney-sweeper [*Duke of SAVOY*] and TOM the Dustman [*King of* PORTUGAL] complained that their Interest was sacrificed.

As for HOCUS's wife [*the Duchess of* MARLBOROUGH], she took a hackney chair, and came to JOHN's house immediately; and fell a scolding at his wife [*Queen* ANNE], like the mother of BEELZEBUB! "You silly, awkward, ill-bred, country sow, you! Have you no more manners than to rail at my husband, that has saved that clodpated, numskulled, ninny-hammer of yours from ruin, and all his Family! It is well known how he has risen early, and sat up late to make him easy; when he was sotting at every alehouse in the town! I knew his last wife! She was a woman of breeding, good-humour, and complaisance! knew how to live in the world; but as for you, you look like a puppet moved by clockwork! Your clothes hang upon you as if they were upon tenter-hooks; and you come into a room as if you were going to steal something! Get you gone into the country, to look after your mother's poultry, to milk the cows, churn the butter, and dress up nosegays for a holiday! and meddle not with matters that you know no more of, than the signpost before your door! It is well known that my husband has an established reputation! He never swore an oath, nor told a lie in all his life! He is grateful to his benefactors, faithful to his friends, liberal to his dependents, and dutiful to his superiors! He values not your money more than the dust under his feet; but he hates to be abused! Once for all, Mrs. MYNX! leave off talking of my husband, or I will put out these saucer eyes of yours! and make that red streaked country face look as raw as an ox-cheek upon a butcher's stall! Remember, I say, that there are pillories and ducking stools!" With this, away she flang; leaving Mrs. BULL no time to reply.

No stone was left unturned to fright JOHN from this Composition [*the Peace, finally settled by the treaties signed at Utrecht, on the* 31*st March of the next year after this tract*]. Sometimes they spread reports at the coffeehouses, that JOHN and his wife had run mad! that they intended to give up house, and make over all their estate to old LEWIS BABOON! that JOHN had been often heard talking to himself, and seen in the streets without shoes or stockings! that he did nothing, from morning to night, but beat his servants; after having been the best master alive! As for his wife, she was a mere natural!

Sometimes JOHN's house was beset with a whole regiment of Attorneys' clerks, bailiffs and bailiffs' followers, and other small retainers of the law; who threw stones at his windows, and dirt at himself as he went along the street.

When JOHN complained of want of ready money to carry on his Suit; they advised him to pawn his plate and jewels, and that Mrs. BULL should sell her linen and wearing clothes!

CHAPTER XIII.

How the lawyers agreed to send Don DIEGO DISMALLO the Conjuror, to JOHN BULL, to dissuade him from making an end of his Lawsuit; and what passed between them.

Bull. HOw does my good friend Don DIEGO [*DANIEL FINCH, Earl of NOTTINGHAM*]?

Don. Never worse! Who can be easy, when their friends are playing the fool?

Bull. But then you may be easy, for I am resolved to play the fool no longer! I wish I had hearkened to your advice, and compounded this Lawsuit sooner.

Don. It is true, I was then against the ruinous ways of this Lawsuit; but looking over my Scheme since, I find there is an error in my calculation. Sol and Jupiter were in a wrong House, but I have now discovered their true places. I tell you I find that the stars are unanimously of opinion, that you will be successful in this Cause, that LEWIS will come to an untimely end, and STRUTT will be turned out of doors by his wife and children.

[*The Satire here is against Lord NOTTINGHAM; and the Party of the High Flyers or the Warm Gentlemen, of which he was one of the leaders. He had, while Secretary of State, in* 1703, *brought DEFOE to the Pillory.*

Then he went on with a torrent of ecliptics, cycles, epicycles, ascendants, trines, quadrants, conjunctions, Bulls, Bears, Goats, Rams, and abundance of hard words; which being put together, signified nothing. JOHN, all this while stood gaping and staring, like a man in a trance.

FINIS

JOHN BULL

in his SENSES:

BEING THE

SECOND PART

OF

Law is a Bottomless Pit.

Printed from a Manuscript found in the Cabinet of the famous Sir HUMPHRY POLESWORTH.

LONDON,

Printed for JOHN MORPHEW, near Stationers' Hall, 1712. Price 3d.

THE CONTENTS.

John Bull *in his Senses.*

CHAPTER I.

Mrs. BULL*'s Vindication of the indispensable duty of cuckoldom* [Resistance to Arbitrary Power] *incumbent upon wives* [Nations] *in case of tyranny, infidelity, or insufficiency of husbands* [Sovereigns]*: being a full Answer to the Doctor's* [SACHEVEREL] *Sermon against Adultery* [Resistance to Arbitrary Power].

JOHN found daily fresh proofs of the infidelity and bad designs of his deceased wife. Amongst other things, one day, looking over his Cabinet, he found the following paper:

It is evident that Matrimony [Government in a State] *is founded upon an Original Contract, whereby the wife makes over the Right she has by the Law of Nature, in favour of the husband, by which he acquires the property of all her posterity. But then the obligation is mutual; and where the Contract is broken on one side, it ceases to bind on the other. Where there is a Right, there must be a Power to maintain it, and to punish the offending party.*

This power, I affirm to be that Original Right, or rather that indispensable duty of cuckoldom [Resistance to Oppression and Arbitrary Power] *lodged in all wives, in the cases above mentioned. No wife is bound* [i. e., People to any Sovereign] *by any law to which she herself has not consented. All œconomical power is lodged originally in the husband and wife* [Sovereign and People]*; the executive part being in the husband. Both have their privileges secured to them by law and reason: but will any man infer from the husband's being invested with the executive power, that the wife is deprived of her share, and that which is the principal branch of it, the original right of cuckoldom* [Resistance to Arbitrary Power]? *and that she has no remedy left but* preces et lachrymæ, *or an appeal to a supreme Court of Judicature?*

No less frivolous are the arguments drawn from the general appellations and terms of Husband and Wife [Sovereign and People]. *A husband denotes several different sorts of Magistrates, according to the usages and customs of different climates and countries. In some Eastern nations, it signifies a Tyrant, with the absolute power of life and death. In Turkey, it denoteth an Arbitrary Governor, with power of perpetual imprisonment. In Italy, it gives the husband the power of poison and padlocks. In the countries of England, France, and Holland, it has quite a different meaning, implying a free and equal Government: securing to the wife, in certain cases, the liberty of cuckoldom* [Resistance], *and the property of pin money and separate maintenance. So that the arguments drawn from the terms of Husband and Wife are fallacious, and by no means fit to support a tyrannical doctrine, as that of Absolute unlimited Chastity* [Passive Obedience] *and conjugal fidelity.*

The general exhortations to chastity in wives are meant only for rules in ordinary cases; but suppose the three conditions of Ability, Justice, and Fidelity in the Husband. Such an unlimited, unconditioned fidelity in the Wife could never be supposed by reasonable men. It seems a reflection upon the Church, to charge her with doctrines that countenance oppression.

The doctrine of the Original Right of cuckoldom is congruous to the Law of Nature, which is superior to all human laws; and for that, I dare appeal to all wives! It is much to the honour of our English wives that they have never given up that Fundamental Point; and that, though in former Ages they were muffled up in darkness and superstition, yet that notion seemed engraven on their minds, and the impression was so strong, that nothing could impair it.

To assert the illegality of cuckoldom [Resistance], *upon any pretence whatever, were to cast odious colours upon the married state, to blacken the necessary means of perpetuating families. Such laws can never be supposed to have been designed to defeat the very end of matrimony, the increase of mankind. I call them necessary means, for in many cases what other means are left? Such a doctrine wounds the honour of families, unsettles the titles to kingdoms, honours, and estates; for if the actions from which such settlements spring were illegal, all that is built upon them must be so too: but the last is absurd, therefore the first must be so likewise. What is the cause that Europe groans, at present, under the heavy load of a cruel and expensive war; but the tyrannical custom of a certain Nation* [Spain] *and the scrupulous nicety of a silly Queen; whereby the Kingdom might have had an heir, and a controverted succession might have been avoided? These are the effects of the narrow maxims of your Clergy, "That one must* not *do evil, that good may come of it."*

From all that has been said, one may clearly perceive the absurdity of the doctrine of the seditious, discontented, hotheaded, ungifted, unedifying Preacher [Doctor SACHEVEREL] *asserting that "the grand security of the matrimonial state, and the pillar upon which it stands, is founded upon the wife's belief of an* absolute unconditional *fidelity to the husband." By which bold assertion he strikes at the root, digs the foundation, and removes the basis upon which the happiness of a married state is built.*

As for his personal reflections, I would gladly know, who are those Wanton Wives he speaks of? who are those Ladies of high stations that he so boldly traduces in his Sermon? It is pretty plain, whom these aspersions are aimed at! for which he deserves the pillory, or something worse.

In confirmation of this doctrine of the indispensable duty of cuckoldom [Resistance], *I could bring the example of the wisest wives of all Ages; who, by these means, have preserved their husbands' families from ruin and oblivion: but what has been said, is a sufficient ground for punishing this pragmatical Parson.*

CHAPTER II.

The two great parties of Wives, the Devotoes and the Hitts.

THE doctrine of unlimited chastity [*non-resistance*] and fidelity in wives, was universally espoused by all husbands [*Sovereigns*]; who went about the country, and made the wives sign papers, signifying their utter detestation and abhorrence of Mrs. BULL's wicked doctrine of the indispensable duty of cuckoldom. Some yielded, others refused to part with their native liberty; which gave rise to two great parties amongst the wives—the Devotoes [*High Church*], and the Hitts [*Low Church*]; though it must be owned that the distinction was more nominal than real. For the Devotoes would abuse freedoms sometimes; and those who were distinguished by the name of Hitts, were often very honest.

At the same time, there was an ingenious treatise, that came out with the title of *Good advice to husbands*. In which they are counselled not to trust too much to their wives' owning the doctrine of unlimited conjugal fidelity, and so to neglect family duty, and a due watchfulness over the manners of their wives; that the greatest security to husbands was a vigorous constitution, good usage of their wives, and keeping them from temptation: many husbands having been sufferers by their trusting too much to general professions; as was exemplified in the case of a foolish and negligent husband [*JAMES II.*], who, trusting to the efficacy of this principle, was undone by his wife's elopement from him [*The Revolution of* 1688].

CHAPTER III.

An account of the Conference between Mrs. BULL and Don DIEGO DISMALLO.

Don Diego. IS IT possible, Cousin BULL! that you can forget the honourable maxims of the Family you are come of, and break your word with three of the honestest, best-meaning persons in the world, Esquire SOUTH, FROG, and HOCUS, that have sacrificed their Interest to yours? It is base to take advantage of their simplicity and credulity, and leave them in the lurch at last!

Mrs. Bull. I am sure, they have left my Family in a bad condition. We have hardly money to go to market, and nobody will take our words for sixpence. A very fine spark, this Esquire SOUTH [*Archduke CHARLES*]! My husband took him in, a dirty boy. It was the business of half the servants to attend to him, the rogue did bawl and make such a noise! Sometimes he fell into the fire, and burnt his face; sometimes broke his shins clambering over the benches: and always came in so dirty, as if he had been dragged through the kennel at a boarding school. He lost his money at chuck-farthing, shuffle-cap, and all-fours; sold his books, and pawned his linen, which we were always forced to redeem. Then the whole generation of him are so in love with bagpipes and puppet-shows! I wish you knew what my husband has paid at the pastrycooks and confectioners, for Naples biscuit, tarts, custards, and sweetmeats. All this while, my husband considered him as a Gentleman of good family that had fallen into decay, gave him a good education, and has settled him in a good credible way of living; having procured him, by his Interest, one of the best places in the country: and what return, think you! does this fine Gentleman make us? He will hardly give me or my husband, a good word or a civil expression! Instead of plain Sir, and Madam; which (though I say it) is our due: he calls us *Goody*, and *Gaffer* such a one! that he did us a great deal of honour to board with us: huffs and dings at such a rate, because we did not spend the little we have left, to get him the title and estate of Lord STRUTT; and then, forsooth! we shall have the honour to be his woollen-drapers.

Don Diego. And would you lose the honour of so noble and generous an undertaking? Would you rather accept the scandalous Composition, and trust that old rogue LEWIS BABOON?

Mrs. Bull. Look you, friend DIEGO! if we law it on till LEWIS turns honest, I am afraid our credit will run low at Blackwall Hall! I wish every man had his own! but I still say, that Lord STRUTT's money shines as bright, and chinks as well as Squire SOUTH's. I don't know any other hold that we Tradesmen have of these Great Folks, but their Interest. *Buy dear, and sell cheap!* and, I'll warrant ye! you will keep your customer. The worst is, that Lord STRUTT's servants have got such a haunt about that old rogue's shop, that it will cost us many a firkin of strong beer to bring them back again: and the longer they are in a bad road, the harder it will be to get them out of it.

Don Diego. But poor FROG! what has he done? On my conscience, if there be an honest, sincere man in the world, it is that FROG!

Mrs. Bull. I think, I need not tell you how much FROG has been obliged to our Family from his childhood. He carries his head high now, but he had never been the man he is, without our help. Ever since the commencement of this Lawsuit, it has been the business of HOCUS, in sharing our expenses, to plead for FROG. "Poor FROG," says he, "is in hard circumstances. He has a numerous family and lives from hand to mouth; his children do not eat a bit of good victuals from one year's end to the other; but live on salt herrings, sour curd, and bore-cole. He does his utmost, poor fellow! to keep things even in the world, and has exerted himself beyond his ability in this Lawsuit: but he really has not wherewithal to go on. What signifies this hundred pounds? place it upon your side of the account! It is a great deal for poor FROG, and a trifle for you."

That has been HOCUS's constant language, and I am sure he has had obligations enough to us, to have acted another part.

Don Diego. No doubt HOCUS meant all this for the best; but he is a tender-hearted charitable man. FROG is indeed in hard circumstances.

Mrs. Bull. Hard circumstances! I swear this is provoking to the last degree. All the time of the Lawsuit, as fast as we have mortgaged, FROG has purchased. From a plain tradesman, with a shop, warehouse, and a country hut with a dirty fishpond at the end of it, he is now grown a very rich Country Gentleman, with a noble landed estate, noble palaces, manors, parks, gardens, and farms finer than any we were ever master of. Is it not strange, when my husband disbursed great sums every Term, FROG should be purchasing some new farm or manor? So that if this Lawsuit lasts, he will be far the richest man in his country.

What is worse than all this, he steals away my customers every day. I have twelve of the richest and the best that have left my shop by his persuasion, and whom to my knowledge, he has under bonds never to return again. Judge you, if this be neighbourly dealing!

Don Diego. FROG is indeed pretty close in his dealings, but very honest! You are so touchy and take things so hotly; I am sure there must be some mistake in this!

Mrs. Bull. A plaguy one indeed! You know, and you have often told me, how HOCUS and those rogues kept my husband, JOHN BULL, drunk for five years together, with punch and strong waters (I am sure he never went one night sober to bed), till they got him to sign the strangest deed that ever you saw in your life. The methods they took to manage him, I'll tell you another time: at present, I only read the writing [*the Barrier Treaty*].

Articles of Agreement between JOHN BULL, *Clothier, and* NICHOLAS FROG, *Linendraper.*

I. *That for maintaining the ancient good correspondence and friendship between the said parties, I,* NICHOLAS FROG, *do solemnly engage and promise to keep peace in* JOHN BULL'*s family: that neither his wife, children, nor servants give him any trouble, disturbance, or molestation whatever; but to oblige them all, to do their duty quietly in their respective stations. And whereas the said* JOHN BULL, *from the assured confidence that he has in my friendship, has appointed me Executor of his last Will and Testament, and Guardian to his children; I do undertake for me, my heirs and assigns, to see the same duly executed and performed, and that it shall be unalterable in all its parts, by* JOHN BULL *or anybody else. For that purpose, it shall be lawful and allowable for me to enter his house at any hour of the day or night, to break open bars, bolts, and doors, chests of drawers and strong boxes, in order to secure the peace of my friend* JOHN BULL'*s family, and to see his Will duly executed.*

II. *In consideration of which kind neighbourly office of* NICHOLAS FROG, *in that he has been pleased to accept of the aforesaid Trust, I,* JOHN BULL, *having duly considered that my friend* NICHOLAS FROG *at this time lives in a marshy soil and unwholesome air, infested with fogs and damps, destructive of the health of himself, wife, and children, do bind and oblige me, my heirs and assigns, to purchase for the said* NICHOLAS FROG, *with the best and readiest of my cash, bonds, mortgages, goods and chattels, a landed estate, with parks, gardens, palaces, rivers, fields, and outlets, consisting of as large extent as the said* NICHOLAS FROG *shall think fit. And whereas the said* NICHOLAS FROG *is at present hemmed in too closely by the grounds of* LEWIS BABOON, *Master of the Science of Defence; I, the said* JOHN BULL, *do oblige myself, with the readiest of my cash, to purchase and enclose the said grounds for as many fields and acres as the said* NICHOLAS *shall think fit; to the extent that the said* NICHOLAS *may have free egress and regress, without let or molestation, suitable to the demands of himself and family.*

III. *Furthermore, the said JOHN BULL obliges himself to make the country neighbours of NICHOLAS FROG allot a certain part of yearly rents to pay for the repairs of the said landed estate, to the intent that his good friend NICHOLAS FROG may be eased of all charges.*

IV. *And whereas the said NICHOLAS FROG did contract with the deceased Lord STRUTT about certain liberties, privileges, and immunities, formerly in the possession of the said JOHN BULL; I, the said JOHN BULL, do freely, by these Presents, renounce, quit, and make over to the said NICHOLAS, the liberties, privileges, and immunities contracted for, as if they never had belonged to me.*

V. *The said JOHN BULL obliges himself, his heirs and assigns, not to sell one rag of broad or coarse cloth to any gentleman within the neighbourhood of the said NICHOLAS, except in such quantities and such rates as the said NICHOLAS shall think fit.*

Signed and sealed,

JOHN BULL,
NIC. FROG.

The reading of this paper put Mrs. BULL in such a passion that she fell down right into a fit, and they were forced to give her a good quantity of the Spirits of Hartshorn before she recovered.

Don Diego. Why in such a passion, Cousin? Considering your circumstances at that time, I don't think such an unreasonable contract. You see FROG, for all this, is religiously true to his bargain! He scorns to hearken to any competition without your privacy.

Mrs. Bull. You know the contrary, read that letter!

(Reads the superscription.) *For LEWIS BABOON, Master of the noble Science of Defence.*

SIR,

I UNDERSTAND that you are, at this time, treating with my friend JOHN BULL, about the restoring of the Lord STRUTT's custom; and besides allowing him certain privileges of parks and fishponds. I wonder how you, that are a man that knows the World, can talk with that simple fellow! He has been my bubble [tool] *these twenty years; and to my certain knowledge, understands no more of his own Affairs than a child in swaddling clothes. I know he has got a sort of a pragmatical silly jade of a wife that pretends to take him out of my hands; but you and she both will find yourselves mistaken. I'll find those that shall manage her! and for him, he dares as well be hanged as make one step in his Affairs without my consent.*

If you will give me what you promised him, I will make all things easy, and stop the Deeds of Ejectment against Lord STRUTT*; if you will not, take what follows! I shall have a good Action against you, for pretending* [designing] *to rob me of my bubble. Take this warning from*

Your loving friend,

NICHOLAS FROG.

I am told, Cousin DIEGO! you are one of those that have undertaken to govern me, and that you have said, you will carry a green bag yourself rather than we shall make an end of our Lawsuit. I'll teach them, and you too, to manage!

Don Diego. For God's sake, Madam! why so choleric! I say, this letter is some forgery! It never entered into the head of that honest man, NIC. FROG, to do any such thing!

Mrs. Bull. I can't abide you! You have been railing, these twenty years, at Esquire SOUTH, FROG, and HOCUS; calling them rogues and pickpockets: and, now, they are turned the honestest fellows in the world! What is the meaning of all this?

Don Diego. Pray tell me, how you came to employ this Sir ROGER in your Affairs, and not think of your old friend DIEGO?

Mrs. Bull. So, so, there it pinches! To tell you the truth, I have employed Sir ROGER in several weighty affairs, and have found him trusty and honest; and the poor man always scorned to take a farthing of me. I have abundance that profess great zeal, but they are greedy of the pence. My husband and I are now in circumstances, that we must be served upon cheaper terms than we have been.

Don Diego. Well, Cousin, I find I can do no good with you! I am sorry that you will ruin yourself, by trusting this Sir ROGER.

CHAPTER IV.

How the Guardians of the deceased Mrs. BULL's three daughters, came to JOHN BULL, and what advice they gave him; wherein is briefly treated the characters of the three daughters. Also JOHN BULL's answer to the three Guardians.

I TOLD you in my First Part [*p.* 285], that Mrs. BULL, before she departed this life, had blessed JOHN with three daughters. I need not repeat their names; neither would willingly use any scandalous reflections upon young ladies, whose reputations ought to be very tenderly handled: but the characters of these were so well known in the neighbourhood, that it is doing them no injury to make a short description of them.

The eldest [*WAR*] was as termagant, imperious, prodigal, lewd, profligate wench as ever breathed. She used to rantipole about the house, pinch the kitten, kick the servants, and torture the cats and dogs. She would rob her father's strong-box for money to give the young fellows she was fond of. She had a noble air, and something great in her mien; but such a noisome infectious breath, as threw all the servants that dressed her into consumption. If she smelt the fresh nosegay, it would shrivel and wither as it had been blighted. She used to come home in her cups, and break the china and the looking-glasses; was of such an irregular temper, and so entirely given to her passion, that you might as well argue with the North Wind as with her Ladyship; and so expensive, that the income of three Dukedoms was not enough to supply her extravagance. HOCUS loved her best.

The second daughter [*DISCORD*], born a year after her sister, was a peevish, froward, ill-conditioned creature as ever was born, ugly as the Devil; lean, haggard, pale; with saucer eyes, a sharp nose, and hunchbacked: but active, sprightly, and diligent about her affairs. Her ill complexion was occasioned by her bad diet, which was coffee, morning, noon, and night [*i.e., Discord fed on the controversies in the Coffeehouses*]. She never rested quietly abed, but used to disturb the whole family with shrieking out in her dreams; and plague them, next day, with interpreting them: for she took them all for Gospel! She would cry out

"Murder!" and disturb the whole neighbourhood; and when JOHN came running downstairs to inquire what the matter was, "Nothing," forsooth! "only her maid had stuck a pin wrong in her gown."

She turned away one servant for putting too much oil in her salad, and another for putting too little salt in her water-gruel. But such as, by flattery, had procured her esteem, she would indulge in the greatest crimes. Her father had two coachmen [*Prime Ministers*]. When one [*HARLEY*] was on the coach-box, if the coach swung but the least to one side, she used to shriek so loud that all the street concluded she was overturned: but, though the other [*GODOLPHIN*] was eternally drunk, and had overturned the whole Family, she was very angry with her father for turning him away.

Then she used to carry tales and stories from one to another, till she had set the whole neighbourhood together by the ears; and this was the only diversion she took pleasure in. She never went abroad but what she brought home such a bundle of monstrous lies, as would have amazed any mortal but such as knew her; of "a whale that had swallowed a fleet of ships"; of "the lions being let out of the Tower, to destroy the Protestant religion"; of "the Pope's being seen in a brandy shop at Wapping"; and a "prodigious strong man that was going to shove down the cupola of St. Paul's"; of "three millions of Five Pound pieces that Esquire SOUTH had found under an old wall"; of "blazing stars," "flying dragons," and abundance of such stuff.

All the servants in the Family made high court to her, for she domineered there; and turned out and in, whom she pleased. Only there was an old grudge between her and Sir ROGER: whom she mortally hated, and used to hire fellows to squirt kennel water upon him, as he passed along the streets; so that he was forced constantly to wear a surtout of oiled cloth, by which means he came home pretty clean, except where the surtout was a little scanty.

As for the third [*USURY*], she was a thief and a common mercenary prostitute. In the practice of her profession, she had amassed vast magazines of all sorts of things. She had above five hundred suits of clothes; and yet went abroad like a cinder-wench. She robbed and starved all the servants, so that nobody could live near her.

So much for JOHN's three daughters; which you will say were rarities to be fond of. Yet Nature will shew itself! Nobody could blame their Relations for taking care of them; and therefore it was that HOCUS, with two other of the Guardians, thought it their duty to take care of the Interest of the three girls, and give JOHN their best advice before he compounded the Lawsuit.

Hocus. What makes you so shy of late, my good friend? There is nobody loves you better than I, nor has taken more pains in your affairs! As I hoped to be saved! I would do anything to serve you! I would crawl upon all fours to serve you! I have spent my health and paternal estate in your service! I have indeed a small pittance left, with which I might retire, and with as good conscience as any man. But the thoughts of this disgraceful Composition so touches me to the quick, that I cannot sleep. After I had brought the Cause to the last stroke, that one verdict more had quite ruined old LEWIS and Lord STRUTT, and put you in the quiet possession of everything: then to Compound! I cannot bear it.

This Cause was my favourite. I had set my heart upon it! It is like an only child, I cannot endure that it should miscarry. For God's sake, consider only to what a dismal condition old LEWIS is brought! He is at an end of all his cash; his Attorneys [*Generals*] have hardly one trick left, they are at an end of all their *chicane*: besides, he has both his law and his daily bread now upon trust. Hold out one Term longer! and, I'll warrant you! before the next, we shall have him in the Fleet. I'll bring him to the pillory! his ears shall pay for his perjuries! For the love of God, don't compound! Let me be hanged, if you have a friend in the World that loves you better than I! there is nobody can say I am covetous! or that I have any Interest to pursue, but yours!

Second Guardian [*Lord GODOLPHIN, the late Lord Treasurer*]. There is nothing so plain than that this LEWIS has a design to ruin all his neighbouring Tradesmen; and at this time, he has such a prodigious income by his trade of all kinds, that if there is not some stop put to his exorbitant riches, he will monopolize everything, and nobody will be able to sell a yard of drapery or mercery ware but himself.

I therefore hold it advisable that you continue the Lawsuit, and burst him at once. My concern for the three poor motherless children obliges me to give you this advice; for their estates, poor girls! depend upon the success of this Cause.

Third Guardian [*Lord* COWPER, *the late Lord Chancellor*]. I own this Writ of Ejectment has cost dear; but then consider it a jewel well worth the purchasing at the price of all you have. None but Mr. BULL's declared enemies can say, he has any other security for his clothing trade but the ejectment of Lord STRUTT. The only question then, that remains to be decided, is, Who shall stand the expenses of the Suit? To which the answer is plain. Who but he that is to have the advantage of the sentence! When Esquire SOUTH has got possession of his title and honour, is not JOHN BULL to be his Clothier? Who then but JOHN, ought to put him in possession! Ask but an indifferent Gentleman, who ought to bear *his* charges at Law? and he will readily answer, "His tradesmen!" I do therefore affirm, and I will go to death with it! that being his Clothier; you ought to put him in quiet possession of his estate! and with the same generous spirit you have begun it, complete the good work! If you persist in the bad measures you are now in, what must become of the three poor orphans? my heart bleeds for the poor girls!

John Bull. You are very eloquent persons, but give me leave to tell you, that you express a great deal more concern for the three girls than for me. I think my Interest ought to be considered in the first place.

As for you, HOCUS! I can't but say you have managed my Lawsuit with great address and much to my honour: and, though I say it! you have been well paid for it! Never was Attorney's bill more extravagant! and, give me leave to say, there are many articles [in it], which the most griping of your profession never demanded. I have trusted you with the disbursing of great sums of money, and you have constantly sunk some into your own pocket. I tell you, I don't like that sinking!

Why must the burden be taken off FROG's back, and laid upon my shoulders? He can drive about his own parks and fields in his gilt chariot; when I have been forced to mortgage my estate! His Note will go further than my

Bond. Is it not matter of fact, that from the richest tradesman in all the country, I am reduced to beg and borrow from Scriveners and Usurers [*The National Debt*], that suck the heart and blood out of me: and what was all this for? Did you like FROG's countenance better than mine? Was not I your old friend and relation? Have I not presented you nobly? Have I not clad your whole family? Have you not had a hundred yards at a time of the finest cloth in my shop? Why must the rest of the Tradesmen be not only indemnified from charges, but forbidden to go on with their own business, and what is more their concern than mine?

As to holding out this Term, I appeal to your own conscience, has not that been your constant discourse these six years, "One Term more, and old LEWIS goes to pot!" If thou art so fond of my Cause, be generous for once! and lend me a brace of thousands. Ah HOCUS! HOCUS! I know thee! Not a *sou*, to save me from gaol, I trow!

Look ye, Gentlemen! I have lived with credit in the World; and it grieves my heart, never to stir out of my doors, but to be pulled by the sleeve, by some rascally dun or another, "Sir, remember my bill!" "There is a small concern of a thousand pounds; I hope you think on it, Sir!" And to have these usurers transact [*sell and buy*] my debts at coffeehouses and alehouses; as if I were going to break up shop. Lord! that ever the rich, the generous JOHN BULL, Clothier, the envy of all his neighbours, should be brought to compound his debts for five shillings in the pound; and to have his name in an advertisement for a statute of Bankrupt! The thought of it makes me mad! I have read somewhere in the *Apocrypha*, that one should *not consult with a woman, touching her of whom she is jealous; nor with a merchant, concerning exchange; nor with a buyer, of selling; nor with an unmerciful man, of kindness; &c.* I could have added one thing more. *Nor with an Attorney, about compounding a Lawsuit.*

This Ejectment of Lord STRUTT will never do! The evidence is crimp [*concocted*]; the witnesses swear backwards and forwards, and contradict themselves; and his tenants [*the people of Spain*] stick by him. If it *were* practicable, is it reasonable that when Esquire SOUTH is losing his money to sharpers and pickpockets, going about the country with fiddlers and buffoons, and squandering his income with hawks and dogs, I should lay out the fruits of my honest industry in a Lawsuit for him, only upon the hopes of being his Clothier? and when the Cause is over, I shall not have the benefit of my project for want of money to go to market!

Look ye, Gentlemen! JOHN BULL is but a plain man; but JOHN BULL knows when he is ill used. I know the infirmity of our Family! We *are* apt to play the boon companion; and throw away our money in our cups. But it was an unfair thing in you, Gentlemen! to take advantage of my weakness; to keep a parcel of roaring bullies about me, day and night, with huzzas and hunting horns, and ringing the changes on butchers' cleavers! never to let me cool! and make me set my hands to papers, when I could hardly hold my pen! There will come a Day of Reckoning for all that proceeding.

In the mean time, Gentlemen! I beg you will let me look into my affairs a little, and that you would not grudge me a very small remainder of a very great estate!

CHAPTER V.

Esquire SOUTH's message and letter to Mrs. BULL.

THE arguments used by HOCUS and the rest of the Guardians had hitherto proved insufficient. JOHN and his wife could not be persuaded to bear the expense of Esquire SOUTH's Lawsuit. They thought it reasonable that, since he was to have the honour and advantage, he should bear the greatest share of the charges; and retrench what he lost to sharpers, and spent upon country dances and puppet-plays, to apply it to that use. This was not very grateful [*agreeable*] to the Esquire [*here standing for the Emperor of AUSTRIA, the father of Archduke CHARLES*].

Therefore, as the last experiment, he was resolved to send Signior BENE-NATO, Master of his Foxhounds [*Prince EUGENE of Savoy, who came to England on this political mission to Queen ANNE, in Jan.–March,* 1711] to Mrs. BULL, to try what good he could do with her.

This Signior BENE-NATO had all the qualities of a fine Gentleman, that were fit to charm a lady's heart; and if any person in the world could have persuaded her, it was he!

But such was her unshaken fidelity to her husband, and the constant purpose of her mind to pursue his Interest, that the most refined arts of gallantry that were practised could not seduce her loyal heart. The necklaces, diamond crosses, and rich bracelets that were offered; she rejected with the utmost scorn and disdain. The music and serenades that were given her, sounded more ungratefully in her ears than the noise of a screech owl. However, she received Esquire SOUTH's letter by the hands of Signior BENE-NATO, with that respect which became his Quality.

The copy of the letter is as follows; in which you will observe, he changes a little his usual style.

MADAM,

THE Writ of Ejectment against PHILIP BABOON pretended Lord STRUTT, is just ready to pass. There want but a few necessary forms, and a Verdict [victory] *or two more, to put me in the quiet possession of my Honour and Estate. I question not but that, according to your wonted generosity and goodness, you will give it the finishing stroke: an honour that I would grudge anybody but yourself.*

In order to ease you of some part of the charges, I promise to furnish pen, ink, and paper; provided you pay for the stamps. Besides, I have ordered my Steward to pay, out of the readiest and best of my rents, £5 10s. a year, till my Suit is finished. I wish you health and happiness, being

With due respect,
Madam,
Your assured friend,
SOUTH.

What answer Mrs. BULL returned to this letter, you shall know in my Third Part: only they were at a pretty good distance in their Proposals. For as Esquire SOUTH only offered to be at the charges of pen, ink, and paper; Mrs. BULL refused any more than to lend her barge to carry his Counsel to Westminster Hall [*the English fleets transporting the forces to Barcelona*].

FINIS.

JOHN BULL

Still

In his SENSES:

BEING THE

THIRD PART

OF

Law is a Bottomless Pit.

Printed from a Manuscript found in the Cabinet of the famous Sir HUMPHRY POLESWORTH*: and published (as well as the two former Parts) by the Author of the* New Atlantis.

LONDON:

Printed for JOHN MORPHEW, near Stationers' Hall, 1712. Price 6d.

THE CONTENTS.

The Publisher's Preface.

THE World is much indebted to the famous Sir HUMPHRY POLESWORTH, for his ingenious and impartial Account of JOHN BULL's Lawsuit; yet there is just cause of complaint against him, in that he retails it only by parcels, and won't give us the whole Work. This forces me, who am only the Publisher, to bespeak the assistance of his friends and acquaintance, to engage him to lay aside that stingy humour, and to gratify the curiosity of the public at once. He pleads in excuse, that "they are only Private Memoirs, written for his own use, in a loose style, to serve as a help to his ordinary conversation."

I represented to him the good reception of the two first Parts had met [with], that though they had been calculated by him only for the meridian of Grub street, yet they were taken notice of by the better sort; that the World was now sufficiently acquainted with JOHN BULL, and interested in his little concerns. He answered with a smile, that "he had, indeed, some trifling things to impart that concerned JOHN BULL's Relations and domestic affairs: if these would satisfy me, he gave me free leave to make use of them! because they would serve to make the History of the Lawsuit more intelligible."

When I had looked over the manuscript, I found likewise some further account of the Composition; which perhaps may not be unacceptable to such as have read the two former Parts.

CHAPTER I.

The Character of JOHN BULL's *mother.*

JOHN had a mother [*the Church of England*] whom he loved and honoured extremely; a discreet, grave, sober, good-conditioned, cleanly old Gentlewoman as ever lived. She was none of your cross-grained, termagant scolding Jades that one had as good be hanged, as live in the house with! such as are always censuring the conduct, and telling scandalous stories, of their neighbours; extolling their own good qualities, and undervaluing those of others. On the contrary, she was of a meek spirit: and as she was strictly virtuous herself, so she always put the best construction upon the words and actions of her neighbours; except where they were irreconcilable to the rules of honesty and decency. She was neither one of your precise prudes, nor one of your phantastical old belles that dress themselves like girls of fifteen: as she neither wore a ruff, forehead cloth, nor high-crowned hat, so she had laid aside feathers, flowers, and crimpt ribbons in her head-dress, furbelow [*flounce*], scarfs, and hooped petticoats. She scorned to patch [*wear black spots on the face*] and paint; yet she loved to keep her hands and her face clean. Though she wore no flaunting laced ruffles, she would not keep herself in a constant sweat with greasy flannel. Though her hair was not stuck with jewels, she was not ashamed of a diamond cross. She was not, like some ladies, hung about with toys and trinkets, twiser [*tweezer*] cases, pocket-glasses, and essence-bottles! she used only a gold watch, and an *Almanack* to mark the hours and the Holy Days.

Her furniture was neat and genteel, well fancied with a *bon goût*. As she affected not the grandeur of a State with a canopy, she thought there was no offence in an elbow-chair. She had laid aside your carving, gilding, and Japan [*japanned*] work, as being too apt to gather dirt: but she never could be prevailed upon to part with plain wainscot and clean hangings. There are some ladies who affect to smell a stink in everything; they are always highly perfumed, and continually burning frankincense in their rooms [*Roman Catholic worship*]: she was above such affectation; yet she never would lay aside the use of brooms and scrubbing brushes, and scrupled not to lay her linen in fresh lavender.

She was no less genteel in her behaviour, well bred without affectation; in the due mean between one of your affected curtseying pieces of formality [*Nonconformity*], and your romps that have no regard to the common rules of civility. There are some ladies that affect a mighty regard for their relations. "We must not eat to-day, for my uncle TOM or my cousin BETTY died this time ten years! [*Saints Days*]." "Let us have a ball to-night, it is my neighbour Such-a-one's birthday!" She looked upon all this as a grimace [*mask*], yet she constantly observed her Husband's birthday [*Christmas Day*], her wedding day [? *Whitsunday*], and some few more.

Though she was a truly good woman, and had a sincere motherly love for her son JOHN; yet there wanted not those who endeavoured to create a misunderstanding between them: and they had so far prevailed with him once [*in the time of the Commonwealth*] that he had turned her out of doors [*exclusion of the Episcopacy from the House of Lords in* 1644]; to his great sorrow, as he found afterwards, for his affairs went all at sixes and sevens.

She was no less judicious in the turn of her conversation, and choice of her studies, in which she far exceeded all her sex [*all other Churches*]. Your rakes that hate the company of all sober grave Gentlewomen, would bear hers: and she would, by her handsome manner of proceeding, sooner reclaim, than some that were more sour and reserved [*Nonconformists*]. She was a zealous preacher up of Chastity and Conjugal Fidelity in wives [*obedience and submission to the King*]; and by no means a friend to the new-fangled doctrine of the "Indispensable Duty of Cuckoldom" [*Resistance to Arbitrary Power*]. Though she advanced her opinions with a becoming assurance; yet she never ushered them in, as some positive creatures do, with dogmatic assertions, "This is infallible!" "I cannot be mistaken!" "None but a rogue can deny it!" It has been observed, that such people are oftener in the wrong than anybody.

Though she had a thousand good qualities, she was not without her faults: amongst which, one might perhaps reckon too great lenity to her servants; to whom she always gave good counsel, but often too gentle correction.

I thought I could not say less of JOHN BULL's mother, because she bears a part in the following transactions.

CHAPTER II.

The Character of JOHN BULL's sister PEG, with the quarrels that happened between Master and Miss in their childhood.

JOHN has a sister [*the Kirk of Scotland*], a poor girl that had been starved at nurse. Anybody would have guessed Miss to have been bred up under the influence of a cruel step-dame, and JOHN to be the fondling of a tender mother. JOHN looked ruddy and plump, with a pair of cheeks like a trumpeter; Miss looked pale and wan, as if she had the green sickness: and, no wonder, for JOHN was the darling! He had all the good bits, was crammed with good pullet, chicken, pig, goose, and capon: while Miss had only a little oatmeal and water, or a dry crust without butter. JOHN had his golden pippins, peaches, and nectarines; poor Miss a crab apple, sloe, or a blackberry. Master lay in the best apartment, with his bedchamber [*England*] towards the south sun: Miss lodged in a garret [*Scotland*], exposed to the north wind, which shrivelled her countenance. However this usage, though it stunted the girl in her growth, gave her a hardy constitution.

She had life and spirit in abundance, and knew when she

was ill used. Now and then, she would seize upon JOHN'S commons, snatch a leg of a pullet or a bit of good beef: for which they were sure to go to fisticuffs. Master was indeed too strong for her, but Miss would not yield in the least point; but even when Master had got her down, she would scratch and bite like a tiger. When he gave her a cuff on the ear, she would prick him with her knitting needle. JOHN brought a great chain, one day, to tie her to the bed-post: for which affront, Miss aimed a penknife at his heart. In short, these quarrels grew up to rooted aversions. They gave one another nicknames. She called him "GUNDY-GUTS!" and he called her "Lousy PEG!"

Though the girl was a tight clever wench, as any was: and, through her pale looks, you might discern spirit and vivacity, which made her, not indeed a perfect beauty, but something that was agreeable.

It was barbarous in parents, not to take notice of these early quarrels, and make them live better together: such domestic feuds proving afterwards the occasions of misfortunes to them both.

PEG had indeed some odd humours and comical antipathy; for which JOHN would jeer her. "What do you think of my sister PEG," says he, "that faints at the sound of an organ! and yet will dance and frisk at the noise of a bagpipe?"

"What is that to you, GUNDY-GUTS!" quoth PEG, "everybody is to choose their own music!"

Then PEG had taken a fancy, not to say her *Paternoster*; which made people imagine strange things of her.

Of the three brothers that have made such a clutter in the world, Lord PETER, MARTIN, and JACK [*the names by which* SWIFT *in his* Tale of a Tub *distinguished the Roman Catholics, the Church of England, and the Fanatics* (Dissenters)], JACK had, of late, been her inclination. Lord PETER she detested, nor did MARTIN stand much better in her good graces; but JACK had found the way to her heart. I have often admired [*wondered*] what charms she discovered in that awkward booby! till I talked with a person that was acquainted with the intrigue, who gave me the following account of it.

CHAPTER III.

JACK's Charms, or the method by which he gained PEG's heart.

IN THE first place, JACK [*the Fanatics* (Dissenters)] was a very young fellow, by much the youngest of the three brothers; and people indeed wondered how such a young upstart jackanapes [*puppy*] should grow so pert and saucy, and take so much upon him.

2. JACK bragged of greater abilities than other men. He was well gifted! as he pretended. I need not tell you, what secret influence that has upon the ladies.

3. JACK had a most scandalous tongue, and persuaded PEG that all mankind besides himself was diseased by that scarlet-faced whore, Signiora BUBONIA [*the Pope*]. "As for his brother, Lord PETER; the tokens were evident in him, blotches, scabs, and the corona [*the tonsure*]! His brother MARTIN, though he was not quite so bad, had some nocturnal pains; which his friends pretended were only scorbutical, but he was sure proceeded from a worse cause."

By such malicious insinuations, he had possessed [*persuaded*] the lady, that he was the only man in the world of a sound pure and untainted Constitution; though there were some that stuck not to say, that Signiora BUBONIA and JACK railed at one another, only the better to hide an intrigue; and that JACK had been found with Signiora under his cloak, carrying her home in a dark stormy night.

4. JACK was a prodigious ogler. He would ogle you the outside of his eye inward, and the white upward!

5. JACK gave himself out for a man of great estate in the Fortunate Islands [*Heaven*], of which the sole property was vested in his person. By this trick, he cheated abundance of poor people of small sums, pretending to make over plantations in the said Islands: but when the poor wretches came there with JACK's *Grant*, they were beaten, mocked, and turned out of doors.

6. I told you that PEG was whimsical, and loved anything that was particular [*peculiar*]. In that way, JACK was her man! for he neither thought, spoke, dressed, nor acted like other mortals. He was for your "bold strokes"! He railed

at fops, though himself the most affected in the World; instead of the common fashion, he would visit his mistress in a mourning cloak, band, short cuffs, and a peaked beard. He invented a way of coming into a room backwards, which he said "shewed more humility and less affectation." Where other people stood, he sat [*in singing*]; where they sat, he stood [*in prayer*]. When he went to Court, he used to kick away the State, and sit down by his Prince, cheek by jowl. "Confound these States," says he, "they are a modern invention!"

When he spoke to his Prince, he always turned his back upon him. If he were advised to fast for his health, he would eat roast beef. If he was allowed a more plentiful diet; then he would be sure, that day! to live upon water-gruel. He would cry at a wedding, and laugh and make jests at a funeral.

He was no less singular in his opinions. You would have burst your sides, to hear him talk politics. "All Government," says he, "is founded upon the right distribution of punishments; decent executions keep the world in awe: for that reason, the majority of mankind ought to be hanged every year! For example, I suppose the Magistrate ought to pass an irreversible sentence upon all blue-eyed children from the cradle [*Predestination*]: but that there may be some shew of justice in this proceeding, these children ought to be trained up by masters appointed for that purpose, to all sorts of villainy, that they may deserve their fate; and the execution of them may serve as an object of terror to the rest of mankind."

As to giving pardons, he has this singular method:

That when the wretches had the ropes about their necks, it should be inquired [of them] Who believed they should be hanged? and Who not? The first were to be pardoned, the latter hanged outright. Such as were once pardoned, were never to be hanged afterwards, for any crime whatever.

He had such skill in physiognomy, that he would pronounce, peremptorily, upon a man's face. "That fellow," says he, "do what he will, cannot avoid hanging! He has a hanging look!" By the same Art, he would prognosticate a Principality to a scoundrel.

He was no less particular in the choice of his studies. They were generally bent toward exploded Chimeras, the *perpetuum mobile*, the circular shot, philosopher's stone, and silent gunpowder; making chains for fleas, nets for flies, and instruments to unravel cobwebs and split hairs.

Thus I think I have given you a distinct account of the methods he practised upon PEG.

Her brother would, now and then, ask her, "What a Devil! dost thou see in that pragmatical [*busybody of a*] coxcomb, to make thee so in love with him? He is a fit match for a tailor's or a shoemaker's daughter; but not for you, that are a Gentlewoman!"

"Fancy is free!" quoth PEG, "I will take my awn way, do you take yours! I do not care for your flaunting beaus that gang with their breast open, and their sarks [? *shirts*] over their waistcoats! that accost me with set speeches out of SIDNEY's *Arcadia*, or *The Academy of Compliments*! JACK is a sober, grave young man: though he has none of your studied harangues, his meaning is sincere. He has a great regard to his father's Will; and he that shews himself a good son, will make a good husband! Besides, I know he has the *original* Deed of Conveyance to the Fortunate Islands: the others are counterfeits!"

There is nothing so obstinate as young ladies in their amours; the more you cross them, the worse they are!

CHAPTER IV.

How the Relations reconciled JOHN and his sister PEG; and what return PEG made to JOHN's message.

JOHN BULL, otherwise a good-natured man, was very hard hearted to his sister Peg; chiefly from an aversion he had conceived in his infancy. While he flourished, kept a warm house, and drove a plentiful trade; poor PEG was forced to go hawking and peddling about the streets, selling knives, scissors, and shoe-buckles; now and then carried a basket of fish to the market; sewed, span, and knitted for a poor livelihood till her fingers' ends were sore. And when she could not get bread for her family, she was forced to hire them out at journeywork to their neighbours [*the emigration of the Scotch to other countries*]. Yet in these, her poor circumstances, she still preserved the air and mien of a Gentlewoman, a certain decent pride that extorted respect from the haughtiest of her neighbours. When she came into any full assembly, she would not yield the *pas* to the best of them! If one asked her, "Are not you related to JOHN BULL?" "Yes," says she, "he has the honour to be my brother!"

So PEG's affairs went on, till all the Relations cried out "Shame!" on JOHN, for his barbarous usage of his own flesh and blood: that it was an easy matter for him to put her in a creditable way of living, not only without hurt, but with advantage to himself; she being an industrious person, and might be serviceable to him in his way of business.

"Hang her! Jade!" quoth JOHN, "I cannot endure her, as long as she keeps that rascal JACK's company!"

They told him the way to reclaim her was to take him into his house [*the Act of Toleration in* 1689], that by conversation, the childish humours of their younger days might be worn out.

These arguments were enforced by a certain incident. It happened that JOHN was, at that time, making his Will [*the Act of Settlement in* 1700], the very same in which NIC. FROG is named Executor. Now his sister PEG's name being in the entail [*the right of the Succession to the Scottish Crown, if Queen ANNE should die childless*], he could not make a thorough Settlement without her consent.

There was indeed a malicious story went about, as if JOHN's last Wife [*the GODOLPHIN Administration*] had fallen in love with JACK, as he was eating custards on horseback;* that she persuaded JOHN to take his sister PEG into the house, the better to drive on her intrigue with JACK, concluding he would follow his Mistress, PEG. All I can infer from this story is, that when one has got a bad character in the World,

* [Dean SWIFT in the Fifth edition of the *Tale of a Tub*, p. 133, 1710, has in the Text]

How JACK's tatters came into fashion in Court and City. How he got upon a great horse, and eat custard.

[And in the notes to the same]

Sir HUMPHRY EDWYN, a Presbyterian, was some years ago [1697] Lord Mayor of London; and had the insolence to go in his formalities to a conventicle, with the ensigns of his office.

Custard is a famous dish at a Lord Mayor's feast.

people will report and believe anything of them, true or false. But to return to my story.

When PEG received JOHN'S message, she huffed and stormed like the Devil!

"My brother JOHN," quoth she, "is grown wondrous kind-hearted, all of a sudden! but I meikle doubt whether it be not mair for his awn conveniency than my good! He draws up his weits and his deeds, forsooth; and I mun set my hand to them unsight unseen! I like the young man [*the House of Hanover*] he has settled upon well enough; but I think I ought to have a valuable consideration for my consent. He wants my poor little farm [*Scotland*], because it makes a nook in his park wall [*Great Britain*]. Ye may e'en tell him, he has mair than he makes good use of! He gangs up and down drinking, roaring, and quarrelling through all the country markets! making foolish bargains in his cups, which he repents when he is sober! like a thriftless wretch, spending the goods and gear that his forefathers wan with the sweat of their brows! 'light come, light go,' he cares not a farthing! But why should I stand surety for his silly contracts? The little I have is free, and I can call it my own! 'Hame's hame, be it never so hamely!' I ken him well enough! he could never abide me: and when he has his ends, he'll e'en use me as he did before! I am sure I shall be treated like a poor drudge! I shall be set to tend the bairns, darn the hose, and mend the linen!

"Then there's no living with that old carline [? *thistle*] his mother! She rails at JACK, and JACK is an honester man than any of her kin! I shall be plagued with her spells and *Paternosters*, and silly auld warld Ceremonies! I mun never pair my nails on a Friday, nor begin a journey on Childermass [*Christmas*] Day! and I mun stand becking and binging [*bowing and scraping*] as I gang out and into the hall [*Church*].

"Tell him he may e'en gan his gait! I'll have nothing to do with him! I'll stay, like the poor country mouse, in my own habitation!"

So PEG talked. But for all that, by the interposition of good friends; and by many a bonny thing that was sent, and many more that was promised PEG, the matter was concluded: and PEG was taken into the House, upon certain Articles [*Act of Union between England and Scotland*, 1707] one of which

That she might have the freedom of JACK's conversation, and might take him for better and for worse, if she pleased; provided always, he did not come into the house at unseasonable hours; and disturb the rest of the old woman, JOHN's mother.

CHAPTER V.

Of some quarrels that happened after PEG was taken into the Family.

IT IS an old observation, that the quarrels of relations are harder to reconcile than any other; injuries from friends fret and gall more, and the memory of them is not so easily obliterated. This is cunningly represented by one of your old sages, called ESOP, in the story of the bird that was grieved extremely for being wounded with an arrow feathered with his own wing; as also of the oak that let many a heavy groan, when he was cleft with a wedge of his own timber.

There was no man in the world less subject to rancour than JOHN BULL, considering how often his good nature had been abused: yet I don't know but he was too apt to hearken to tattling people that carried tales between him and his sister PEG, on purpose to sow jealousies and set them together by the ears.

They say, that there were some hardships put upon PEG, that had been better let alone; but it was the business of good people to restrain the injuries on one side, and moderate the resentments on the other. A good friend acts both parts; the one without the other will not do!

The purchase money of PEG's farm was ill paid. Then PEG loved a little good liquor, and the servants shut up the wine cellar: but for that PEG found a trick; for she made a false key [*Occasional Conformity*]. PEG's servants complained that they were debarred from all manner of business, and never suffered to touch the least thing within the house. If they offered to come into the warehouse, then straight went the yard [*measuring rod*] slap over their noddle! If they ventured into the counting-house, a fellow would throw an ink-bottle at their head! If they came into the best apartment, to set anything there in order; they were saluted with a broom! If they meddled with anything in the kitchen, it was odds but the cook laid them over the pate with a ladle! One that would have gone into the stables, was met by two rascals, who fell to work with him, with a brush and a curry comb! Some climbing up into the coach box, were told that "one of their companions had been there before, that could not drive!" then slap went the long whip about their ears!

On the other hand, it was complained that PEG's servants were always asking for drink money! that they had more than their share of the Christmas Box. To say the truth, PEG's lads bustled pretty hard for that: for when they were endeavouring to lock it up, they got in their great fists, and pulled out handfuls of half-crowns, some shillings and sixpences; others in the scramble picked up guineas and broad pieces.

But there happened a worse thing than this. It was complained that PEG's servants had great stomachs [*Fanatics* (Dissenters) *getting into places of trust*], and brought too many of their friends and acquaintance to the table, that JOHN's family was like[ly] to be eaten out of house and home.

Instead of regulating this matter as it ought to be, PEG's young men were thrust from the table [*Fanatics excluded by the passing of the Occasional Conformity Act, in* 1711]. Then there was the Devil and all to do! spoons, plates and dishes flew about the room like mad; and Sir ROGER [*ROBERT HARLEY*], who was now *Major Domo*, had enough to do to quiet them.

PEG said this was contrary to agreement, whereby she was, in all things, to be treated like a child of the family. Then she called upon those that had made her such fair promises, and undertook for her brother JOHN's good behaviour; but, alas, to her cost, she found that they were the first and readiest to do her the injury.

JOHN, at last, agreed to this regulation, that PEG's footmen might sit with his book-keeper, journeymen, and apprentices; and PEG's better sort of servants might sit with his footmen, if they pleased.

Then, they began to order plum-porridge and minced pies

for PEG's dinner [*the Act of 1712, restoring the ancient rights of Patrons in the bestowal of Scotch ecclesiastical presentations; which had been, of late, in the power of the Kirk*]. PEG told them, "She had an aversion to that sort of food; that upon the forcing down of a mess of it some years ago, it threw her into a fit until she brought it up again." Some alleged it was nothing but humour, that the same mess should be served up again for supper, and breakfast next morning: others would have made use of a horn. But the wiser sort bid let her alone, and she might take to it of her own accord.

CHAPTER VI.

The Conversation between JOHN BULL and his wife, [Queen ANNE].

Mrs. Bull. THOUGH our affairs, Honey! are in a bad condition; I have a better opinion of them, since you seem to be convinced of the ill course you have been in, and are resolved to submit to proper remedies. But when I consider your immense debts, your foolish bargains, and the general disorder of your business; I have a curiosity to know, what Fate or Chance has brought you into this condition?

John Bull. I wish you would talk of some other subject. The thoughts of it make me mad! Our Family must have their run!

Mrs. Bull. But such a strange thing as this, never happened to any of your Family before! They have had Lawsuits [*wars*]; but though they spent the income, they never mortgaged the Stock [*Capital*]! Sure, you must have some of the Norman or Norfolk blood in you: prithee, give me some account of these matters!

John Bull. Who could help it? There lives not such a fellow by bread, as that old LEWIS BABOON! It is the cheatingest, [most] contentious rogue upon the face of the earth!

You must know, one day, as NIC. FROG and I were over a bottle, making up an old quarrel, the old knave would needs have us drink a bottle of his Champagne: and so, one after another, till my friend NIC. and I, not being used to such heady stuff, got drunk. LEWIS, all the while, either by the strength of his brain or flinching his glass, kept himself sober as a judge.

"My worthy friends," quoth LEWIS, "henceforth, let us live neighbourly! I am as peaceable and quiet as a lamb, of my own temper; but it has been my misfortune to live among quarrelsome neighbours. There is but one thing that can make us fall out, and that is the Inheritance of Lord STRUTT's estate. I am content, for peace sake, to waive my right, and submit to any expedient to prevent a Lawsuit. I think an equal division will be the fairest way!"

"Well moved, old LEWIS!" quoth FROG, "and I hope my friend JOHN here, will not be refractory!" At the same time, he clapped me on the back, and slabbered me all over, from cheek to cheek, with his great tongue.

"Do as you please, Gentlemen!" quoth I; "it is all one to JOHN BULL!"

We agreed, to part that night, and next morning to meet at the corner of Lord STRUTT's park wall, with our surveying instruments: which accordingly we did [*the negotiations for the first Treaty of Partition in* 1698].

Old LEWIS carried a chain and a semicircle; NIC., paper, rulers, and a lead pencil; and I followed at some distance with a long pole.

We began first surveying the meadow grounds; afterwards, we measured the cornfields, close [*field*] by close; then we proceeded to the woodlands, the copper and tin mines [*the West Indies*]. All this while, NIC. laid down everything exactly, upon paper, and calculated the acres and roods to a great nicety. When we finished the land, we were going to break into the house and gardens, to take an inventory of his plate, pictures, and other furniture.

Mrs. Bull. What said Lord STRUTT to all this?

John Bull. As we had almost finished our concern, we were accosted by some one of Lord STRUTT's servants. "Hey day! what's here? What a Devil! is the meaning of all these trangrams and gimcracks, Gentlemen? What, in the name of wonder! are you going about, jumping over my Master's hedges, and running your lines across his grounds?

If you are at any field pastime, you might have asked leave! my Master is a civil well bred person as any is!"

Mrs. Bull. What could you answer to this?

John Bull. Why, truly, my neighbour FROG and I were still hot-headed. We told him, "His Master was an old doating puppy that minded nothing of his own business! that we were surveying his estate, and settling it for him; since he would not do it himself!"

Upon this, there happened a quarrel; but we being stronger than they, sent them away with a flea in their ear.

They went home, and told their Master. "My Lord!" say they, "there are three odd sort of fellows going about your grounds, with the strangest machines that ever we beheld in our life. We suppose they are going to rob your orchard, fell your trees, or drive away your cattle. They told us strange things, about 'settling your estates.' One [*LEWIS BABOON*] is a lusty old fellow in a black wig with a black beard, and without teeth. There's another [*NICHOLAS FROG*] thick squat fellow in trunk hose [*knee-breeches*]. The third is a little long-nosed thin man (I was then lean, being just come out of a fit of sickness [? *the war* 1689—1697]). We suppose it is fit to send after them, lest they carry something away!"

Mrs. Bull. I fancy this put the old fellow in a rare tweag [*passion*]!

John Bull. Weak as he was, he called for his long Toledo [sword], swore, and bounced about the room, "'Sdeath! what am I come to, to be affronted so by my tradesmen? I know the rascals! My barber, linendraper, and clothier dispose of my estate! Bring hither my blunderbuss! I'll warrant ye, you shall see daylight through them! Scoundrels! dogs! the scum of the earth! FROG! that was my father's kitchen-boy; he pretend to meddle with my estate! with my Will! Ah, poor STRUTT! what art thou come to at last! Thou hast lived too long in the world to see thy age and infirmity so despised! How will the ghosts of my noble ancestors receive these tidings? they cannot, they must not sleep quietly in their graves!" In short, the old gentleman was carried off in a fainting fit; and, after bleeding in both arms, hardly recovered.

Mrs. Bull. Really, this was a very extraordinary way of proceeding: I long to hear the rest of it!

John Bull. After we had come back to the tavern, and taken the other bottle of Champagne, we quarrelled a little about the division of the estate. LEWIS hauled and pulled the map on one side, and FROG and I on the other; till we had like to have torn the parchment to pieces.

At last, LEWIS pulled out a pair of tailor's great shears, and clipped off a corner for himself [*Guipuscoa and Sicily went to France, by the First Partition Treaty of* 1698], which he said was a Manor that lay convenient for him: and left FROG and me the rest to dispose of as we pleased.

We were overjoyed to think that LEWIS was contented with so little, not smelling what was at the bottom of the plot.

There happened, indeed, an incident that gave us some disturbance. A cunning fellow, one of my servants, two days after, peeping through the keyhole, observed that old LEWIS had stole away our part of the map, and saw him fiddling and turning the map from one corner to the other, trying to join the two pieces again. He was muttering something to himself, which he did not well hear, only these words, "'Tis a great pity! 'tis a great pity!" My servant added, that he believed this had some ill meaning.

I told him, "He was a coxcomb, always pretending to be wiser than his companions! LEWIS and I are good friends. He is an honest fellow; and, I dare say! will stand to his bargain.

The sequel of the story proved this fellow's suspicion to be too well grounded. For LEWIS revealed our whole secret to the deceased Lord STRUTT, who (in reward to his treachery, and revenge to FROG and me), settled his whole estate upon the present PHILIP BABOON [*PHILIP, Duke of ANJOU, afterwards PHILIP V.*]. Then we understood what he meant by piecing the map together.

Mrs. Bull. And were you surprised at this? Had not Lord STRUTT reason to be angry? Would you have been contented to have been so used yourself?

John Bull. Why, truly, Wife! it was not easily reconciled to the common methods! but then it was the fashion to do such things.

I have read of your Golden Age, your Silver Age, &c.: one might justly call this, the Age of the Lawyers [*Claimants*]. There is hardly a man of substance in all the country, but had a Counterfeit that pretended to his estate. As the philosophers say, that there is a duplicate of every terrestial animal, at sea; so it was in this Age of Lawyers, there were, at least, two of everything. Nay, on my conscience! I think there were three Esquire HACKUMS [kings of Poland] at one time.

LEWIS BABOON entertained a fellow [*the Chevalier ST. GEORGE, afterwards called the Old Pretender*] that called himself JOHN BULL's Heir. I knew him no more than the child unborn; yet he brought me into some trouble and expense. There was another that pretended to be Esquire SOUTH [*Emperor of AUSTRIA*]: and two Lord STRUTTS, you know!

In short, it was usual for a parcel of fellows to meet and dispose of the whole estates in the country.

"This lies convenient for me, TOM!" "Thou would do more good with that, DICK! than the old fellow that has it!" So to law they went with the true owners. The lawyers got well by it: everybody else was undone.

It was a common thing for an honest man, when he came home at night, to find another fellow domineering in his family, hectoring his servants, and calling for his supper. In every house, you might observe two *SOSIAS* quarrelling who was Master! For my own part, I am still afraid of the same treatment! that I should find somebody behind my counter selling my broadcloth.

Mrs. Bull. There are a sort of fellows that they call Banterers and Bamboozlers, that play such tricks; but it seems these fellows were in earnest!

John Bull. I begin to think that Justice is a better rule than Conveniency, for all some people make so slight on it:

CHAPTER VII.

Of the hard shifts Mrs. BULL was put to, to preserve the Manor of Bullock's Hatch; with Sir ROGER's method to keep off importunate duns.

AS JOHN BULL and his wife were talking together, they were surprised with a sudden knocking at the door.

"Those wicked Scriveners and Lawyers, no doubt!" quoth JOHN. And so it was; some asking for the money that he owed, and others warning to prepare for the approaching Term.

"What a cursed life do I lead!" quoth JOHN. "Debt is like deadly sin. For GOD's sake! Sir ROGER! get me rid of these fellows!"

"I'll warrant you!" quoth Sir ROGER, "leave them to me!"

And indeed it was pleasant enough to observe Sir ROGER's method with those importunate duns. His sincere friendship for JOHN BULL, made him submit to many things, for his service, which he would have scorned to have done for himself.

Sometimes he would stand at the door with his long pole, to keep off the duns, till JOHN got out at the back door. When the lawyers and Tradesmen [*the Allies*] brought extravagant bills, Sir ROGER used to bargain beforehand for leave to cut off a quarter of a yard in any part of the bill he pleased: he wore a pair of scissors in his pocket for this purpose, and would snip it off so nicely, as you cannot imagine! Like a true goldsmith, he kept all your holidays [*i.e., to gain more time*]: there was not one wanting in his Calendar! When ready money was scarce, he would set them a telling [*counting*] a Thousand Pounds in sixpences, groats, and threepenny pieces. It would have done your heart good to have seen him charge through an army of Lawyers, Attorneys, Clerks, and Tradesmen! sometimes with sword in hand, at other nuzzling like an eel in the mud. When a fellow stuck like a burr that there was no shaking him off, he used to be mighty inquisitive about the health of his uncles and aunts in the country! he would call them all by their names: for he knew everybody, and could talk to them in their own way. The extremely impertinent, he would send them away to see some strange sight, as the dragon at Hockley the Hole, or bid him call the 30th of next February.

Now and then, you would see him in the kitchen, weighing the beef and butter, paying ready money that the maids might not run a [*on*] tick at the market, and the butchers (by bribing of them) sell damaged and light meat. Another time, he would slip into the cellar, and gauge the casks.

In his leisure minutes, he was posting his books, and

gathering in his debts: such frugal methods were necessary where money was so scarce, and duns so numerous.

All this while, JOHN kept his credit, could show his head both at the Change and Westminster Hall; no man protested his bill, nor refused his bond: only the Sharpers and Scriveners, the Lawyers and other Clerks pelted Sir ROGER as he went along. The Squirters were at it, with their kennel water; for they were mad for the loss of their bubble [*victim*], and that they could not get him to mortgage the Manor of Bullock's Hatch [*to repeal the Sacramental Test Act of* 1673].

Sir ROGER shook his ears, and nuzzled along; well satisfied within himself that he was doing a charitable work, in rescuing an honest man from the claws of harpies and blood-suckers.

Mrs. BULL did all that an affectionate wife and a good housewife could do. Yet the boundaries of virtues are indivisible lines. It is impossible to march up close to the frontiers of frugality, without entering the territories of parsimony. Your good housewives are apt to look into the minutest things. Therefore some blamed Mrs. BULL for new heelpiecing of her shoes, grudging a quarter of a pound of soap and sand to scour the rooms: but especially that she would not allow her maids and apprentices the benefit of *JOHN BUNYAN*, *the London Apprentice*, or *the Seven Champions* in the black letter [*the Act for restraining the Press, against seditious pamphlets*].

CHAPTER VIII.

A continuation of the Conversation betwixt JOHN BULL and his wife.

Mrs. Bull. IT IS a most sad life we lead, my Dear! to be so teazed, paying interest for old debts, and still contracting new ones. However, I do not blame you for vindicating your honour, and chastizing old LEWIS. To curb the insolent, protect the oppressed, recover one's own, and defend what one has, are good effects of the Law. The only thing I want to know is, how you come to make an end of your money, before you have finished your Suit?

John Bull. I was told by the Learned in the Law, that my Suit stood upon three firm pillars: *More Money for more Law, more Law for more Money, and no Composition.* "More Money for more Law," was plain to a demonstration; for who can go to Law without money? and it was as plain, that any man that has Money, may have Law for it! The third was as evident as the other two: for what Composition [*Peace*] could be made with a rogue that never kept a word he said?

Mrs. Bull. I think you are most likely to get out of this labyrinth by the second door, by want of ready money to purchase this precious commodity! But you seem not only to have bought too much of it, but to have paid too dear for what you have bought! else how was it possible to run so much in debt, when, at this very time, the yearly income that is mortgaged to those usurers, would discharge HOCUS's bills, and give you your bellyful of Law for all your life, without running one sixpence in debt! You have been bred up to business! I suppose you can cypher! I wonder you never used your pen and ink!

John Bull. Now, you urge me too far! Prithee, dear wife! hold thy tongue! Suppose a young heir, heedless, raw, and inexperienced; full of spirit and vigour, with a favourite passion, in the hands of Money Scriveners [*Money Lenders*]! Such fellows are like your wire-drawing mills! if they get hold of a man's finger they will pull in his whole body at last, till they squeeze the heart, blood, and bowels out of him. When I wanted money, half a dozen of these fellows were always waiting in my antechamber, with their securities ready drawn. I was tempted with the "ready"! Some farm or other went to pot! I received with one hand, and paid it away with the other, to Lawyers that, like so many hell-hounds, were ready to devour me. Then the rogues would plead poverty and scarcity of money. That always ended in [my] receiving Ninety for the Hundred! After they had gotten possession of my best rents, they were able to supply me with my own money! But what was worse, when I looked into my securities [*Perpetual Consols*], there was no clause of redemption.

Mrs. Bull. "No Clause of Redemption," say you! that's hard!

John Bull. No great matter, for I cannot pay them! They had got a worse trick than that! The same man bought and sold to himself, paid the money, and gave the acquittance. The same man was Butcher and Grazier, Brewer and Butler, Cook and Poulterer. There is something still worse than all this. There came twenty bills on me, at once; which I had given money to discharge. I was like[ly] to be pulled to pieces by Brewer, Butcher, and Baker; even my Herb-Woman dunned me as I went along the streets (thanks to my friend Sir ROGER! else I must have gone to gaol). When I asked the meaning of this, I was told, "The money went to the Lawyers; Counsel won't tick [*give credit*], Sir!" HOCUS was urging, my Bookkeeper [*Lord Treasurer* GODOLPHIN] sat sotting all day, playing at Putt and All Fours. In short, by griping Usurers, devouring Lawyers, and negligent Servants, I am brought to this pass!

Mrs. Bull. This was hard usage; but, methinks, the least reflection might have retrieved you!

John Bull. 'Tis true! yet consider my circumstances! My honour was engaged, and I did not know how to get out! Besides, I was, for five years, often drunk; always muddled! They carried me from tavern to tavern, to ale-houses and brandy-shops; and brought me acquainted with such strange dogs! "There goes the prettiest fellow in the world," says one, "for managing a jury; make him yours!" "There is another can pick you up witnesses!" "Serjeant Such-a-One has a silver tongue at the bar!" I believe in time I should have retained every single person within the Inns of Court!

The night after a trial, I treated the Lawyers, their wives, and daughters, with fiddles, hautboys, drums, and trumpets. I was always hot-headed! Then they placed me in the middle; the Attorneys and their Clerks dancing about me, whooping and holloaing, "Long live JOHN BULL! the glory and support of the Law!"

Mrs. Bull. Really, Husband! you went through a very notable course!

John Bull. One of the things that first alarmed me, was that they shewed a spite against my poor old Mother.

"Lord!" quoth I, "what makes you so jealous of a poor old innocent Gentlewoman that minds only her *Prayers* and her *Practice of Piety*? She never meddles in any of your concerns!"

"Foh!" say they, "to see a handsome, brisk, genteel, young fellow so much governed by a doating old woman! Why don't you go and suck the bubby [*breasts.* Bu bu *is the cry of the child needing its mother's milk*]? Do you consider she keeps you out of a good jointure! She has the best of your estate settled upon her for a rent-charge [*tithes*]! Hang her, old thief! turn her out of doors! seize her lands! and let her go to Law if she dares!"

"Soft and fair, Gentlemen!" quoth I; "my mother is my mother! Our Family is not of an unnatural temper! Though I don't take all her advice, I won't seize her jointure! Long may she enjoy it, good woman! I don't grudge it her! She allows me, now and then, a brace of Hundreds [*taxation of the Clergy*] for my Lawsuit; that is pretty fair!"

About this time, the old Gentlewoman fell ill of an odd sort of a distemper [*deterioration and worldliness of the Established Clergy*]. It began with a coldness and numbness in her limbs; which, by degrees, affected the nerves (I think the Physicians call them), seized the brain, and at last ended in a lethargy. It betrayed itself, at first, in a sort of indifference and carelessness in all her actions, coldness to her best friends, and an aversion to stir or go about the common offices of life. She that would sometimes rattle off her servants pretty sharply; now if she saw them drink, or heard them talk profanely, never took any notice of it. Instead of her usual charities to deserving persons, she threw away her money upon roaring swearing bullies and randy beggars that went about the streets.

"What is the matter with the old Gentlewoman?" said everybody; "she never used to do in this manner!"

At last, the distemper grew more violent, and threw her downright into raving fits [*Complaints against Moderation*]; in which, she shrieked out so loud, that she disturbed the whole neighbourhood. In her fits, she call out upon Sir WILLIAM [*WILLIAM III.*]: "O, Sir WILLIAM! thou hast betrayed me! killed me! stabbed me! sold me! See, see, *CLUM* with his bloody knife! seize him! seize him! stop him! Behold the Fury with her hissing snakes! Where is my son JOHN? Is he well? is he well? Poor man, I pity him!" And abundance more of such strange stuff that nobody could make anything of.

I knew little of the matter; for when I inquired about her health, the answer was, "She was in a good moderate way!"

Physicians were sent for in haste: Sir ROGER with great difficulty brought R[ADCLI]FF [*the Tory party*]. G[AR]TH [*the Whig party*] came upon the first message. There were several others called in: but, as usual upon such occasions, they differed strangely at the Consultation.

At last they divided into two parties; one sided with G[AR]TH, and the other with R[ADCLI]FF.

Dr. G[AR]TH. This case seems to me, to be plainly hysterical. The old woman is whimsical; it is a common thing for your old women to be so! I'll pawn my life! Blisters with the Steel diet will recover her!

Others suggested strong purging and letting of blood, because she was plethoric. Some went so far as to say the old woman was mad; and that nothing would do better than a little corporal correction.

R[ADCLI]FF. Gentlemen, you are mistaken in this case. It is plainly an acute distemper! and she cannot hold out three days, without she is supported with strong cordials!

I came into her room with a good deal of concern, and asked them, "What they thought of my mother?"

"In no manner of danger, I vow to God!" quoth G[AR]TH, "the old woman is hysterical, fanciful, Sir, I vow to God!"

"I tell you, Sir!" says R[ADCLI]FF, "she can't live three days to an end, unless there is some very effectual course taken with her! She has a malignant fever!"

Then "Fool!" "Puppy!" and "Blockhead!" were the best words they gave. I could hardly restrain them from throwing the ink-bottles at one another's heads.

I forgot to tell you, that one party of the physicians desired I should take my sister PEG into the house to nurse her; but the old Gentlewoman would not hear of that.

At last, one physician asked, "If the Lady had ever been used to take laudanum?"

Her maid answered, "Not that she knew!" that "indeed there was a High German liveryman of hers, one YAN

PTSCHIRNSOOKER [*Inviting over the Palatines*] that gave her a sort of a Quack powder."

The physician desired to see it; "Nay," says he, "there is opium in this, I am sure!"

Mrs. Bull. I hope you examined a little into this matter!

John Bull. I did indeed! and discovered a great mystery of iniquity.

The witnesses made oath, that they had heard some of the liverymen frequently railing at their Mistress. They said "She was a troublesome fiddle faddle old woman, and so ceremonious that there was no bearing of her! They were so plagued with bowing and cringing, as they went in and out of the room, that their backs ached! She used to scold at one, for his dirty shoes: at another, for his greasy hair, and not combing his head! Then she was so passionate and fiery in her temper, that there was no living with her! She wanted something to sweeten her blood! They never had a quiet night's rest, for getting up in the morning to early sacraments! They wished they could find some way or another to keep the old woman quiet in her bed!"

Such discourses were so often overheard among the liverymen, that the said YAN PTSCHIRNSOOKER had undertaken this matter.

A maid made affidavit, that she "had seen the said YAN PTSCHIRNSOOKER, one of the liverymen, frequently making up of medicines, and administering them to all the neighbours"; that she "saw him, one morning, make up the powder which her mistress took," that she "had the curiosity to ask him, whence he had the ingredients?"

"They come," says he, "from several parts of de world. Dis I have from Geneva! dat from Rome! this white powder from Amsterdam! and the red from Edinburgh: but the chief ingredient of all comes from Turkey!"

It was likewise proved, that the said YAN PTSCHIRNSOOKER had been frequently seen at the *Rose* with JACK, who was known to bear an inveterate spite to his Mistress; that he brought a certain powder to his Mistress, which the Examinant believes to be the same, and spoke the following words: *Madam, here is grand secret van de warld! my sweetning powder! It does temperate de humour, despel de windt, and cure de vapour! It lulleth and quieteth de animal spirits, procuring rest and pleasant dreams! It is de infallible receipt for de scurvy, all heats in de bloodt, and breaking out upon de skin! It is de true bloodt stauncher, stopping all fluxes of de bloodt! If you do take this, you will never ail anything! it will cure you of all diseases!* and abundance more to this purpose, which the Examinant does not remember.

JOHN BULL was interrupted in his story by a porter, that brought him a letter from NICHOLAS FROG; which is as follows:

CHAPTER IX.

A copy of NICHOLAS FROG's letter to JOHN BULL.

JOHN BULL reads

Friend JOHN!

What schellum is it, that makes thee jealous of thy old friend NICHOLAS? Hast thou forgot how, some years ago, he took thee out of the Sponging-house [The Revolution of 1688].

'Tis true, my friend NIC. did so, and I thank him! but he made me pay a swinging reckoning.

Thou beginst now to repent the bargain that thou wast so fond of! and, if thou durst, would foreswear thy own hand and seal. Thou sayst that "thou hast purchased me too great an estate already!" when, at the same time, thou knowest I have only a mortgage [the Spanish Netherlands]. *'Tis true, I have possession, and the tenants own me for Master; but has not Esquire SOUTH the equity of redemption?*

No doubt, and will redeem it very speedily! Poor NIC. has only possession; eleven points of the Law!

As for the turnpikes [the prohibition of trade to all but the English] *I have set up; they are for other people, not for my friend JOHN! I have ordered my servant constantly to attend, to let thy carriages through, without paying anything; only I hope thou wilt not come too heavy ladened, to spoil my ways!*

Certainly, I have just cause of offence against thee, my friend! for supposing it possible that thou and I should ever quarrel. What houndsfoot is it, that puts these whims in thy head? Ten thousand lasts [a Last was estimated to contain 10,000 herrings] *of devils haul me, if I do not love thee as I love my life!*

No question! as the Devil loves holy water!

Does not thy own hand and seal oblige thee to purchase for me, till I say "It is enough!" Are not these words plain? I say, it is not *enough! Dost thou think thy friend* NICHOLAS FROG *made a child's bargain! Marks the words of thy contract,* tota pecunia, *with all thy money!*

Very well! I have purchased with my own money, my children's, and my grandchildren's money: is that not enough? Well, *tota pecunia*, let it be! for, at present, I have none at all! He would not have me purchase with other people's money, sure! Since *tota pecunia* is the bargain, I think it is plain "no more money, no more purchase!"

And, whatever the World may say! NICHOLAS FROG *is but a poor man in comparison of the rich, the opulent* JOHN BULL, *great Clothier of the World!*

I have had many losses! Six of my best sheep were drowned; and the water has come into my cellar, and spoiled a pipe of my best brandy. It would be a more friendly act in thee, to carry a Brief *about the country, to repair the losses of thy poor friend! Is it not evident to all the World, that I am still hemmed in by* LEWIS BABOON? *Is he not just upon my borders?*

And so he will be, if I purchase a thousand acres more; unless he gets somebody betwixt them!

I tell thee, friend JOHN! *thou hast flatterers that persuade thee thou art a man of business. Do not believe them! If thou wouldst still leave thy affairs in my hands, thou shouldst see how handsomely I would deal by thee! That ever* thou *shouldst be dazzled with the Enchanted Islands* [the South Seas, *i.e.*, the Spanish Colonies in the Pacific] *and mountains of gold, that old* LEWIS *promises thee! 'Dswounds! why dost thou not lay out thy money to purchase a place at Court, of honest* ISRAEL*? I tell thee, thou must not so much as think of a Composition* [Peace].

Not think of a Composition, that is hard indeed! I cannot help thinking of it, if I would!

Thou complainest of want of money, let thy wife and daughters burn the gold lace upon their petticoats! sell thy fat cattle! retrench but a sirloin of beef and a peck-loaf in a week, from thy gormandizing stomach!

Retrench my beef, a dog! retrench my beef! Then it is plain the rascal has an ill design upon me! He would starve me!

Mortgage thy Manor of Bullock's Hatch, or pawn thy crop for ten years!

A rogue! Part with my country seat, my patrimony, all that I have left in the world! I'll see thee hanged first!

Why hast thou changed thy Attorney! Can any man manage thy Cause better for thee?

Very pleasant! Because a man has a good Attorney, he must never make an end of his Lawsuit!

Ah, JOHN! JOHN! *I wish thou knewst thy own mind! Thou art as fickle as the wind! I tell thee, thou hadst better let this Composition alone, or leave it to thy*

Loving friend,

NIC. FROG.

CHAPTER X.

Of some extraordinary things that passed at the Salutation *tavern, in the Conference between* BULL, FROG, *Esquire* SOUTH, *and* LEWIS BABOON.

FROG had given his word that he would meet the above-mentioned company at the *Salutation* [*the Congress at Utrecht*], to talk of this Agreement. Though he durst not directly break his appointment, he made many a shuffling excuse. One time, he pretended to be seized with the gout in his right knee; then he got a great cold that had struck him deaf of one ear: afterwards two of his coach horses fell sick, and he durst not go by water for fear of catching an ague.

JOHN would take no excuse; but hurried him away. "Come NIC.!" says he, "let us go and hear at least, what this Old Fellow has to propose! I hope there is no hurt in that!"

"Be it so," says NIC., "but if I catch any harm, woe be to you! My wife and children will curse you as long as they live!"

When they were come to the *Salutation*, JOHN concluded all was sure, then! and that he should be troubled no more with law affairs. He thought everybody as plain and sincere as he was.

"Well, neighbours!" quoth he, "let us now make an end of all matters, and live peaceably together for the time to come! If everybody is as well inclined as I, we shall quickly come to the upshot of our affair!" And so, pointing to FROG to say something: to the great surprise of all the company, FROG was seized with a dead palsy in the tongue.

JOHN began to ask him some plain questions, and whooped and holloaed in his ear.

John Bull. Let us come to the point, NIC.! Who wouldst thou have to be Lord STRUTT? Wouldst thou have PHILIP BABOON?

NIC. shook his head, and said nothing.

John Bull. Wilt thou then have Esquire SOUTH to be Lord STRUTT?

NIC. shook his head a second time.

John Bull. Then who, the Devil! wilt thou have? Say something or another!

NIC. opened his mouth, and pointed to his tongue; and cried, "A! a! a! a!"; which was as much as to say he could not speak.

John Bull. Shall I serve PHILIP BABOON with broadcloth; and accept of the Composition that he offers, with the liberty of his parks and fishponds?

Then NIC. roared like a bull, "O! o! o! o!"

John Bull. If thou wilt not let me have them, wilt thou take them thyself?

Then NIC. grinned, cackled, and laughed, till he was like to kill himself; and seemed to be so pleased that he fell a frisking and dancing about the room.

John Bull. Shall I leave all this matter to thy management, Nic.! and go about my business?

Then NIC. got up a glass and drank to JOHN; shaking him by the hand till he had like to have shaken his shoulder out of joint.

John Bull. I understand thee, NIC.! but I shall make thee speak before I go!

Then NIC. put his finger to his cheek, and made it cry "Buck!": which is as much as to say, "I care not a farthing for thee!"

John Bull. I have done, NIC.! If thou wilt not speak, I will make my own terms with old LEWIS here!

Then NIC. lolled out his tongue, and turned his back to him.

JOHN perceiving that FROG would not speak, turned to old LEWIS, "Since we cannot make this obstinate fellow speak, LEWIS! pray condescend a little to his humour, and set down thy meaning upon paper, that he may answer it on another scrap!"

"I am infinitely sorry," quoth **Lewis**, "that it happens so unfortunately! for, playing a little at cudgels the other day, a fellow has given me such a rap over the right arm that I am quite lame [*disabled*]. I have lost the use of my forefinger and my thumb, so that I cannot hold my pen."

John Bull. That is all one, let me write for you!

Lewis. But I have a misfortune that I cannot read anybody's hand but my own.

John Bull. Try what you can do with your left hand!

Lewis. That is impossible! It will make such a scrawl that it will not be legible!

As they were talking of this matter, in came Esquire SOUTH, all dressed up in feathers and ribbons, stark staring mad, brandishing his sword as if he would have cut off their heads; crying, "Room, room, boys! for the grand Esquire of the world! the flower of Esquires! What! covered in my Presence! I will crush your souls, and crack you like lice!"

With that, he had like to have struck JOHN BULL's hat into the fire; but JOHN, who was pretty strong fisted, gave him such a squeeze, as made his eyes water.

He still went on with his pranks, "When I am Lord of the Universe, the sun shall prostrate and adore me! Thou, FROG! shalt be my bailiff! LEWIS! my tailor! and thou JOHN BULL! shalt be my fool!"

All this while, FROG laughed in his sleeve, gave the Esquire the other noggin of brandy, and clapped him on the back; which made him ten times madder.

Poor JOHN stood in amaze, talking thus to himself, "Well, JOHN! thou art got into rare company! One has a dumb devil! the other a mad devil! and the third, a spirit of Infirmity! An honest man has a fine time of it amongst such rogues! What art thou asking of them, after all? some mighty boon, one would think! Only to sit quietly at thy own fireside. 'Sdeath! what have I to do with such fellows? JOHN BULL, after all his losses and crosses, can live better without them; than they can, without him! Would to God! I lived a thousand leagues off them! but the Devil is in it."

As he was talking to himself, he observed FROG and old LEWIS edging towards one another to whisper; so that JOHN was forced to sit with his arms akimbo to keep them asunder.

Some people advised JOHN to bleed FROG under the tongue: or take away his bread and butter, which would certainly make him speak; to give Esquire SOUTH, hellebore: as for LEWIS, some were for emollient pultas's [*poultices*]; others for opening his arm with an incision knife.

I could not obtain from Sir HUMPHRY, at this time, a copy of JOHN's letter, which he sent to his nephew by the young Necromancer; wherein he advises him not to eat butter and ham, and drink old hock in the morning with the Esquire and FROG, for fear of giving him a sour breath.

FINIS.

AN

APPENDIX

TO

JOHN BULL

Still

In his SENSES:

OR

Law is a Bottomless Pit.

Printed from a Manuscript found in the Cabinet of the famous Sir HUMPHRY POLESWORTH: *and published (as well as the Three former Parts) by the Author of the* New Atlantis.

LONDON,

Printed for JOHN MORPHEW, near Stationers' Hall, 1712. Price 3d.

AN APPENDIX TO JOHN BULL *Still in his Senses, &c.*

CHAPTER I.

The apprehending, examination, and imprisonment of JACK, *for suspicion of poisoning.*

THE attentive Reader cannot have forgotten that, in my last Part, the Story of YAN PTSCHIRNSOOKER's Powder, was interrupted by a message from FROG. I have a natural compassion for curiosity, being much troubled with the distemper myself; therefore, to gratify that uneasy itching sensation in my Reader, I have procured the following account of that matter.

YAN PTSCHIRNSOOKER came off, as rogues usually do upon such occasions, by peaching [*turning evidence on*] his partner; and being extremely forward to bring him to the gallows, JACK was accused as the contriver of all the roguery.

And, indeed, it happened, unfortunately for the poor fellow, that he was known to bear a most inveterate spite against the old Gentlewoman; and, consequently, that never any ill accident happened to her, but he was suspected to be at the bottom of it. If she pricked her finger; Jack, to be sure, laid the pin in the way! If some noise in the street disturbed her rest; who could it be but Jack? in some of his nocturnal rambles. If a servant ran away, Jack had debauched [*corrupted*] him! Every tittle tattle that went about, JACK was always suspected for the author of it!

However all was nothing to this last affair of the

Temperating Moderating Powder. The Hue and Cry went after JACK, to apprehend him, dead or alive, wherever he could be found. The Constables looked out for him, in all his usual haunts; but to no purpose! Where, do you think, did they find him at last? Even smoking his pipe very quietly, at his brother MARTIN's! from whence, he was carried, with a vast mob at his heels, before the Worshipful Mr. Justice OVERDO.

Several of his neighbours made oath, that, of late, the prisoner had been observed to lead a very dissolute life, renouncing even his usual hypocrisy and pretences to sobriety; that he frequented taverns and eating-houses, and had been often guilty of drunkenness and gluttony at my Lord Mayor's table [*the Dissenters holding Civic appointments*]; that he had been seen in the company of lewd women; that he had transferred his usual religious care of the engrossed copy of his father's Will [*the printed* Bible], to Bank Bills, Orders for Tallies, and Debentures [*Dissenters becoming worldly minded*]; these he now affirmed, with more literal truth, to be *meat, drink, and cloth; the Philosopher's Stone, and the Universal Medicine**; that he was so far from shewing his customary reverence to the Will, that he kept company with those [? *sceptics*] that called his Father a "cheating rogue!" and his Will "a forgery!"; that he not only sat quietly and heard his Father railed at, but often chimed in with the discourse, and hugged the authors as his bosom friends; that instead *of asking for blows at the corners of the streets*,† he bestowed them as plentifully as he begged them before. In short, that he was grown a mere rake, and had nothing left in him of old JACK, except his spite to JOHN BULL's mother.

* *Tale of the Tub.*

† *Tale of the Tub.*

Another witness made oath, that JACK had been overheard bragging of a trick he had found out to manage the "old formal Jade," as he used to call her. "D—— this numbed skull of mine," quoth he, "that I could not light on it sooner! As long as I go in this ragged tattered coat, I am so well known that I am hunted away from the old woman's door by every barking cur about the house; they bid me defiance! There is no doing mischief as an open enemy! I must find some way or another of getting within doors! and then I shall have better opportunities of playing my pranks, besides the benefit of good keeping! [*The suggestion here is, that the Dis-*

senters turned Low Church, for the sake of the good things in the Establishment.]

Two witnesses swore, that several years ago, there came to their mistress's door, a young fellow in a tattered coat, that went by the name of TIMOTHY TRIM; whom they did, in their conscience, believe to be the very prisoner, resembling him in shape, stature, and the features of his countenance; that the said TIMOTHY TRIM being taken into the family, clapped their mistress's livery over his own tattered coat [*Church forms over Dissenting principles*]; that the said TIMOTHY was extremely officious about their mistress's person, endeavouring by flattery and tale-bearing, to set her against the rest of their servants. Nobody was so ready to fetch anything that was wanted, or reach what was dropped! that he used to shove and elbow his fellow servants, to get near his mistress: especially when money was a paying or receiving, then he was never out of the way! That he was extremely diligent about everybody's business but his own.

That the said TIMOTHY, while he was in the Family, used to be playing roguish tricks. When his mistress's back was turned, he would loll out his tongue, make mouths, and laugh at her, walking behind her like a harlequin, ridiculing her motions and gestures: if his mistress look about, he put on a grave, demure countenance, as [if] he had been in a fit of devotion. That he used often to trip upstairs so smoothly that you could not hear him tread, and put all things out of order; that he would pinch the children and servants, when he met them in the dark, so hard that he left the print of his forefingers and thumb in black and blue; and then slink into a corner, as if nobody had done it. Out of the same malicious design, he used to lay chairs and joint-stools in their way, that they might break their noses by falling over them. The more young and unexperienced, he used to teach to talk saucily and call names.

During his stay in the Family, there was much plate missing; that being catched with a couple of silver spoons in his pocket, with their handles wrenched off, he said, "He was only going to carry them to the goldsmith's to be mended!"

That the said TIMOTHY was hated by all the honest servants, for his ill-conditioned, splenetic tricks: but especially for his slanderous tongue; traducing them to his mistress, as drunkards and thieves.

That the said TIMOTHY, by lying stories, used to set all the Family together by the ears; taking delight to make them fight and quarrel. Particularly, one day sitting at table, he spoke words to this effect:

"I am of opinion," quoth he, "that little short fellows, such as we are, have better hearts, and could beat the tall fellows. I wish it came to a fair trial! I believe these long fellows, as sightly as they are, should find their jackets well thwacked!" A parcel of tall fellows, who thought themselves affronted by this discourse, took up the question: and to it they went! the Tall Men [*High Church*] and the Low Men [*Low Church. These ecclesiastical badges first sprang up in Queen ANNE's reign*]; which continues still a faction in the Family, to the great disorder of our mistress's affairs.

That the said TIMOTHY carried this frolic so far, that he proposed to his mistress, that she should entertain no servant that was above four feet seven inches high; and for that purpose he prepared a gauge, by which they were to be measured.

That the good old Gentlewoman was not so simple as to go into his projects. She began to smell a rat. "This TRIM," quoth she, "is an odd sort of a fellow! Methinks, he makes a strange figure with that ragged tattered coat appearing under his livery! Can't he go spruce and clean, like the rest of the servants? The fellow has a roguish leer with him, which I don't like by any means. Besides he has such a twang in his discourse, and such an ungraceful way of speaking through the nose, that one can hardly understand him! I wish [*hope*] the fellow be not tainted with some bad disease!"

The witnesses further made oath, that the said TIMOTHY lay out a nights, and went abroad often at unseasonable hours; that it was credibly reported, he did business in another family; that he pretended to have a squeamish stomach, and could not eat at table with the rest of the servants [? *the strict Communion of some Dissenters*], though this was but a pretence to provide some nice bit for himself; that he refused to dine upon salt fish, only to have an opportunity to eat a calf's head, his favourite dish, in private [*alluding to the Calf's Head Club*]; that for all his tender stomach, when he was got by himself, he would devour capons, turkeys, and sirloins of beef, like a cormorant.

Two other witnesses gave the following evidence. That in his officious attendance upon his mistress, he had tried to slip in a powder into her drink; and that once he was catched endeavouring to stifle her with a pillow as she was asleep: that he and PTSCHIRNSOOKER were often in close conference, and that they used to drink together at the *Rose*, where it seems he was well enough known by the true name of JACK.

The prisoner had little to say in his defence. He endeavoured to prove him *alibi*; so that the trial turned upon this single question, Whether the said TIMOTHY TRIM and JACK were the same person? which was proved by such plain tokens, and particularly by a mole under the left pap, that there was no withstanding the evidence. Therefore the worshipful Mr. Justice committed him, in order to his trial.

CHAPTER II.

How JACK's friends came to visit him in prison, and what advice they gave him.

JACK hitherto had passed in the World, for a poor, simple, well-meaning, half-witted, crack-brained fellow. People were strangely surprised to find him in such a roguery; that he should disguise himself under a false name, hire himself out for a servant to an old Gentlewoman, only for an opportunity to poison her! They said that it was more generous to profess an open emnity, than, under a profound dissimulation, to be guilty of such a scandalous breach of trust, and of the sacred rights of hospitality.

In short, the action was universally condemned by his best friends. They told him, in plain terms, that "this was come as a judgement upon him, for his loose life, his gluttony, drunkenness, and avarice, laying aside his Father's Will in an old mouldy trunk, and turning stock-jobber, newsmonger, and busybody, meddling with other people's affairs, shaking off his old serious friends, and keeping company with buffoons and pickpockets, his Father's sworn enemies!" that "he had best throw himself upon the mercy of the Court, repent, and change his manners!"

To say truth, JACK heard these discourses with some compunction; however he resolved to try what his new acquaintance would do for him.

They sent HABBAKUK SLYBOOTS [? Lord Somers] who delivered him the following message, as the peremptory commands of his trusty companions.

Habbakuk. Dear JACK! I am sorry for thy misfortune! Matters have not been carried on with due secrecy; however, we must make the best of a bad bargain! Thou art in the utmost jeopardy, that is certain! *hang! draw!* and *quarter!* are the gentlest things they talk of. However, thy faithful friends, ever watchful for thy security, bid me tell thee, that they have one infallible expedient left to save thy life. Thou must know, we have got into some understanding with the enemy, by means of Don DIEGO DISMALLO. He assures us, there is no mercy for thee, and that there is only one way left to escape. It is indeed somewhat out of the common road: however, be assured it is the result of most mature deliberation!

Jack. Prithee, tell me quickly! for my heart is sunk down into the very bottom of my belly.

Habbakuk. It is the unanimous opinion of your friends, that you make as if you hanged yourself! they will give it out that you are quite dead, and convey your body out of prison in a bier; and that JOHN BULL, being busied with his Lawsuit, will not inquire further into the matter.

Jack. How do you mean, "make as if I had hanged myself"?

Habbakuk. Nay, but you must really hang yourself up in a true genuine rope, that there may appear no trick in it; and leave the rest to your friends.

Jack. Truly this is a matter of some concern, and my friends, I hope, won't take it ill, if I inquire into the means by which they intend to deliver me. A rope and a noose are no jesting matters!

Habbakuk. Why so mistrustful! Hast thou ever found us false to thee? I tell thee, there is one ready to cut thee down!

Jack. May I presume to ask, who it is, that is entrusted with that important office?

Habbakuk. Is there no end of thy "Hows?" and thy "Whys?" That is a secret!

Jack. A secret, perhaps, that I may be safely trusted with! for I am not like[ly] to tell it again! I tell you plainly, it is no strange thing for a man, before he hangs himself up, to inquire who is to cut him down!

Habbakuk. Thou suspicious creature! If thou must needs know it, I tell thee, it is Sir ROGER! He has been in tears ever since thy misfortune. Don DIEGO and we have laid it so, that he is to be in the next room; and before the rope is well about thy neck, rest satisfied he will break in, and cut thee down! Fear not, old boy! we'll do it, I warrant thee!

Jack. So I must hang myself up, upon hopes that Sir ROGER will cut me down; and all this, upon the credit of Don DIEGO! A fine stratagem indeed to save my life, that depends upon hanging, Don DIEGO, and Sir ROGER!

Habbakuk. I tell thee there is a mystery in all this, my friend! a piece of profound policy! If thou knew what good this will do to the common Cause, thy heart would leap for joy! I am sure thou wouldst not delay the experiment one moment!

Jack. This is to the tune of *All for the better!* What is your Cause to me, when I am to be hanged?

Habbakuk. Refractory mortal! If thou wilt not trust thy friends, take what follows! Know assuredly, before next full moon, that thou wilt be hung up in chains, or thy quarters perching upon the most conspicuous places of the kingdom! Nay, I don't believe they will be contented with hanging! they talk of *impaling!* or *breaking on the wheel!* and thou choosest that, before a gentle suspending of thyself for one minute! Hanging is not so painful a thing as thou imaginest. I have spoken with several that have undergone it. They all agree it is no manner of uneasiness! Be sure thou take good notice of the symptoms; the relation will be curious! It is but a kick or two with thy heels, and a wry mouth or so! Sir ROGER will be with thee, in the twinkling of an eye!

Jack. But what if Sir ROGER should not come? will my friends be there to succour me?

Habbakuk. Doubt it not! I will provide everything against to-morrow morning! Do thou keep thy own secret! say nothing! I tell thee, it is absolutely necessary for the common good, that thou shouldst go through this operation.

CHAPTER III.

How JACK hanged himself up, by the persuasion of his friends; who broke their word, and left his neck in the noose.

JACK was a professed enemy to Implicit Faith; and yet I dare say, it was never more strongly exerted, nor more basely abused, than upon this occasion. He was now with his friends, in the state of a poor disbanded Officer after a Peace, or rather a wounded soldier after a battle; like an old favourite of a cunning Minister after the job is over, or a decayed beauty to a cloyed lover in quest of new game: or like a hundred such things that one sees every day. There were new intrigues, new views, new projects on foot. JACK's life was the purchase of DIEGO's friendship; much good may it do them! The Interest of HOCUS and Sir WILLIAM CRAWLEY [Sunderland], which was now more at heart, made this operation upon poor JACK absolutely necessary.

You may easily guess that his rest, that night, was but small, and much disturbed: however the remaining part of his time, he did not employ, as his custom was formerly, in prayer, meditation, or singing a double verse of a *Psalm*; but amused himself with disposing of his Bank Stock.

Many a doubt, many a qualm overspread his clouded imagination. "Must I then," quoth he, "hang up my own personal, natural, individual Self, with these two hands! *Durus Sermo*! What if I should be cut down, as my friends tell me; there is something infamous in the very attempt! The world will conclude I had a guilty conscience. Is it possible that good man, Sir ROGER, can have so much pity upon an unfortunate scoundrel that has persecuted him so many years? No, it cannot be! I don't love favours that pass through Don DIEGO's hands! On the other side, my blood chills about my heart, at the thought of these rogues with their hands pulling out my very entrails! Hang it! for once, I'll trust my friends!"

So JACK resolved; but he had done more wisely to have put himself upon the trial of his country, and made his defence in form. Many things happen between the cup and the lip. Witnesses might have been bribed, juries managed, or prosecution stopped.

But so it was. JACK, for this time, had a sufficient stock of Implicit Faith, which led him to his ruin, as the sequel of the story shews.

And now the fatal day was come, in which he was to try this hanging experiment. His friends did not fail him at the appointed hour, to see it put in practice.

HABBAKUK brought him a smooth strong tough rope made of many a ply of wholesome Scandinavian hemp, compactly twisted together, with a noose that slipped as glib as a bird-catcher's gin.

JACK shrank and grew pale at first sight of it. He handled it, measured it, stretched it, fixed it against the iron bar of the window to try its strength; but no familiarity could reconcile him to it! He found fault with the length, the thickness, and the twist: nay, the very colour did not please him!

"Will nothing less than hanging serve?" quoth JACK. "Won't my enemies take bail for my good behaviour? Will they accept of a fine, or be satisfied with the pillory and imprisonment, a good sound whipping, or burning in the cheek?"

Habbakuk. Nothing but your blood will appease their rage! Make haste, else we shall be discovered! There is nothing like surprising the rogues! How they will be disappointed, when they hear that thou hast prevented their revenge, and hanged thine own self!

Jack. That is true! but what if I should do it in effigies? Is there never an old Pope or Pretender to hang up in my stead? We are not so unlike but it may pass!

Habbakuk. That can never be put upon Sir ROGER!

Jack. Are you sure he is in the next room? Have you provided a very sharp knife in case of the worst?

Habbakuk. Dost thou take me for a common liar! Be satisfied no damage can happen to your person! Your friends will take care of that!

Jack. Mayn't I quilt the rope! It galls me strangely. Besides, I don't like this running knot; it holds too tight! I may be stifled all of a sudden!

Habbakuk. Thou hast so many "Ifs" and "Ands!" Prithee, despatch! it might have been over before this time!

Jack. But now I think on it, I would fain settle some affairs for fear of the worst: have a little patience!

Habbakuk. There is no having patience: thou art such a fainting silly creature!

Jack. O thou most detestable abominable Passive Obedience! did I ever imagine I should become thy votary in so pregnant an instance! How will my brother MARTIN laugh at this story, to see himself outdone in his own calling! He has taken the doctrine, and left me the practice!

No sooner had he uttered these words, but like a man of true courage, he tied the fatal cord to the beam, fitted the noose, and mounted upon the bottom of a *Tub*, the inside of which he had often graced in his prosperous days. This footstool, HABBAKUK kicked away; and left poor JACK swinging like the pendulum of Paul's clock. The fatal noose performed its office, and, with most strict ligature, squeezed the blood into his face, till it assumed a purple dye.

While the poor man heaved from the very bottom of his belly for breath, HABBAKUK walked with great deliberation into both the upper and lower room, to acquaint his friends; who received the news with great temper [*equanimity*], and with jeers and scoffs instead of pity.

"JACK has hanged himself!" quoth they, "let us go and see how the poor rogue swings!"

Then they called Sir ROGER.

"Sir ROGER!" quoth **Habbakuk,** "JACK has hanged himself; make haste and cut him down!"

Sir ROGER turned, first one ear, and then the other, not understanding what he said.

Habbakuk. I tell you, JACK has hanged himself up!

Sir Roger. Who is hanged?

Habbakuk. JACK!

Sir Roger. I thought this had not been hanging day!

Habbakuk. But the poor fellow has hanged himself!

Sir Roger. Then let him hang! I don't wonder at it: the fellow has been mad these twenty years!

With this, he slank away.

Then JACK's friends began to hunch and push one another.

"Why don't you go and cut the poor fellow down?"

"Why don't you?"

And "Why don't you?"

"Not I!" quoth one.

"Not I!" quoth another.

"Not I!" quoth a third, "he may hang till Doomsday before I relieve him!"

Nay it is credibly reported that they were so far from succouring their poor friend in this his dismal circumstance, that PTSCHIRNSOOKER and several of his companions went in and pulled him by the legs, and thumped him on the breast.

Then they began to rail at him for the very thing which they had both advised and justified before; viz., his getting into the old Gentlewoman's family, and putting on her livery.

The Keeper who performed the last office, coming up, found JACK swinging with no life in him. He took down the body gently, and laid it on a bulk, and brought out the rope to the company.

"This, Gentlemen! is the rope that hanged JACK! What must be done with it?"

Upon which, they ordered it to be laid among the curiosities of Gresham College; and it is called "JACK's rope" to this very day.

However, JACK, after all, had some small tokens of life in him: but lies, at this time, past hopes of a total recovery; with his head hanging on one shoulder, without speech or motion.

The Coroner's Inquest supposing him dead, brought him in *Non Compos*.

CHAPTER IV.

The Conference between Don DIEGO DISMALLO and JOHN BULL.

DURING the time of the foregoing transaction, Don DIEGO was entertaining JOHN BULL.

Don Diego. I hope, Sir, this day's proceedings will convince you of the sincerity of your old friend DIEGO, and the treachery of Sir ROGER.

John Bull. What's the matter now?

Don Diego. You have been endeavouring for several years, to have justice done upon that rogue JACK; but, what through the remissness of Constables, Justices, and packed juries, he has always found the means to escape.

John Bull. What then?

Don Diego. Consider, then, who is your best friend, he that would have brought him to condign punishment, or he that has saved him? By my persuasion, JACK had hanged himself, if Sir ROGER had not cut him down!

John Bull. Who told you that Sir ROGER has done so?

Don Diego. You seem to receive me coldly! Methinks, my services deserve a better return!

John Bull. Since you value yourself upon hanging this poor scoundrel; I tell you, when I have any more hanging work, I will send for thee! I have some better employment for Sir ROGER. In the meantime, I desire the poor fellow may be looked after.

When he first came out of the North country into my Family, under the pretended name of TIMOTHY TRIM, the fellow seemed to mind his loom and his spinning-wheel till somebody turned his head. Then he grew so pragmatical, that he took upon him the government of my whole Family [*the Commonwealth*]. I could never order anything within or without doors; but he must be always giving his counsel, forsooth! Nevertheless, tell him I will forgive what is past! and if he would mind his business for the future, and not meddle out of his own sphere; he will find that JOHN BULL is not of a cruel disposition!

Don Diego. Yet all your skilful physicians say that nothing can recover your mother, but a piece of JACK's liver boiled in her soup!

John Bull. Those are Quacks! My mother abhors such cannibal's food! She is in perfect health at present. I would have given many a good pound to have had her so well, some time ago.

There are indeed two or three troublesome old nurses, that because they believe I am tender-hearted, will never let me have a quiet night's rest, with knocking me up, "Oh, Sir! your mother is taken extremely ill! She is fallen into a fainting fit! She has a great emptiness, and wants sustenance!" [*The Tory cry of "The Church is in danger!"*] This is only to recommend themselves, for their great care. JOHN BULL, as simple as he is, understands a little of a pulse.

FINIS.

LEWIS BABOON
Turned Honest,
AND
JOHN BULL
POLITICIAN.
Being
The FOURTH PART
OF
Law is a Bottomless Pit.

Printed from a Manuscript found in the Cabinet of the famous Sir H*UMPHRY* P*OLESWORTH: and published (as well as the Three former Parts and* Appendix*) by the Author of the* New Atlantis.

LONDON: Printed for JOHN MORPHEW, near Stationers' Hall, 1712. Price 6d.

THE CONTENTS.

THE PREFACE.

WHEN I was first called to the Office of Historiographer to JOHN BULL, *he expressed himself to this purpose, "Sir* HUMPHRY*! I know you are a plain dealer! It is for that reason that I have chosen you for this important trust! Speak the truth, and spare not!"*

That I might fulfil those his honourable intentions, I obtained leave to repair to, and attend him in his most secret retirements: and I put the Journals of all transactions into a strong box, to be opened at a fitting occasion; after the manner of the Historiographers of some Eastern monarchs. This I thought was the safest way; though I declare I was never afraid to be chopped [off] by my Master, for telling the truth.

It is from those Journals, that my Memoirs are compiled. Therefore let not Posterity, a thousand years hence, look for truth in the voluminous Annals *of pedants, who are entirely ignorant of the secret springs of great actions! If they do, let me tell them, they will be* nebused*!*

With incredible pains have I endeavoured to copy the several beauties of the ancient and modern historians, the impartial temper of HERODOTUS, *the gravity, austerity, and strict morals of* THUCYDIDES, *the extensive knowledge of* XENOPHON, *the sublimity and grandeur of* TITUS LIVIUS; *and to avoid the careless style of*

POLYBIUS! I have borrowed considerable ornaments from DIONYSIUS Harlicarnasseus and DIODORUS SICULUS! The specious gilding of TACITUS, I have endeavoured to shun! MARIANA, D'AVILA, and Fra PAULO are those among the Moderns, whom I thought most worthy of imitation; but I cannot be so disingenuous, as not to own the infinite obligations I have to the Pilgrim's Progress *of JOHN BUNYAN, and the* Tenter Belly *of the Rev. JOSEPH HALL.*

From such encouragement and helps, it is easy to guess, to what a degree of perfection I might have brought this great Work, had it not been nipped in the bud, by some illiterate people in both Houses of Parliament: who, envying the great figure I was to make in future Ages, under pretence of raising money for the war, have padlocked [by the Stamp Act] *all those very pens that were to celebrate the actions of their heroes, by silencing at once the whole University of Grub street. I am persuaded that nothing but the prospect of an approaching Peace could have encouraged them to make so bold a step. But suffer me, in the name of the rest of the Matriculates of that famous University, to ask them some plain questions. Do they think that Peace will bring along with it a Golden Age? Will there be never a dying speech of a Traitor? Are CETHEGUS and CATALINE turned so tame that there will be no opportunity to cry about the streets, "A dangerous Plot!"? Will Peace bring such Plenty that no gentleman will have occasion to go upon the highway, or break into a house?*

I am sorry that the World should be so much imposed upon, by the dreams of a false prophet, as to imagine the Millenium is at hand. O Grub street! thou fruitful nursery of towering geniuses! how do I lament thy downfall! Thy ruin could never be meditated by any who meant well to English Liberty! No modern Lycæum will ever equal thy glory, whether in soft Pastorals thou sangst the flames of pampered apprentices and coy cookmaids, or mournful

Ditties of departing lovers! or if to Mœonian strains, thou raisedst thy voice, to record the stratagems, the arduous exploits, and the nocturnal scalade of needy heroes, the terror of your peaceful citizen! describing the powerful BETTY, *or the artful* PICKLOCK, *or the secret caverns and grottoes of* VULCAN *sweating at his forge and stamping the Queen's image on viler metals, which he retails for beef and pots of ale! or if thou wert content in simple Narrative to relate the cruel acts of implacable revenge; or the complaints of ravished virgins blushing to tell their adventure before the listening crowd of City damsels: whilst, in thy faithful History, thou interminglest the gravest counsels and the purest morals! nor less acute and piercing wert thou in thy search and pompous description of the Works of Nature; whether, in proper and emphatic terms, thou didst paint the blazing comet's fiery tail, the stupendous force of dreadful thunder and earthquakes, and the unrelenting inundations! Sometimes, with Machiavellian sagacity, thou unravelledst the intrigues of State, and the traitorous conspiracies of rebels; giving wise counsel to Monarchs! How didst thou move our terror and our pity with thy passionate scenes between* JACK CATCH *and the heroes of the Old Bailey! how didst thou describe their intrepid march up Holborn Hill! Nor didst thou shine less in thy Theological capacity, when thou gavest ghostly counsel to dying felons, and recorded the guilty pangs of Sabbath-breakers! How will the noble Arts of* JOHN OVERTON'S *painting and sculpture now languish! where rich invention, proper expression, correct design, divine altitudes, and artful contrast, heightened with the beauties of Clar Obscur* [Chiar obscuro] *imbellish thy celebrated pieces, to the delight and astonishment of the judicious multitude!*

Adieu, persuasive Eloquence! The quaint Metaphor, the poignant Irony, the proper Epithet, and the lively Simile are fled to Burleigh on the Hill!

*Instead of these, we shall have I know not what! "The illiterate will tell the rest with pleasure."**

I hope the Reader will excuse this digression, due, by way of condolence, to my worthy brethren of Grub street, for the approaching barbarity that is likely to overspread all its regions, by this oppressive and exorbitant tax [the Stamp duty]. *It has been my good fortune to receive my education there; and so long as I preserved some figure and rank among the Learned of that Society, I scorned to take my degree either at Utrecht or Leyden, though I were offered it gratis by the Professors there.*

* Vide [WILLIAM FLEETWOOD] the Bishop of ST ASAPH'S *Preface* [to his *Four Sermons*].

LEWIS BABOON
Turned Honest,
AND
JOHN BULL
POLITICIAN.

CHAPTER I.

The Sequel of the History of the Meeting at the Salutation:

WHERE, I think I left JOHN BULL sitting between NIC. FROG and LEWIS BABOON, with his arms akimbo, in great concern to keep LEWIS and NIC. asunder.

As watchful as he was, NIC. found means, now and then, to steal a whisper; and, by a cleanly conveyance under the table, to slip a short note into LEWIS's hand: which LEWIS as slyly, put into JOHN's pocket, with a pinch or a jog to warn him what he was about.

JOHN had the curiosity to retire into a corner, to peruse

these *billet-doux* of NIC.'s; wherein he found that NIC. had used great freedoms, both with his Interest and reputation.

One contained these words:

Dear LEWIS,

Thou seest clearly that this blockhead can never bring his matters to bear! Let thee and me talk to-night by ourselves at the Rose, *and I will give thee satisfaction!*

Another was thus expressed:

Friend LEWIS,

Has thy sense quite forsaken thee, to make BULL *such offers? Hold fast! part with nothing! and I will give thee a better bargain, I'll warrant thee!*

In some of his billets, he told LEWIS that *JOHN BULL was under his guardianship!* that *the best part of his servants were at his command!* that *he could have JOHN gagged and bound, whenever he pleased, by the people of his own Family!*

In all these epistles, *blockhead! dunce! ass! coxcomb!* were the best epithets he gave poor JOHN.

In others, he threatened that, *he, Esquire* SOUTH, *and the rest of the Tradesmen* [the Allies] *would lay* LEWIS *down upon his back, and beat out his teeth, if he did not retire immediately, and break up the meeting!*

I fancy I need not tell my reader that JOHN often changed colour as he read, and that his fingers itched to give NIC. a good slap on the chops: but he wisely moderated his choleric temper.

"I saved this fellow," quoth he, "from the gallows, when he ran away from his last master [*the rise of the Dutch Republic with English help*]; because I thought he was harshly treated: but the rogue was no sooner safe under my protection, than he began to lie, pilfer, and steal, like the Devil!

"When I first set him up in a warm house; he had hardly put up his Sign, when he began to debauch [*entice*] my best customers from me. Then it was his constant practice to rob my fish-ponds [*Dutch fishing for herrings off the English coast*]; not only to feed his family, but to trade with the fishmongers. I connived at the fellow, till he began to tell me that 'they were his, as much as mine!'

"In my Manor of Eastcheap [*East Indies*], because it

lay at some distance from my constant inspection, he broke down my fences, robbed my orchards, and beat my servants. When I used to reprimand him for his tricks; he would talk saucily, lie, and brazen it out as if he had done nothing amiss. 'Will nothing cure thee of these pranks, NIC.?' quoth I. 'I shall be forced, some time or another, to chastise thee!' The rogue got up his cane and threatened me; and was well thwacked for his pains [*the wars with the Dutch in* 1652, 1665, *and* 1671].

"But I think his behaviour at this time, worst of all! After I have almost drowned myself, to keep his head above water; he would leave me sticking in the mud, trusting to his goodness to help me out! After I have beggared myself with this troublesome Lawsuit, he takes it in mighty dudgeon, because I have brought him here, to end matters amicably! and because I won't let him make me over, by deed and indenture, as his lawful cully [*dupe*]! which to my certain knowledge, he has attempted several times.

"But, after all, canst thou *gather grapes from thorns*? NIC. does not pretend to be a Gentleman! He is a tradesman, a self-seeking wretch! But how comest thou to bear all this, JOHN? The reason is plain; thou conferrest the benefits, and he receives them: the first produces love, and the last ingratitude.

"Ah, NIC.! thou art a dog, that is certain! Thou knowest too well, that I will take care of thee, else thou wouldst not use me thus. I won't give thee up, it is true: but, as true it is, that thou shalt not sell me, according to thy laudable custom!"

While JOHN was deep in this soliloquy, NIC. broke out into the following protestation:

"Gentlemen,

I believe everybody here present, will allow me to be a very just and disinterested person. My friend JOHN BULL here, is very angry with me; forsooth, because I won't agree to his foolish bargains. Now I declare to all mankind, I should be ready to sacrifice my own concerns to his quiet; but the care of his Interest and that of the honest Tradesmen [*the Allies*] that are embarked with us, keeps me from entering into this Composition. What shall become of those poor creatures? The thought of their impending ruin disturbs my night's rest! Therefore I desire they may speak for themselves. If they are willing to give up this affair, I shan't make two words of it!"

JOHN BULL begged him to lay aside that immoderate concern for him: and withal, put him in mind that the Interest of those Tradesmen had not sat quite so heavy upon him, some years ago, on a like occasion.

NIC. answered little to that, but immediately pulled out a boatswain's whistle. Upon the first whiff, the Tradesmen came jumping in the room, and began to surround LEWIS like so many yelping curs about a great boar: or, to use a modester simile, like duns at a great Lord's levee, the morning he goes into the country. One pulled him by the sleeve! another by the skirt! a third holloaed in his ear! They began to ask him for all that had been taken from their forefathers, by stealth, fraud, force, or lawful purchase! Some asked for Manors! Others, for acres that lay convenient for them! that he would pull down his fences! level his ditches! All agreed in one common demand, that he should be purged, sweated, vomited, and starved, till he came to a sizeable bulk like that of his neighbours.

One modestly asked him leave to call him "Brother!" NIC. FROG demanded two things, to be his Porter and his Fishmonger; to keep the keys of his gates, and furnish his kitchen. JOHN's sister, PEG, only desired that he would let his servants [*French Protestants*] sing *Psalms* a Sundays. Some descended even to the asking of old clothes, shoes and boots, broken bottles, tobacco pipes, and ends of candles.

"Monsieur BULL," quoth LEWIS, "you seem to be a man of some breeding! For God's sake! use your Interest with these Messieurs, that they would speak but one at once! for if one had a hundred pair of hands and as many tongues, he cannot satisfy them all, at this rate!"

JOHN begged they might proceed with some method.

Then they stopped all of a sudden, and would not say a word.

"If this be your play," quoth JOHN, "that we may not be like a Quaker's dumb meeting; let us begin some diversion! What do ye think of Rouly Pouly, or a Country Dance? What if we should have a match at football? I am sure we shall never end matters at this rate!"

CHAPTER II.

How JOHN BULL and NICHOLAS FROG settled their accounts.

John Bull. DURING this general cessation of talk, what if you and I, NIC.! should inquire how money matters stand between us?

Nic. Frog. With all my heart! I love exact dealing; and let HOCUS audit! he knows how the money was disbursed.

John Bull. I am not for that, at present! We will settle it between ourselves! Fair and square, NIC.! keeps friends together. There have been laid out in this Lawsuit, at one time, 36,000 pounds and 40,000 crowns. In some cases, I, in others you, bear the greater proportion.

Nic. Right! I pay Three-fifths of the greater number; and you pay Two-thirds of the lesser number. I think this is "fair and square" as you call it.

John. Well, go on!

Nic. Two-thirds of 36,000 pounds is 24,000 pounds for your share; and there remains 12,000 pounds. Again, of the 40,000 crowns, I pay 24,000; which is Three-fifths; and you pay only 16,000, which is Two-fifths. 24,000 crowns make 6,000 pounds, and 16,000 crowns make 4,000 pounds: 12,000 and 6,000 make 18,000; 24,000 and 4,000 make 28,000. So there are 18,000 pounds to my share of the expenses, and 28,000 pounds to yours."

After NIC. had bamboozled JOHN a while about the 18,000 and the 28,000; JOHN called for counters. But what with sleight of hand, and taking from his own score and adding to JOHN'S, NIC. wrought the balance always on his own side.

John Bull. Nay, good friend NIC., though I am not quite so nimble in the figures, I understand ciphering as well as you! I will produce my accounts one by one, fairly written out of my own books.

And here I begin with the first. You must excuse me, if I don't pronounce the Law terms right.

John reads.

		£	s.	d.
Fees to the Lord Chief Justice and other Judges, by way of dividend...		200	10	6
Fees to *puisne* Judges ...		50	0	0
To Esquire SOUTH,	for *post Terminums* ...	100	10	6
To ditto	for *Non est factums* ...	200	0	0
To ditto	for Discontinuance, *Noli prosequi*, and *Retraxit* ...	80	10	6
To ditto	for a *Non Omittas*, and filing a *post Diem* ...	50	0	0
To HOCUS,	for a *Dedimus protestatem* ...	300	0	0
To ditto	for *Casas* and *Fifas* after a *Devastavit* ...	500	0	0
To ditto	for a *Capias ad computandum* ...	100	10	6
To FROG's New tenants [*the Barrier towns*],	*per* Account to HOCUS, for *Audita querelas* ...	200	0	0
	On the said Account, for Writs of Ejectment and *Destringas* ...	300	0	0
To Esquire SOUTH's quota	for a Return of a *Non est inventus* and *nulla habet bona* ...	150	10	0
To ———	for a Pardon *in formâ pauperis* ...	200	0	0
To JACK	for a *Melius inquirendum* upon a *Felo de se* ...	100	0	0
To Don DIEGO	for a *Deficit*...	50	0	0
To Coach hire	...	500	0	0
For treats to Juries and Witnesses ...		300	0	0
	Sum	£3,382	12	0
	Due by NIC. FROG	£1,691	6	0
	Of which, paid by NIC. FROG	1,036	11	0
	Remains due by NIC. FROG	£654	15	0

Then NIC. FROG pulled out his bill out of his pocket, and began to read

NICHOLAS FROG's Account.

Remains to be deducted out of the former Account :	£	s.	d.
To HOCUS for Entries of a *Rege inconsulto* ...	200	0	0
To JOHN BULL's Nephew [*the Old Pretender*] for a *Venire Facias*: the money not yet all laid out	300	0	0
The coach hire for my wife and family, and the carriage of my goods during the time of this Lawsuit	200	10	6
For the extraordinary expenses of feeding my family, during this Lawsuit...	500	0	0
To *Major AB.*	300	0	0
To *Major WILL.*	200	0	0
Sum	£1,700	10	6
From which deduct	1,691	6	0
There remains due to NIC. FROG	£9	4	6

Besides; recollecting, I believe I paid for DIEGO's *Deficit.*

John Bull. As for your *Venire facias*, I have paid you for one already! In the other, I believe you will be nonsuited. I'll take care of my nephew myself. Your coach hire and family charges are most unreasonable deductions! At that rate, I can bring in any man in the world, my debtor! But who, the Devil! are those two *Majors* that consume all my money? I find they always run away with the balance in all accounts.

Nic. Frog. Two very honest Gentlemen, I assure you! that have done me some service.

To tell you plainly, *Major AB.* denotes thy "greater Ability," and *Major WILL.*, thy "greater Willingness," to carry on this Lawsuit. It was but reasonable, thou shouldst pay both for thy Power and thy Positiveness!

John Bull. I believe I shall have those two honest Majors' discount on my side, in a little time.

Nic. Frog. Why all this higgling with thy friend, about

such a paltry sum? Does this become the generosity of the noble and rich JOHN BULL? I wonder thou art not ashamed! O HOCUS! HOCUS! where art thou? It used to go anotherguess manner in thy time! When a poor man has almost undone himself for thy sake; thou art for fleecing him, and fleecing him! Is that thy conscience, JOHN?

John Bull. Very pleasant indeed! It is well known thou retainest thy Lawyers by the year; so that a fresh Lawsuit adds but little to thy expense. They are thy customers: I hardly ever sell them a farthing's worth of anything! Nay, thou hast set up an eating-house, where the whole tribe of them spend all they can rap or run [*i.e., all the ready money they can chink, and all the credit they can run*]. If it were well reckoned, I believe thou gettest more of my money than thou spendest of thy own. However, if thou wilt needs plead poverty, own at least that thy Accounts are false.

Nic. Frog. No, marry! won't I! I refer myself to these honest Gentlemen [*the Tradesmen, i.e., the Allies*]! Let them judge between us! Let Esquire SOUTH speak his mind, Whether my accounts are not right? and Whether we ought not to go on with the Lawsuit?

John Bull. *Consult the butchers about keeping of Lent!* I tell you, once for all, JOHN BULL knows where his shoe pinches. None of your Esquires shall give him the law, as long as he wears this trusty weapon by his side, or has an inch of broad-cloth in his shop!

Nic. Frog. Why, there it is! You will be Judge and Party! I am sorry thou discoverest so much of thy headstrong humour before these strange Gentlemen! I have often told you, that it would prove thy ruin some time or another!

JOHN saw clearly he should have nothing but wrangling; and that he should have as little success in settling his accounts as in ending the Composition.

"Since they will needs overload my shoulders," quoth JOHN, "I shall throw down the burden with a squash amongst them; take it up who dares! A man has a fine time of it, among a combination of sharpers that vouch for one another's honesty! JOHN, look to thyself! Old LEWIS makes reasonable offers! When thou hast spent the small pittance that is left, thou wilt make a glorious figure, when thou art brought to live upon NIC. FROG's and Esquire SOUTH's generosity and gratitude. If they use thee thus, when they want thee; what will they do, when thou wantest them? I say again, JOHN look to thyself!"

JOHN wisely stifled his resentments; and told the company that, "in a little time, he should give them law, or something better!"

All. Law! Law! Sir, by all means! What are twenty-two poor years towards the finishing a Lawsuit? For the love of God! more Law, Sir!

John Bull. Prepare your demands, how many years more of Law you want! that I may order my affairs accordingly. In the meanwhile, farewell!

CHAPTER III.

How JOHN BULL found all his Family in an uproar at home.

NIC. FROG (who thought of nothing but of carrying JOHN to the market, and there disposing of him as his own proper goods) was mad to find that JOHN thought himself now of age to look after his own affairs. He resolved to traverse this new project, and to make him uneasy in his own Family. He had corrupted or deluded most of his servants into the most extravagant conceits in the world, that their Master was run mad! and wore a dagger in one pocket, and poison in the other! he had sold his wife and children to LEWIS! disinherited his heir! and was going to settle his estate upon a parish boy! that if they did not look after their Master, he would do some very mischievous thing!

When JOHN came home, he found a more surprising scene than any he had yet met with [*the national excitement as to the Hanoverian Succession*]; and that, you will say, was somewhat extraordinary.

He called his cook-maid BETTY to bespeak his dinner.

BETTY told him that "she begged his pardon, she could not dress dinner till she knew what he intended to do with his Will [*the Act of Settlement, ensuring the Hanoverian Succession*]!"

"Why, BETTY, forsooth, thou art not run mad! art thou? My will at present, is to have dinner."

"That may be," quoth BETTY, "but my conscience won't allow me to dress it, till I know whether you intend to do righteous things by your heir [*the Princess SOPHIA*]?"

"I am sorry for that, BETTY!" quoth JOHN, "I must find somebody else then!"

Then he called JOHN the barber.

"Before I begin," quoth JOHN, "I hope your Honour won't be offended, if I ask you, Whether you intend to alter your Will? If you won't give me a positive answer, your beard may grow down to your middle, for me!"

"I gad, and so it shall!" quoth BULL, "for I will never trust my throat in such a mad fellow's hands!"

"Where is DICK the butler?"

"Look ye!" quoth DICK, "I am very willing to serve you in my calling, do ye see! but there are strange reports, and plain dealing is best, do you see! I must be satisfied if you intend to leave all to your nephew, and if NIC. FROG is still your executor, do you see! If you will not satisfy me as to these points, do you see! you may drink with the ducks!"

"And so I will!" quoth JOHN, "rather than keep a butler that loves my heir better than myself."

HOB the shoemaker and PRICKET the tailor told him that they "would most willingly serve him in their several stations, if he would promise them, never to talk with LEWIS BABOON, and let NICHOLAS FROG, linendraper, manage his concerns!" that they "could neither make shoes nor clothes to any that were not in good correspondence with their worthy friend NICHOLAS."

John Bull. Call ANDREW my journeyman! How go affairs, ANDREW? I hope the Devil has not taken possession of thy body too!

Andrew. No, Sir! I only desire to know, what you would do if you were dead?

John Bull. Just as other dead folks do, ANDREW!

[*Aside*. This is amazing

Andrew. I mean if your nephew shall inherit your estate?

John Bull. That depends upon himself! I shall do nothing to hinder him!

Andrew. But will you make it sure?

John Bull. Thou meanest that I should put him in possession; for I can make no surer without that! He has all the Law can give him!

Andrew. Indeed, Possession, as you say, would make it much surer. They say "it is eleven points of the Law!"

JOHN began now to think they were all enchanted. He inquired about the age of the moon? if NIC. had not given them some intoxicating potion? or if old mother JENISA was not still alive?

"No, on my faith!" quoth HARRY, "I believe there is no potion in the case but a little *aurum potabile.* You will have more of this, by and by!"

He had scarce spoken the word, when, of a sudden, Don DIEGO, followed by a great multitude of his tenants and workpeople, came rushing into the room.

Don Diego. Since those worthy persons, who are as much concerned for your safety as I am, have employed me as their Orator; I desire to know whether you will have it, by way of Syllogism, Enthymeme [a *syllogism drawn from probable premisses, and which therefore does not pretend to be demonstrative*], Dilemma [*an argument in which the adversary is caught between two difficulties*], or Sorites [*a heap of syllogisms, the conclusion of the one forming the premiss of the next*].

JOHN now began to be diverted with their extravagance.

John Bull. Let us have a Sorites, by all means! though they are all new to me!

Don Diego. It is evident to all that are versed in history, that there were two sisters that played the whore two thousand years ago: therefore it follows, that it is not lawful for JOHN BULL to have any manner of intercourse with LEWIS BABOON. If it is not lawful for JOHN BULL to have any manner of intercourse (correspondence if you will! that is much the same thing!); then, *a fortiori,* it is much more unlawful for the said JOHN to make over his wife and children to the said LEWIS. If his wife and children are not to be made over, he is not to wear a dagger and ratsbane in his pockets. If he wears a dagger and a ratsbane, it must be to do mischief to himself or somebody else. If he intends to do mischief, he ought to be under Guardians: and there are none so fit as myself and some other worthy persons, who have a commission for that purpose from NIC. FROG, the Executor of his Will and Testament.

John Bull. And this is your Sorites, you say!

With that, he snatched a good oaken cudgel, and began to brandish it. Then happy was the man that was first at the door! Crowding to get out, they tumbled down stairs: and it is credibly reported, some of them dropped very valuable things in the hurry, which were picked up by others of the Family.

"That any of these rogues," quoth JOHN, "should imagine, I am not as much concerned as they, about having my affairs in a settled condition; or that I would wrong my heir, for I know not what! Well, NIC.! I really cannot but applaud thy diligence! I must own this is really a pretty sort of a trick; but it shan't do thy business, for all that!"

CHAPTER IV.

How LEWIS BABOON came to visit JOHN BULL, and what passed between them.

I THINK it is but ingenuous to acquaint the reader, that this chapter was not written by Sir HUMPHRY himself, but by another very able Pen of the University of Grub street.

JOHN had, by some good instructions that were given him, got the better of his choleric temper; and wrought himself up to a great steadiness of mind to pursue his own Interest through all impediments that were thrown in the way. He began to leave off some of his old acquaintance, his roaring and bullying about the streets. He put on a serious air, knitted his brows: and, for a time, had made a very considerable progress in politics; considering that he had been kept a stranger to his own affairs. However, he could not help discovering some remains of his nature, when he happened to meet with a foot-ball, or a match at cricket: for which Sir ROGER was sure to take him to task.

JOHN was walking about his room, with folded arms and a most thoughtful countenance, when his servant brought him word, that one LEWIS BABOON, below, wanted to speak with him.

JOHN had got an impression that LEWIS was so deadly a cunning a man, that he was afraid to venture himself alone with him. At last, he took heart of grace. "Let him come up," quoth he, "it is but sticking to my point, and he can never overreach me!"

Lewis Baboon. Monsieur BULL! I will frankly acknowledge that my behaviour to my neighbours has been somewhat uncivil; and I believe you will readily grant me! that I have met with usage accordingly. I was fond of backsword and cudgel-play from my youth; and I now bear in my body, many a black and blue gash and scar, God knows! I had as good a warehouse and as fair possessions as any of my neighbours, though I say it! but a contentious temper, flattering servants, and unfortunate stars, have brought me into circumstances that are not unknown to you.

These my misfortunes are heightened by domestic calamities that I need not relate. I am a poor old battered fellow; and I would willingly end my days in peace! But, alas, I see but small hopes of that! for every new circumstance affords an argument to my enemies to pursue their revenge! Formerly, I was to be banged, because I was too strong; and now, because I am too weak to resist! I am to be brought down, when too rich; and oppressed, when too poor! NIC. FROG has used me like a scoundrel! You are a Gentleman, and I freely put myself in your hands, to dispose of me as you think fit.

John Bull. Look you, Master BABOON! as to your usage of your neighbours, you had best not dwell too much upon that chapter! let it suffice, at present, that you have been met with. You have been rolling a great stone uphill all your life; and, at last, it has come tumbling down till it is like[ly] to crush you to pieces.

Plain dealing is best. If you have any particular mark, Monsieur BABOON! whereby one may know when you fib, and when you speak truth; you had best tell it me! that one may proceed accordingly. But since, at present, I know of none such, it is better that you should trust me, than that I should trust you!

Lewis Baboon. I know of no particular mark of veracity amongst us Tradesmen, but Interest: and it is manifestly mine, not to deceive you at this time. You may safely trust me, I can assure you!

John Bull. The trust I give is, in short, this. I must have something in hand, before I make the bargain; and the rest, before it is concluded.

Lewis Baboon. To shew you I deal fairly, name your something!

John Bull. I need not tell thee, old boy! thou canst guess!

Lewis Baboon. Ecclesdown Castle, I'll warrant you! because it has been formerly in your family! [*Dunkirk, sold by* CHARLES *II. to France, in* 1662, *for* £500,000]. Say no more, you shall have it!

John Bull. I shall have it to mine own self!

Lewis Baboon. To thine own self!

John Bull. Every wall, gate, room, and inch of Ecclesdown Castle, you say!

Lewis Baboon. Just so!

John Bull. Every single stone of Ecclesdown Castle to mine own self, speedily!

Lewis Baboon. When you please! What need more words!

John Bull. But tell me, old boy! hast thou laid aside all thy Equivocals and Mentals [*reservations*] in this case?

Lewis Baboon. There is nothing like matter of fact. Seeing is believing.

John Bull. Now thou talkest to the purpose! let us shake hands, old boy! Let me ask thee one question more! What hast thou to do with the affairs of my Family, to dispose of my estate, old boy?

Lewis Baboon. Just as much as you have to do with the affairs of Lord STRUTT!

John Bull. Ay, but my trade, my very being was concerned in that!

Lewis Baboon. And my Interest was concerned in the other. But let us drop both our pretences! for I believe it is a moot point whether I am more likely to make a Master BULL; or you, a Lord STRUTT.

John Bull. Agreed, old boy! but then I must have

security that I shall carry my broadcloth to market, old boy!

Lewis Baboon. That you shall! Ecclesdown Castle! Ecclesdown, remember that! Why wouldst thou not take it, when it was offered thee, some years ago?

John Bull. I would not take it, because they told me thou wouldst not give to me!

Lewis Baboon. How could Monsieur BULL be so gross abused by downright nonsense! They that advised you to refuse, must have believed I intended to give! else why would they not make the experiment? But I can tell you more of that matter, than perhaps you know at present.

John Bull. But what sayst thou as to the Esquire, NIC. FROG, and the rest of the Tradesmen [*the Allies*]? I must take care of them.

Lewis Baboon. Thou hast but small obligations to NIC., to my certain knowledge. He has not used me like a Gentleman!

John Bull. NIC., indeed, is not very nice in your punctilios of ceremony: he is clownish, as a man may say. Belching and calling of names have been allowed him, time out of mind, by prescription. But however, we are engaged in one common cause, and I must look after him.

Lewis Baboon. All matters that relate to him and the rest of the Plaintiffs in this Lawsuit, I will refer to youı justice!

CHAPTER V.

NICHOLAS FROG's letter to JOHN BULL; wherein he endeavours to vindicate all his conduct with relation to JOHN BULL and the Lawsuit.

NIC. perceived now that his cully [*dupe*] had eloped, that JOHN intended henceforth to deal without a broker; but he was resolved to leave no stone unturned to recover his bubble.

Among other artifices, he wrote a most obliging letter, which he sent him printed in a fair character [*type*].

Dear friend,

When I consider the late ill usage I have met with from you,

I am reflecting, What it was that could provoke you to it? but upon a narrow inspection into my conduct, I can find nothing to reproach myself with, but too partial a concern for your Interest. You no sooner set this Composition afoot, but I was ready to comply, and prevented [anticipated] *your every wishes: and the Affair might have been ended before now, had it not been for the greater concerns of Esquire* SOUTH *and the other poor creatures embarked in the same common Cause, whose safety touches me to the quick.*

You seemed a little jealous that I had dealt unfairly with you in money matters, till it appeared, by your own accounts, that there was something due to me upon the balance.

Having nothing to answer to so plain a demonstration, you began to complain as if I had been familiar with your reputation: when it is well known, not only I, but the meanest servant in my family, talk of you with the utmost respect. I have always, as far as in me lies, exhorted your servants and tenants to be dutiful: not that I any ways meddle in your domestic affairs, which were very unbecoming for me to do. If some of your servants express their great concern for you in a manner that is not so polite, you ought to impute it to their extraordinary zeal, which deserves a reward rather than a reproof.

You cannot reproach me for want of success at the Salutation; *since I am not master of the passions and Interests of other folks. I have beggared myself with this Lawsuit, undertaken merely in complaisance to you! and, if you would have had but a little patience, I had greater things in reserve that I intended to have done for you.*

I hope what I have said will prevail with you to lay aside your unreasonable jealousies; and that we may have no more meetings at the Salutation, *spending our time and money to no purpose. My concern for your welfare and prosperity almost makes me mad! You may be assured, I will continue to be,*

Your affectionate friend and servant,

NICHOLAS FROG.

JOHN received this with a good deal of *sang froid*.

"*Transeat*," quoth JOHN, "*cum cœteris erroribus!*"

He was now at his ease. He saw he could now make a very good bargain for himself, and a very safe one for other folks.

"My shirt," quoth he, "is near me, but my skin in nearer! Whilst I take care of the welfare of other folks, nobody can blame me for applying a little balsam to my own sores! It is a pretty thing, after all, for a man to do his own business: a man has such a tender concern for himself, there is nothing like it! This is somewhat better, I trow! that for JOHN BULL to be standing in the market like a great dray horse, with FROG's paws upon his head, 'What will ye give me for this beast?'

"*Serviteur* NIC. FROG! though JOHN BULL has not read your ARISTOTLES, PLATOS, and MACHIAVELLIS, he can see as far into a millstone as another!" With that, JOHN began to chuckle and laugh, till he was like to burst his sides.

CHAPTER VI.

The discourse that passed between NICHOLAS FROG and Esquire SOUTH, which JOHN BULL overheard.

JOHN thought every minute a year till he got into Ecclesdown Castle. He repaired to the *Salutation*, with a design to break matter the gently to his partners. Before he entered, he overheard NIC. and the Esquire in a very pleasant conference.

Esquire South. O the ingratitude and injustice of mankind! That JOHN BULL, whom I have honoured with my friendship and protection so long, should flinch at last; and pretend that he can disburse no more money for me! that the family of the SOUTHS, by his sneaking temper, should be kept out of their own!

Nic. Frog. An [*if*] it like your Worship! I am in amaze at it! I think the rogue should be compelled to do his duty

Esquire South. That he should prefer his scandalous self, the dust and dregs of the earth, to the prosperity and grandeur of my family!

Nic. Frog. Nay, he is mistaken there too! for he would quickly lick himself whole again, by his vails [*tips*]. It is strange he should prefer LEWIS BABOON's custom to Esquire SOUTH's.

Esquire South. As you say, that my clothier, that is to

get so much by the purchase, should refuse to put me in possession! Did you ever know any man's tradesmen serve him so before?

Nic. Frog. No, indeed, an it please your Worship! it is a very unusual proceeding! and I would not have been guilty of it for the world! If your Honour had not a great stock of moderation and patience, you would not bear it so well as you do!

Esquire South. It is most intolerable, that is certain, NIC.! and I will be revenged!

Nic. Frog. Methinks, it is strange that PHILIP BABOON'S tenants [*the Spaniards*] do not all take your Honour's part, considering how good and gentle a master you are!

Esquire South. True, NIC.! but few are sensible of merit in this world. It is a great comfort to have so faithful a friend as thyself in so critical a juncture.

Nic. Frog. If all the world should forsake you, be assured NIC. FROG never will! Let us stick to our point, and we will manage BULL, I'll warrant ye!

Esquire South. Let me kiss thee, dear NIC.! I have found one honest man among a thousand at last!

Nic. Frog. If it were possible, your Honour has it in your power to wed me still closer to your interest!

Esquire South. Tell me quickly, dear NIC.!

Nic. Frog. You know I am your tenant. The difference between my lease and an inheritance is such a trifle, as I am sure you will not grudge your poor friend! That will be an encouragement to go on! Besides, it will make BULL as mad as the Devil. You and I shall be able to manage him then, to some purpose!

Esquire South. Say no more! It shall be done, NIC.! to thy heart's content!

JOHN, all this while, was listening to this comical dialogue; and laughed heartily in his sleeve, at the pride and simplicity of the Esquire, and the sly roguery of his friend NIC.

Then, of a sudden, bolting into the room, he began to tell them that he believed he had brought LEWIS to reasonable terms, if they would be pleased to hear them.

Then they all bawled out aloud, "No Composition! Long live Esquire SOUTH and the Law!"

As JOHN was going to proceed, some roared, some stamped

with their feet, and others stopped their ears with their fingers.

"Nay, Gentlemen," quoth JOHN, "if you will but stop your proceeding for a while, you shall judge yourselves whether LEWIS's proposals are reasonable.

All. Very fine indeed! Stop proceeding, and so loose a Term [*a campaign*].

John Bull. Not so, neither! We have something by way of advance. He will put us in possession of his Manor and Castle of Ecclesdown.

Nic. Frog. What dost thou talk of Us, thou meanest thyself!

John Bull. When FROG took possession of anything, it was always said to be for Us; and why may not JOHN BULL be Us, as well as NIC. FROG was Us? I hope JOHN BULL is no more confined to Singularity than NIC. FROG! or take it so, the constant doctrine that Thou hast preached up, for many years, was that thou and I are One; and why must we be supposed Two in this case, that were always One before? It is impossible thou and I can fall out, NIC.! we must trust one another! I have trusted thee with a great many things; prithee, trust me with this one trifle!

Nic. Frog. That principle is true in the main; but there is some speciality in this case that makes it highly inconvenient for us both.

John Bull. Those are your jealousies, that common enemies sow between us. How often hast thou warned me of those rogues, NIC.! that would make us mistrustful of one another?

Nic. Frog. This Ecclesdown Castle is only a bone of contention!

John Bull. It depends upon you to make it so! For my part, I am as peaceable as a lamb.

Nic. Frog. But do you consider the unwholesomeness of the air and soil, the expenses of reparations and servants! I would scorn to accept of such a quagmire!

John Bull. You are a great man, NIC.! but in my circumstances, I must be even content to take it as it is.

Nic Frog. And are you really so silly as to believe the old cheating rogue will give it you!

John Bull. I believe nothing but matter of fact. I stand and fall by that! I am resolved to put him to it.

Nic. Frog. And so relinquish the hopefullest Cause in the world! a claim that will certainly, in the end, make thy fortune for ever!

John Bull. Wilt thou purchase it, NIC.? Thou shalt have a bumping pennyworth! Nay, rather than we should differ, I'll give thee something to take it off my hands!

Nic. Frog. If thou wouldst but moderate that hasty impatient temper of thine, thou shouldst quickly see a better thing than all that! What shouldst thou think to find old LEWIS turned out of his paternal estates and mansion house of Clay Pool [*Paris*]? Would not that do thy heart good, to see thy old friend NIC. FROG, Lord of Clay Pool? Then thou and thy wife and children shall walk in my gardens, buy toys, drink lemonade; and now and then we should have a country dance.

John Bull. I love to be plain. I'd as lief see myself in Ecclesdown Castle, as thee in Clay Pool! I tell you again, LEWIS gives this as a pledge of his sincerity: if you won't stop proceeding, to hear him, I will!

CHAPTER VII.

The rest of NICHOLAS's fetches to keep JOHN out of Ecclesdown Castle.

WHEN NIC. could not dissuade JOHN by argument, he tried to move his pity. He pretended to be sick and likely to die; that he should leave his wife and children in a starving condition, if JOHN did abandon him; that he was hardly able to crawl after such a troublesome business as this Lawsuit: and therefore begged that his good friend would not leave him!

When he saw that JOHN was still inexorable, he pulled out a case-knife, with which he used to *sneaker-snee*; and threatened to cut his own throat. Thrice he aimed the knife to his windpipe with a most determined threatening air. "What signifies life!" quoth he, "in this languishing condition? It will be some pleasure that my friends will revenge my death upon this barbarous man, that has been the cause of it!"

All this while, JOHN looked sedate and calm, neither offering in the least to snatch the knife, nor stop his blow; trusting to the tenderness NIC. had for his own person.

When he perceived that JOHN was immoveable in his purpose, he applied himself to LEWIS.

"Art thou," quoth he, "turned bubble [*a deluder*] in thy old age, from being a sharper in thy youth? What occasion hast thou to give up Ecclesdown Castle to JOHN BULL? his friendship is not worth a rush! Give it me, and I'll make it worth thy while! If thou dislikest that proposition, keep it thyself! I had rather thou shouldst have it, than he! If thou hearkenest not to my advice, take what follows. Esquire SOUTH and I will go on with the Lawsuit in spite of JOHN BULL's teeth!"

Lewis Baboon. Monsieur BULL has used me like a Gentleman! and I am resolved to make good my promise, and trust him for the consequences.

Nic. Frog. Then I tell thee thou art an old doating fool!

With that, NIC. bounced up with a spring equal to that of one of your nimblest tumblers or rope dancers, falls foul upon JOHN BULL to snatch the cudgel he had in his hand, that he might thwack LEWIS with it. JOHN held it fast, so that there was no wrenching it from him. At last Esquire SOUTH buckled to, to assist his friend NIC.

JOHN hauled on one side, and they two on the other. Sometimes they were like to pull JOHN over: then it went, all of a sudden, again on JOHN's side. So they went seesawing up and down, from one end of the room to the other. Down tumbled the tables, bottles, glasses, and tobacco pipes. The wine and the tobacco were all spilt about the room; and the little fellows were almost trod under foot: till more of the Tradesmen [*Allies*] joining with NIC. and the Esquire, JOHN was hardly able to pull against them all. Yet he never quitted hold of his trusty cudgel; which by the contranitent force of two so great Powers broke short in his hands.

NIC. seized the longer end, and with it began to bastinado old LEWIS: who had slank into a corner, waiting the event of this squabble. NIC. came up to him with an insolent, menacing air; so that the old fellow was forced to scuttle out of the room, and retire behind a dung-cart. He called to NIC. "Thou insolent jackanapes! Time was when thou durst not have used me so! Thou now takest me unprovided, but old and infirm as I am, I shall find a weapon, by and by, to chastise thy impudence!"

When JOHN BULL had recovered his breath, he began to parley with NIC. "Friend NIC.! I am glad to find thee so strong after thy great complaints! Really thy motions, NIC.! are pretty vigorous for a consumptive man! As for thy worldly affairs, NIC.! if it can do thee any service, I freely make over to thee this profitable Lawsuit; and I desire all these Gentlemen to bear witness to this my act and deed, yours be all the gain! as mine have been the charges. I have brought it to bear finely! However, all I have laid out upon it goes for nothing; thou shalt have it with all its appurtenances! I ask nothing but leave to go home!

Nic. Frog. The Counsel are fee-ed, and all things prepared for a trial: thou shalt be forced to stand the issue! It shall be pleaded in thy name as well as mine! Go home, if thou canst! The gates are shut, the turnpikes locked, and the roads barricadoed [*Dutch refusal to admit English goods in the district of the Barrier towns*].

John Bull. Even these very ways, NIC.! that thou toldest me, "were as open to me as thyself!" If I can't pass with my own equipage, what can I expect for my goods and waggons? I am denied passage through those very grounds, that I have purchased with my own money! However, I am glad I have made the experiment, it may serve me in some stead.

JOHN BULL was so overjoyed that he was going to take possession of Ecclesdown, that nothing could vex him, "NIC.!" quoth he, "I am just going to leave thee! cast a kind look upon me at parting!"

NIC. looked sour and glum, and would not open his mouth.

John Bull. I wish thee all the success that thy heart can desire! and that these Gentlemen of the long robe may have their bellyful of Law!

NIC. could stand it no longer; but flang out of the room with disdain, and beckoned the lawyers to follow him.

John Bull. Bye! bye, NIC.! Not one poor smile at parting! Won't you like to shake you *day-day*, NIC.? Bye, NIC.!

With that, JOHN marched out of the common road, across the country, to take possession of Ecclesdown.

CHAPTER VIII.

Of the great joy that JOHN expressed when he got possession of Ecclesdown.

WHEN JOHN had got into his Castle, he seemed like ULYSSES upon his plank, after he had been well soused in cold water; who, as HOMER says, was as glad as a Judge going to sit down to dinner, after hearing a long cause upon the Bench. I dare say JOHN BULL's joy was equal to that of either of the two. He skipped from room to room, ran upstairs and downstairs, from the kitchen to the garrets, and from the garrets to the kitchen. He peeped into every cranny. Sometimes he admired the beauty of the architecture, and the vast solidity of the mason's work: at other times, he commended the symmetry and proportion of the rooms. He walked about the gardens. He bathed himself in the Canal; swimming, diving, and beating the liquid element, like a milk-white swan. The hall resounded with the sprightly violin and the martial hautboy. The Family tripped it about, and capered like hailstones bounding from a marble floor. Wine, Ale, and October [beer] flew about as plentifully as kennel-water.

Then a frolic took JOHN in the head, to call up some of NIC. FROG's pensioners [*the Whigs*], that had been so mutinous in his Family.

John Bull. Are you glad to see your master in Ecclesdown Castle?

All. Yes, indeed, Sir!

John Bull. Extremely glad?

All. Extremely glad!

John Bull. Swear to me that ye are so!

Then they began to sink their souls to the lowest pit of hell, if any person in the world rejoiced more than they did!

John Bull. Now, hang me! if I don't believe you are a parcel of perjured rascals! However, take this bumper of October, to your master's health!

Then JOHN got upon the battlements; and looking over, he called to NIC. FROG:

"How do you do, NIC.! Do you see where I am, NIC.? I hope the Cause goes on swimmingly, NIC.! When dost thou intend to go to Clay Pool, NIC.? Wilt thou buy there some high-heads of the newest cut, for my daughters? How comest thou to go with thy arm tied up? Has old LEWIS given thee a rap over the finger ends? Thy weapon was a good one when I wielded it; but the butt end remains for my hands. I am so busy in packing up my goods, that I have no time to talk with thee any longer! It would do thy heart good, to see what waggon loads I am preparing for market! If thou wantest any good office of mine; for all that has happened, I will use thee well, NIC.! Bye, NIC.!"

*** *JOHN BULL's thanks to Sir ROGER, and NIC. FROG's malediction upon all shrews, the original cause of his misfortunes, are reserved for the next volume.*

FINIS.